ANNUAL EDITIONS

Marketing

Thirtieth Edition

08/09

EDITOR

John E. Richardson
Pepperdine University

Dr. John E. Richardson is Professor of Marketing in The George L. Graziadio School of Business and Management at Pepperdine University. He is president of his own consulting firm and has consulted with organizations such as Bell and Howell, Dayton-Hudson, Epson, and the U.S. Navy as well as with various service, nonprofit, and franchise organizations. Dr. Richardson is a member of the American Marketing Association, the American Management Association, the Society for Business Ethics, and Beta Gamma Sigma honorary business fraternity.

 **Higher Education**

Boston   Burr Ridge, IL   Dubuque, IA   New York   San Francisco   St. Louis
Bangkok   Bogotá   Caracas   Kuala Lumpur   Lisbon   London   Madrid   Mexico City
Milan   Montreal   New Delhi   Santiago   Seoul   Singapore   Sydney   Taipei   Toronto

The McGraw-Hill Companies

Higher Education

ANNUAL EDITIONS: MARKETING, THIRTIETH EDITION

Published by McGraw-Hill, a business unit of The McGraw-Hill Companies, Inc., 1221 Avenue of the Americas, New York, NY 10020.

Some ancillaries, including electronic and print components, may not be available to customers outside the United States.

Annual Editions® is a registered trademark of the McGraw-Hill Companies, Inc.
Annual Editions is published by the **Contemporary Learning Series** group within the McGraw-Hill Higher Education division.

1 2 3 4 5 6 7 8 9 0 QPD/QPD 0 9 8

ISBN 978–0–07–336946–4
MHID 0–07–336946–2
ISSN 0730–2606

Managing Editor: *Larry Loeppke*
Production Manager*: Beth Kundert*
Developmental Editor: *Dave Welsh*
Editorial Assistant: *Nancy Meissner*
Production Service Assistant: *Rita Hingtgen*
Permissions Coordinator: *Shirley Lanners*
Senior Marketing Manager: *Julie Keck*
Marketing Communications Specialist: *Mary Klein*
Marketing Coordinator: *Alice Link*
Project Manager: *Jean Smith*
Design Specialist: *Tara McDermott*
Senior Administrative Assistant: *DeAnna Dausener*
Senior Operations Manager: *Pat Koch Krieger*
Cover Graphics: *Maggie Lytle*

Compositor: Laserwords Private Limited
Cover Image: Royalty-Free/CORBIS

Library in Congress Cataloging-in-Publication Data
Main entry under title: Annual Editions: Marketing. 2008/2009.
  1. Marketing—Periodicals. I. Richardson, John E., *comp.* II. Title: Marketing.
658'.05

www.mhhe.com

Editors/Advisory Board

Members of the Advisory Board are instrumental in the final selection of articles for each edition of ANNUAL EDITIONS. Their review of articles for content, level, currentness, and appropriateness provides critical direction to the editor and staff. We think that you will find their careful consideration well reflected in this volume.

Preface

In publishing ANNUAL EDITIONS we recognize the enormous role played by the magazines, newspapers, and journals of the public press in providing current, first-rate educational information in a broad spectrum of interest areas. Many of these articles are appropriate for students, researchers, and professionals seeking accurate, current material to help bridge the gap between principles and theories and the real world. These articles, however, become more useful for study when those of lasting value are carefully collected, organized, indexed, and reproduced in a low-cost format, which provides easy and permanent access when the material is needed. That is the role played by ANNUAL EDITIONS.

The new millennium should prove to be an exciting and challenging time for the American business community. Recent dramatic social, economic, and technological changes have become an important part of the present marketplace. These changes—accompanied by increasing domestic and foreign competition—are leading a wide array of companies and industries toward the realization that better marketing must become a top priority now to assure their future success.

How does the marketing manager respond to this growing challenge? How does the marketing student apply marketing theory to the real world practice? Many reach for the *Wall Street Journal*, *BusinessWeek*, *Fortune*, and other well-known sources of business information. There, specific industry and company strategies are discussed and analyzed, marketing principles are often reaffirmed by real occurrences, and textbook theories are supported or challenged by current events.

The articles reprinted in this edition of *Annual Editions: Marketing 08/09* have been carefully chosen from numerous public press sources to provide current information on marketing in the world today. Within these pages you will find articles that address marketing theory and application in a wide range of industries. In addition, the selections reveal how several firms interpret and utilize marketing principles in their daily operations and corporate planning.

The volume contains a number of features designed to make it useful for marketing students, researchers, and professionals. These include the *topic guide* to locate articles on specific marketing subjects; *Internet References* pages; the *table of contents* abstracts, which summarize each article and highlights key concepts; and a *glossary* of key marketing terms.

The articles are organized into four units. Selections that focus on similar issues are concentrated into subsections within the broader units. Each unit is preceded by a list of unit selections, as well as a list of key points to consider that focus on major themes running throughout the selections, Web links that provide extra support for the unit's data, and an overview that provides background for informed reading of the articles and emphasizes critical issues.

This is the thirtieth edition of *Annual Editions: Marketing*. Since its first edition in the mid-1970s, the efforts of many individuals have contributed toward its success. We think this is by far the most useful collection of material available for the marketing student. We are anxious to know what you think. What are your opinions? What are your recommendations? Please take a moment to complete and return the *article rating form* on the last page of this volume. Any book can be improved and this one will continue to be, annually.

John E. Richardson
Editor

Contents

UNIT 1
Marketing in the 2000s and Beyond

The concepts in bold italics are developed in the article. For further expansion, please refer to the Topic Guide.

UNIT 2
Research, Markets, and Consumer Behavior

The concepts in bold italics are developed in the article. For further expansion, please refer to the Topic Guide.

UNIT 3
Developing and Implementing Marketing Strategies

The concepts in bold italics are developed in the article. For further expansion, please refer to the Topic Guide.

The concepts in bold italics are developed in the article. For further expansion, please refer to the Topic Guide.

UNIT 4
Global Marketing

The concepts in bold italics are developed in the article. For further expansion, please refer to the Topic Guide.

Topic Guide

This topic guide suggests how the selections in this book relate to the subjects covered in your course. You may want to use the topics listed on these pages to search the Web more easily.

On the following pages a number of Web sites have been gathered specifically for this book. They are arranged to reflect the units of this *Annual Edition*. You can link to these sites by going to the student online support site at *http://www.mhcls.com/online/*.

ALL THE ARTICLES THAT RELATE TO EACH TOPIC ARE LISTED BELOW THE BOLD-FACED TERM.

Advertising
1. Hot Stuff
7. The Big Opportunity
13. 6 Strategies Marketers Use to Get Kids to Want Stuff *Bad*
18. A New Age for the Ad Biz
25. In Praise of the Purple Cow
26. Starbucks' 'Venti' Problem
31. The Old Pillars of New Retailing
35. The Online Ad Surge
37. Got Advertising That Works
41. Three Dimensional

Branding
1. Hot Stuff
3. The Next 25 Years
4. Customers at Work
8. Listening to Starbucks
10. Nonprofits Can Take Cues from Biz World
11. Fidelity Factor
12. Trust in the Marketplace
20. Gen Y Sits on Top of Consumer Food Chain
22. Marketing: Consumers in the Mist
24. He Came. He Sawed. He Took on the Whole Power-Tool Industry
25. In Praise of the Purple Cow
26. Starbucks' 'Venti' Problem
27. Making Cents of Pricing
29. Boost Your Bottom Line by Taking the Guesswork Out of Pricing
32. Why Costco Is So Damn Addictive
33. A Sales Channel They Can't Resist
35. The Online Ad Surge
37. Got Advertising That Works
39. Segmenting Global Markets: Look Before You Leap
41. Three Dimensional
43. The Great Wal-Mart of China

Competition
14. Wrestling With Ethics
23. The Very Model of a Modern Marketing Plan
27. Making Cents of Pricing
29. Boost Your Bottom Line by Taking the Guesswork Out of Pricing
30. Pricing Gets Creative
31. The Old Pillars of New Retailing
37. Got Advertising That Works
38. Managing Differences
39. Segmenting Global Markets: Look Before You Leap
40. How China Will Change Your Business
42. Tech's Future

Consumer behavior
1. Hot Stuff
4. Customers at Work
6. Customer Connection
11. Fidelity Factor
15. The Science of Desire
19. The Halo Effect
20. Gen Y Sits on Top of Consumer Food Chain
22. Marketing: Consumers in the Mist
29. Boost Your Bottom Line by Taking the Guesswork Out of Pricing
30. Pricing Gets Creative
35. The Online Ad Surge
37. Got Advertising That Works

39. Segmenting Global Markets: Look Before You Leap
41. Three Dimensional

Consumer demographics
1. Hot Stuff
7. The Big Opportunity
13. 6 Strategies Marketers Use to Get Kids to Want Stuff *Bad*
17. Eight Tips Offer Best Practices for Online MR
18. A New Age for the Ad Biz
19. The Halo Effect
20. Gen Y Sits on Top of Consumer Food Chain
41. Three Dimensional
42. Tech's Future
43. The Great Wal-Mart of China
44. Selling to the Poor

Direct marketing
12. Trust in the Marketplace
25. In Praise of the Purple Cow
34. Direct Mail Still Has Its Place
35. The Online Ad Surge
42. Tech's Future

Distribution planning
31. The Old Pillars of New Retailing
33. A Sales Channel They Can't Resist
44. Selling to the Poor

Economic environment
10. Nonprofits Can Take Cues from Biz World
14. Wrestling With Ethics
29. Boost Your Bottom Line by Taking the Guesswork Out of Pricing
33. A Sales Channel They Can't Resist
38. Managing Differences
39. Segmenting Global Markets: Look Before You Leap
40. How China Will Change Your Business
42. Tech's Future

Exportation
40. How China Will Change Your Business
42. Tech's Future
44. Selling to the Poor

Focus groups
22. Marketing: Consumers in the Mist
37. Got Advertising That Works

Franchising
4. Customers at Work
8. Listening to Starbucks
18. A New Age for the Ad Biz
41. Three Dimensional
44. Selling to the Poor

Global marketing
2. The World's Most Innovative Companies
15. The Science of Desire
30. Pricing Gets Creative
32. Why Costco Is So Damn Addictive
35. The Online Ad Surge

Correlation Guide

The **Annual Editions** series provides students with convenient, inexpensive access to current, carefully selected articles from the public press. **Annual Editions: Marketing 08/09** is an easy-to-use reader that presents articles on important topics such as the *future of marketing* and *developing marketing strategies.* For more information on **Annual Editions** and other **McGraw-Hill Contemporary Learning Series** titles visit **www. mhcls.com.** This convenient guide matches the Units in **Annual Editions: Marketing 08/09** with corresponding chapters in **FOUR** best-selling **McGraw-Hill Marketing** texts.

	Grewal/Levy: Marketing, 1e	Kerin: Marketing: The Core, 2e	Perreault: Basic Marketing, 16e	Perreault: Essentials of Marketing, 10e
Unit 1: Marketing in the 2000s and Beyond	Chapter 1: Overview of Marketing—pg. 2 Chapter 3: Marketing Ethics—pg. 58	Chapter 1: Creating Customer Relationships and Value Through Marketing—pg. 4 Chapter 4: Ehtics and Social Responsibility in Marketing—pg. 78	Chapter 1: Marketing's Value to Consumers, Firms, and Society—pg. 2 Chapter 4: Evaluating Opportunities in the Changing Marketing Environment—pg. 88 Chapter 22: Ethical Marketing in a Consumer-Oriented World: Appraisal and Challenges—pg. 598	Chapter 1: Marketing's Value to Consumers, Firms, and Society—pg. 4
Unit 2: Research, Markets, and Consumer Behavior	Chapter 5: Consumer Behavior—pg. 116 Chapter 9: Marketing Research and Information Systems—pg. 240	Chapter 5: Consumer Behavior—pg. 98 Chapter 6: Organizational Markets and Buyer Behavior—pg. 120 Chapter 8: Marketing Research: From Information to Action—pg. 160	Chapter 6: Final Consumers and Their Buying Behavior—pg. 150 Chapter 7: Business and Organizational Customers and Their Buying Behavior—pg. 176 Chapter 8: Improving Decisions with Marketing Information—pg. 206	Chapter 3: Focusing Marketing Strategy with Segmentation and Positioning—pg. 57 Chapter 5: Final Consumers and Their Buying Behavior—pg. 110 Chapter 7: Improving Decisions with Marketing Information—pg. 166
Unit 3: Developing and Implementing Strategies	Chapter 8: Segmentation, Targeting, and Positioning—pg. 208 Chapter 10: Product, Branding, and Packaging Decisions—pg. 268 Chapter 13: Pricing Concepts for Establishing Value—pg. 354 Chapter 14: Strategic Pricing Methods—pg. 382 Chapter 18: Advertising and Sales Promotion—pg. 486	Chapter 10: Developing New Products and Services—pg. 208 Chapter 11: Managing Products, Services and Brands—pg. 234 Chapter 12: Pricing, Products, Services and Brands—pg. 260 Chapter 16: Advertising, Sales Promotion, and Public Relations—pg. 352	Chapter 9: Elements of Product Planning for Goods and Services—pg. 234 Chapter 10: Product Management and New-Product Development—pg. 262 Chapter 12: Distribution Customer Services and Logistics—pg. 312 Chapter 14: Promotion—Introduction to Integrated Marketing Communications—pg. 366 Chapter 17: Pricing Objectives and Policies—pg. 454	Chapter 9: Product Management and New-Product Management—pg. 218 Chapter 11: Distribution Customer Service and Logistics—pg. 268 Chapter 12: Retailers, Wholesalers, and Their Strategy Planning—pg.290 Chapter 13: Promotion—Introduction to Integrated Marketing Communications—pg. 318 Chapter 17: Price Setting in the Business World—pg. 427
Unit 4: Global Marketing	Chapter 7: Global Marketing—pg. 174	Chapter 7: Reaching Global Markets—pg. 138	Chapter 5: Demographic Dimensions of Global Consumer Marketing—pg. 120	Chapter 1: Marketing's Value to Consumers, Firms, and Society—pg. 4

Internet References

The following Internet sites have been carefully researched and selected to support the articles found in this reader. The easiest way to access these selected sites is to go to our student online support site at *http://www.mhcls.com/online/*.

AE: Marketing 08/09

The following sites were available at the time of publication. Visit our Web site—we update our student online support site regularly to reflect any changes.

General Sources

Baruch College Business Week–Harris Poll Demographics
http://www.businessweek.com/1997/18/b352511.htm

The Baruch College–Harris poll commissioned by *Business Week* is used at this site to show interested businesses that are on the Net in the United States.

General Social Survey
http://webapp.icpsr.umich.edu/cocoon/ICPSR-SERIES/00028.xml

The GSS (see DPLS Archive: http://DPLS.DACC.WISC.EDU/SAF/) is an almost annual personal interview survey of U.S. households that began in 1972. More than 35,000 respondents have answered 2,500 questions. It covers a broad range of variables, many of which relate to microeconomic issues.

BestOfAdvertising.net
http://www.bestofadvertising.net/

This is a complete list of sites that include information on marketing research, marketing on the Internet, demographic sources, and organizations and associations. The site also features current books on the subject of marketing.

STAT-USA/Internet Site Economic, Trade, Business Information
http://www.stat-usa.gov

This site, from the U.S. Department of Commerce, contains Daily Economic News, Frequently Requested Statistical Releases, Information on Export and International Trade, Domestic Economic News and Statistical Series, and Databases.

U.S. Census Bureau Home Page
http://www.census.gov

This is a major source of social, demographic, and economic information, such as income/employment data and the latest indicators, income distribution, and poverty data.

UNIT 1: Marketing in the 2000s and Beyond

American Marketing Association Code of Ethics
http://www.marketingpower.com/

At this American Marketing Association site, use the search mechanism to access the organization's Code of Ethics for marketers.

Futures Research Quarterly
http://www.wfs.org/frq.htm

Published by the World Future Society, this publication describes future research that encompasses both an evolving philosophy and a range of techniques, with the aim of assisting decision-makers in all fields to understand better the potential consequences of decisions by developing images of alternative futures. From this page explore the current and back issues and What's Coming Up!

Center for Innovation in Product Development (CIPD)
http://web.mit.edu/cipd/research/prdctdevelop.htm

CIPD is one of the National Science Foundation's engineering research centers. It shares the goal of future product development with academia, industry, and government.

UNIT 2: Research, Markets, and Consumer Behavior

Canadian Innovation Centre
http://www.innovationcentre.ca/

The Canadian Innovation Centre has developed a unique mix of innovation services that can help a company from idea to market launch. Their services are based on the review of 12,000 new product ideas through their technology and market assessment programs over the past 20 years.

BizMiner—Industry Analysis and Trends
http://www.bizminer.com/market_research.asp

The importance of using market research databases and pinpointing local and national trends, including details of industry and small business startups, is emphasized by this site of the Brandow Company that offers samples of market research profiles.

Small Business Center—Articles & Insights
http://www.bcentral.com/articles/krotz/123.asp

This article discusses five market intelligence blunders made by the giant retailer K-Mart. "There were warning signs that K-Mart management mishandled, downplayed or just plain ignored," Joanna L. Krotz says.

Maritz Marketing Research
http://www.maritzresearch.com

Maritz Marketing Research Inc. (MMRI) specializes in custom-designed research studies that link the consumer to the marketer through information. Go to Maritz Loyalty Marketing in the Maritz Companies menu to find resources to identify, retain, and grow your most valuable customers. Also visit Maritz Research for polls, stats, and archived research reports.

USADATA
http://www.usadata.com

This leading provider of marketing, company, advertising, and consumer behavior data offers national and local data covering the top 60 U.S. markets.

WWW Virtual Library: Demography & Population Studies
http://demography.anu.edu.au/VirtualLibrary/

More than 150 links can be found at this major resource to keep track of information of value to researchers in the fields of demography and population studies.

www.mhcls.com/online/

UNIT 3: Developing and Implementing Marketing Strategies

American Marketing Association Homepage
http://www.marketingpower.com

This site of the American Marketing Association is geared to managers, educators, researchers, students, and global electronic members. It contains a search mechanism, definitions of marketing and market research, and links.

Consumer Buying Behavior
http://www.courses.psu.edu/mktg/mktg220_rso3/sls_cons.htm

The Center for Academic Computing at Penn State posts this course data that includes a review of consumer buying behaviors; group, environment, and internal influences; problem-solving; and post-purchasing behavior.

UNIT 4: Global Marketing

International Trade Administration
http://www.ita.doc.gov

The U.S. Department of Commerce is dedicated to helping U.S. businesses compete in the global marketplace, and at this site it offers assistance through many Web links under such headings as Trade Statistics, Cross-Cutting Programs, Regions and Countries, and Import Administration.

World Chambers Network
http://www.worldchambers.net

International trade at work is viewable at this site. For example, click on Global Business eXchange (GBX) for a list of active business opportunities worldwide or to submit your new business opportunity for validation.

World Trade Center Association On Line
http://iserve.wtca.org

Data on world trade is available at this site that features information, services, a virtual trade fair, an exporter's encyclopedia, trade opportunities, and a resource center.

We highly recommend that you review our Web site for expanded information and our other product lines. We are continually updating and adding links to our Web site in order to offer you the most usable and useful information that will support and expand the value of your Annual Editions. You can reach us at: *http://www.mhcls.com/annualeditions/*.

UNIT 1

Marketing in the 2000s and Beyond

Unit Selections

Key Points to Consider

- Dramatic changes are occurring in the marketing of products and services. What social and economic trends do you believe are most significant today, and how do you think these will affect marketing in the future?

- Theodore Levitt suggests that as times change the marketing concept must be reinterpreted. Given the varied perspectives of the other articles in this unit, what do you think this reinterpretation will entail?

- In the present competitive business arena, is it possible for marketers to behave ethically in the environment and both survive and prosper? What suggestions can you give that could be incorporated into the marketing strategy for firms that want to be both ethical and successful?

Student Web Site

www.mhcls.com/online

Internet References

Further information regarding these Web sites may be found in this book's preface or online.

American Marketing Association Code of Ethics
http://www.marketingpower.com/
Futures Research Quarterly
http://www.wfs.org/frq.htm
Center for Innovation in Product Development (CIPD)
http://web.mit.edu/cipd/research/prdctdevelop.htm

"If we want to know what a business is we must start with its purpose.... There is only one valid definition of business purpose: to create a customer. What business thinks it produces is not of first importance—especially not to the future of the business or to its success. What the customer thinks he is buying, what he considers 'value' is decisive—it determines what a business is, what it produces, and whether it will prosper."

—Peter Drucker, *The Practice of Management*

When Peter Drucker penned these words in 1954, American industry was just awakening to the realization that marketing would play an important role in the future success of businesses. The ensuing years have seen an increasing number of firms in highly competitive areas—particularly in the consumer goods industry—adopt a more sophisticated customer orientation and an integrated marketing focus.

The dramatic economic and social changes of the last decade have stirred companies in an even broader range of industries—from banking and air travel to communications—to the realization that marketing will provide them with their cutting edge. Demographic and lifestyle changes have splintered mass, homogeneous markets into many markets, each with different needs and interests. Deregulation has made once-protected industries vulnerable to the vagaries of competition. Vast and rapid technological changes are making an increasing number of products and services obsolete. Intense international competition, rapid expansion of the Internet-based economy, and the growth of truly global markets have many firms looking well beyond their national boundaries.

Indeed, it appears that during the new millennium marketing will take on a unique significance—and not just within the industrial sector. Social institutions of all kinds, which had thought themselves exempt from the pressures of the marketplace, are also beginning to recognize the need for marketing in the management of their affairs. Colleges and universities, charities, museums, symphony orchestras, and even hospitals are beginning to give attention the marketing concept—to provide what the consumer wants to buy.

The selections in this unit are grouped into four areas. Their purposes are to provide current perspectives on marketing, discuss differing views of the marketing concept, analyze the use of marketing by social institutions and nonprofit organizations, and examine the ethical and social responsibilities of marketing.

The articles in the first subsection provide significant clues about salient approaches and issues that marketers need to address in the future in order to create, promote, and sell their products and services in ways that meet the expectation of consumers.

The selections that address the marketing concept include Levitt's now classic "Marketing Myopia," which first appeared in the *Harvard Business Review* in 1960. This version includes the author's retrospective commentary, written in 1975, in which he

The McGraw-Hill Companies, Inc./Christopher Kerrigan, photographer

discusses how shortsightedness can make management unable to recognize that there is no such thing as a growth industry. The second article provides five strategies for focusing on customers. "The Big Opportunity" describes the challenge of marketing to the needs of overweight consumers. The last article in this subsection, "Listening to Starbucks," discloses that there are close parallels between the way Starbucks is developing a new music business and the way Howard Shultz developed the core coffee business.

In the *Services & Social Marketing* subsection, the first article reveals why learning the importance of how to manage angry customers is a significant part of today's service landscape. The final article in this subsection emphasizes the importance of nonprofits having a carefully developed brand.

In the final subsection, a careful look is taken at the strategic process and practice of incorporating ethics and social responsibility into the marketplace. "The Fidelity Factor" underlines the importance of ensuring customer relationships by infusing them with trust. "Trust in the Marketplace" discusses the importance of gaining and maintaining customers' trust. The last article in this subsection provides some things for parents and their kids to look out for concerning the questionable practices of some marketers during the holiday season.

Hot Stuff

Make These Top Trends Part of Your Marketing Mix

Gwen Moran

Still using the same marketing tactics you were using five years ago? Those won't work with today's shifting demographics and preferences. The U.S. population is older, more multicultural, more time-pressed and more jaded toward overt sales pitches than ever before. And your marketing strategy should be built accordingly.

So what's working? After consulting over a dozen experts in the field, we've uncovered the following hot trends in marketing.

Market on the Move

According to the Mobile Marketing Association, by 2008, 89 percent of brands will use text and multimedia messaging to reach their audiences, with nearly one-third planning to spend more than 10 percent of their marketing budgets on advertising in the medium. As phones with video capability become more prevalent, expect more rich media marketing options. Plus, now that mobile phone service providers are dipping their toes into the credit card pool—soon your phone or PDA may make plastic obsolete—customers will be relying on these devices more than ever.

"There are some low-cost mobile marketing onramps for small businesses," says Kim Bayne, author of *Marketing Without Wires*. "Businesses can implement opt-in text messaging services and coupons with their loyal customers. We've already seen local restaurants send the day's specials to nearby lunch patrons. The cost is fairly low, and it can be done from a PC, without involving a pricey service provider."

Go Online

"Think globally, act locally" is now the mantra for entrepreneurs advertising online. Online ad spending is up as much as 33 percent over last year, says David J. Moore, chairman and CEO of digital marketing firm 24/7 Real Media Inc. in New York City. Earlier this year, Google announced a new local advertising program linked to its map service and AdWords program, allowing businesses to drive some of Google's traffic to their brick-and-mortar locations.

"[Entrepreneurs] should pay attention to any targeting that allows them to increase advertising efficiency by reaching users in their particular geographic area," says Moore. Online ads are also migrating to podcasts and blogs, where advertisers can reach very specific niche audiences. And with increased access to broadband and the falling cost of video production, Moore foresees a rise in online video ads for businesses as well.

Court the Boom

A baby boomer turns 50 every 7 seconds—joining a population segment that will grow by 25 percent in the next decade while other segments remain flat.

Matt Thornhill, founder of consulting firm The Boomer Project, which helps businesses reach adults born between 1946 and 1964, says it's time for marketers to recalibrate their thinking about marketing to older adults. Boomers are a dynamic group that's much more open to new experiences and brands than previous generations of older adults have been.

Stephanie Lakhani found that to be true at her upscale Breathe Wellness Spas (www.breathetoheal.com) in Boise, Idaho. Catering primarily to boomers, the two spas bring in about $1.2 million per year. She says boomers are an excellent target, with disposable income and a tendency to refer business. "They expect perfect service," says Lakhani, 35, who adds, "They tend to travel and buy in groups, so giving them an incentive to refer a friend in the form of an upgrade or a thank you [gesture] works very well. They are also very responsive to direct mail."

Thornhill adds that marketers should target boomers by what they're doing instead of how old they are. "Boomers are living such cyclical lives. In their 40s or 50s, they could be going back to college, be empty nesters or be married a second time and raising a young family," he explains. "You wouldn't sell the same vacation package to all these people. So pick the lifestyle segment you're targeting, and focus on that."

Sindicate Simply

For something that's named Really Simple Syndication, few tools are more misunderstood or misused than RSS. Provided by such companies as Bloglines (www.bloglines.com) and NewsGator (www.newsgator.com), RSS lets you send and receive information without using e-mail. Instead, the information is sent directly to a subscriber, who receives it through an RSS reader. With browsers like Internet Explorer integrating such readers, we'll be seeing more information feeds. That could be a good thing—or not—depending on whether businesses use them properly.

"You don't need to blog to offer an RSS feed," says online marketing consultant Debbie Weil, author of *The Corporate Blogging Book*. "But you should have a blogging mind-set. Show the reader what's in it for them. Write clear and interesting headlines. There's a bit of an art to writing RSS [content]." She adds that you should break up your feeds by audience—customers, investors, media and the like—just as you would any other message distribution.

Jim Edwards, 38, uses a blog and RSS to promote his business, Guaranteed Response Marketing. "Whenever I publish an article, either through my blog [www.igottatellyou.com/blog] or through another site's RSS feeder, I expect to get 100 to 300 references back to me in a week," says Edwards, whose $2 million Lightfoot, Virginia, business provides electronic tutorials and publications. "It's a quick way to get links back to you, as well as to get on sites that people are actively looking at."

Use Social Networks

Customers are making friends online through social networking sites like MySpace.com. The massive site—boasting millions of users, all segmented by age, geography and interests—offers an unbridled opportunity for marketers, according to Libby Pigg, senior account manager at Edelman Interactive in New York City.

"You [can] launch a profile for your business and give it a personality," says Pigg, who has launched MySpace marketing campaigns for major consumer products companies. "It's simi-

lar to a dating site, where you tell people a bit about yourself. Then, you use the search function to find the group you want to target—maybe single people in New York [City] between 24 and 30—and contact them to become your 'friends.'"

A MySpace profile helped Taylor Bond generate interest in Egismoz.com, the electronics division of his $20 million retail company, Children's Orchard, in Ann Arbor, Michigan. Earlier this year, Bond sent invitations to some of the site's young, tech-savvy users. The key to maintaining their interest, he says, is to provide fresh content and special offers.

"We're seeing more people come into the store saying that they saw us on MySpace," says Bond, 44. "We're definitely seeing more traffic and feedback on the profile, and we're getting some incredible feedback about what's hot and what people want, so it's good for market research, too." Opportunities also exist on other networking sites like Friendster.com, LinkedIn.com, and even niche sites like Adholcs.com, which focuses on the advertising community.

Advertise in Unusual Places

From valet tickets and hubcaps to T-shirts emblazoned with video displays, advertising is popping up in new places. A March survey of marketing executives by Blackfriars Communications entitled "Marketing 2006: 2006's Timid Start" found that business spending on traditional advertising continued its decline, and spending on nontraditional marketing methods—from online promotions to buzz marketing—rose 12 percent since late 2005.

Scott Montgomery, principal and creative director of Bradley and Montgomery, an advertising and branding firm in Indianapolis, says the shift in ad spending will continue as advertisers look to make their ad dollars more effective.

Make it Stick

Tap these marketing trends to get into customers' hearts and minds.

- **Multicultural Market:** By 2010, the buying power of American blacks and Hispanics is expected to exceed the gross domestic product of Canada, according to the Selig Center for Economic Growth at the University of Georgia in Athens. Make sure you're not overlooking this market. Rochelle Newman-Carrasco, CEO of Enlace Communications, a Los Angeles multicultural marketing firm, advises companies not only to translate materials when appropriate, but also to be conscious of cultural images: "In lifestyle shots, go beyond multicultural casting. Show scenes where the clothing, food and other backgrounds reflect different cultures."
- **Experiential Marketing:** Kathy Sherbrooke, president of Circles, an experiential marketing firm in Boston, says businesses must figure out the key messages of their brand and find ways for their staffs and locations to reflect that image—young and trendy, sophisticated and elegant, and so on. "Create an environment that's consistent with your brand," she says. She points to Apple Computer's retail stores, where clerks use handheld

checkout machines and pull product bags out of their back pockets to reinforce the ease-of-use and streamlined processes for which Apple is known.
- **Customer Evangelism:** From hiring word-of-mouth marketing companies to creating incentives for customer referrals, businesses are placing more importance on customer evangelism, says Andrew Pierce, senior partner at New York City branding firm Prophet. "Companies need to be customer-centric for this to happen," he explains. "If you're not finding ways to increase value and inspire loyalty, it won't work."

At the simplest level, Pierce advises using customer testimonials to add credibility to marketing efforts, including webinars where customers talk about your company. More extreme examples include buzz marketing campaigns where happy customers talk up the product, or inviting customers to trade shows or other events where they can show their enthusiasm in person.

Montgomery and his team were the first to develop advertising programs on electrical outlets in airports. Reasoning that business travelers—one of the holy grail audiences marketers love—power up portable technology while waiting for their planes, it seemed a natural place to reach them.

"Smart marketers are looking [for] places where people are engaged," says Montgomery. "You have to target your message in a way that makes sense for [how] people behave."

Premium-ize Your Brand

Brands like Coach and Grey Goose vodka have mastered the art of taking everyday items and introducing luxe versions at much higher price points. Now, growing businesses are also going upscale with their products or services.

Andrew Rohm, professor of marketing at Northeastern University's College of Business Administration in Boston, says smaller businesses can often "trickle up" more easily than large brands, which may find that customers are resistant to accepting their more expensive offerings. "A small brand can reinvent itself without having to swim upstream against its image," says Rohm.

To posh up your product, he advises the same best practices as with any new offering: Do your research, and make sure there's a market for the product or service before you make your brand go bling.

Blog On

With the blogosphere more than 43.1 million blogs strong, according to blog search engine Technorati, it appears everyone and his grandmother are blogging. Robert Scoble, technical evangelist at Microsoft and author of *Naked Conversations: How Blogs Are Changing the Way That Businesses Talk With Customers,* believes blogs are important for businesses that want direct customer feedback. And development blogs, where businesses get direct input about products and services from readers, will soon become even more important, he says.

Scoble predicts a rise in regional blogs linked to Google's new local advertising program and Mapquest.com for quick access to directions, giving people more insight into the local businesses they want to frequent. He also says we'll see more video blogs, which won't replace text blogs but will more effectively communicate with some audiences. "If I'm trying to explain to you what [video game] Halo 2 is, I can write 10,000 words and I'm not going to get it right, but you can see a 2-minute video and you'll understand," he says.

Take these trends into consideration as you plan for the coming year. Not every idea may apply to your company, but most are market forces you can't afford to ignore.

GWEN MORAN is Entrepreneur's "Retail Register" and "Quick Pick" columnist.

The World's Most Innovative Companies

Their creativity goes beyond products to rewiring themselves. *BusinessWeek* and the Boston Consulting Group rank the best.

JENA McGREGOR

It was a fitting way to wrap up the first day of IBM's innovation-themed leadership forum, held in Rome in early April. Guests were treated to small group tours of the Vatican Museum, including Michelangelo's frescoes in the Sistine Chapel. They sipped cocktails on a patio in the back of St. Peter's, the vast dome of the basilica outlined by the light of the moon. They dined in a marble-statue-filled hall inside the Vatican. What better place than Italy to hold a global confab on innovation, the topic *di giorno* among corporate leaders? It was, after all, the birthplace of the Renaissance, another period of great innovation and change.

The next day, at the Auditorium Parco della Musica, 500-odd corporate executives, government leaders, and academics listened as a diverse group of innovative leaders took the stage. Sunil B. Mittal, chief executive officer of Indian telecom company Bharti Tele-Ventures Ltd., described his radical business model, which outsources everything but marketing and customer management, charges 2 cents a minute for calls, and is adding a million customers a month. Yang Mingsheng, CEO of Agricultural Bank of China, the country's second-biggest commercial bank, spoke of building a banking powerhouse from a modest business making micro loans to peasant farmers.

Their stories echoed a comment IBM CEO Samuel J. Palmisano had made the day before: "The way you will thrive in this environment is by innovating—innovating in technologies, innovating in strategies, innovating in business models."

Palmisano, to be sure, was making a subtle pitch for IBM and its ability to help the assembled leaders do well in an increasingly challenging business environment. But he also summed up the broad focus of innovation in the 21st century.

Today, innovation is about much more than new products. It is about reinventing business processes and building entirely new markets that meet untapped customer needs. Most important, as the Internet and globalization widen the pool of new ideas, it's about selecting and executing the right ideas and bringing them to market in record time.

In the 1990s, innovation was about technology and control of quality and cost. Today, it's about taking corporate organizations built for efficiency and rewiring them for creativity and growth. "There are a lot of different things that fall under the rubric of innovation," says Vijay Govindarajan, a professor at Dartmouth College's Tuck School of Business and author of *Ten Rules for Strategic Innovators: From Idea to Execution.* "Innovation does not have to have anything to do with technology."

The Quick and the Blocked

To discover which companies innovate best—and why—*BusinessWeek* joined with The Boston Consulting Group to produce our second annual ranking of the 25 most innovative companies. More than 1,000 senior managers responded to the global survey, making it our deepest management survey to date on this critical issue.

The new ranking has companies evoking all types of innovation. There are technology innovators, such as BlackBerry maker and newcomer Research In Motion Ltd., which makes its debut on our list at No. 24. There are business model innovators, such as No. 11 Virgin Group Ltd., which applies its hip lifestyle brand to ho-hum operations such as airlines, financial services, and even health insurance. Process innovators are there, too: Rounding out the ranking is Southwest Airlines Co. at No. 25, a whiz at wielding operational improvements to outfly its competitors.

At the top of the list are the masters of many genres of innovation. Take Apple Computer Inc., once again the creative king. To launch the iPod, says innovation consultant Larry Keeley of Doblin Inc., Apple used no fewer than seven types of innovation. They included networking (a novel agreement among music companies to sell their songs online), business model (songs sold for a buck each online), and branding (how cool are those white ear buds and wires?). Consumers love the ease and feel of the iPod, but it is the simplicity of the iTunes software platform that turned a great MP3 player into a revenue-gushing phenomenon.

Toyota Motor Corp., which leapt 10 spots this year to No. 4, is becoming a master of many as well. The Japanese auto giant is best known for an obsessive focus on innovating its manufacturing processes. But thanks to the hot-selling Prius, Toyota is earning even more respect as a product innovator. It is also collaborating more closely with suppliers to generate innovation. Last year, Toyota launched its Value Innovation strategy. Rather than work with suppliers just to cut costs of individual parts, it is delving further back in the design process to find savings spanning entire vehicle systems.

OPEN YOUR LABS AND EXPAND YOUR OPPORTUNITIES
Corporate R&D labs are opening their doors—collaborating with suppliers and customers, sharing software code with programmers, and tapping networks of scientists and entrepreneurs for the world's best ideas.

The *BusinessWeek*-BCG survey is more than just a Who's Who list of innovators. It also focuses on the major obstacles to innovation that executives face today. While 72% of the senior executives in the survey named innovation as one of their top three priorities, almost half said they were dissatisfied with the returns on their investments in that area.

The No. 1 obstacle, according to our survey takers, is slow development times. Fast-changing consumer demands, global outsourcing, and open-source software make speed to market paramount today. Yet companies often can't organize themselves to move faster, says George Stalk Jr., a senior vice-president with BCG who has studied time-based competition for 25 years. Fast cycle times require taking bets even when huge payoffs aren't a certainty. "Some organizations are nearly immobilized by the notion that [they] can't do anything unless it moves the needle," says Stalk. In addition, he says, speed requires coordination from the hub: "Fast innovators organize the corporate center to drive growth. They don't wait for [it] to come up through the business units."

Indeed, a lack of coordination is the second-biggest barrier to innovation, according to the survey's findings. But collaboration requires much more than paying lip service to breaking down silos. The best innovators reroute reporting lines and create physical spaces for collaboration. They team up people from across the org chart and link rewards to innovation. Innovative companies build innovation cultures. "You have to be willing to get down into the plumbing of the organization and align the nervous system of the company," says James P. Andrew, who heads the innovation practice at BCG.

Procter & Gamble Co. (No. 7) has done just that in transforming its traditional in-house research and development process into an open-source innovation strategy it calls "connect and develop." The new method? Embrace the collective brains of the world. Make it a goal that 50% of the company's new products come from outside P&G's labs. Tap networks of inventors, scientists, and suppliers for new products that can be developed in-house.

The radically different approach couldn't be shoehorned into managers' existing responsibilities. Rather, P&G had to tear apart and restitch much of its research organization. It created new job classifications, such as 70 worldwide "technology entrepreneurs," or TEs, who act as scouts, looking for the latest breakthroughs from places such as university

PLAYBOOK: BEST-PRACTICE IDEAS

Ideas from the Innovators

Take a page from some of the world's most respected creative companies:

Bring them together	Think traits as well as numbers	Make a seat at the table	Preserve oral traditions	Get involved on the ground
BMW relocates between 200 and 300 engineers, designers, and managers to its central research and innovation center to design cars. **Face-to-face teams reduce late-stage conflicts and speed development times.**	Tracking innovation results is crucial for any growth-focused company. **But when evaluating managers, subjective metrics, such as risk tolerance or GE's measure of "imagination and courage," can be a better way.**	Infosys **selects nine employees under 30 each year to participate in its senior management sessions.** These young guns present their ideas for new services and ways to improve the company's processes.	Old-timers at 3M are expected to **hand down tales of the company's long innovation tradition** to new engineers. Before long, every new 3Mer can quote the philosophies of former CEO William McKnight.	Research In Motion co-CEO Mike Lazaridis personally heads engineering teams and hosts weekly innovation-themed "vision" sessions to excite the troops. **A culture of innovation starts from the top.**

labs. TEs also develop "technology game boards" that map out where technology opportunities lie and help P&Gers get inside the minds of its competitors.

To spearhead the connect-and-develop efforts, Larry Huston took on the newly created role of vice-president for innovation and knowledge. Each business unit, from household care to family health, added a manager responsible for driving cultural change around the new model. The managers communicate directly with Huston, who also oversees the technology entrepreneurs and managers running the external innovation networks. "You want to have a coherent strategy across the organization," says Huston. "The ideas tend to be bigger when you have someone sitting at the center looking at the company's growth goals."

Asking the Right Questions

Coordinating innovation from the center is taken literally at BMW Group, No. 16 on the list. Each time BMW begins developing a car, the project team's members—some 200 to 300 staffers from engineering, design, production, marketing, purchasing, and finance—are relocated from their scattered locations to the auto maker's Research and Innovation Center, called FIZ, for up to three years. Such proximity helps speed up communications (and therefore car development) and encourages face-to-face meetings that prevent late-stage conflicts between, say, marketing and engineering. In 2004 these teams began meeting in the center's new Project House, a unique structure that lets them work a short walk from the company's 8,000 researchers and developers and alongside life-size clay prototypes of the car in development.

For many companies, cross-functional collaborations last weeks or months, not years. Southwest recently gathered people from its in-flight, ground, maintenance, and dispatch operations. For six months they met for 10 hours a week, brainstorming ideas to address a broad issue: What are the highest-impact changes we can make to our aircraft operations?

BECOME INNOVATORS-IN-CHIEF
More than 50% of survey respondents said the CEO or chairman was responsible for driving innovation. Without heavy fire cover from the top, innovation efforts will get lost in the shuffle of short-term demands.

The group presented 109 ideas to senior management, three of which involve sweeping operational changes. One solution about to be introduced will reduce the number of aircraft "swaps"—disruptive events that occur when one aircraft has to be substituted for another during mechanical problems. Chief Information Officer Tom Nealon says the diversity of the people on the team was crucial, mentioning one director from the airline's schedule planning division in particular. "He had almost a naive perspective," says Nealon. "His questions were so fundamental they challenged the premises the maintenance and dispatch guys had worked on for the last 30 years."

Managers are scrambling to come up with ways to measure and raise the productivity of their innovation efforts. Yet the *BusinessWeek*-BCG survey shows widespread differences over which metrics—such as the ratio of products that succeed, or the ROI of innovation projects—should be used and how best to use them. Some two-thirds of the managers in the survey say metrics have the most impact in the selection of the right ideas to fund and develop. About half say they use metrics best in assessing the health of their company's innovation portfolio. But as many as 47% said measurements on the impact of innovation after products or services have been launched are used only sporadically.

Actually, most managers in the survey aren't monitoring many innovation metrics at all; 63% follow five gauges or fewer. "Two or three metrics just don't give you the visibility to get down to root causes," says BCG's Andrew. Then there are companies that track far too many. Andrew says one of the top innovators on our list—he's mum as to which one—collects 85 different innovation metrics in one of its businesses. "That means they manage none of them," he says. "They default to a couple, but they spend an immense amount of time and effort collecting those 85."

The sweet spot is somewhere between 8 and 12 metrics, says Andrew. That's about the number that Samsung Electronics Co. uses, says Chu Woosik, a senior vice-president at the South Korean company. Chu says the most important metrics are price premiums and how quickly they can bring to market phones that delight customers. Samsung also watches the allocation of investments across projects and its new-product success ratio. That, Chu says, has nearly doubled in the last five years. "You want to see it from every angle," he says. "A lot of companies fall into the trap that they thought things were really improving, but in the end, it didn't work out that way. We don't want to make that mistake."

Awards and Ethnography

One of the biggest mistakes companies may make is tying managers' incentives too directly to specific innovation metrics. Tuck's Govindarajan warns that linking pay too closely to hard innovation measures may tempt managers to game the system. A metric such as the percentage of revenue from new products, for instance, can lead to incremental brand extensions rather than true breakthroughs. In addition, innovation is such a murky process that targets are likely to change. "There's a dialogue that needs to happen," says Govindarajan. "Operating plans may need to be reviewed, or you may need to change plans because a new competitor came into your space."

Susan Schuman, CEO of Stone Yamashita Partners, which works with CEOs on innovation and change, says that besides numbers-driven metrics, some clients are adding subjective assessments related to innovation, such as a manager's risk tolerance, to performance evaluations. "It's not just about results," she says. "It's how did you lead people to get to those results."

That's one reason the bastion of Six Sigma-dom, General Electric Co., has begun evaluating its top 5,000 managers on "growth traits" that include innovation-oriented themes such as "external focus" and "imagination and courage." GE has also added more flexibility into its traditionally rigid performance

7

rankings. GE will now have to square its traditional Six Sigma metrics, which are all about control, with its new emphasis on innovation, which is more about managing risk. That's a major change in culture.

How do you build an innovation culture? Try carrots. Several companies on our list have formal rewards for top innovators. Nokia Corp. inducts engineers with at least 10 patents into its "Club 10," recognizing them each year in a formal awards ceremony hosted by CEO Jorma Ollila.

3M has long awarded "Genesis Grants" to scientists who want to work on outside projects. Each year more than 60 researchers submit formal applications to a panel of 20 senior scientists who review the requests, just as a foundation would review academics' proposals. Twelve to 20 grants, ranging from $50,000 and $100,000 apiece, are awarded each year. The researchers can use the money to hire supplemental staff or acquire necessary equipment.

MEASURE WHAT MATTERS
Tracking innovation results is hard: You can't reduce it to a single number, and balancing risk is always part of the equation. Just 30% of survey takers said they measure ROI on innovation investments.

Of course, rewards won't help if the inventions aren't focused on customer needs. Getting good consumer insight is the fourth most cited obstacle to innovation in our survey. Blogs and online communities now make it easier to know what customers are thinking. Hiring designers and ethnographers who observe customers using products at work or at home helps, too. But finding that Holy Grail of marketing, the "unmet need" of a consumer, remains elusive. "You need time, just thinking time, to step out of the day to day to see what's going on in the world and what's going on with your customers," says Stone Yamashita's Schuman.

The World Is Your Lab

Try learning journeys. That's what Starbucks Corp., up 10 spots from 2005 to No. 9, does. While the coffee company began doing ethnography back in 2002 and relies on its army of baristas to share customer insights, it recently started taking product development and other cross-company teams on "inspiration" field trips to view customers and trends. Two months ago, Michelle Gass, Starbucks' senior vice-president for category management, took her team to Paris, Düsseldorf, and London to visit local Starbucks and other restaurants to get a better sense of local cultures, behaviors, and fashions. "You come back just full of different ideas and different ways to think about things than you would had you read about it in a magazine or e-mail," says Gass.

A close watch of customer insights can also bring innovation to even the most iconic and established products. Back in 2003, 3M began noticing and monitoring two consumer trends. One

was troubling: Customers were using laptops, cell phones, and BlackBerrys to send quick memos or jot down bits of information. Every thumb-tapped message or stylus-penned note on a personal digital assistant meant one less Post-it note.

The other trend, however, was encouraging: The rise of digital photography. While observing consumers, 3M researchers asked to see their photos. What followed was always a clunky process: Consumers would scroll through screen upon screen of photos or have to dig through a drawer for the few shots they printed. Nine months later a team of one marketer and two lab scientists hit upon the idea of Post-it Picture Paper, or photo paper coated with adhesive that lets people stick their photos to a wall for display. "We listened carefully to what consumers didn't say and observed what they did," says Jack Truong, vice-president of 3M's office supply division.

To get a sense of the value of customer research, imagine you're a Finnish engineer trying to design a phone for an illiterate customer on the Indian subcontinent. That's the problem Nokia faced when it began making low-cost phones for emerging markets. A combination of basic ethnographic and long-term user research in China, India, and Nepal helped Nokia understand how illiterate people live in a world full of numbers and letters. The result? A new "iconic" menu that lets illiterate customers navigate contact lists made up of images.

COORDINATE AND COLLABORATE
There's no simple innovation "on" switch. Building creative companies takes synchronization from the center, cross-boundary collaboration, and structural changes to the org chart.

Other innovative ideas followed. By listening to customers in poorer countries, Nokia learned that phones had to be more durable, since they're often the most expensive item these customers will buy. To function in a tropical climate, it made the phones more moisture-resistant. It even used special screens that are more legible in bright sunlight.

Consumers increasingly are doing the innovation themselves. Consider Google Inc., our No. 2 innovator, and its mapping technology, which it opened to the public. This produced a myriad of "mash-ups" in which programmers combine Google's maps with anything from real estate listings to local poker game sites.

Google's mash-ups are just one example of the escalating phenomenon of open innovation. These days the world is your R&D lab. Customers are co-opting technology and morphing products into their own inventions. Many companies are scouting for outside ideas they can develop in-house, embracing the open-source movement, and joining up with suppliers or even competitors on big projects that will make them more efficient and more powerful. "When you work with outside parties, they bear some of the costs and some of the risks, and can accelerate the time to market," says Henry W. Chesbrough, the University of California at Berkeley Haas School of Business professor

8

who helped establish the concept with his 2003 book, *Open Innovation.*

India and China are growing sources of innovation for companies, too. The *BusinessWeek*-BCG survey shows that they are nearly as popular as Europe among innovation-focused executives. When asked where their company planned to increase R&D spending, 44% answered India, 44% said China, and 48% said Western Europe. Managers tended to look to the U.S. and Canada for idea generation, while a lower percentage looked to Europe for the same tasks. India and China, though, are still seen as centers for product development.

Few companies have embraced the open innovation model as widely as IBM, No. 10 on our list. While the company's proprietary technology is still a force to behold—Big Blue remains the world's largest patent holder, with more than 40,000—the company is opening up its technology to developers, partners, and clients. Last year it made 500 of its patents, mainly for software code, freely available to outside programmers. And in November it helped fund the Open Invention Network, a company formed to acquire patents and offer them royalty-free to help promote the open-source software movement.

Why the generosity? IBM believes that by helping to create technology ecosystems, it will benefit in the long run. "We want to do things that encourage markets to grow," says Dr. John E. Kelly III, senior vice-president for technology and intellectual property at IBM. By helping nurture those markets, says Kelly, "we know we'll get at least our fair share."

Going Outside for Ideas

P&G has helped establish several outside networks of innovators it turns to for ideas the company can develop in-house. These networks include NineSigma, which links up companies with scientists at university, government, and private labs; YourEncore Inc., which connects retired scientists and engineers with businesses; and yet2.com Inc., an online marketplace for intellectual property.

Only a CEO can change a business culture at top speed, and in Alan G. Lafley, P&G has its own innovator-in-chief. Lafley sits in on all "upstream" R&D review meetings, 15 a year, that showcase new products. He also spends three full days a year with the company's Design Board, a group of outside designers who offer their perspective on upcoming P&G products. "He's sort of the chief innovation officer," says P&G's Huston. "He's very, very involved."

That sort of support from the CEO is essential, says Jon R. Katzenbach, co-founder of New York-based management consultancy Katzenbach Partners LLC. "The CEO determines the culture," he says. "If the CEO is determined to [improve] the surfacing of ideas and determined to make critical choices, then the chances of an [organization's] figuring that out are much, much greater."

Infosys Technologies Ltd., the Bangalore-based information technology services company that popped up at No. 10 on our

Asia-Pacific list, takes a direct approach to making sure management stays involved in the innovation process. Chairman and "chief mentor" N.R. Narayana Murthy introduced the company's "voice of youth" program seven years ago. Each year the company selects nine top-performing young guns—each under 30—to participate in its eight yearly senior management council meetings, presenting and discussing their ideas with the top leadership team. "We believe these young ideas need the senior-most attention for them to be identified and fostered," says Sanjay Purohit, associate vice-president and head of corporate planning. Infosys CEO Nandan M. Nilekani concurs: "If an organization becomes too hierarchical, ideas that bubble up from younger people [aren't going to be heard]."

MINE CUSTOMER INSIGHTS
Getting inside the minds of customers is essential for "aha!" moments that lead to innovation. While ethnographers and designers are increasingly helping companies, true insight remains elusive: One quarter of our respondents still call customer awareness an innovation obstacle.

Mike Lazaridis, president and co-CEO of Research In Motion, hosts an innovation-themed, invitation-only "Vision Series" session in the Waterloo (Ont.)-based company's 100-seat auditorium each Thursday. The standing-room-only meetings focus on new research and future goals for the company that gave us the BlackBerry.

Lazaridis is likely the only chief executive of a publicly traded company who has an Academy Award for technical achievement. (He won it in 1999 for an innovative bar-code reader that he helped invent that expedites film editing and production.) He has donated $100 million of his own money to fund a theoretical physics institute and an additional $50 million to a university quantum computing and nanotechnology engineering center in Waterloo. He has even appeared in an American Express commercial, scratching complex equations across a blackboard while proclaiming his commitment to the creative process. "I think we have a culture of innovation here, and [engineers] have absolute access to me," says Lazaridis. "I live a life that tries to promote innovation." As the *BusinessWeek*-BCG survey demonstrates, it is a life every manager around the world must embrace.

JENA MCGREGOR, with MICHAEL ARNDT and ROBERT BERNER in Chicago, IAN ROWLEY and KENJI HALL in Tokyo, GAIL EDMONDSON in Frankfurt, STEVE HAMM in Rome, MOON IHLWAN in Seoul, and ANDY REINHARDT in Paris.

The Next 25 Years

Population projections calculated exclusively for *American Demographics* for the next quarter century forecast a larger, older and more diverse nation, one with many opportunities—and challenges—for businesses.

ALISON STEIN WELLNER

In 2025, the oldest Baby Boomers will celebrate their 79th birthday. The youngest members of Gen Y will mark their 31st birthday, and the oldest Gen Xers will be two years away from being eligible for Social Security benefits—assuming they still exist.

It's always difficult to predict the future, and crystal balls are particularly cloudy when it comes to speculation about what this country will be like politically, socially and culturally a quarter century from now. In statistician-speak, too many variables are interacting in unpredictable ways for a steady hand to paint a detailed picture of tomorrow. But there is an exception: demographics. The demographic book on 2025 is already written, as most of the people who will be alive in 22 years in this country are alive today.

So what are the fundamental demographic trends that will shape the consumer market over the next 25 years? To help answer that question, *American Demographics* teamed up with MapInfo, a Troy, N.Y.-based market research firm, to create population projections to 2025. We found that the trends likely to influence business agendas of tomorrow are already gaining momentum today—and the smartest companies have started developing strategies to suit the three largest and most likely demographic trends that will shape the marketplace of tomorrow. Even in a down economy, these companies are aware that they'll need to meet the needs of a population that's growing at a feverish pace. They're tweaking marketing plans to suit a nation that will increasingly be dominated by people over age 65. They're working to understand emerging ethnic groups now, instead of waiting another 10 years, realizing that the majority white population is on its way to becoming a minority.

But even demographic projections are fallible: Consumers have the ability to throw them off course. By definition, projections make assumptions based on past behavior, and future behavior may or may not follow the same patterns. To create projections such as these, demographers analyze birth rates, death rates and immigration, and project forward three different numbers—one that indicates the highest possible number, one that indicates the lowest and one that's in between, a number known as "the middle series." The projections that follow mostly rely on the middle series—which means they assume people will continue to have children at about the same rate, deaths will continue at about the same rate and immigration will fall between the current rate and its highest number. To the extent that demographics are destiny, here's what's in the cards.

America the Crowded

On the business agenda:

- More opportunity, more niche markets
- Environmental concerns moving front and center

If your idea of America conjures up visions of unlimited wide, open spaces, or of houses on acres and acres of land, you may be in for quite a shock during the next two decades. By 2025, the

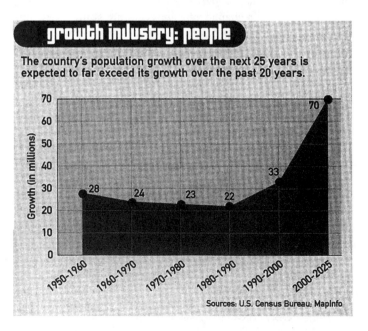

growth industry: people

The country's population growth over the next 25 years is expected to far exceed its growth over the past 20 years.

Growth (in millions): 70, 60, 50, 40, 30, 20, 10, 0

1950–1960: 28
1960–1970: 24
1970–1980: 23
1980–1990: 22
1990–2000: 33
2000–2025: 70

Sources: U.S. Census Bureau; MapInfo

U.S. population is expected to exceed 350 million people—an increase of about 70 million and a boost of 25 percent, according to projections by MapInfo.

This puts the nation on a growth trajectory that's similar to the one experienced just after World War II, when the GIs came home and helped create the Baby Boom in the 1950s and 1960s. Population growth slowed during the 1970s and 1980s but experienced a surge during the 1990s. Expect record-shattering growth to continue, as Americans live longer, birth rates hold steady and immigration continues apace. This wide expanse of growing humanity means that nearly every market segment will expand in numbers over the next 25 years, because more people means more pocketbooks.

However, this *massive* market does not herald a return to the *mass* market. "This [population] growth will combine with increasing diversity to create an ever-growing list of market segments," says Josh Calder, chief editor of the Global Lifestyles project, a research venture of Social Technologies, an Arlington, Va.-based consultancy. "I saw a professionally made bumper sticker the other day that said, 'Proud to be Sikh and American.' Such niches driven by ethnicity, attitudes and interest will proliferate," he adds.

As the population increases, niche markets may become unwieldy for businesses to target with a single marketing strategy. For example, many companies have one marketing strategy to reach Hispanic consumers. But by 2025, the Hispanic market will double, to 70 million consumers. As a result, the niche market of today will become a mass market in its own right, segmented not only by nationality (i.e., Mexican, Guatemalan) but also by spending behavior and other psychographic characteristics. Vickie Abrahamson, cofounder and executive vice president of Minneapolis-based Iconoculture, a trends consulting firm, dubs this movement "beehiving." Says Abrahamson, "Beehiving is the growth of tight-knit, alternative communities sharing common values and passions. Marketers must tap in to beehive rituals, customs and language to build trust and patronage."

Of course, population growth can present some challenges. "Don't you ever wonder how we'll have all the resources to take care of everyone on this planet? It's stunning to think about," says Richard Laermer, marketing expert and author of *TrendSpotting* (Perigee, 2002). A larger U.S. population will require more water and more land to provide food; it also means that more pollution will be created, according to a 2001 report by Lori Hunter, an analyst at the Santa Monica, Calif.-based think tank RAND. Indeed, population growth means that natural resources will be stretched in the coming years, says Dan McGinn, president of the McGinn Group, a marketing communications firm in Arlington, Va. "More people means more demand for resources, which means shortages of resources. Land, water, power—there will be less to go around," he adds. Expect to see escalating conflicts at the local level over land use, in which the benefits of population growth will be pitted against the cost to the environment. Also expect products and services to be scrutinized more closely for their environmental impact.

Table 1 The Graying Future

Those over the age of 60 will likely dominate by 2025.

	2000	2025	Difference	Percent Difference
Total	281,421,906	351,070,000	69,648,094	24.7%
Under 5 years	19,175,798	23,183,000	4,007,202	20.9%
5–9	20,549,505	22,845,000	2,295,495	11.2%
10–14	20,528,072	23,166,000	2,637,928	12.9%
15–19	20,219,890	23,449,000	3,229,110	16.0%
20–24	18,964,001	22,481,000	3,516,999	18.5%
25–29	19,381,336	21,257,000	1,875,664	9.7%
30–34	20,510,388	21,615,000	1,104,612	5.4%
35–39	22,706,664	22,728,000	21,336	0.1%
40–44	22,441,863	22,374,000	−67,863	−0.3%
45–49	20,092,404	21,031,000	938,596	4.7%
50–54	17,585,548	19,318,000	1,732,452	9.9%
55–59	13,469,237	18,452,000	4,982,763	37.0%
60–64	10,805,447	18,853,000	8,047,553	74.5%
65–69	9,533,545	19,844,000	10,310,455	108.1%
70–74	8,857,441	17,878,000	9,020,559	101.8%
75–79	7,415,813	14,029,000	6,613,187	89.2%
80–84	4,945,367	9,638,000	4,692,633	94.9%
85+	4,239,587	8,930,000	4,690,413	110.6%

Source: MapInfo and American Demographics

The Mighty Mature Market

On the business agenda:

- The senior market gaining new allure
- Creating ageless multigenerational brands

The biggest growth market, by far, will be the 65 and older set. In 2000, this group included 35 million people, about 12 percent of the population. By 2025, as Baby Boomers age and life expectancy continues to increase, the number of seniors will double, to more than 70 million people. To put this in perspective, the U.S. will have twice as many seniors in 2025 as it has African Americans today.

The graying of America means that companies will have to do more than pay lip service to the idea of marketing to older people. "The era of youth domination in business and marketing will be over," contends Maddy Dychtwald, the author of *Cycles: How We Will Live, Work, and Buy* (Free Press, 2003). "We've always been very youth focused because the percentage of young people has always overwhelmed the percentage of older adults. Since this domination will be balancing out, we will see more industries and companies begin to seek customers outside of the 18-to-34 demographic," she says. Dychtwald cites a recent Pepsi commercial as an indication of things to come. The ad features a teenage boy in the middle of a mosh pit at a rock concert. He turns around to discover his father rocking out nearby. "The Pepsi Generation is not just about youth anymore," she says. "In fact, it's becoming multigenerational, which is good news for business. It increases their potential target market dramatically."

Still, businesses are not going to suddenly lose all interest in the 18-to-34 demographic. "America loves youth—and all things associated with it," points out Ann A. Fishman, president of Generational Target Marketing Corp., in New Orleans. Adds Rob Duboff, senior vice president of Bowne Decision Quest, based in Waltham, Mass., "Even if there is no increase in the 18-and-under age segment, many marketers will continue to target it as these people start to establish their adult buying habits."

Table 2   The Mixed Society

By 2025, white non-Hispanics will hold a mere 60 percent majority.

	White, Non-Hispanic	Black, Non-Hispanic	Asian/Pacific Islander, Non-Hispanic	Native American, Non-Hispanic	Hispanic
Population, all ages	210,984	45,567	23,564	2,787	68,168
Percent of total population	60.1%	13.0%	6.7%	0.8%	19.4%
Population, under 5 years	11,872	3,103	1,642	196	6,370
5–9	12,034	3,065	1,583	199	5,964
10–14	12,319	3,180	1,677	221	5,769
15–19	12,495	3,359	1,652	224	5,719
20–24	11,985	3,170	1,641	213	5,472
25–29	11,418	2,907	1,703	201	5,028
30–34	11,993	2,865	1,780	187	4,790
35–39	12,938	3,198	1,771	190	4,631
40–44	13,311	3,176	1,634	202	4,051
45–49	12,834	2,836	1,524	180	3,657
50–54	11,888	2,596	1,356	148	3,330
55–59	11,664	2,419	1,263	130	2,976
60–64	12,502	2,343	1,141	114	2,753
65–69	13,838	2,413	978	107	2,508
70–74	13,071	1,978	800	93	1,936
75–79	10,531	1,429	606	72	1,391
80–84	7,471	816	400	49	902
85–89	3,950	385	217	29	496
90–94	1,859	199	118	17	264
95–99	745	90	54	10	116
100+	267	41	22	6	45
Median age	43.2 years	36.9 years	35.3 years	33.8 years	29.8 years

Note: Population numbers in thousands
Source: MapInfo

Instead, companies will have to learn to establish brands that attract older consumers without alienating younger ones, says Dychtwald. "It's becoming clear that people aren't over the hill at 50 anymore. Smart marketers will capitalize on this knowledge and create the image of an ageless society where people define themselves more by the activities they're involved in than by their age." Although grandparents can be age 45, 65 or 85, what they have in common is that they all want to buy gifts for their grandchildren, she reports. "You could have college students ages 20, 30 and 60. It's all part of a more cyclic life, where people cycle in and out of different life-stage events based on their interests rather than their age," explains Dychtwald.

The Consumer Kaleidoscope

On the business agenda:

- Devising marketing campaigns that appeal to many demographic segments
- Figuring out how to address the shrinking white majority

By 2025, the term "minority," as it's currently used, will be virtually obsolete. Non-Hispanic whites will still be the majority race in America—but just barely. According to MapInfo's projections, the share of non-Hispanic whites will fall to 60 percent by 2025, from 70 percent today. And the Hispanic population will almost double, to more than 68 million, from 35 million today, growing to 19 percent of the population from 12 percent. The number of Asians in the U.S. will also double, reaching 24 million, or 7 percent of the population, from its current 4 percent.

Companies that have not yet developed a multicultural marketing strategy will have to "wake up and smell the Thai tacos," quips Abrahamson. "If a company today is concentrating solely on a white audience, then it is living in another galaxy, far, far away," she says. Indeed, as the multicultural market becomes a multibillion-dollar market, companies that are already focusing on nonwhite consumers will find themselves at a distinct advantage, says Mark Seferian, director of business development at EchoboomX, a marketing firm based in Denver. "The companies that are currently working to understand emerging

Table 3   Magnet Markets

Metros with a high diversity quotient, or that have a large senior population are expected to grow the fastest over the next 25 years; areas with a low diversity quotient are more likely to shrink.

METROPOLITAN AREA	2000	2005	2010	2015	2020	2025	CHANGE	Percent Change
Laredo, TX	194,636	227,570	261,073	295,656	331,176	367,815	173,179	89.0%
Punta Gorda, FL	142,297	166,531	190,665	215,186	240,104	265,542	123,245	86.6%
Las Vegas, NV-AZ	1,581,525	1,836,721	2,093,204	2,355,460	2,622,811	2,897,008	1,315,483	83.2%
Austin-San Marcos, TX	1,259,929	1,452,492	1,645,797	1,843,311	2,044,712	2,251,148	991,219	78.7%
Provo-Orem, UT	370,532	423,693	476,961	531,378	586,832	643,683	273,151	73.7%
Phoenix-Mesa, AZ	3,276,401	3,689,337	4,105,093	4,531,884	4,968,122	5,416,621	2,140,220	65.3%
Naples, FL	253,806	285,648	317,698	350,581	384,177	418,739	164,933	65.0%
Medford-Ashland, OR	181,824	203,962	226,198	248,931	272,152	295,966	114,142	62.8%
West Palm Beach-Boca Raton, FL	1,137,775	1,275,564	1,412,373	1,551,564	1,692,865	1,837,450	699,675	61.5%
Wilmington, NC	234,816	262,761	290,765	319,409	348,657	378,676	143,860	61.3%
Orlando, FL	1,654,675	1,847,142	2,042,204	2,243,626	2,450,435	2,663,763	1,009,099	61.0%
Huntington-Ashland WV-KY-OH	315,379	315,296	315,753	317,042	319,011	321,537	6,158	2.0%
Toledo, OH	618,056	617,729	618,309	620,615	623,998	628,522	10,466	1.7%
Pittsburgh, PA	2,356,378	2,354,353	2,355,811	2,363,989	2,376,583	2,393,744	37,366	1.6%
Buffalo-Niagara Falls, NY	1,168,948	1,167,651	1,168,075	1,171,903	1,177,887	1,186,172	17,224	1.5%
Jamestown, NY	139,663	139,488	139,511	139,933	140,634	141,593	1,930	1.4%
Lawton, OK	114,886	114,695	114,692	115,022	115,523	116,298	1,412	1.2%
Muncie, IN	118,722	118,689	118,752	119,037	119,485	120,099	1,377	1.2%
Parkersburg-Marietta, WV-OH	151,138	150,877	150,821	151,185	151,848	152,807	1,669	1.1%
Youngstown-Warren, OH	594,416	593,378	593,165	594,563	597,065	600,601	6,185	1.0%
Sharon, PA	120,219	119,972	119,890	120,154	120,620	121,271	1,052	0.9%
Binghamton, NY	251,897	250,751	249,948	249,860	250,236	251,055	−842	−0.3%

Source: Woods & Poole Economics; MapInfo 2003

ethnic groups will have a huge advantage over the companies that wait another 10 years," he says. (This will be particularly true in fast-growing metro areas, which will tend to be more diverse. See Table 2, "The Mixed Society.")

Many businesses will not be able to adapt to the realities of the new marketplace, argues McGinn. "Diversity will be much more than a buzzword—diversity will be the key to economic survival," he says. Ethnic newspapers, magazines, television and radio will see phenomenal growth over the coming decades, McGinn believes, and the mainstream media will have to join forces with these ethnic specialists to stay in business. "Companies will not be able to keep swimming in the mainstream, because there is no mainstream. Instead, it's a series of parallel creeks, some constantly filling, some drying up a little," he says.

One of those "drying" creeks will be the declining majority—the white consumer market, which will experience slow growth over the next 25 years. Companies that market to white America will have to rethink their strategies, according to Rob Frankel, a branding expert based in Los Angeles. "The more cynical side of me suspects a subtle 'white market' will define itself, probably premium-positioned, probably leveraging white angst at lost population dominance," he says. If the current gap in wealth and income between white and nonwhite consumers holds for the next 25 years, businesses will find ample reason to target the nation's 210 million non-Hispanic white consumers.

Will tomorrow's multicultural marketing strategies continue to be segmented by race, with one strategy for "mainstream," one for African American consumers, another for Asians, another for Hispanics? Or will an increasingly multicultural population prefer inclusive, "fusion" strategies that attempt to encompass many different nationalities or racial identities in one campaign, such as those pioneered by clothing retailers Benetton and The Gap? The answer will depend on how Americans come to view their racial identity over the next two and a half decades. For instance, the increasing number of multiracial consumers may not necessarily lead to a consumer culture that blends racial identities, because there's growing evidence that multiracial consumers will think of themselves as a distinct racial group. Former Census Bureau director Kenneth Prewitt points to a growing number of organizations on college campuses aimed at helping multiracial students assert their group identity.

It will become a major challenge for businesses to grasp such subtle matters of cultural identity. To do this, companies will have to rely more heavily on in-depth market research techniques, such as ethnographic research, or new qualitative methods that rely on cognitive science, which promise to give markets an understanding of their consumer's culture, says Seferian. Ethnography enables marketers to understand a culture other than their own through direct observation, absorbing subtle differences in communication styles, behavior patterns and lifestyle. (For more on ethnography, see "Watch Me Now," *American Demographics,* July/August 2002, and "The New Science of Focus Groups," in the March 2003 issue.)

In a nation no longer dominated by one group, most businesses will be marketing to a consumer base that will include a patchwork of racial and ethnic identities. Understanding the differences in consumers' cultural identities will make the difference between failure and success.

Customers at Work

Self-service customers can reduce costs and become cocreators of value.

PETER C. HONEBEIN AND ROY F. CAMMARANO

I n today's marketplace, companies are asking customers to do more. Home Depot offers self checkout, Southwest Airlines offers self check-in, Dell Inc. provides Web-enabled tools allowing customers to configure their systems, Bank of America encourages customers to manage their accounts online, and HealthCheckUSA supplies customers with special kits for performing their own genetic testing.

Although customers previously expected companies to complete a lot of the work for them, a paradigm shift in the economy means the reverse is true. And when companies effectively design the new brand experience, customers respond enthusiastically. They often find that performing tasks themselves is faster and more efficient, affords a larger sense of control, and in some cases presents greater customization of the results. In other words, customers are able to unlock more value from purchased goods and services when they can successfully complete tasks themselves.

Executive Briefing

Companies are asking their customers to do more work. But if customers fail to perform tasks well, then satisfaction, trust, loyalty, and lifetime value are threatened. This article explores the jobs do-it-yourself customers execute, and the brand experiences companies wrap around goods and services. Through vision, access, incentive, and expertise, companies can create coproduction experiences that ensure customers are cocreators of value.

Customers aren't the only ones who benefit from this shift. Airlines estimate that they save $3.52 when a customer buys a ticket online and $2.70 when a customer conducts self check-in. Software companies, banks, and even local cable providers can save more than $9 when customers manage services and receive support with self-service Web sites, instead of by speaking with someone.

Companies also can benefit from increases in customer lifetime value. When do-it-yourself customers invest in learning company products, technology, and processes, the experience becomes "sticky": Usage of services increases, frequency of consumable purchasing is higher, acquisition of add-ons and accessories is more likely, and defecting to a competitor is less probable.

These advantages are moot, however, if customers can't perform. Jupiter Research estimates that 91% of customers with a bad experience on a self-service site won't return. Customers must be coached and trained for success, the same way that employees are at the best companies in the world. They need vision to know what they're expected to accomplish, access to tools enabling them to perform, incentive to motivate desired performances, and expertise to competently execute tasks. The orchestration of these strategies is a "coproduction experience," the cornerstone for developing customers who are cocreators of value.

Customer Work

Coproduction reflects different levels of customer involvement with companies. Some experiences, such as those at full-service restaurants, find companies carrying the majority of the effort. As companies begin to ask customers to take on more work, experiences will be shared. (For example, at Build-A-Bear Workshops, children and store employees share tasks to create a personalized teddy bear. And Quickbooks software requires that customers complete quite a bit of work, but conveniently handles the messy part of payroll and taxes.) Other experiences involve labor that's solely conducted by customers, such as online banking and self checkout.

Another way of looking at coproduction experiences is by examining the roles customers play.

Transactionals. They like to execute everyday business themselves. They use self checkout at the grocery store, eat at buffets, and book travel online.

Traditionals. They favor do-it-yourself in terms of home improvement, gardening, financial management, auto repair, and so on. They frequent Home Depot, Smith & Hawken, Charles Schwab Corp., and Kragen Auto Parts.

Conventionals. They acquire tangible, self-contained products that enable them to perform tasks independently. For example, a Viking stove facilitates gourmet cooking, and a snow blower clears snow from a driveway.

Intentionals. They engage in coproduction experiences to customize goods and services (e.g., at Build-A-Bear, or at the Nike iD.com design center where customers can create their own pair of athletic shoes).

Radicals. They take coproduction experiences to new extremes. This is the man in California who modified his Toyota Prius' batteries to achieve 80 miles per gallon, and the Apple iPod aficionados who create podcasts (audio programs featuring comedy, music, and sports).

Customer Experiences

All companies engage their customers as coproducers, codesigners, or cocreators in some way. Consider the story of Al Yeganeh, the soup purveyor immortalized as the "Soup Nazi" on *Seinfeld*. For more than 20 years, Yeganeh has created an extraordinarily successful business at a small storefront in New York. Because of his unrelenting focus on high quality, there is strong demand: A line stretches around the block. This yields a transaction process that is high on efficiency but low on accustomed social graces. To ensure that everyone who wants soup gets it, Yeganeh designed a rigid, militaristic coproduction experience.

Here is the established ordering procedure:

- When you walk in, immediately move to the right.
- Order your soup with no enthusiasm at all.
- Put your money on the counter and move to the left.
- Take your soup and don't make any comments.

Failure to follow these rules results in expulsion and the admonishment, "No soup for you!" (the catchphrase popularized by *Seinfeld*). Although this might not seem like much of an experience, the outcome is satisfactory for all involved; everyone who wants soup gets it. And customer compliance with the stringent policies is consistently reinforced: Current customers serve as trainers for new customers. The consequences for non-performance, although extreme, ensure obedience.

Whether customers are ordering soup, getting a haircut, or managing personal investments, their ability to perform well has a significant bearing on their results. Obviously, customers don't want to fail (miss out on soup, receive a bad haircut, or lose money on investments). The experience companies wrap around customer goals substantially affects what customers achieve and what companies gain. Designed experiences are better than default experiences in attaining desired outcomes.

Default experiences. These reflect an absence of systematic design. Because of this, the likelihood that customers will fail in them is high. Default experiences are relatively easy to identify, meeting one or more of the following conditions:

- The experience isn't written as a script, plan, or process.
- The experience hasn't been tested.
- Employee tasks associated with the experience aren't covered in training.
- "Who decided it should work this way?" is answered with "he did," "she did," or "don't know, it just happened." (Designs typically are created by a stakeholder committee, not individuals.)

The result of default experiences is chaos—for customers and employees. One familiar fast-food restaurant, with a location in a large truck stop, employed a simple design for selling soda: The cashier would hand customers a cup and lid, and they'd fill the cup at a soda dispenser shared between the restaurant and truck stop. One day, the restaurant manager decided that it would be more efficient for customers to take their own cups. The idea was to save time in the transaction. However, customers would forget to take a cup; instead, they'd walk to the soda dispenser and use a cup from the truck stop. But this cup was a signal to the truck-stop cashier to charge for the soda, for which customers already had paid. Patrons were furious. Another common scenario was that customers would take the cup, but not the lid. After filling the cup, they'd grab a lid from the truck stop—a lid incompatible with the restaurant's cups. This resulted in not only angry customers, but also crumpled lids littering the floor by the soda dispenser.

Designed experiences. Here, leaders of coproduction experiences take a systematic, multidimensional view of the situation: They establish internal cross-functional teams, and integrate customer information and experiences into the design process. These teams truly must understand the customer perspective. Many employees don't have a clue what it's like to be customers of their company; they think they understand what customers go through, but they're usually wrong.

The Coproduction-Experience Model

You can understand the coproduction experiences of your customers, and improve their encounters by design, through the orchestration of four key tactics: vision, access, incentive, and expertise. This coproduction-experience model provides a lens for not only assessing such experiences, but also designing them.

For example, when Southwest Airlines implemented its e-commerce strategy (southwest.com) in the 1990s, customers were set for success. Regarding vision, various promotional channels communicated an attractive, novel goal: Book your own tickets. For access, the Web site presented the tool and a simple interface for completing transactions. The incentive to perform was the double "rapid reward" credit, which enabled customers to earn free flights twice as fast. And expertise was supplied with step-by-step booking instructions on the Web site. In 2004, Southwest Airlines reported that southwest.com generated 59% of its revenue. Customer conditioning was so successful that it was able to eliminate the incentive without negatively affecting the site's revenue percentage.

The Vision

In Ken Blanchard and Sheldon Bowles' book *Raving Fans* (William Morrow, 1993), customers are encouraged to develop a vision of how they would use products. Through this vision, they articulate their goals and the tasks/actions they expect to execute for achieving them. In coproduction experiences, companies must help customers shape their goals in a way that balances customer needs and company capabilities.

Goals. The retirement planning advice that San Francisco-based Charles Schwab Corp. offers is a great example of how to help customers shape goals. For most customers, accumulating $1 million by the time they are 65 years old seems out of reach. Hence, the expectation is that customers won't perform. However, if Schwab makes the goal more reasonable, then it can stimulate appropriate customer performance. To accomplish this, it localizes investment goals to four age ranges: 20s, 30s, 40–45, and older than 45. For each, Schwab suggests suitable yearly savings goals, as a percentage of salary. For example, if you start saving when you are age 22, then you should put aside 10% of your yearly salary. If you are age 28, then the percentage jumps to 14%. If you are age 36, then you should sock away 23%. And if you are older than 45, then you fall into the "ouch" category: Your rate can be 58% or higher.

Feedback. Vision isn't just about goals; it's also about the feedback customers obtain as they attempt to achieve them. In a classic experiment by psychologists Albert Bandura and Daniel Cervone, subjects experienced different combinations of goals and feedback in relation to an exercise task. The researchers divided subjects into four groups and asked everyone to ride an exercise bike. This provided a baseline measure. The researchers then asked the subjects to ride the bike again. The first group received neither the goal nor feedback, the second group received only feedback, the third group received only the goal, and the fourth group received both the goal and feedback. Which group performed best? The first three groups had a performance increase of about 20%. The fourth group, however, had a performance increase of 60%.

A Dutch power company replicated Bandura and Cervone's results. The performance it wanted from customers was energy conservation. It set a goal for customers to reduce energy consumption by 10%. For feedback, customers assessed their performance using a real-time monitoring device, monthly report, or diary of their electrical meter. (A control group didn't receive feedback.) As expected, all groups receiving feedback performed better than the control group. But only one group, the customers with a real-time monitoring device, exceeded the 10% goal. The closer the feedback is to performance, the more likely the goal will be achieved.

The Access

Winston Churchill said in the early days of World War II, "We shall not fail or falter; we shall not weaken or tire. . . . Give us the tools and we will finish the job." Many customers share this sentiment when trying to use goods and services. Access reflects the resources companies supply so that customers can perform. It consists of eight critical tactics: policies, processes, procedures, people, tools, interfaces, information, and nuances.

Policies provide the rules for the coproduction experience, and processes and procedures provide the script for how customers are expected to act (and how companies respond to their performance). Because coproduction involves people, companies retain some choice in who performs coproduction tasks.

To make work simpler or more convenient, tools such as self-service technologies are used to supplement or enhance experiences. Interfaces, such as a store's floor plan or a product's ergonomic design, affect the ability of customers to complete tasks. And information, such as nutritional labeling on food, helps customers make better choices. Coproduction experiences are rounded out with nuances, which subtly influence performance through sights, sounds, smells, and tastes.

Think for a moment: Have you ever met someone who received a bad sandwich at a Subway restaurant? We asked hundreds of people this question and always were given the same response: "no." One of Subway's secrets is a specific procedure combined with a well-designed interface. Its customers play the role of director: They guide the sandwich maker through each step of the process (e.g., type of bread and sandwich, assortment and quantity of extras). Via the interface—a glass counter through which customers observe every action—customers receive feedback and make adjustments as needed, before approving the creation. It's difficult to complain about a sandwich, when you directed the design.

The Incentive

Customers sometimes need a kick in the pants to conduct more work. Incentives can be powerful motivators for convincing them to try new items or stop bad behavior. Rewards are the typical incentive of choice in coproduction experiences, and they range from simple recognition to cold, hard cash.

Recognition rewards. Alpine Home Air Products in Rockford, Ill. (a manufacturer and distributor of heating, air-conditioning, and air cleaning products), uses a recognition reward for customer jobs well-done. It keeps a Web page that is titled, "Help us celebrate our customers' success!" Do-it-yourself customers are invited to submit a photograph of their product installation and a short story of their experience. Customer Don Neslon wrote: "The instructions and video made installation very easy. The entire job took about two hours. The added humidity has made winters almost enjoyable in New England."

It's difficult to complain about a sandwich, when you directed the design.

Cash rewards. Banks such as Citibank, Wells Fargo, and Bank of America use a cash reward to get customers paying bills online. For the most part, these online services are free; the problem is getting customers to shift their work from paper to cyberspace. Citibank offers the richest purse, up to $200, depending on how many bills customers pay. And U.S. Bancorp entered online bankers into a contest with a $10,000 prize. Those who use online banking are better customers: They maintain more accounts and higher balances, and make fewer calls to support lines and branches.

Disincentives. Companies aren't limited to rewards in shaping customer performance. Disincentives, in the form of punishments, can prevent customer behaviors that are incompatible with the coproduction experience expected by companies and other customers. An overdrawn checking account might trigger a $30 charge; an overdue video might cost another day's rental fee. And for six years, the Carnival cruise line punished no-smoking policy violators with a $250 fine and disembarkation at the next port (such guests would need to find their own way home).

The Expertise

Although customers might possess vision to perform, access to necessary resources, and an incentive, performance won't be forthcoming if they lack expertise. This is the knowledge/skills customers must retain to execute work required by the coproduction experience.

No one knows this better than Atlanta-based Home Depot. As the leader in the craze of do-it-yourself home improvement, it provides customers many ways to develop expertise. Weekend in-store clinics teach them how to lay ceramic tile or install hardwood floors, point-of-sale job aids help with product selection, and orange-aproned associates mentor customers one-on-one. Also, a Web site—with tutorials, videos, and step-by-step instructions—presents the just-in-time knowledge that customers need in the middle of a job.

As Home Depot illustrates, companies can choose from a variety of customer-education solutions to build customer expertise. Customers typically start with basic tools, such as an instruction manual. Tools embedded in the product, such as user assistance or voice-driven prompts, provide on-the-spot knowledge. And if customers run into difficulties during execution, then problem tools (e.g., a telephone customer-service representative) help them navigate these areas. Together, these three solutions help customers develop the minimum expertise necessary for initial success with goods and services.

For longer-term development and expertise enhancement, two other education solutions come into play. Premium tools usually involve formal training, and are included in the system if product tasks are complex or require physical skill. And support tools are items such as Web-based information and tutorials.

Age of Sophistication

Do-it-yourself customers are steadily increasing. Because customers determine the value of goods and services through usage, sophisticated customers can hold a significant advantage over unsophisticated customers: They can perform more effectively as cocreators of value. Companies that adopt the coproduction-experience model's principles create conditions for customers to flourish. This forms a value chain resulting in maximized customer satisfaction, trust, loyalty, and lifetime value.

PETER C. HONEBEIN and ROY F. CAMMARANO are principals of the Customer Performance Group, a strategy consultancy in Reno, Nev. They are also authors of *Creating Do-It-Yourself Customers: How Great Customer Experiences Build Great Companies* (Thomson Texere, 2005). Both may be reached at peter@doityourselfcustomers.com.

From *Marketing Management,* Vol. 15, No. 1, January/February 2006, pp. 26, 28–31. Copyright © 2006 by American Marketing Association. Reprinted by permission.

Marketing Myopia
(with Retrospective Commentary)

Shortsighted managements often fail to recognize that in fact there is no such thing as a growth industry

THEODORE LEVITT

How can a company ensure its continued growth? In 1960 "Marketing Myopia" answered that question in a new and challenging way by urging organizations to define their industries broadly to take advantage of growth opportunities. Using the archetype of the railroads, Mr. Levitt showed how they declined inevitably as technology advanced because they defined themselves too narrowly. To continue growing, companies must ascertain and act on their customers' needs and desires, not bank on the presumptive longevity of their products. The success of the article testifies to the validity of its message. It has been widely quoted and anthologized, and HBR has sold more than 265,000 reprints of it. The author of 14 subsequent articles in HBR, Mr. Levitt is one of the magazine's most prolific contributors. In a retrospective commentary, he considers the use and misuse that have been made of "Marketing Myopia," describing its many interpretations and hypothesizing about its success.

Every major industry was once a growth industry. But some that are now riding a wave of growth enthusiasm are very much in the shadow of decline. Others which are thought of as seasoned growth industries have actually stopped growing. In every case the reason growth is threatened, slowed, or stopped is *not* because the market is saturated. It is because there has been a failure of management.

Fateful purposes: The failure is at the top. The executives responsible for it, in the last analysis, are those who deal with broad aims and policies. Thus:

- The railroads did not stop growing because the need for passenger and freight transportation declined. That grew. The railroads are in trouble today not because the need was filled by others (cars, trucks, airplanes, even telephones), but because it was *not* filled by the railroads themselves. They let others take customers away from them because they assumed themselves to be in the railroad business rather than in the transportation business. The reason they defined their industry wrong was because they were railroad-oriented instead of transportation-oriented; they were product-oriented instead of customer-oriented.

- Hollywood barely escaped being totally ravished by television. Actually, all the established film companies went through drastic reorganizations. Some simply disappeared. All of them got into trouble not because of TV's inroads but because of their own myopia. As with the railroads, Hollywood defined its business incorrectly. It thought it was in the movie business when it was actually in the entertainment business. "Movies" implied a specific, limited product. This produced a fatuous contentment which from the beginning led producers to view TV as a threat. Hollywood scorned and rejected TV when it should have welcomed it as an opportunity—an opportunity to expand the entertainment business.

Today TV is a bigger business than the old narrowly defined movie business ever was. Had Hollywood been customer-oriented (providing entertainment), rather then product-oriented (making movies), would it have gone through the fiscal purgatory that it did? I doubt it. What ultimately saved Hollywood and accounted for its recent resurgence was the wave of new young writers, producers, and directors whose previous successes in television had decimated the old movie companies and toppled the big movie moguls.

There are other less obvious examples of industries that have been and are now endangering their futures by improperly defining their purposes. I shall discuss some in detail later and analyze the kind of policies that lead to trouble. Right now it may help to show what a thoroughly customer-oriented management can do to keep a growth industry growing, even after the obvious opportunities have been exhausted; and here there are two examples that have been around for a long time. They are nylon and glass—specifically, E. I. duPont de Nemours & Company and Corning Glass Works.

Both companies have great technical competence. Their product orientation is unquestioned. But this alone does not explain their success. After all, who was more pridefully product-oriented and product-conscious than the erstwhile New England textile companies that have been so thoroughly massacred? The DuPonts and the Cornings have succeeded not primarily because of their product or research orientation but because they have been thoroughly customer-oriented also. It is constant watchfulness for opportunities to apply their technical knowhow to the creation of customer-satisfying uses which accounts for their prodigious output of successful new products. Without a very sophisticated eye on the customer, most of their new products might have been wrong, their sales methods useless.

Aluminum has also continued to be a growth industry, thanks to the efforts of two wartime-created companies which deliberately set about creating new customer-satisfying uses. Without Kaiser Aluminum & Chemical Corporation and Reynolds Metals Company, the total demand for aluminum today would be vastly less.

Error of analysis: Some may argue that it is foolish to set the railroads off against aluminum or the movies off against glass. Are not aluminum and glass naturally so versatile that the industries are bound to have more growth opportunities than the railroads and movies? This view commits precisely the error I have been talking about. It defines an industry, or a product, or a cluster of know-how so narrowly as to guarantee its premature senescence. When we mention "railroads," we should make sure we mean "transportation." As transporters, the railroads still have a good chance for very considerable growth. They are not limited to the railroad business as such (though in my opinion rail transportation is potentially a much stronger transportation medium than is generally believed).

What the railroads lack is not opportunity, but some of the same managerial imaginativeness and audacity that made them great. Even an amateur like Jacques Barzun can see what is lacking when he says:

"I grieve to see the most advanced physical and social organization of the last century go down in shabby disgrace for lack of the same comprehensive imagination that built it up. [What is lacking is] the will of the companies to survive and to satisfy the public by inventiveness and skill."[1]

Shadow of Obsolescence

It is impossible to mention a single major industry that did not at one time qualify for the magic appellation of "growth industry." In each case its assumed strength lay in the apparently unchallenged superiority of its product. There appeared to be no effective substitute for it. It was itself a runaway substitute for the product it so triumphantly replaced. Yet one after another of these celebrated industries has come under a shadow. Let us look briefly at a few more of them, this time taking examples that have so far received a little less attention:

- *Dry cleaning*—This was once a growth industry with lavish prospects. In an age of wool garments, imagine being finally able to get them safely and easily clean. The boom was on.

  Yet here we are 30 years after the boom started and the industry is in trouble. Where has the competition come from? From a better way of cleaning? No. It has come from synthetic fibers and chemical additives that have cut the need for dry cleaning. But this is only the beginning. Lurking in the wings and ready to make chemical dry cleaning totally obsolescent is that powerful magician, ultrasonics.

- *Electric utilities*—This is another one of those supposedly "no-substitute" products that has been enthroned on a pedestal of invincible growth. When the incandescent lamp came along, kerosene lights were finished. Later the water wheel and the steam engine were cut to ribbons by the flexibility, reliability, simplicity, and just plain easy availability of electric motors. The prosperity of electric utilities continues to wax extravagant as the home is converted into a museum of electric gadgetry. How can anybody miss by investing in utilities, with no competition, nothing but growth ahead?

  But a second look is not quite so comforting. A score of nonutility companies are well advanced toward developing a powerful chemical fuel cell which could sit in some hidden closet of every home silently ticking off electric power. The electric lines that vulgarize so many neighborhoods will be eliminated. So will the endless demolition of streets and service interruptions during storms. Also on the horizon is solar energy, again pioneered by nonutility companies.

  Who says that the utilities have no competition? They may be natural monopolies now, but tomorrow they may be natural deaths. To avoid this prospect, they too will have to develop fuel cells, solar energy, and other power sources. To survive, they themselves will have to plot the obsolescence of what now produces their livelihood.

- *Grocery stores*—Many people find it hard to realize that there ever was a thriving establishment known as the "corner grocery store." The supermarket has taken over with a powerful effectiveness. Yet the big food chains of the 1930s narrowly escaped being completely wiped out by the aggressive expansion of independent supermarkets. The first genuine supermarket was opened in 1930, in Jamaica, Long Island. By 1933 supermarkets were thriving in California, Ohio, Pennsylvania, and elsewhere. Yet the established chains pompously ignored them. When they chose to notice them, it was with such derisive descriptions as "cheapy," "horse-and-buggy," "cracker-barrel storekeeping," and "unethical opportunists."

The executive of one big chain announced at the time that he found it "hard to believe that people will drive for miles to shop for foods and sacrifice the personal service chains have perfected and to which Mrs. Consumer is accustomed."[2] As late as 1936, the National Wholesale Grocers convention and the New Jersey Retail Grocers Association said there was nothing to fear. They said that the supers' narrow appeal to the price buyer limited the size of their market. They had to draw from miles around. When imitators came, there would be wholesale liquidations as volume fell. The current high sales of the supers was said to be partly due to their novelty. Basically people wanted convenient neighborhood grocers. If the neighborhood stores "cooperate with their suppliers, pay attention to their costs, and improve their service," they would be able to weather the competition until it blew over.[3]

It never blew over. The chains discovered that survival required going into the supermarket business. This meant the wholesale destruction of their huge investments in corner store sites and in established distribution and merchandising methods. The companies with "the courage of their convictions" resolutely stuck to the corner store philosophy. They kept their pride but lost their shirts.

Self-deceiving cycle: But memories are short. For example, it is hard for people who today confidently hail the twin messiahs of electronics and chemicals to see how things could possibly go wrong with these galloping industries. They probably also cannot see how a reasonably sensible businessman could have been as myopic as the famous Boston millionaire who 50 years ago unintentionally sentenced his heirs to poverty by stipulating that his entire estate be forever invested exclusively in electric streetcar securities. His posthumous declaration, "There will always be a big demand for efficient urban transportation," is no consolation to his heirs who sustain life by pumping gasoline at automobile filling stations.

Yet, in a casual survey I recently took among a group of intelligent business executives, nearly half agreed that it would be hard to hurt their heirs by tying their estates forever to the electronics industry. When I then confronted them with the Boston streetcar example, they chorused unanimously, "That's different!" But is it? Is not the basic situation identical?

In truth, *there is no such thing* as a growth industry, I believe. There are only companies organized and operated to create and capitalize on growth opportunities. Industries that assume themselves to be riding some automatic growth escalator invariably descend into stagnation. The history of every dead and dying "growth" industry shows a self-deceiving cycle of bountiful expansion and undetected decay. There are four conditions which usually guarantee this cycle:

1. The belief that growth is assured by an expanding and more affluent population.

2. The belief that there is no competitive substitute for the industry's major product.

3. Too much faith in mass production and in the advantages of rapidly declining unit costs as output rises.

4. Preoccupation with a product that lends itself to carefully controlled scientific experimentation, improvement, and manufacturing cost reduction.

I should like now to begin examining each of these conditions in some detail. To build my case as boldly as possible, I shall illustrate the points with reference to three industries—petroleum, automobiles, and electronics—particularly petroleum, because it spans more years and more vicissitudes. Not only do these three have excellent reputations with the general public and also enjoy the confidence of sophisticated investors, but their managements have become known for progressive thinking in areas like financial control, product research, and management training. If obsolescence can cripple even these industries, it can happen anywhere.

Population Myth

The belief that profits are assured by an expanding and more affluent population is dear to the heart of every industry. It takes the edge off the apprehensions everybody understandably feels about the future. If consumers are multiplying and also buying more of your product or service, you can face the future with considerably more comfort than if the market is shrinking. An expanding market keeps the manufacturer from having to think very hard or imaginatively. If thinking is an intellectual response to a problem, then the absence of a problem leads to the absence of thinking. If your product has an automatically expanding market, then you will not give much thought to how to expand it.

One of the most interesting examples of this is provided by the petroleum industry. Probably our oldest growth industry, it has an enviable record. While there are some current apprehensions about its growth rate, the industry itself tends to be optimistic.

But I believe it can be demonstrated that it is undergoing a fundamental yet typical change. It is not only ceasing to be a growth industry, but may actually be a declining one, relative to other business. Although there is widespread unawareness of it, I believe that within 25 years the oil industry may find itself in much the same position of retrospective glory that the railroads are now in. Despite its pioneering work in developing and applying the present-value method of investment evaluation, in employee relations, and in working with backward countries, the petroleum business is a distressing example of how complacency and wrongheadedness can stubbornly convert opportunity into near disaster.

One of the characteristics of this and other industries that have believed very strongly in the beneficial consequences of an expanding population, while at the same time being industries with a generic product for which there has appeared to be no competitive substitute, is that the individual companies have sought to outdo their competitors by improving on what they are already doing. This makes sense, of course, if one assumes that sales are tied to the country's population strings, because the customer can compare products only on a feature-by-feature basis. I believe it is significant, for example, that not since John D. Rockefeller sent free kerosene lamps to China has the oil industry done anything really outstanding to create a demand for its product. Not even in product improvement has it showered itself with eminence. The greatest single improvement—namely, the development of tetraethyl lead—came from outside the industry, specifically from General Motors and DuPont. The big contributions made by the industry itself are confined to the technology of oil exploration, production, and refining.

Asking for trouble: In other words, the industry's efforts have focused on improving the *efficiency* of getting and making its product, not really on improving the generic product or its marketing. Moreover, its chief product has continuously been defined in the narrowest possible terms, namely, gasoline, not energy, fuel, or transportation. This attitude has helped assure that:

• Major improvements in gasoline quality tend not to originate in the oil industry. Also, the development of superior alternative fuels comes from outside the oil industry, as will be shown later.

- Major innovations in automobile fuel marketing are originated by small new oil companies that are not primarily preoccupied with production or refining. These are the companies that have been responsible for the rapidly expanding multipump gasoline stations, with their successful emphasis on large and clean layouts, rapid and efficient driveway service, and quality gasoline at low prices.

Thus, the oil industry is asking for trouble from outsiders. Sooner or later, in this land of hungry inventors and entrepreneurs, a threat is sure to come. The possibilities of this will become more apparent when we turn to the next dangerous belief of many managements. For the sake of continuity, because this second belief is tied closely to the first, I shall continue with the same example.

Idea of indispensability: The petroleum industry is pretty much persuaded that there is no competitive substitute for its major product, gasoline—or if there is, that it will continue to be a derivative of crude oil, such as diesel fuel or kerosene jet fuel.

There is a lot of automatic wishful thinking in this assumption. The trouble is that most refining companies own huge amounts of crude oil reserves. These have value only if there is a market for products into which oil can be converted—hence the tenacious belief in the continuing competitive superiority of automobile fuels made from crude oil.

This idea persists despite all historic evidence against it. The evidence not only shows that oil has never been a superior product for any purpose for very long, but it also shows that the oil industry has never really been a growth industry. It has been a succession of different businesses that have gone through the usual historic cycles of growth, maturity, and decay. Its overall survival is owed to a series of miraculous escapes from total obsolescence, of last-minute and unexpected reprieves from total disaster reminiscent of the Perils of Pauline.

Perils of petroleum: I shall sketch in only the main episodes.

First, crude oil was largely a patent medicine. But even before that fad ran out, demand was greatly expanded by the use of oil in kerosene lamps. The prospect of lighting the world's lamps gave rise to an extravagant promise of growth. The prospects were similar to those the industry now holds for gasoline in other parts of the world. It can hardly wait for the underdeveloped nations to get a car in every garage.

In the days of the kerosene lamp, the oil companies competed with each other and against gaslight by trying to improve the illuminating characteristics of kerosene. Then suddenly the impossible happened. Edison invented a light which was totally nondependent on crude oil. Had it not been for the growing use of kerosene in space heaters, the incandescent lamp would have completely finished oil as a growth industry at that time. Oil would have been good for little else than axle grease.

Then disaster and reprieve struck again. Two great innovations occurred, neither originating in the oil industry. The successful development of coal-burning domestic central-heating systems made the space heater obsolescent. While the industry reeled, along came its most magnificent boost yet—the internal combustion engine, also invented by outsiders. Then when the prodigious expansion for gasoline finally began to level off in

the 1920s, along came the miraculous escape of a central oil heater. Once again, the escape was provided by an outsider's invention and development. And when that market weakened, wartime demand for aviation fuel came to the rescue. After the war the expansion of civilian aviation, the dieselization of railroads, and the explosive demand for cars and trucks kept the industry's growth in high gear.

Meanwhile, centralized oil heating—whose boom potential had only recently been proclaimed—ran into severe competition from natural gas. While the oil companies themselves owned the gas that now competed with their oil, the industry did not originate the natural gas revolution, nor has it to this day greatly profited from its gas ownership. The gas revolution was made by newly formed transmission companies that marketed the product with an aggressive ardor. They started a magnificent new industry, first against the advice and then against the resistance of the oil companies.

By all the logic of the situation, the oil companies themselves should have made the gas revolution. They not only owned the gas; they also were the only people experienced in handling, scrubbing, and using it, the only people experienced in pipeline technology and transmission, and they understood heating problems. But, partly because they knew that natural gas would compete with their own sale of heating oil, the oil companies pooh-poohed the potentials of gas.

The revolution was finally started by oil pipeline executives who, unable to persuade their own companies to go into gas, quit and organized the spectacularly successful gas transmission companies. Even after their success became painfully evident to the oil companies, the latter did not go into gas transmission. The multibillion dollar business which should have been theirs went to others. As in the past, the industry was blinded by its narrow preoccupation with a specific product and the value of its reserves. It paid little or no attention to its customers' basic needs and preferences.

The postwar years have not witnessed any change. Immediately after World War II the oil industry was greatly encouraged about its future by the rapid expansion of demand for its traditional line of products. In 1950 most companies projected annual rates of domestic expansion of around 6% through at least 1975. Though the ratio of crude oil reserves to demand in the Free World was about 20 to 1, with 10 to 1 being usually considered a reasonable working ratio in the United States, booming demand sent oil men searching for more without sufficient regard to what the future really promised. In 1952 they "hit" in the Middle East; the ratio skyrocketed to 42 to 1. If gross additions to reserves continue at the average rate of the past five years (37 billion barrels annually), then by 1970 the reserve ratio will be up to 45 to 1. This abundance of oil has weakened crude and product prices all over the world.

Uncertain future: Management cannot find much consolation today in the rapidly expanding petrochemical industry, another oil-using idea that did not originate in the leading firms. The total United States production of petrochemicals is equivalent to about 2% (by volume) of the demand for all petroleum products. Although the petrochemical industry is now expected to grow by about 10% per year, this will not offset other drains on the growth of crude oil consumption. Furthermore, while petrochemical products are many and growing, it is well to remember that there are nonpetroleum sources of the basic raw material, such as coal. Besides, a lot of plastics can be produced with relatively little oil. A 5,000-barrel-per-day oil refinery is now considered the absolute minimum size for efficiency. But a 5,000-barrel-per-day chemical plant is a giant operation.

Oil has never been a continuously strong growth industry. It has grown by fits and starts, always miraculously saved by innovations and developments not of its own making. The reason it has not grown in a smooth progression is that each time it thought it had a superior product safe from the possibility of competitive substitutes, the product turned out to be inferior and notoriously subject to obsolescence. Until now, gasoline (for motor fuel, anyhow) has escaped this fate. But, as we shall see later, it too may be on its last legs.

The point of all this is that there is no guarantee against product obsolescence. If a company's own research does not make it obsolete, another's will. Unless an industry is especially lucky, as oil has been until now, it can easily go down in a sea of red figures—just as the railroads have, as the buggy whip manufacturers have, as the corner grocery chains have, as most of the big movie companies have, and indeed as many other industries have.

The best way for a firm to be lucky is to make its own luck. That requires knowing what makes a business successful. One of the greatest enemies of this knowledge is mass production.

Production Pressures

Mass-production industries are impelled by a great drive to produce all they can. The prospect of steeply declining unit costs as output rises is more than most companies can usually resist. The profit possibilities look spectacular. All effort focuses on production. The result is that marketing gets neglected.

John Kenneth Galbraith contends that just the opposite occurs.[4] Output is so prodigious that all effort concentrates on trying to get rid of it. He says this accounts for singing commercials, desecration of the countryside with advertising signs, and other wasteful and vulgar practices. Galbraith has a finger on something real, but he misses the strategic point. Mass production does indeed generate great pressure to "move" the product. But what usually gets emphasized is selling, not marketing. Marketing, being a more sophisticated and complex process, gets ignored.

The difference between marketing and selling is more than semantic. Selling focuses on the needs of the seller, marketing on the needs of the buyer. Selling is preoccupied with the seller's need to convert his product into cash, marketing with the idea of satisfying the needs of the customer by means of the product and the whole cluster of things associated with creating, delivering, and finally consuming it.

In some industries the enticements of full mass production have been so powerful that for many years top management in effect has told the sales departments, "You get rid of it; we'll worry about profits." By contrast, a truly marketing-minded firm tries to create value-satisfying goods and services that consumers will want to buy. What it offers for sale includes not only the generic product or service, but also how it is made available to the customer, in what form, when, under what conditions, and at what terms of trade. Most important, what it offers for sale is determined not by the seller but by the buyer. The seller takes his cues from the buyer in such a way that the product becomes a consequence of the marketing effort, not vice versa.

Lag in Detroit: This may sound like an elementary rule of business, but that does not keep it from being violated wholesale. It is certainly more violated than honored. Take the automobile industry.

Here mass production is most famous, most honored, and has the greatest impact on the entire society. The industry has hitched its fortune to the relentless requirements of the annual model change, a policy that makes customer orientation an especially urgent necessity. Consequently the auto companies annually spend millions of dollars on consumer research. But the fact that the new compact cars are selling so well in their first year indicates that Detroit's vast researches have for a long time failed to reveal what the customer really wanted. Detroit was not persuaded that he wanted anything different from what he had been getting until it lost millions of customers to other small car manufacturers.

How could this unbelievable lag behind consumer wants have been perpetuated so long? Why did not research reveal consumer preferences before consumers' buying decisions themselves revealed the facts? Is that not what consumer research is for—to find out before the fact what is going to happen? The answer is that Detroit never really researched the customer's wants. It only researched his preferences between the kinds of things which it had already decided to offer him. For Detroit is mainly product-oriented, not customer-oriented. To the extent that the customer is recognized as having needs that the manufacturer should try to satisfy, Detroit usually acts as if the job can be done entirely by product changes. Occasionally attention gets paid to financing, too, but that is done more in order to sell than to enable the customer to buy.

As for taking care of other customer needs, there is not enough being done to write about. The areas of the greatest unsatisfied needs are ignored, or at best get stepchild attention. These are at the point of sale and on the matter of automotive repair and maintenance. Detroit views these problem areas as being of secondary importance. That is underscored by the fact that the retailing and servicing ends of this industry are neither owned and operated nor controlled by the manufacturers. Once the car is produced, things are pretty much in the dealer's inadequate hands. Illustrative of Detroit's arm's-length attitude is the fact that, while servicing holds enormous sales-stimulating, profit-building opportunities, only 57 of Chevrolet's 7,000 dealers provide night maintenance service.

Motorists repeatedly express their dissatisfaction with servicing and their apprehensions about buying cars under the present selling setup. The anxieties and problems they encounter during the auto buying and maintenance processes are probably more intense and widespread today than 30 years ago. Yet the automobile companies do not *seem* to listen to or take their cues from the anguished consumer. If they do listen, it must be through the filter of their own preoccupation with production.

23

The marketing effort is still viewed as a necessary consequence of the product, not vice versa, as it should be. That is the legacy of mass production, with its parochial view that profit resides essentially in low-cost full production.

What Ford put first: The profit lure of mass production obviously has a place in the plans and strategy of business management, but it must always *follow* hard thinking about the customer. This is one of the most important lessons that we can learn from the contradictory behavior of Henry Ford. In a sense Ford was both the most brilliant and the most senseless marketer in American history. He was senseless because he refused to give the customer anything but a black car. He was brilliant because he fashioned a production system designed to fit market needs. We habitually celebrate him for the wrong reason, his production genius. His real genius was marketing. We think he was able to cut his selling price and therefore sell millions of $500 cars because his invention of the assembly line had reduced the costs. Actually he invented the assembly line because he had concluded that at $500 he could sell millions of cars. Mass production was the *result* not the cause of his low prices.

Ford repeatedly emphasized this point, but a nation of production-oriented business managers refuses to hear the great lesson he taught. Here is his operating philosophy as he expressed it succinctly:

"Our policy is to reduce the price, extend the operations, and improve the article. You will notice that the reduction of price comes first. We have never considered any costs as fixed. Therefore we first reduce the price to the point where we believe more sales will result. Then we go ahead and try to make the prices. We do not bother about the costs. The new price forces the costs down. The more usual way is to take the costs and then determine the price; and although that method may be scientific in the narrow sense, it is not scientific in the broad sense, because what earthly use is it to know the cost if it tells you that you cannot manufacture at a price at which the article can be sold? But more to the point is the fact that, although one may calculate what a cost is, and of course all of our costs are carefully calculated, no one knows what a cost ought to be. One of the ways of discovering . . . is to name a price so low as to force everybody in the place to the highest point of efficiency. The low price makes everybody dig for profits. We make more discoveries concerning manufacturing and selling under this forced method than by any method of leisurely investigation."[5]

Product provincialism: The tantalizing profit possibilities of low unit production costs may be the most seriously self-deceiving attitude that can afflict a company, particularly a "growth" company where an apparently assured expansion of demand already tends to undermine a proper concern for the importance of marketing and the customer.

The usual result of this narrow preoccupation with so-called concrete matters is that instead of growing, the industry declines. It usually means that the product fails to adapt to the constantly changing patterns of consumer needs and tastes, to new and modified marketing institutions and practices, or to product developments in competing or complementary industries. The industry has its eyes so firmly on its own specific product that it does not see how it is being made obsolete.

The classical example of this is the buggy whip industry. No amount of product improvement could stave off its death sentence. But had the industry defined itself as being in the transportation business rather than the buggy whip business, it might have survived. It would have done what survival always entails, that is, changing. Even if it had only defined its business as providing a stimulant or catalyst to an energy source, it might have survived by becoming a manufacturer of, say, fanbelts or air cleaners.

What may some day be a still more classical example is, again, the oil industry. Having let others steal marvelous opportunities from it (e.g., natural gas, as already mentioned, missile fuels, and jet engine lubricants), one would expect it to have taken steps never to let that happen again. But this is not the case. We are now getting extraordinary new developments in fuel systems specifically designed to power automobiles. Not only are these developments concentrated in firms outside the petroleum industry, but petroleum is almost systematically ignoring them, securely content in its wedded bliss to oil. It is the story of the kerosene lamp versus the incandescent lamp all over again. Oil is trying to improve hydrocarbon fuels rather than develop *any* fuels best suited to the needs of their users, whether or not made in different ways and with different raw materials from oil.

Here are some things which nonpetroleum companies are working on:

- Over a dozen such firms now have advanced working models of energy systems which, when perfected, will replace the internal combustion engine and eliminate the demand for gasoline. The superior merit of each of these systems is their elimination of frequent, time-consuming, and irritating refueling stops. Most of these systems are fuel cells designed to create electrical energy directly from chemicals without combustion. Most of them use chemicals that are not derived from oil, generally hydrogen and oxygen.

- Several other companies have advanced models of electric storage batteries designed to power automobiles. One of these is an aircraft producer that is working jointly with several electric utility companies. The latter hope to use off-peak generating capacity to supply overnight plug-in battery regeneration. Another company, also using the battery approach, is a medium-size electronics firm with extensive small-battery experience that it developed in connection with its work on hearing aids. It is collaborating with an automobile manufacturer. Recent improvements arising from the need for high-powered miniature power storage plants in rockets have put us within reach of a relatively small battery capable of withstanding great overloads or surges of power. Germanium diode applications and batteries using sintered-plate and nickel-cadmium techniques promise to make a revolution in our energy sources.

- Solar energy conversion systems are also getting increasing attention. One usually cautious Detroit auto executive recently ventured that solar-powered cars might be common by 1980.

As for the oil companies, they are more or less "watching developments," as one research director put it to me. A few are doing a bit of research on fuel cells, but almost always confined to developing cells powered by hydrocarbon chemicals. None of them are enthusiastically researching fuel cells, batteries, or solar power plants. None of them are spending a fraction as much on research in these profoundly important areas as they are on the usual run-of-the-mill things like reducing combustion chamber deposit in gasoline engines. One major integrated petroleum company recently took a tentative look at the fuel cell and concluded that although "the companies actively working on it indicate a belief in ultimate success . . . the timing and magnitude of its impact are too remote to warrant recognition in our forecasts."

One might, of course, ask: Why should the oil companies do anything different? Would not chemical fuel cells, batteries, or solar energy kill the present product lines? The answer is that they would indeed, and that is precisely the reason for the oil firms having to develop these power units before their competitors, so they will not be companies without an industry.

Management might be more likely to do what is needed for its own preservation if it thought of itself as being in the energy business. But even that would not be enough if it persists in imprisoning itself in the narrow grip of its tight product orientation. It has to think of itself as taking care of customer needs, not finding, refining, or even selling oil. Once it genuinely thinks of its business as taking care of people's transportation needs, nothing can stop it from creating its own extravagantly profitable growth.

'Creative destruction': Since words are cheap and deeds are dear, it may be appropriate to indicate what this kind of thinking involves and leads to. Let us start at the beginning—the customer. It can be shown that motorists strongly dislike the bother, delay, and experience of buying gasoline. People actually do not buy gasoline. They cannot see it, taste it, feel it, appreciate it, or really test it. What they buy is the right to continue driving their cars. The gas station is like a tax collector to whom people are compelled to pay a periodic toll as the price of using their cars. This makes the gas station a basically unpopular institution. It can never be made popular or pleasant, only less unpopular, less unpleasant.

To reduce its unpopularity completely means eliminating it. Nobody likes a tax collector, not even a pleasantly cheerful one. Nobody likes to interrupt a trip to buy a phantom product, not even from a handsome Adonis or a seductive Venus. Hence, companies that are working on exotic fuel substitutes which will eliminate the need for frequent refueling are heading directly into the outstretched arms of the irritated motorist. They are riding a wave of inevitability, not because they are creating something which is technologically superior or more sophisticated, but because they are satisfying a powerful customer need. They are also eliminating noxious odors and air pollution.

Once the petroleum companies recognize the customer-satisfying logic of what another power system can do they will see that they have no more choice about working on an efficient, long-lasting fuel (or some way of delivering present fuels without bothering the motorist) than the big food chains had a choice about going into the supermarket business, or the vacuum tube companies had a choice about making semiconductors. For their own good the oil firms will have to destroy their own highly profitable assets. No amount of wishful thinking can save them from the necessity of engaging in this form of "creative destruction."

I phrase the need as strongly as this because I think management must make quite an effort to break itself loose from conventional ways. It is all too easy in this day and age for a company or industry to let its sense of purpose become dominated by the economies of full production and to develop a dangerously lopsided product orientation. In short, if management lets itself drift, it invariably drifts in the direction of thinking of itself as producing goods and services, not customer satisfactions. While it probably will not descend to the depths of telling its salesmen, "You get rid of it; we'll worry about profits," it can, without knowing it, be practicing precisely that formula for withering decay. The historic fate of one growth industry after another has been its suicidal product provincialism.

Dangers of R&D

Another big danger to a firm's continued growth arises when top management is wholly transfixed by the profit possibilities of technical research and development. To illustrate I shall turn first to a new industry—electronics—and then return once more to the oil companies. By comparing a fresh example with a familiar one, I hope to emphasize the prevalence and insidiousness of a hazardous way of thinking.

Marketing shortchanged: In the case of electronics, the greatest danger which faces the glamorous new companies in this field is not that they do not pay enough attention to research and development, but that they pay *too much* attention to it. And the fact that the fastest growing electronics firms owe their eminence to their heavy emphasis on technical research is completely beside the point. They have vaulted to affluence on a sudden crest of unusually strong general receptiveness to new technical ideas. Also, their success has been shaped in the virtually guaranteed market of military subsidies and by military orders that in many cases actually preceded the existence of facilities to make the products. Their expansion has, in other words, been almost totally devoid of marketing effort.

Thus, they are growing up under conditions that come dangerously close to creating the illusion that a superior product will sell itself. Having created a successful company by making a superior product, it is not surprising that management continues to be oriented toward the product rather than the people who consume it. It develops the philosophy that continued growth is a matter of continued product innovation and improvement.

A number of other factors tend to strengthen and sustain this belief:

1. Because electronic products are highly complex and sophisticated, managements become top-heavy with engineers and scientists. This creates a selective bias in favor of research and production at the expense of

marketing. The organization tends to view itself as making things rather than satisfying customer needs. Marketing gets treated as a residual activity, "something else" that must be done once the vital job of product creation and production is completed.

2. To this bias in favor of product research, development, and production is added the bias in favor of dealing with controllable variables. Engineers and scientists are at home in the world of concrete things like machines, test tubes, production lines, and even balance sheets. The abstractions to which they feel kindly are those which are testable or manipulatable in the laboratory, or, if not testable, then functional, such as Euclid's axioms. In short, the managements of the new glamour-growth companies tend to favor those business activities which lend themselves to careful study, experimentation, and control—the hard, practical realities of the lab, the shop, the books.

What gets shortchanged are the realities of the *market*. Consumers are unpredictable, varied, fickle, stupid, shortsighted, stubborn, and generally bothersome. This is not what the engineer-managers say, but deep down in their consciousness it is what they believe. And this accounts for their concentrating on what they know and what they can control, namely, product research, engineering, and production. The emphasis on production becomes particularly attractive when the product can be made at declining unit costs. There is no more inviting way of making money than by running the plant full blast.

Today the top-heavy science-engineering-production orientation of so many electronics companies works reasonably well because they are pushing into new frontiers in which the armed services have pioneered virtually assured markets. The companies are in the felicitous position of having to fill, not find markets; of not having to discover what the customer needs and wants, but of having the customer voluntarily come forward with specific new product demands. If a team of consultants had been assigned specifically to design a business situation calculated to prevent the emergence and development of a customer-oriented marketing viewpoint, it could not have produced anything better than the conditions just described.

Stepchild treatment: The oil industry is a stunning example of how science, technology, and mass production can divert an entire group of companies from their main task. To the extent the consumer is studied at all (which is not much), the focus is forever on getting information which is designed to help the oil companies improve what they are now doing. They try to discover more convincing advertising themes, more effective sales promotional drives, what the market shares of the various companies are, what people like or dislike about service station dealers and oil companies, and so forth. Nobody seems as interested in probing deeply into the basic human needs that the industry might be trying to satisfy as in probing into the basic properties of the raw material that the companies work with in trying to deliver customer satisfactions.

Basic questions about customers and markets seldom get asked. The latter occupy a stepchild status. They are recog-

nized as existing, as having to be taken care of, but not worth very much real thought or dedicated attention. Nobody gets as excited about the customers in his own backyard as about the oil in the Sahara Desert. Nothing illustrates better the neglect of marketing than its treatment in the industry press.

The centennial issue of the *American Petroleum Institute Quarterly*, published in 1959 to celebrate the discovery of oil in Titusville, Pennsylvania, contained 21 feature articles proclaiming the industry's greatness. Only one of these talked about its achievements in marketing, and that was only a pictorial record of how service station architecture has changed. The issue also contained a special section on "New Horizons," which was devoted to showing the magnificent role oil would play in America's future. Every reference was ebulliently optimistic, never implying once that oil might have some hard competition. Even the reference to atomic energy was a cheerful catalogue of how oil would help make atomic energy a success. There was not a single apprehension that the oil industry's affluence might be threatened or a suggestion that one "new horizon" might include new and better ways of serving oil's present customers.

But the most revealing example of the stepchild treatment that marketing gets was still another special series of short articles on "The Revolutionary Potential of Electronics." Under that heading this list of articles appeared in the table of contents:

- "In the Search for Oil"
- "In Production Operations"
- "In Refinery Processes"
- "In Pipeline Operations"

Significantly, every one of the industry's major functional areas is listed, *except* marketing. Why? Either it is believed that electronics holds no revolutionary potential for petroleum marketing (which is palpably wrong), or the editors forgot to discuss marketing (which is more likely, and illustrates its stepchild status).

The order in which the four functional areas are listed also betrays the alienation of the oil industry from the consumer. The industry is implicitly defined as beginning with the search for oil and ending with its distribution from the refinery. But the truth is, it seems to me, that the industry begins with the needs of the customer for its products. From that primal position its definition moves steadily back-stream to areas of progressively lesser importance, until it finally comes to rest at the "search for oil."

Beginning & end: The view that an industry is a customer-satisfying process, not a goods-producing process, is vital for all businessmen to understand. An industry begins with the customer and his needs, not with a patent, a raw material, or a selling skill. Given the customer's needs, the industry develops backwards, first concerning itself with the physical *delivery* of customer satisfactions. Then it moves back further to *creating* the things by which these satisfactions are in part achieved. How these materials are created is a matter of indifference to the customer, hence the particular form of manufacturing, processing, or what-have-you cannot be considered as a vital aspect of the industry. Finally, the industry moves back still further to *finding* the raw materials necessary for making its products.

The irony of some industries oriented toward technical research and development is that the scientists who occupy the high executive positions are totally unscientific when it comes to defining their companies' overall needs and purposes. They violate the first two rules of the scientific method—being aware of and defining their companies' problems, and then developing testable hypotheses about solving them. They are scientific only about the convenient things, such as laboratory and product experiments.

The reason that the customer (and the satisfaction of his deepest needs) is not considered as being "the problem" is not because there is any certain belief that no such problem exists, but because an organizational lifetime has conditioned management to look in the opposite direction. Marketing is a stepchild.

I do not mean that selling is ignored. Far from it. But selling, again, is not marketing. As already pointed out, selling concerns itself with the tricks and techniques of getting people to exchange their cash for your product. It is not concerned with the values that the exchange is all about. And it does not, as marketing invariably does, view the entire business process as consisting of a tightly integrated effort to discover, create, arouse, and satisfy customer needs. The customer is somebody "out there" who, with proper cunning, can be separated from his loose change.

Actually, not even selling gets much attention in some technologically minded firms. Because there is a virtually guaranteed market for the abundant flow of their new products, they do not actually know what a real market is. It is as if they lived in a planned economy, moving their products routinely from factory to retail outlet. Their successful concentration on products tends to convince them of the soundness of what they have been doing, and they fail to see the gathering clouds over the market.

Conclusion

Less than 75 years ago American railroads enjoyed a fierce loyalty among astute Wall Streeters. European monarchs invested in them heavily. Eternal wealth was thought to be the benediction for anybody who could scrape a few thousand dollars together to put into rail stocks. No other form of transportation could compete with the railroads in speed, flexibility, durability, economy, and growth potentials.

As Jacques Barzun put it, "By the turn of the century it was an institution, an image of man, a tradition, a code of honor, a source of poetry, a nursery of boyhood desires, a sublimest of toys, and the most solemn machine—next to the funeral hearse—that marks the epochs in man's life."[6]

Even after the advent of automobiles, trucks, and airplanes, the railroad tycoons remained imperturbably self-confident. If you had told them 30 years ago that in 30 years they would be flat on their backs, broke, and pleading for government subsidies, they would have thought you totally demented. Such a future was simply not considered possible. It was not even a discussable subject, or an askable question, or a matter which any sane person would consider worth speculating about. The very thought was insane. Yet a lot of insane notions now have matter-of-fact acceptance—for example, the idea of 100-ton tubes of metal moving smoothly through the air 20,000 feet above the earth, loaded with 100 sane and solid citizens casually drinking martinis—and they have dealt cruel blows to the railroads.

What specifically must other companies do to avoid this fate? What does customer orientation involve? These questions have in part been answered by the preceding examples and analysis. It would take another article to show in detail what is required for specific industries. In any case, it should be obvious that building an effective customer-oriented company involves far more than good intentions or promotional tricks; it involves profound matters of human organization and leadership. For the present, let me merely suggest what appear to be some general requirements.

Visceral feel of greatness: Obviously the company has to do what survival demands. It has to adapt to the requirements of the market, and it has to do it sooner rather than later. But mere survival is a so-so aspiration. Anybody can survive in some way or other, even the skid-row bum. The trick is to survive gallantly, to feel the surging impulse of commercial mastery; not just to experience the sweet smell of success, but to have the visceral feel of entrepreneurial greatness.

No organization can achieve greatness without a vigorous leader who is driven onward by his own pulsating *will to succeed*. He has to have a vision of grandeur, a vision that can produce eager followers in vast numbers. In business, the followers are the customers.

In order to produce these customers, the entire corporation must be viewed as a customer-creating and customer-satisfying organism. Management must think of itself not as producing products but as providing customer-creating value satisfactions. It must push this idea (and everything it means and requires) into every nook and cranny of the organization. It has to do this continuously and with the kind of flair that excites and stimulates the people in it. Otherwise, the company will be merely a series of pigeonholed parts, with no consolidating sense of purpose or direction.

In short, the organization must learn to think of itself not as producing goods or services but as *buying customers,* as doing the things that will make people *want* to do business with it. And the chief executive himself has the inescapable responsibility for creating this environment, this viewpoint, this attitude, this aspiration. He himself must set the company's style, its direction, and its goals. This means he has to know precisely where he himself wants to go, and to make sure the whole organization is enthusiastically aware of where that is. This is a first requisite of leadership, for *unless he knows where he is going, any road will take him there.*

If any road is okay, the chief executive might as well pack his attaché case and go fishing. If an organization does not know or care where it is going, it does not need to advertise that fact with a ceremonial figurehead. Everybody will notice it soon enough.

Retrospective Commentary

Amazed, finally, by his literary success, Isaac Bashevis Singer reconciled an attendant problem: "I think the moment you have published a book, it's not any more your private property. . . . If it has value, everybody can find in it what he finds, and I cannot tell the man I did not intend it to be so." Over the past 15 years, "Marketing Myopia" has become a case in point. Remarkably, the article spawned a legion of loyal partisans—not to mention a host of unlikely bedfellows.

Its most common and, I believe, most influential consequence is the way certain companies for the first time gave serious thought to the question of what businesses they are really in.

The strategic consequences of this have in many cases been dramatic. The best-known case, of course, is the shift in thinking of oneself as being in the "oil business" to being in the "energy business." In some instances the payoff has been spectacular (getting into coal, for example) and in others dreadful (in terms of the time and money spent so far on fuel cell research). Another successful example is a company with a large chain of retail shoe stores that redefined itself as a retailer of moderately priced, frequently purchased, widely assorted consumer specialty products. The result was a dramatic growth in volume, earnings, and return on assets.

Some companies, again for the first time, asked themselves whether they wished to be masters of certain technologies for which they would seek markets, or be masters of markets for which they would seek customer-satisfying products and services.

Choosing the former, one company has declared, in effect, "We are experts in glass technology. We intend to improve and expand that expertise with the object of creating products that will attract customers." This decision has forced the company into a much more systematic and customer-sensitive look at possible markets and users, even though its stated strategic object has been to capitalize on glass technology.

Deciding to concentrate on markets, another company has determined that "we want to help people (primarily women) enhance their beauty and sense of youthfulness." This company has expanded its line of cosmetic products, but has also entered the fields of proprietary drugs and vitamin supplements.

All these examples illustrate the "policy" results of "Marketing Myopia." On the operating level, there has been, I think, an extraordinary heightening of sensitivity to customers and consumers. R&D departments have cultivated a greater "external" orientation toward uses, users, and markets—balancing thereby the previously one-sided "internal" focus on materials and methods; upper management has realized that marketing and sales departments should be somewhat more willingly accommodated than before, finance departments have become more receptive to the legitimacy of budgets for market research and experimentation in marketing, and salesmen have been better trained to listen to and understand customer needs and problems, rather than merely to "push" the product.

A Mirror, Not a Window

My impression is that the article has had more impact in industrial-products companies than in consumer-products companies—perhaps because the former had lagged most in customer orientation. There are at least two reasons for this lag: (1) industrial-products companies tend to be more capital intensive, and (2) in the past, at least, they have had to rely heavily on communicating face-to-face the technical character of what they made and sold. These points are worth explaining.

Capital-intensive businesses are understandably preoccupied with magnitudes, especially where the capital, once invested, cannot be easily moved, manipulated, or modified for the production of a variety of products—e.g., chemical plants, steel mills, airlines, and railroads. Understandably, they seek big volumes and operating efficiencies to pay off the equipment and meet the carrying costs.

At least one problem results: corporate power becomes disproportionately lodged with operating or financial executives. If you read the charter of one of the nation's largest companies, you will see that the chairman of the finance committee, not the chief executive officer, is the "chief." Executives with such backgrounds have an almost trained incapacity to see that getting "volume" may require understanding and serving many discrete and sometimes small market segments, rather than going after a perhaps mythical batch of big or homogeneous customers.

These executives also often fail to appreciate the competitive changes going on around them. They observe the changes, all right, but devalue their significance or underestimate their ability to nibble away at the company's markets.

Once dramatically alerted to the concept of segments, sectors, and customers, though, managers of capital-intensive businesses have become more responsive to the necessity of balancing their inescapable preoccupation with "paying the bills" or breaking even with the fact that the best way to accomplish this may be to pay more attention to segments, sectors, and customers.

The second reason industrial products companies have probably been more influenced by the article is that, in the case of the more technical industrial products or services, the necessity of clearly communicating product and service characteristics to prospects results in a lot of face-to-face "selling" effort. But precisely because the product is so complex, the situation produces salesmen who know the product more than they know the customer, who are more adept at explaining what they have and what it can do than learning what the customer's needs and problems are. The result has been a narrow product orientation rather than a liberating customer orientation, and "service" often suffered. To be sure, sellers said, "We have to provide service," but they tended to define service by looking into the mirror rather than out the window. They *thought* they were looking out the window at the customer, but it was actually a mirror—a reflection of their own product-oriented biases rather than a reflection of their customers' situations.

A Manifesto, Not a Prescription

Not everything has been rosy. A lot of bizarre things have happened as a result of the article:

- Some companies have developed what I call "marketing mania"—they've become obsessively responsive to every fleeting whim of the customer. Mass production operations have been converted to approximations of job shops, with cost and price consequences far exceeding the willingness of customers to buy the product.

- Management has expanded product lines and added new lines of business without first establishing adequate control systems to run more complex operations.

- Marketing staffs have suddenly and rapidly expanded themselves and their research budgets without either getting sufficient prior organizational support or, thereafter, producing sufficient results.

- Companies that are functionally organized have converted to product, brand, or market-based organizations with the expectation of instant and miraculous results. The outcome has been ambiguity, frustration, confusion, corporate infighting, losses, and finally a reversion to functional arrangements that only worsened the situation.

- Companies have attempted to "serve" customers by creating complex and beautifully efficient products or services that buyers are either too risk-averse to adopt or incapable of learning how to employ—in effect, there are now steam shovels for people who haven't yet learned to use spades. This problem has happened repeatedly in the so-called service industries (financial services, insurance, computer-based services) and with American companies selling in less-developed economies.

"Marketing Myopia" was not intended as analysis or even prescription; it was intended as manifesto. It did not pretend to take a balanced position. Nor was it a new idea—Peter F. Drucker, J. B. McKitterick, Wroe Alderson, John Howard, and Neil Borden had each done more original and balanced work on "the marketing concept." My scheme, however, tied marketing more closely to the inner orbit of business policy. Drucker—especially in *The Concept of the Corporation* and *The Practice of Management*—originally provided me with a great deal of insight.

My contribution, therefore, appears merely to have been a simple, brief, and useful way of communicating an existing way of thinking. I tried to do it in a very direct, but responsible fashion, knowing that few readers (customers), especially managers and leaders, could stand much equivocation or hesitation.

I also knew that the colorful and lightly documented affirmation works better than the tortuously reasoned explanation.

But why the enormous popularity of what was actually such a simple preexisting idea? Why its appeal throughout the world to resolutely restrained scholars, implacably temperate managers, and high government officials, all accustomed to balanced and thoughtful calculation? Is it that concrete examples, joined to illustrate a simple idea and presented with some attention to literacy, communicate better than massive analytical reasoning that reads as though it were translated from the German? Is it that provocative assertions are more memorable and persuasive than restrained and balanced explanations, no matter who the audience? Is it that the character of the message is as much the message as its content? Or was mine not simply a different tune, but a new symphony? I don't know.

Of course, I'd do it again and in the same way, given my purposes, even with what more I now know—the good and the bad, the power of facts and the limits of rhetoric. If your mission is the moon, you don't use a car. Don Marquis's cockroach, Archy, provides some final consolation: "an idea is not responsible for who believes in it."

Notes

1. Jacques Barzun, "Trains and the Mind of Man," *Holiday*, February 1960, p. 21.
2. For more details see M. M. Zimmerman, *The Super Market: A Revolution in Distribution* (New York, McGraw-Hill Book Company, Inc., 1955), p. 48.
3. Ibid., pp. 45.–47.
4. *The Affluent Society* (Boston, Houghton Mifflin Company, 1958), pp. 152–160.
5. Henry Ford, *My Life and Work* (New York, Doubleday, Page & Company, 1923), pp. 146–147.
6. Jacques Barzun, "Trains and the Mind of Man," *Holiday*, February 1960, p. 20.

At the time of the article's publication, **THEODORE LEVITT** was lecturer in business administration at the Harvard Business School. He is the author of several books, including *The Third Sector: New Tactics for a Responsive Society* (1973) and *Marketing for Business Growth* (1974).

Customer Connection

We started winning when we listened to customers.

ANNE M. MULCAHY

I came by my passion for the customer naturally. I began my Xerox career in sales, and I have never stopped selling Xerox. Staying connected with customers is part of my DNA, and I'm trying to keep it a part of the Xerox DNA. As our founder, Joe Wilson, said: "Customers determine whether we have a job or not. Their attitude determines our success." This legacy is what saved Xerox from our worst crisis. We got into trouble by losing sight of the customer, and we got out of trouble by redoubling our focus on the customer.

Just five years ago, the prospect of bankruptcy loomed over us. Revenue and profits were declining. Cash was shrinking. Debt was mounting. Customers were irate. Employees were defecting. The day the value of Xerox stock had been cut in half (May 11, 2000), I was named president and COO.

One of the first things I did was call Warren Buffet to get his advice. He told me, "You've been drafted into a war you didn't start. Focus on your customers and lead your people as though their lives depended on your success."

Fortunately, I had not one but two aces in the hole: 1) a loyal customer base that wanted Xerox to survive, and 2) a talented and committed workforce—people who love Xerox and would do anything to help save the company and return it to greatness.

And so we went to work. We spent lots of time with customers, industry experts, and employees—listening. Customers told us we had great technology, but our response to them had slipped. Industry experts told us our technology was leading-edge, but we had to focus on doing a few things very well. And employees told us they would do whatever it took to save the company, but they needed clear direction.

We laid out a bold plan to turn Xerox around. The results have been stunning in magnitude and swiftness. We cut our debt by more than half; most of what remains is in the form of receivables. We more than doubled our equity. We took more than $2 billion out of our cost base through tough choices. And we increased earnings—building value for our shareholders, customers, and employees. Four years ago we lost $273 million. Last year we made $978 million. Our margins are healthy. We have money in the bank, and we're buying back stock.

Leading Xerox has been the opportunity of a lifetime, and I've learned that you can't do enough communications; that you need to change the bad and leverage the good in your culture; that you need to articulate a vision of where you are taking the company; that bad leadership can ruin a company overnight, and good leadership can move mountains over time; and that good people, aligned around a common set of objectives, can do almost anything. Mostly I learned that the customer is the center of our universe. Forget that and nothing much else matters: employees lose jobs, shareholders lose value, suppliers lose business, the brand deteriorates, and the firm spirals downward.

Consider the value of customer service: 1) If you can retain 5 percent more of your customers than you currently do, your bottom-line profit will grow from 25 to 50 percent; and 2) it takes five times more money and effort to attract a new customer as it does to retain an old one. We all know that customers are the reason we exist, yet we don't always behave that way. That's what got Xerox in trouble. We made decisions that didn't have the customer in mind. We weren't listening to our customers, and we started to take them for granted. We learned a powerful lesson the hard way.

Five Strategies

We've since made the customer our priority by focusing on five strategies:

Strategy 1: Listen and leant what your customers are facing—what their problems and opportunities are. It's not something you can delegate. It starts at the top. Every week I sit down with some of our key customers. In 2005 and 2006, I spent 25 percent of my time in direct contact with customers. Our entire leadership team at Xerox shares the same passion. Our 500 major accounts are assigned to our top executives. All our executives are involved. Each executive is responsible for communicating with at least one of our customers—understanding their concerns and requirements, and making sure that Xerox resources are marshaled to fix problems, address issues, and capture opportunities.

All of our officers do something to keep in touch with customers. There are about 20 of us, and we rotate responsibility to be "Customer Officer of the Day." It works out to about a day a month. When you're in the box, you assume responsibility for dealing with complaints from customers who have had a bad experience. They're angry, frustrated, and calling headquarters as their court of last resort. The "Officer of the Day" is required to listen, resolve the problem, and fix the underlying cause. It keeps us in touch with the real world, permeates our decision-making, impacts the way we allocate resources, and keeps us passionate about serving our customers.

Strategy 2: Even in the worst of times, invest in the best of times. As proud as I am of out financial turnaround, what gives me even greater satisfaction is the progress we've made on strengthening our core business to ensure future growth. Even as we dramatically reduced our costs, we maintained R&D spending in our core business. This was not a universally applauded decision: our financial advisors thought that slashing R&D was necessary; the bankers thought I didn't understand the problem; but our customers knew it would be a hollow victory if we avoided financial bankruptcy today only to face a technology drought tomorrow.

So we continued to invest in innovation. We're glad we did. In recent years, we have brought to market scores of new products and services. These investments are paying off. In fact, three-quarters of our revenues are coming from offerings that were introduced in the past two years.

Strategy 3: Align: Focus all your employees on creating customer value. A CEO I met with during our turnaround advised me to ask the question: "Would the customer pay for this? Would the customer think this was helpful?" I've tried to use that as a guideline. It has a double-payoff—streamlined costs and customer focus.

Top to bottom, Xerox people are tightly connected to our customers and their businesses. For us, it's personal. Our customers are real people with aspirations that we want to help them realize. We treat each customer as an individual—using our own technology to communicate with them one-to-one.

Strategy 4: Deliver value: Don't sell the customer your products, offer them solutions to their problems. In the recent decades, organizations have poured billions of dollars into technology. And the ROI hasn't always lived up to the promise because the focus was always on the technology. Our focus is on what really matters—information and what our customers do with it. We focus not on hardware and technology for the sake of technology, but on reducing cost and complexity while improving the customer experience. And the customer experience is more about striving problems.

Strategy 5: Serve: Provide service beyond the customer's expectations. About 75 percent of customers who defect say they were satisfied. When our customers tell us they are *very* satisfied, they are six times more likely to continue doing business with us than those who arc merely "satisfied." If you're providing your customers with good service, they're probably satisfied. But only about 40 percent of satisfied people repurchase! This should set off alarm bells. In a world of increasing competition and expectations, standards like *good* and *satisfied* don't cut it.

We realize that our customers have choices about whom they do business with, that their expectations continue to escalate, and that our competitors continue to improve.

We embrace those challenges. We now that our success depends on customer loyalty. Customers put a lot of trust in us, and we're on a crusade to give them a good return on trust.

The idea of putting the customer first is powerful, and we stray from it at our own peril. Our recent successes all stem from putting the customer at the center of decision-making.

ANNE M. MULCAHY is chairman and CEO of Xerox Corporation. This article is adapted from her speech at the World Business Forum, October 25, 2006. Frankfurt, Germany. Visit www.xerox.com or call 203-968-3000.

The Big Opportunity

KRYSTEN CRAWFORD

Tim Barry had no intention of launching a company, much less building a million-dollar business. He was just frustrated.

Several years ago, as the 55-year-old management consultant boarded a plane in Boston bound for San Francisco, he heard flight attendants discussing how they would handle an especially sensitive problem with seating. At 6-foot-1 and 365 pounds, the stout Barry and several other heavyset passengers needed seatbelt extenders—standard equipment on most airplanes to accommodate larger customers. But flight attendants didn't have enough to go around, and Barry overheard the humiliating options being considered: They might ask the bigger passengers to squeeze into a standard belt, or, if they couldn't, boot them off the flight.

Crisis was averted after airline workers found some extra belt extenders inside the terminal. But Barry didn't want to ever be put in the same situation again. He decided he would buy his own seatbelt extenders and make them part of his travel kit, along with his noise-reduction headphones and Tom Clancy novels. Barry hunted around the Web, in catalogs and travel magazines, and even at private airports. No luck. There was, it seemed to Barry, a nationwide shortage of airline seatbelt extenders on the retail market—and it was then that Barry's frustration began to give way to the invigorating tingle that hits every business veteran at the first whiff of an entrepreneurial opportunity.

Barry first contacted the manufacturers that supply the airlines. Soon thereafter he began mapping out plans to launch a retail site, called Extend-Its.com, from a small warehouse near his home outside Vancouver, Wash., to provide seatbelt extenders directly to the abundant numbers of people who need them. To date, Barry has shipped more than 10,000 belt extenders at $60 to $70 a pop. And he's launched two other sites, Scale-It.com and SuperSizeWorld.com, to sell household supplies and hard-to-find convenience items for heavyset customers: $20 Hangerzillas that hold coats weighing as much as 100 pounds, high-capacity scales, extra-large plush bath towels that go for $60 apiece. This year, with just two employees, Barry expects to hit $1 million in sales. "I've done nothing but Google ads," he says. "The demand is there, and the market is wide open."

Indeed it is. There is no polite way to say this: Americans are fat, and they're getting fatter. Government statistics show that more than 60 million Americans already qualify as obese,

up from 23 million in 1980. Another 28 million are expected to join their ranks by 2013. Forget the stereotypes: It's not just people in low-income neighborhoods who are packing on the pounds at McDonald's. Researchers at the University of Iowa have found that obesity rates are rising most rapidly among urbanites who earn $60,000 or more per year.

Fat Americans have become our fastest-growing consumer segment. To many, that's an unpleasant surprise. To entrepreneurial mavericks, it's a market of potentially immense proportions.

Heretofore, the main business response to this overwhelming demographic trend has been the $49 billion weight-loss industry—huge and profitable, but in many ways narrowly targeted. Now a much broader segment of corporate America has begun to see the nation's fattening for what it is: a potentially powerful driver of consumer demand across a wide swath of the economy. Just as baby boomers have driven business and shaped the economy during the past half century, the "plus-size" population is likely to dictate marketing trends through much of the 21st.

Already, greater girth is forcing American business to rethink—albeit carefully—the way it designs and sells everything from sofas and toilets to clothes and nights on the town. The new Toyota Rav4 comes with seats up to 3 inches wider than prior models. Select Comfort, the high-end mattress maker, now sells a grand king size that's 30 percent bigger than a traditional king. Market research firm Mintel estimates that U.S. sales of women's plus-size apparel jumped 50 percent during the past five years to nearly $32 billion. Dana Buchman, Tommy Hilfiger, and Ralph Lauren now make clothes to fit larger women, and even Jessica Simpson has slapped her name on a new brand of big-bottom jeans. In several major cities around the country, popular new "size acceptance" nightclubs are becoming profit machines, not just safe havens for outcasts.

The opportunities, in short, seem about as unlimited and surefire as these things get. "I just don't see how I can lose," Barry says. "If we know anything about medical history, once you get past a certain weight, you're probably not going to lose it. You'll be my customer for life."

It is breathtaking—and, of course, alarming for the state of public health—how rapidly the overweight are becoming a powerhouse consumer class. Up until the early 1980s, Americans' body sizes had remained relatively stable, growing by just a third of a pound between 1962 and 1980. In 1980 the average adult male weighed in at 174 pounds. The typical woman was 145 pounds. Then came a kind of unholy alliance of societal trends: bigger portions of cheaper, fattier food; more dual-income households that scarfed more restaurant grub and cooked less at home; and suburban sprawl that turned formerly active urban dwellers into sedentary drivers and couch potatoes. Today nearly a third of adult men and more than a third of adult women are considered obese, defined as having a body mass index of 30 or higher. That's the equivalent of a 5-foot-4 woman tipping the scales at 175 pounds or a 5-foot-9 male weighing 205 pounds. And since no one has yet found a magic cure for weight gain, there seems very little chance that the trend will reverse itself.

Outside of the lucrative trade in peddling diet aids and health club memberships to people eternally searching for ways to lose weight, U.S. business was slow to pick up on the trend. But as in any new industry, there were pioneers—namely retailers who realized that bigger bodies still had to be clothed. At first, most department stores and top retailers had little to offer larger customers and were happy to let niche players like Lane Bryant, which began as a seller of maternity clothes more than a century ago, handle the market. And as the nation's waistlines expanded,

Lane Bryant expanded right along with them. By 2000 the chain had grown to more than 690 stores and $930 million in sales. The following year Pennsylvania-based Charming Shoppes, now a $2.8 billion retailer that owns two other plus-size clothing chains (Catherines Plus Sizes and Fashion Bug), snapped up Lane Bryant for $335 million.

The acquisition was a turning point. "Clothing retailers didn't think it was chic to be fat," says Kurt Barnard, president of Barnard's Retail Consulting Group. "But then they realized they were losing tons of business." Now women who wear sizes 14 and larger make up more than half of the overall market, and plus-size apparel is the fastest-growing segment of the clothing industry. Retailers big and small are launching new plus-size lines for brides, shorter women, and expectant mothers. San Francisco-based Old Navy has rolled out a line of oversize clothes for adults to 250 stores over the past two years; it recently added "husky" sizes for teenage boys and plus sizes for girls. Wal-Mart, too, made sure to include plus sizes last year when it launched Metro 7, its new line of hip fashions for adult women.

The trend has also given rise to at least one successful niche player: Torrid, a division of the $725 million youth clothing retailer Hot Topic, sells Baby Phat tube tops and Hot Kiss gaucho pants to large women in their 20s at mall-based stores around the country. Betsy McLaughlin, Hot Topic's CEO, decided to launch a separate brand after her female customers started clamoring for bigger sizes in the late 1990s. "There was no place they could shop," McLaughlin says. "They either made their own clothes or wore men's clothes." Since launching with six stores in 2001, Torrid has seen its revenue grow to more than $70 million, according to analysts, and it plans to end 2006 with 130 stores.

As Americans Get Fatter . . .

Obesity rates have climbed at an unprecedented clip since 1980—so fast, in fact, that big business is only now starting to catch on.

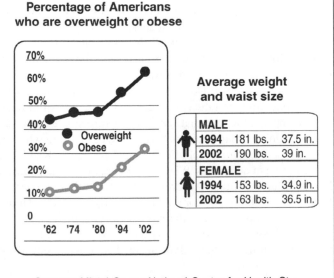

Percentage of Americans who are overweight or obese

Average weight and waist size

MALE		
1994	181 lbs.	37.5 in.
2002	190 lbs.	39 in.
FEMALE		
1994	153 lbs.	34.9 in.
2002	163 lbs.	36.5 in.

Sources: Mintel Group; National Center for Health Statistics; NPD Group; University of Iowa; Business 2.0 analysis

. . . So Does the Market

Obesity is soaring among the middle class, helping clothing chains like Lane Bryant and others outpace the overall market.

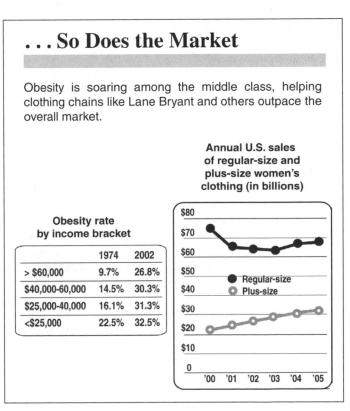

Obesity rate by income bracket

	1974	2002
> $60,000	9.7%	26.8%
$40,000-60,000	14.5%	30.3%
$25,000-40,000	16.1%	31.3%
<$25,000	22.5%	32.5%

Annual U.S. sales of regular-size and plus-size women's clothing (in billions)

Charming Shoppes, meanwhile, is fast becoming a retail giant on par with Limited Brands and Abercrombie & Fitch. Already the country's third-largest specialty retailer, the company recently announced plans to do battle with Victoria's Secret by opening 50 Cacique lingerie shops in 2006. Sales of its 48DDD bras and other intimates hit $227 million last year, up from nothing a decade ago, according to Gayle Coolick, Charming Shoppes's director of investor relations. "And that's when lingerie was hidden in the back of the store," Coolick adds. When Charming Shoppes tested the Cacique line in select stores last year, undergarment sales took off and the effort drew even more customers into Lane Bryant outlets, "Women are starved for this product," Coolick says. So are investors: Charming Shoppes's share price has doubled in the past year.

The prize for retailers isn't just increased sales but also loyal customers who aren't as price-sensitive as their slimmer counterparts. That's especially important at $4.8 billion fashion brand Liz Claiborne, where growth of mainstream lines has stalled in the face of fierce competition from department stores and big-box retailers. The company is counting on specialty stores, such as its 29 plus-size Elisabeth boutiques, for future growth. "This business was so underserved for so long," says Barry Zelman, general manager of specialty retail. "A plus-size woman sticks with a brand she likes, and she doesn't mind paying full price for it."

That kind of loyalty can extend well beyond clothes. Anne Corning, a 40-year-old Seattle resident, describes life as an overweight consumer as a series of seemingly endless frustrations and hassles. Buying clothes, she says, has been getting a lot easier. What she really wants now are conveniences like chairs without armrests, spas that offer bigger robes, restaurants with wider booths, and couches that don't sink so much. "There are definitely moments when I'm in a low-slung sofa and I'm thinking, 'Oh, shit, how am I going to get out of this?'" Corning says.

Entrepreneurs—many of them overweight themselves—have begun racing to alleviate those kinds of nightmares. While Tim Barry and several other retailers sell household convenience items, Aitan Levy is making the same kind of bet with bathroom fixtures, another market that big business has been slow to adapt to the obese. The owner of a small plumbing manufacturer based outside Los Angeles, Levy had heard people complain for years that standard toilet seats are too small, uncomfortable, and fragile for stout customers. So three years ago he designed the Big John Toilet Seat, a 19-inch throne made of reinforced plastic, and started making the seats himself. In the first two months, he sold about 2,000 commodes at $88 apiece, and he has since rolled out a newer $170 model and added a $160 open-front version. Demand has doubled over the last six months. "All you have to do is look around to see that people are bigger," Levy says. "But where are all the products and services?" Levy's toilet line is not yet profitable, but he expects it to be by year's end. Industry heavyweights Kohler and American Standard, meanwhile, have yet to unveil rival products.

Seating for overweight consumers is just as big a problem in the living room or office as it is in the bathroom—and businesses are starting to tackle that too. Brayton International—a subsidiary of Steelcase, the world's largest office furniture maker, with $2.9 billion in annual revenue—began selling waiting-room chairs designed for heavier builds in 2003 and is looking to add wider, sturdier office chairs in response to growing demand. "We're taking a hard look at what it's going to take to accommodate a larger-framed society." says Cia Mooney, Brayton's VP for product development.

Most likely, that means more market research. Nemschoff, a privately held maker of health-care equipment based in Sheboygan, Wis., started offering extra-large furniture several years ago when surgery became a popular treatment for obesity. As the number of surgeries rose, hospitals have raced to build bariatric wings with wider door frames, bigger gurneys, and sturdier waiting-room furniture. But when Nemschoff came out with its first plus-size seating—a line of reinforced chairs that didn't appear much different from standard chairs—heavyset customers mistook them for standard equipment that might buckle. "We didn't want the chairs to scream out 'I'm the one for you' when a heavy person walked into a room," says CEO Mark Nemschoff. Understanding the goof, he followed up with newer, wider models. Nemschoff sold 1,800 bariatric chairs last year—a 40 percent jump from 2004.

Nemschoff's early misstep underscores some of the difficulties in marketing to the obese. Large consumers want the mass market to respond to their needs, but products that reflect too much reality—that remind them that they're overweight—often bomb. At the same time, companies don't want to be seen as enablers of an increasingly fat society. For some, the answer is to design bigger products for big people without advertising them or even talking about them. When Toyota outfitted its Rav4 mini SUV with tilting steering wheels and wider seats—popular features with heavy set drivers—it billed the cars as nothing more than "roomier." Paul Williamsen, Toyota's product education manager, puts it delicately: "Some products of ours may be seen to be more appropriate for different body shapes."

Other companies have tackled the challenges of marketing products for the obese using traditional Madison Avenue savvy. Last year Unilever plastered New York and several other U.S. cities with ads for new Dove skin-firming creams that featured women flaunting their curves in bras and panties. Lost to many consumers was the fact that the models were smaller than the average adult woman is today. "So you're celebrating who you are—but selling an anticellulite cream?" says Mira Kaddoura, an executive at ad agency Wieden & Kennedy. "That's weird." Maybe. But it works. According to Information Resources, Dove's sales jumped more than 12 percent in the United States—far outpacing growth in its category. Those results suggest that plus-size consumers, like the rest of us, respond better to pretty portraits of themselves in ads than to what they see in the bathroom mirror.

Despite success stories like Dove's, some businesses remain reluctant to make themselves more fat-friendly. The airlines, for instance, face a rising number of large passengers—but as Tim Barry's experience shows, the industry has been among the least willing to openly market to the overweight, out of fear of alienating smaller passengers. Southwest Airlines, for instance, still enforces a 30-year-old policy that requires extra-large passengers to buy a second seat if they can't fold down their armrests. Brandy King, a Southwest spokeswoman, says the airline gets more complaints about encroaching seatmates than it does about the two-ticket policy. Mike Boyd, an independent aviation consultant in Evergreen, Colo., explains that the obesity epidemic won't hit airlines anytime soon. "If the average American's girth is growing a couple of centimeters a year," Boyd says, "are airlines going to have to accommodate that? No, they're not."

The headaches associated with air travel help explain why another nascent plus-size market—vacation resorts—hasn't taken off. Three years ago Julio Rincon, a longtime hotel manager in Cancún, Mexico, opened the world's first "fat friendly" resort. Called Freedom Paradise, it was a beach complex with 112 rooms where extra-large vacationers could relax in the sun away from the disapproving stares of others. (The resort's slogan was "Live large, live free.") Rincon spent $2 million outfitting the place with features like reinforced beds, wide restaurant chairs without armrests, and a staff that had undergone sensitivity training.

Overweight consumers want the mass market to respond to their needs, but companies don't want to be seen as enablers of the obesity epidemic.

But after Freedom Paradise launched with much fanfare and press coverage, the crowds never materialized. Rincon says he seldom got the vacancy rate below 50 percent. His mistake, he says now, was underestimating how much plus-size travelers dread long-distance air travel, especially during peak months when planes are packed. So last fall, Rincon abandoned the fat-only concept, renamed the resort Maya Tankah, and opened the place to all comers. The rooms are now full, but Rincon isn't giving up on his original idea. He's been checking out resorts closer to the U.S. border, as well as in Spain and Germany. "I'm convinced the market is growing, and not just in the U.S.," Rincon says. "But right now a lot of plus-size people do their vacationing close to home."

That isn't to suggest that they're homebodies, though. On a recent Saturday night in the Orange County, Calif., suburb of Costa Mesa, luxury cars jam the parking lot of the Butterfly Lounge as stretch limos glide along the palm-lined street. Inside the club, young couples bump and grind to Usher's hit "Yeah!," while bartenders pour vodka-and-Red Bulls. The club is no magnet for the rail-thin blonds and buff hunks you'll find on *The O.C.*, though. Butterfly advertises itself as a "size acceptance" nightspot, with high stools set around elevated tables to make seating easier. Almost everyone weighs more than 250 pounds. The club is profitable, drawing crowds of 300 or more on weekends. "Ninety percent of the folks here have tried everything to be thin," says one male customer who's come to the Butterfly after reading about it on the Web. "At some point you've just got to live."

KRYSTEN CRAWFORD (kcrawford@business2.com) is an associate editor at Business 2.0.

Listening to Starbucks

With a big, bold push into music, Howard Schultz is really thinking outside the cup. Is it time to reimagine *your* business?

ALISON OVERHOLT

So this girl walks into a bar. She holds a tall iced coffee in one hand, and her blond hair is piled high in a ponytail, neon bikini strings peeking out from her tank top. At this bar, however, headphones hang above the stools, and computer screens are embedded in the countertop. The girl looks at the "bartender" quizzically. "So you can burn music here and it's, like, legal and everything?" she asks. The bartender smiles and nods. "Omigod, so you have, like, every song, ever?" Well, not every song, but quite a few: approaching 150,000—about 20,000 albums' worth. The girl settles onto a stool and grabs a headset, taking a long drag on the straw in her drink as she starts tapping away on a screen. "That's awwwesome."

It's awesome indeed, this new-concept music store on the trendy Third Street Promenade in Santa Monica, California. It's a beautiful space with warm lighting and wood paneling—a place where you can buy regular old CDs, or linger with a drink while you listen to music and sift through thousands of songs stored in a computer database to create your very own personalized, mixed-CD masterpiece. In about five minutes, a freshly burned CD, complete with your chosen title and funky artwork on both the disc and the jacket (plus liner notes!) will be ready to take home. It all happens very smoothly, and yet it's a novel and startling experience. But what's most startling about this remarkable new place to buy music is this: It's a Starbucks.

The Hear Music Coffeehouse, as it's known, opened last March as the first of several fully integrated café-music stores that Starbucks is launching with its wholly owned subsidiary, retailer Hear Music. This August, Starbucks will install individual music-listening stations, with CD-burning capabilities, in 10 existing Starbucks locations in Seattle. From there, the concept rolls out to Texas in the fall, including Starbucks stores in the music mecca of Austin. With the help of technology partner Hewlett-Packard, Starbucks plans to have 100 coffee shops across the country enabled with Hear Music CD-burning stations by next Christmas, and more than 1,000 locations up and running by the end of 2005. Think iTunes meets Tower Records. With lattes.

Chairman and chief global strategist Howard Schultz's ambitions for this new business operation are vast; it's not just about selling a few CDs from a coffee shop (Starbucks has been doing that, successfully, for about five years already). Schultz wants Starbucks customers to make their own CDs, yes, but he also thinks they will someday use Starbucks' enormous Wi-Fi footprint to buy and store music from the network on any device imaginable—from laptops and iPods to phones and PDAs. He hopes record labels will develop proprietary material just for the Starbucks network. And that Starbucks itself may help break new artists and develop original material. Indeed, Howard Schultz plans nothing less than to turn the entire music industry upside down. "We are the most frequented retailer in the world," he says. "With hundreds of thousands of songs digitally filed and stored, these Hear Music coffeehouses combined with our existing locations can become the largest music store in any city that we have a Starbucks in. And because of the traffic, the frequency, and the trust that our customers have in the experience and the brand, we believe strongly that we can transform the retail record industry."

There's something even more intriguing going on here, though. This push into music is the start of a daring effort to reinvent one of the world's best-known brands. It is an experiment that asks whether that brand is powerful enough, and Starbucks' relationships with the 30 million customers who pass through its 8,000 stores every week durable enough, that they can be used to completely transform the business.

"Great companies are defined by their discipline and their understanding of who they are and who they are not," Schultz says. "But also, great companies must have the courage to examine strategic opportunities that are transformational—as long as they are not inconsistent with the guiding principles and values of the core business." And so Schultz finds himself on a precipice, at the edge of just such an opportunity, where he celebrates coffee as both the origins and the core of his business, and yet has dreams of transcending those origins to become something much more.

In effect, Schultz is asking the question famously posed by Theodore Levitt, the Harvard Business School professor and father of modern marketing: What business are you really in? Levitt explained that the once-powerful railroads, for example, were blindsided first by automobiles and then by the airlines. It happened because they had defined themselves too narrowly as being in the railroad business rather than the transportation business. As railroads, they were entrenched and invulnerable; as transportation, they were wide open to attack. Theirs was a failure of imagination—the inability to reconceive themselves based on the business they were really in.

"Great companies recognize who they are and who they are not. But they must have the courage to examine transformational opportunities."

Over the years, a handful of companies have taken Levitt's words to heart, reimagining the very definitions of their businesses and their industries each time they reached a critical turning point. Disney was once a little studio that turned out cartoon shorts. Then Walt Disney opened a theme park unlike anything anyone had ever known. Now his company develops, produces, and distributes films of all kinds; has a network of theme parks; and runs a vast media empire. Virgin's Richard Branson turned a little music magazine into a music superstore, then launched an airline, and, most recently, a cell-phone company. And before her ImClone disgrace, Martha Stewart was among this select few: Her home-catering operation became a series of cookbooks, then gave birth to a multimedia company and a lifestyle-products line that sold everything from hand towels to patio furniture at Kmart.

In each case, as the company reached a plateau in one industry category, a visionary-leader looked past the original product or service to redefine, in the broadest terms, the business it was in. Disney, Branson, and Stewart reimagined their cartoon, magazine, and food-service operations as entertainment enterprises. Then, when entertainment itself became too constricting, they blew apart traditional industry characterizations altogether. Now what they really sell is a lifestyle. Disney and its idealized view of wholesome, all-American family life; Virgin and its vision of youth, sexiness, adventure, and exuberance; Martha Stewart and her promise that you, too, can lead the elegant, good life. They sell you the dream, then the full suite of products, services, and experiences to achieve it.

And Schultz would like Starbucks to join them. He aims to achieve what so few are able to do—to reimagine his company as something bigger, better, and more significant than it has ever been. In fact, forget joining them. Schultz plans to surpass them all. "We have the potential to become the most recognizable and respected brand in the world," he says flatly.

That may be hubris, or it may be an attainable goal. Either way, Schultz must still answer Levitt's question: What business is Starbucks really in? Clearly, it's more than coffee shops. Like those other successful marketers, Schultz is selling his own lifestyle dream, one of affluence and comfort, a forward-looking but not-too-trendy community experience wrapped around a steaming cup of coffee in a cozy living room that exists on every block between home and work.

This wouldn't be the first time Schultz has transformed his company with a quantum leap of imagination. When he arrived at Starbucks in 1982 as the director of marketing and retail sales, the company was a coffee roaster and wholesaler. Back then, coffee was a 40-cent cup of brownish water, and Maxwell House reigned supreme. Now millions of coffee drinkers think nothing of paying $4 for a tall vanilla latte. Sure, it tastes better than coffee from the 1980s, but is it really worth 10 times as much? Probably not. And Schultz knows it, because he's not really selling the coffee. What he's really persuading us to pay for is that relaxing world of velvet armchairs and afternoon chats with friends in a home away from home that's filled with . . . yes, music. Or as he puts it, "We've known for a long time now that Starbucks is more than just a wonderful cup of coffee. It's the experience."

And those $4 lattes, with their extra-foamy triple-caffeinated profit margins, sure do add up. Since its IPO in 1992, Starbucks has been a stellar performer by nearly every measure. The stock is up 3,500%, with a market capitalization that increased from $400 million to about $15 billion this year. Starbucks opens three new stores every single day, and now has about 8,000 coffee shops around the world (up from 165 in 1992). It has racked up more than 12 consecutive years of sales growth in existing stores; in each of the last five years, same-store sales have increased by 5% or more. Far from showing signs of flagging, this critical measure of retail performance is looking even better lately. Same-store sales rose 9% in 2003.

And yet it's hard not to wonder whether Starbucks' cup won't someday run dry. With a shop on what seems like every corner, can market saturation be far behind? Schultz dismisses the notion; he's fond of pointing out that Starbucks has just a 7% share of the North American coffee market, which would suggest that there's lots of room to grow. And despite some setbacks, Starbucks has 1,867 stores overseas and has big hopes for China.

"Of course no chief executive wants to say, 'Yes, our market is saturated,'" scoffs Geoffrey Moore, a partner at the Silicon Valley venture-capital firm Mohr, Davidow Ventures and author of the business classic *Crossing the Chasm* (HarperBusiness, 1991). "But the notion that 7% market share means he still has a big field to go after is silly. His market is not all coffee drinkers. His market is people who buy into an upscale 21st-century café society experience, which is much smaller."

Whether or not Starbucks' own railroad moment is waiting just around the bend, now is probably not a bad time to be thinking of some new and different ways to grow. "Schultz is doing

Redefining Your Business

To Howard Schultz, Starbucks isn't in the coffee business. It's in the people business. Once you start looking at things that way, the horizons get a lot wider. Here's Schultz's guide to contemplating life beyond the cup.

Think like an athlete.

Whenever you reach a plateau, it's time to rethink. If you're number one or number two in your category, maybe it's time to reconsider the category in which you compete: Create a broader definition of the industry, and develop a new plan to conquer it.

Team up with like-minded partners.

Hear Music and Don MacKinnon approach their business the same way Starbucks does: Customer interaction is vital, intimacy is important, and the shopping experience is everything. That's what made launching a music service together smart, not crazy.

Dream big.

A corollary to finding a new industry definition: Make its boundaries as wide as possible. "We have the potential to become the most recognizable and respected brand in the world," Schultz says. Not the biggest coffee company but the biggest brand, period. "When you're building a business, you have to dream as big as you can possibly imagine—otherwise, what's the point?"

Stay small.

Everyone loves the convenience of a widely available product or service; no one likes to feel anonymous. Even as Starbucks goes global, adding new products and new businesses, Schultz and his team strive to maintain the intimacy and personalized feel of every single Starbucks encounter. "Our biggest challenge is to get big but stay small," he says.

something quite unusual in business," says Adrian Slywotzky, a partner at Mercer Management Consulting and coauthor of *How to Grow When Markets Don't* (Warner Books, 2003). "He's already looking ahead, doing the arithmetic and saying, 'Well, our current model is not forever.' There are probably a few more years of growth left in coffee shops, and he's asking, 'How do we manage that inevitable slowdown a couple of years from now?'"

There are several ways Starbucks might answer that question, Slywotzky says. It could expand grocery operations, increase corporate sales, or explore entirely new markets. The company has already had some success in the first two categories. It sells bottled coffee drinks, coffee-flavored ice creams, and coffee beans in grocery chains nationwide. And it sells to foodservice companies that supply coffee on airlines and in hotels and restaurants.

But all told, these businesses don't add up to a very big hill of beans for Starbucks. They amount to something like 8% of total revenues. And profit margins are slim.

Schultz stumbled on another answer five years ago when he walked into the Stanford Shopping Center in Palo Alto. He was on an idea-hunting trip, the sort of expedition he and other Starbucks executives frequently go on. "At our core, we're merchants," he says. "And that means we travel the world all the time, looking at and examining the best retailers and merchants, whatever they might be." That day, Schultz walked into a Hear Music record store and fell in love.

It wasn't huge by the standards of superstores such as Tower Records, HMV, or Virgin Megastore. Instead of ringing up CDs by the latest top-40 bubblegum princesses, the store clerks talked to Schultz about such artists as jazz greats Ella Fitzgerald and Dinah Washington. "When I think about the average music-shopping experience, what I would call the sense of romance about music is gone," Schultz recalls. "But when I saw Hear Music that first time, it was clear that they had cracked the code on the sense of discovery that music should have."

What Schultz had come across was a group of music stores with something of a cult following in the Bay Area. Hear Music was one of the first stores in the country to introduce the now-universal concept of the "listening station," those headphone-equipped CD stations where shoppers can try their music before they buy. Though the stores carry fewer titles than the music superstores, Hear Music prides itself on introducing customers to music from off-the-beaten-path artists, and the people who work there are passionate about music. A Hear Music employee can almost always suggest singers you might like if you tell him what music you already own. If you don't know the name of a particular tune, he can probably track it down for you.

In its intimacy, quality, and customer focus, Hear Music must have reminded Schultz very much of his own company. And the rest of the music industry, with its commoditization, standardization, and concentration on shoveling millions of Hilary Duff CDs out the door, must have looked a lot like Maxwell House. "We never dreamed we'd be sitting on the unique opportunity we're sitting on now," he says. "We just saw that they were doing for music what we had done for coffee."

On some level, of course, it hardly took a flash of blinding insight to see that music and coffeehouses were made for each other. "Our customers respond to music," says Anne Saunders, senior vice president of marketing. "Part of why they come is as an entertainment destination, for a respite, a break with friends, as a place for community gathering. The idea for the music service is very grounded in why people come to Starbucks."

Since acquiring the company in 1999, Starbucks has sold Hear Music compilation CDs in its stores. And it launched a popular series of CDs called "Artist's Choice," in which musicians from Lucinda Williams to the Rolling Stones share their

A Coffee-Klatsch with Mr. Schultz

Words of wisdom from the architect of Starbucks' phenomenal success:

"Customer loyalty is not an entitlement."

Whether you have 30 customers or 30 million (like Starbucks), customers are fickle. They're bombarded with newer products and snazzier messages every day. Companies must continue to prove their worth—or lose it. Says Schultz: "We know we need to win back our customers' loyalty every day. Our success is based on their continued trust in our people and our environment over long periods of time."

"Great brands aren't built on ads or promotions."

Redefining the industry you're playing in doesn't just mean hiring an agency to think up a fancy new slogan. To make it work, you have to offer high-quality new products and services that customers actually want, and that will reinforce the value offered by your core brand and expand the emotional connection your customers feel with it.

"It's no fun being a pioneer."

When launching a new product, service, or business unit, remember that experience still counts. Even though the Hear Music Coffeehouse experience is unique, developing it with folks familiar with the music business was vital. "It's always best to surround yourself with people who've done it before, in some form or another," Schultz says.

"Stay humble, there is no room for arrogance."

Customers can tell when a new product or service is an authentic outgrowth of the company's mission, and when it's an overblown gimmick designed to feed the buzz machine. Be aggressive with your business performance goals—not your ego.

favorite songs. Nearly 400,000 copies have been sold at Starbucks stores. It was after seeing those results that Schultz and Don MacKinnon, one of the founders of Hear Music and now Starbucks' vice president of music and entertainment (doesn't that title tell you something?), began to wonder whether there was a bigger opportunity to explore.

Schultz and MacKinnon came to believe that the core Starbucks customer, an affluent 25- to 50-year-old who's likelier to be tuned in to NPR than to MTV or one of the nine gazillion radio stations owned by Clear Channel Communications Inc., probably feels ignored by the music industry. The shopping experience at most record stores is off-putting, with customers overwhelmed by the volume of stuff but still unable to discover great new music. At the same time, the consolidated radio industry has gone as bland and homogenized as low-fat milk. "What you're left with is this very broad audience made up of the core Starbucks customer, who loves music and can't find it," Schultz says. "We have a unique opportunity to take advantage of this."

There are clear parallels between the way Starbucks is developing this new music business and the way Schultz developed the core coffee business.

Follow that blond girl into the Hear Music Coffeehouse in Santa Monica, and you'll start to see what Schultz means. Down on the Promenade, it's early on a Sunday afternoon, and the cobblestone sidewalks are full of people. They flock to the Starbucks storefront between Broadway and Santa Monica boulevards for iced-coffee confections. Customers order at an outdoor bar, and are directed inside the store to pick up their drinks on the other side of the doorway. More often than not, once folks step inside, they decide to stay.

A smooth R&B tune is grooving over the sound system, and a quick look at the wall over the music bar reveals a projected-light sign: "Now Playing: 'When It Hurts So Bad,' by Lauryn Hill, from the album *The Miseducation of Lauryn Hill.*" The store is crowded. More than 60 people are in the small space—3,000 square feet, just large enough to accommodate the coffee and music bars, two short aisles of CD racks, plus space to mill around near the center of the store.

Now take a peek around the corner, at the Tower Records on Santa Monica Boulevard. It's easily four times as big as the Hear Music Coffeehouse, and there are just 10 people inside. None are interacting with a Tower employee, and none are using the listening stations—perhaps because three of them are broken. (Tower's parent company filed for Chapter 11 bankruptcy in February.) And here's the Borders, just three doors down from Hear Music. It has an entire floor dedicated to music and movies, but there are no employees and just two customers—both looking at DVDs.

Back at the coffeehouse, each of the seven listening stations at the CD-burning music bar is in use, and—though you wouldn't believe there was enough space for this many—all of the 55 other HP Tablet PC-based listening stations around the store are in use, too. Three more stations outside at the coffee bar make 65 places in all where customers can listen to as many songs as they have the patience to sample.

There are no restrictions on what songs you can listen to, or for how long. Pick up any CD from the racks, wave its bar code under the scanner at the bottom of the listening stations, and a complete list of the songs on the album appears on screen, along with a description of the artist and links to other records. "The

The Chairman's Mix

Howard Schultz drinks a double-short, nonfat latte, three-quarters full. Here's what he'd burn on his CD.

Mack the Knife	Bobby Darin
Mood Indigo	Duke Ellington
I Get a Kick Out of You	Nat King Cole
Homeward Bound	Simon & Garfunkel
Peel Me a Grape Some	Diana Krall
Some Kind of Wonderful	Joss Stone
So What	Miles Davis
Angel	Sarah McLachlan

scanning thing is pretty rad," says Nathan Hill, 26, who comes by often to check out the selection. "It helps me find stuff." If Hear Music has written reviews about, conducted interviews with, or produced compilations that include the artist, those are linked, too. The tablets are simple ATM-style touch screens. And often there are recommendations: "If you like Norah Jones, you might try Shelby Lynne."

There are clear parallels between the way Starbucks is developing this new music business and the way Schultz developed the core coffee business over the past two decades. Though his ambitions are global and his product is mass market, each coffee drink is personalized and created individually. Like all Starbucks executives, Saunders, the marketing chief, worked in a store when she first arrived on the job. "I waited on hundreds of customers while working the cash register and was struck by how every single one of them ordered something different," she says. "A flavor shot, extra hot, half-caf, maybe all those things together. Every single person coming in here has a different experience, designed the way they want it."

At the Hear Music Coffeehouse, the personalization is even more . . . personal. Choose your cover art. Create an album title. Select your songs. Move them around into a different order. Pick music by mood, by artist, or by genre—it's your choice. "We have a marketing tagline on the wall to reinforce how important we think that personalized experience is," says Saunders. "It reads: 'It'll be your favorite CD because you picked every song." And the product itself is high quality and perfectly packaged. "So many people aren't ready for digital music if they approach it on their own," says MacKinnon. "Here, there is no barrier to exploration, and you take something home that is tangible and beautiful."

And here's who MacKinnon has in mind: a woman with a head of unruly gray hair who has been tapping intently on a screen at the music bar for nearly two hours now. It's Mother's

Day, and Kerry Smallwood, 47, just received a gift certificate to the store. A friend brought her here when the Hear Music Coffeehouse first opened. Today is her sixth visit. "I pretty much just listen to the CDs I make here now," Smallwood says. Her play list so far has songs by Norah Jones, Rufus Wainwright, Sting, and Oscar Petersen.

Has she ever burned a CD for herself on a computer at home? Smallwood's expression is completely blank. "No, no, I've never done that. I don't know how." She's exactly why Starbucks thinks it can go up against Apple's more technology-oriented iTunes service. Smallwood will never know that there is a mini server farm hidden behind the service door at the back of the store. She just knows that for $6.99 for her first five tracks and $1 for each additional song, plus about a five-minute wait, she gets another beautifully packaged, personalized CD.

It's all very smooth, it's all very seamless, and it all seems to make so much sense. But does it? Can Schultz and his team carry off a transformation like this? Is it really a smart move for a coffee company to reimagine itself as a lifestyle-entertainment enterprise and to start by serving up music? After all, the mere fact that a certain sort of music and a certain sort of coffee appeal to the same sort of customer doesn't necessarily mean that they should be sold at the same store. By such logic, what would stop Starbucks from selling, say, hiking shoes, or take-'em-home versions of the new-agey furniture in its stores, or earth-friendly kids' toys? That's why Mohr, Davidow Ventures' Moore cautions Schultz to tread carefully. "It's a very interesting experiment, but if I was on their board of directors, I'd be more concerned that they not corrupt the brand," he says. "If Starbucks is just trying to find more ways to monetize the traffic that comes through, this is a bad idea. At some point the customers will start to feel abused."

Though he acknowledges the risk, Schultz sees his company poised at a turning point—and he's confident the music service is the next step along Starbucks' path toward becoming, yes, the world's biggest brand. "The hardest thing is to stay small while you get big, to figure out how to stay intimate with your customers and your people, even as your reach gets bigger. We want to be a respectful merchant so that we're not trying to sell anything that would in any way dilute the experience," he says. The music business won't do that, he vows; rather, it will enhance that experience. "Great retailers recognize that they're in the business of constantly surprising and delighting their customers," he says. This big, bold push into music, he expects, will do both.

ALISON OVERHOLT (aoverholt@fastcompany.com) is a FAST COMPANY staff writer with a penchant for tall soy lattes and compilations of jazzy lounge music.

Surviving in the Age of Rage

Learning to manage angry customers is a crucial part of today's service landscape.

STEPHEN J. GROVE, RAYMOND P. FISK, AND JOBY JOHN

We seem to live in an age of rage. What once were isolated incidents of volatile customer behavior have become commonplace. News reports from around the world chronicle a growing number of customer rage incidents. These incidents create serious problems for managers of service organizations. Consider the following episodes:

Checkout counter rage. A woman had half her nose bitten off by a fellow shopper when she insisted on remaining in an express lane with more than the 12 permitted items.

Parking rage. Youths screamed, swore at, and verbally abused a man in a dispute over a parking space in front of a Costco store and later severely scratched his automobile.

Air rage. A disruptive passenger who attempted to break into the cockpit on a Southwest Airlines flight to Salt Lake City was beaten, choked, and eventually killed by other passengers. (This happened before Sept. 11, 2001.)

Snowplow rage. Frustrated by the never-ending snowfall and the snowplow generated mountain of white blocking his driveway, a Framingham, Mass., man beat the town's plow driver with his snow shovel.

Pub rage. Incensed for being refused service at a pub at closing time, a man with a tractor repeatedly smashed into the establishment, causing the pub's walls to crumble.

ATM rage. When a bank machine at a convenience store swallowed his card, an enraged patron stuck the ATM machine with a utility knife, cursed a nearby clerk, hurled the knife at a cashier, and smashed an adjacent fax machine to the ground. These incidents only hint at the breadth and severity of customer rage. Damage caused by rage episodes varies from verbal indignation, to vandalism, to physical injury, and even death. Fellow patrons and workers alike have been unsuspecting targets of rage. Clearly, disruptive customer behaviors pose severe problems for businesses afflicted by rage episodes. These problems might include negative publicity, costs of legal actions, and the untold ramifications of traumatized customers and employees.

Service organizations should have policies and procedures to prevent or reduce the occurrence of customer rage.

Many customer rage incidents go unreported, so the precise number of rage episodes is difficult to determine. Indications are, however, that customer rage is on the upswing. Consider the airline industry prior to Sept. 11. A *New York Times* article reported that Swissair witnessed nearly a 100% increase over a three-year period in the occurrence of passenger interference with crew members' in-flight duties. CNN reported that an estimated 4,000 air rage episodes occurred in the United States (where airlines are not required to register such instances) in the year 2000 alone. While the number of air rage incidents has declined since 2001 according to the Federal Aviation Administration, a new phenomenon called "ground rage" is growing. Aggressive behavior toward airline personnel on the ground is now so prevalent that British Airways issues soccer-style yellow cards as a final warning to disruptive travelers that any further disturbance will result in refusal of service.

On another front, a recent survey of call center personnel found that nearly 60% of the respondents reported an increased incidence of phone rage over the past five years. Regardless of the range or severity of customer rage, it's the service sector that is most frequently afflicted with rage incidents. Service organizations, such as hotels, banks, restaurants, airlines, and theme parks, require interaction between customers and employees, often in the presence of multiple consumers sharing a common service setting. In addition, service quality provided by such organizations is notoriously variable due to the "real time" character of service delivery and the many uncontrollable elements that combine to create customers' service experience. Further, service organizations are often capacity constrained. It's not surprising then that service encounters are a veritable petri dish for customer rage. According to a 2002 study by the Public Agenda research group, shopping malls, airports, airplanes, and government offices are particularly vulnerable to rude or disrespectful behavior.

Customer behaviors in service settings can range from those that are too friendly to those that constitute rage. Obviously, pleasant interactions between customers and employees are

Executive Briefing

With civility on a seemingly downward path, customer rage has become a common problem for many service organizations. This article discusses "the four Ts of customer rage," which include the targets of customer rage behavior, the influence of temperament on customers expressing rage, the triggers that spark customers' rage, and the treatments for preventing or managing customer rage. In this environment, smart service managers are doing all they can to improve the service environment for their customers.

desirable. However, if customers are excessively friendly, they can be a major distraction to employees and may delay service to subsequent customers. Under such circumstances, the service process bogs down and workers search for ways to chill customers' friendly advances. Hence, we label the boundary line between too friendly and the range of acceptable behaviors as the freezing point. Toward the other extreme of acceptable behaviors, unfriendly situations occur when customers are irritating or rude to employees. Unfriendly interactions can escalate to rage if the customer or the employee hits the other's hot button with an inappropriate comment, misguided gesture, or other affront. We label the boundary line between rage and the range of acceptable behaviors as the boiling point.

The Four Ts of Customer Rage

Targets. Since customer rage is a common service phenomenon, it's not surprising that the targets of customer rage are other customers, employees, or elements of the service environment. In reality, no aspect of a service organization is immune from rage. In most cases, the rage exhibited far exceeds the transgression that triggered the anger. An unsolicited comment or an accidental bump by a fellow patron may unleash astonishing fury. Harried employees who snub or overlook demanding customers may experience their uncontrolled wrath. Not even innocent bystanders are sheltered from customer rage. Bottled up angst may find an outlet in the nearest unsuspecting soul. Sometimes it's the adjacent passenger, fellow shopper, or exuberant fan that draws the rage of nearby customers. Sharing the service setting with one who is predisposed to rage is not unfathomable.

When fellow customers or employees are not targets of rage, fury may be directed at inanimate objects or others' possessions. Angry ATM users relentlessly pound the machine that swallowed their debit card. Frustrated golfers hurl the clubs that humiliate them into the nearest water hazard. Enraged diners slam tables and toss food on the floor when offended by a waiter. Clearly, when anger boils over, neither people nor property is safe.

Temperament. Service organizations that cater to large numbers of customers simultaneously must be aware that some

people are prone to customer rage. Most people know somebody who can "go off" at the slightest provocation. Perhaps it can be traced to personality or maybe other personal factors are at play. Regardless, not all service customers are equally likely to exhibit rage.

Modern technology has created a world where the boundaries between work and leisure are blurred. Where can one escape the responsibilities of the workplace? Cell phones, pagers, laptop computers, and Internet access keep us tethered to obligations that follow us everywhere. We seem to live in a world where we're on stage 24 hours a day, seven days a week, and 365 days a year. These stressful circumstances provide ample kindling to ignite rage in some customers.

> **Unfriendly interactions can escalate to rage if the customer or the employee hits the other's hot button with an inappropriate comment, misguided gesture, or other affront.**

Is it possible that some people fly into rage more quickly? Perhaps. There is some evidence that anger is inherited, yet it seems more likely that rage behaviors are learned via socialization as appropriate responses to certain situations. Some people may have internalized rage as a typical response for some occasions, possibly through a previous experience or by observing others. Further contributing to the likelihood of rage may be the absence of one's spouse or close friends, whose presence might normally keep one's aggressive behavior in check. At the very least, the enraged customer may lack strong social or personal norms that prevent them from boiling over when faced with challenging circumstances.

Many other temperament factors can make some people susceptible to rage. Aggressive personality types are prone to heated verbal exchanges and attempt retribution for even the smallest perceived transgressions. Customers who exhibit type A behavior patterns (i.e., intense achievement strivings, strong sense of competition) often find themselves in situations where their impatience or obsessive nature sparks confrontation. Those who feel controlled by circumstances may be prone to display aggression as well. Even physiological conditions, such as reduced amounts of serotonin and low levels of cholesterol in one's blood system, have been linked with aggressive tendencies. These are just a handful of individual characteristics associated with rage. In short, some customers enter a service encounter with their rage sensors loaded and ready.

The task of identifying likely candidates for rage is fraught with issues. There is an important but subtle difference between engaging in customer segmentation and discrimination. Customer segmentation involves offering different customers different service based on their distinctive characteristics. (Service businesses that provide a more protective environment for parents with small children engage in customer segmentation.) Discrimination occurs when customers are given poor service because of their race, age, sex, religion, or other distinctive characteristic. Discrimination can take the form of "profiling." For instance, a business may decide that males with beards are prone to rage and subject such customers to obtrusive scrutiny. Since Sept. 11, profiling has become a controversial issue. The U.S. Transportation Security Administration's computer-assisted passenger profiling system (or CAPPS II) classifies prospective passengers with a three-level rating— green, yellow, or red. A green rating yields minimal security screening, a yellow rating leads to extensive searches and interrogation, and a red rating prevents boarding the plane.

Triggers. The interactive nature of services offers many potential triggers for customer rage. Some of the strongest triggers occur when customers believe they have been treated unfairly, neglected, or negated in a service encounter. Perceived unjust treatment, such as a later-arriving patron being seated first at a restaurant, may fuel rage. Customers sometimes become angry when their needs are neglected. One who endures a long wait at an unattended customer service counter may commence yelling when the service representative finally arrives. If customers believe they are being treated with disrespect, hostility may ensue. A patronizing attitude from an employee tells customers that they are unimportant and can send the customer into a fury. Ironically, it seems that some organizations knowingly trigger "righteous indignation" from customers and may deserve the rage responses they prompt.

We seem to live in a world where we're on stage 24 hours a day, seven days a week, and 365 days a year. These stressful circumstances provide ample kindling to ignite rage in some customers.

Situational influences on customer behavior, such as those described by Russell Belk, may play a role in triggering rage in any service encounter. Consider the rage-generating effect of these in the following:

- *Physical surrounding:* Aspects of the service environment may rub customers the wrong way. Room temperatures can be oppressively warm or chillingly cold, noise levels can be painfully loud, filthy service settings can anger customers, and/or cramped facilities can make the service setting seem too crowded.
- *Social surroundings:* Other customers often negatively affect each other by violating normative expectations (e.g., standing too close in line or smoking in nonsmoking areas). Crowded service settings can push customers to their limits and may initiate jostling among customers.
- *Temporal perspective:* Long delays or being rushed for time can ignite rage. Time is one of the most sensitive of situational triggers. For example, most customers detest

waiting in line, and time delays can cause tempers to rushed often become aggravated and lash out.
- *Task definition:* Extraordinary obligations Heightened expectations and desires can increase customer sensitivity. For example, a married couple celebrating a special occasion may become quite agitated when things don't go as planned at a fancy restaurant.
- *Antecedent states:* Temporary conditions that customers experience, such as hunger or thirst, may cause people to become easily enraged. But the most troubling of such antecedent states is drunkenness, a circumstance that escalates when businesses such as bars, nightclubs, or sporting events serve large numbers of drinking customers.

Treatment. People's emotions can soar during a rage-precipitating incident to the point where management must get involved during or after the episode. Less astute organizations occasionally find themselves tackling uncomfortable negative publicity and possibly liability issues. Clearly, it's in any organization's best interest to have a well-designed set of procedures and policies to manage customer rage.

The first management step is to prevent customer rage by preempting such situations. To do this, firms should focus on the triggers that activate rage. Organizations that understand the triggers that prompt rage can institute procedures to manage outbursts. For example, an unfulfilled promise of a "freebie" supplemental service, an unbearably long wait for service due to unforeseen circumstances, an aggressive customer in a bad mood, or a poorly trained employee serving an "important customer" may each require different treatment. Consider how Disney Corp. successfully manages waiting time for rides at its theme parks. For years, Disney has communicated average waiting times, kept lines moving, and made the wait entertaining. But the most significant improvement is Disney's Fastpass virtual queue system that allows guests to reserve a place in line without having to queue up.

When rage incidents occur, frontline service staff must scramble to defuse the situation and protect the personal safety of those present. At the very least, customer rage may have harmful effects on frontline employees, on customers who share the service setting, and on the perception of service quality. If an employee is the target of rage, this can affect subsequent encounters with future customers. If other patrons are present, they may witness the rage incident and their own experience may be affected negatively. The 2002 Public Agenda study found that nearly three of every four customers report seeing fellow customers behaving badly toward service personnel, and more than 60% said such incidents bothered them a lot. All in all, the costs of mishandling customer rage are too great to be ignored.

Once a rage episode has occurred, organizations are faced with the difficult task of determining the appropriate remedial action for that specific incident and learning from the event to prevent future occurrences. Service organizations should be attuned to how the nature of services can affect customer rage.

BEFORE

Ensure that people and processes are in place to recognize customers who are prone to rage and potential customer rage situations

DURING

Empower employees with the skills and reward mechanisms to manage customer rage as it occurs

AFTER

Investigate, analyze, and learn from customer rage incidents

Figure 1   Living with Customer Rage

Since services occur in real time, the risk of failure is always high. Therefore, it is imperative that organizations take a systematic approach to managing rage incidents. For example, the C.H.A.R.M. School provides lessons in Customer Hostility and Rage Management. Employees learn various identification techniques to spot potential incidents before they happen and plausible tactics to defuse potentially dangerous customers. Forward thinking organizations that prepare employees for rage through such programs are making a commitment to a better service experience.

In Figure 1, we suggest how firms might establish customer rage management protocols.

There are several managerial actions that organizations can take before, during, or after a customer rage incident occurs.

"Before" Actions

Before customer rage occurs, managers can take preemptive actions to lock the trigger. First, organizations should identify and institute early warning mechanisms and procedures for handling rage episodes. The specific devices involved may vary across service types. Nevertheless, frontline employees need to be trained, motivated, and rewarded for handling difficult customer rage incidents. These actions demonstrate to employees and customers that management takes rage situations seriously. It also facilitates any legal defense if an unfortunate event should occur. As a manager, you might do the following:

- Train employees to anticipate and manage service failures and customer rage.
- Empower employees to act on the incidents without waiting for supervisory assistance.
- Establish reward systems that motivate all employees to attend to customer rage incidents.
- Design early warning mechanisms to anticipate circumstances and situations leading to customer rage.

As an example, Caterpillar Inc. depends a great deal on service enhancements to its products. The company monitors customer equipment remotely, sending electronic warning signals to its service technicians when necessary. These employees are given information indicating the parts and tools needed to make the repair.

What's Next in *Marketing Management*?

May/June

Our May/June issue focuses on managing your brands—a topic that includes examining the value of brands and building and maintaining that value. The issue's feature articles will delve deep into the questions of brand management and offer insights from notable experts in the field. We'll also feature an exclusive interview with Wonya Lucas, the vice president of marketing for The Weather Channel.

And, as always, our columns and departments will provide fresh insights on current marketing topics, including B2B, CRM, branding, services marketing, and marketing law.

"During" Actions

During a rage incident, other procedures may be engaged. Such procedures might include employee actions that seek to respond to the situation. The status of the customer could dictate the type of procedure to invoke. For example, an important client might be handled by senior management with a just amount of apologies and offers for redemption. During a rage incident, you should do the following:

- Take immediate action
- Maintain decorum and remain calm
- Listen to the customer, show empathy, assume responsibility, apologize, and make amends
- Separate or isolate the enraged customer, especially in a shared customer experience
- Document everything about the incident including witness reports
- Involve superiors, if necessary

Marriott, for example, specifies the situations that call for empowered actions based on the nature of the customer problem and the value of the customer to the company. Employees are given "safe zones" for spending up to $2,500 to compensate a customer grievance or inconvenience.

"After" Actions

After a rage incident, management must analyze each episode and follow up with the individuals involved. For long-term actions, incidents must be recorded, categorized by level of severity and frequency of occurrence, stored as information, and then analyzed so that systemic improvements might be designed into the service delivery processes. Managers should take the following steps after an episode of customer rage:

- Investigate causes of the incident
- Follow-up with customers by apologizing, explaining, and reinstating the organization's commitment to preventing similar occurrences in the future

- Depending on the severity and pervasiveness of an incident, involve upper management If service failure was the reason, determine what can be done to prevent it in the future
- If a customer is at fault, determine if an individual or a customer segment should be avoided
- If a service employee is at fault, determine if screening, hiring, training, or supervision is to be changed or improved

Westpac Bank of Melbourne, Australia, has adopted an innovative way to respond to customer rage. It recruits "middle-aged mums" to cool customer rage since mothers tend to have the proper skills from managing their families. They have a general willingness to listen, an increased level of patience, and are naturally empathetic.

Figure 2 outlines the series of steps that firms might formally establish to manage customer rage. Step 1 is to analyze rage incidents to understand what triggered the rage. Process design is Step 2, which requires designing and implementing methods for preempting customer rage. Step 3 stresses action during rage incidents by employing prevention methods to manage raging customers. Taking action after a rage incident is Step 4, following up with individuals who became enraged. This is essentially a damage control step. If the customer was enraged about legitimate complaints, then corrective actions must be taken. If, however, the customer was primarily to blame for the rage incident, then it might be necessary to ask the customer to take their patronage elsewhere. Step 5 is process improvement. The organization should follow up on any lessons learned regarding managing customer rage.

The Prognosis

In some ways, it's surprising that the customer rage problem isn't worse. Civility seems to be scarce in modern times. The 2002 Public Agenda study documented a perception of growing rudeness in America with 80% of Americans surveyed viewing rudeness as a very serious problem. Among the reasons that customers become rude or even enraged is that their public and private lives leave them pressed for time. In addition, rising education levels have led to rising customer expectations. Information age technology will continue to present opportunities

Figure 2 Phases in the Treatment of Customer Rage

for customer rage as it provides new methods for interaction between firm and customer, and for interaction among customers. Against this backdrop, it's clear that more needs to be done to manage and prevent customer rage.

Will service encounters in the future contain even more hostility than today? We believe that customer rage is more likely unless service managers reduce common targets of customer rage, manage customer temperaments, prevent triggers, and pursue treatments for customer rage. Smart services managers will do everything possible to make sure that their customer interactions are characterized by civility rather than marred by rage. They know that customers prefer businesses that provide predictably pleasant service environments.

STEPHEN J. GROVE is professor, department of marketing, college of business, Clemson University, Clemson, S.C. He may be reached at groves@clemson.edu. **RAYMOND P. FISK** is professor and chair of marketing, department of marketing, college of business administration, University of New Orleans. He may be reached at rfisk@uno.edu. **JOBY JOHN** is professor and chair, marketing department, Bentley College, Waltham, Mass. He may be reached at jjohn@bentley.edu.

Nonprofits Can Take Cues from Biz World

Branding roadmap shapes success

LARRY CHIAGOURIS

Individual nonprofit organizations face unique challenges. Consider the following examples:

- A leading provider of social services is confronting a major challenge: It has substantial resources, but its major contributors, who are more than 60 years old on average, are dying off. This charity is not signing up meaningful numbers of baby boomers as members, donors or volunteers. Consequently, its leaders are concerned about future levels of financial support.
- A state-of-the-art science museum is about to open when it receives inquiries from the media, concerning its mission. Will the museum celebrate current global environmental issues or will it speak to the ecological beauty of its location? Will it engage adults about the world or will it raise children's awareness of science and the environment? Its leaders cannot agree on the answers and thus cannot move forward on communications activities.
- An international institution organized to fight hunger recognizes that it needs more than government donations to perform. It conducts a fund-raising project among corporations and the general public. The project is not successful because most people had never heard of the institution.

  Each of these organizations lacked a coherent brand strategy and program. Whether recruiting new members, responding to the media or generating donations, nonprofits are more likely to succeed if their target audiences know who they are and what they stand for. In other words, nonprofits must have a carefully developed brand.

  The pressures on nonprofit brands have increased dramatically over the last decade, for several reasons.

- Many of them are managed with small staffs and tight budgets.
- More than 1.5 million nonprofits now are competing for scarce resources and attention from public and private

donors in the United States. This estimate primarily encompasses charitable causes, universities, foundations, and professional societies and associations. But there are more nonprofits: hospitals, governmental organizations, political candidates and committees, and even branches of the military.

- The Internet offers new and exciting ways to attract volunteers and donations. With new concerns about scams and spam, however, an Internet presence demands a brand be credible and meaningful to prospective supporters.

Establish mission statement, brand promise

Given this challenging environment, what brand components will target audiences view as compelling? What should nonprofits borrow from the commercial sector, to aid them in brand building? To answer these questions, my organization studied the best branding practices of leading nonprofits. We also interviewed several nonprofit managers breaking ground in the branding arena. Brand mission, unique selling proposition and reason to believe, personality, graphic identity and measurement emerged as highly relevant components.

Make a Statement

Nonprofit brands do not have to answer to the vagaries of Wall Street or the short-term demands publicly held companies face daily. In many ways, however, they have to meet more exacting requirements. They are under constant scrutiny to efficiently deliver on missions that answer to a higher calling—delivery that can mean the difference between life and death for some, and improved quality of life for many.

Most consumers don't know or even care what the mission is for Nike, Charmin, McDonald's or other leading brands. But for nonprofits, the lead brand element is its mission. If people are going to donate time or money or become members, they want to know what the brand is all about; they want to know the mission statement.

Specific

Most nonprofit mission statements fail to provide sufficient specificity. For example, many museums state broadly that they will educate the public on their subject matter. They do not differentiate their purpose from that of other museums. In contrast, the Chicago Children's Museum's mission statement is rather specific: "to create a community where play and learning connect." It does not fall in step with so many other routine promises.

Realistic

Another problem is that many nonprofits compose unrealistic mission statements that exceed their abilities. It is wonderful to reach and stretch, but not if it negatively affects credibility. A mission statement to rid the world of a crippling disease may be admirable, but isn't believable if it's coming from a small or unknown entity without a strong track record. A mission statement with a reasonable chance of being accomplished is a major step toward brand credibility.

Show Promise

Nonprofits should then look at what they would like target audiences to take from encounters with the brand, as well as build a case to support such reasoning.

Unique selling proposition (USP)

The USP is central to the brand message. Some call it the brand promise, others refer to it as the net impression. Whatever the label, it is the primary thought the target audience should take from encounters with the brand—a composite of brand attributes and benefits. The most effective commercial sector USPs convey what the brand will do for or give to the consumer. USPs such as "melts in your mouth—not in your hand" (M&M's) or "We try harder" (Avis) live on long after tag lines change.

The USPs of nonprofit brands are quite different. Nonprofit USPs frequently reflect what the brand will do for others—not just the target audience. The benefits are often to be experienced by all. Instead of promising that your skin will look younger or your house will be cleaner, nonprofit brands pledge to make the world better with their work.

Consider the USP of St. Jude Children's Research Hospital: "Finding cures. Saving children." It is clear and specific. It does not promise it will cure the world, but focuses on searching for cures—for children. Not complicated, yet very compelling.

Reason to believe (RTB)

An RTB should always accompany a USP. Some label it the "support." It builds the case for the target audience accepting a USP as true and highly credible. A car buried for months in the Alaskan snow, only to start immediately when the driver turns the ignition key, is an effective image because it prompts the prospective consumer to think, "If this battery can start a car in the middle of an Alaskan winter, it surely can start my car." The RTB can similarly serve nonprofit branding objectives.

So, why should we believe St. Jude's USP? In a recently televised appeal to prospective donors, the spokesperson noted that because of St. Jude's research, the survival rates for childhood cancers have increased substantially in recent years. This proves St. Jude's support is producing results. Other St. Jude's communications, such as press releases, also reveal many research breakthroughs in combating childhood diseases.

The most important consideration for the RTB is that in a highly segmented market, different support points will be called on to convince the different target audiences of the USP's believability. It is acceptable to have several, as long as you don't throw them into the same communication in an "everything but the kitchen sink" style. That will only lead to confusion about the brand.

Multiple Personality

Brand personality is a valuable way to enhance the relationship between organization and target audience. Key personality attributes will vary according to the nonprofit's mission: Hospitals and social service organizations benefit if consumers see them as caring and maternal; museums benefit if consumers see them as highly competent and knowledgeable.

Just as one attribute is not enough to capture a person's essence, so it is with brand personality. For example, it's important for people to view museum staff as competent, but it's even more important for them to view the staff as accessible. Visitors do not want tour guides or personnel to treat them in a condescending manner. They want them to courteously answer their questions and encourage their curiosity. A museum supportive in this multidimensional way is likely to receive more visitors and donor contributions.

Values

A nonprofit's values can also make a difference in brand perception. Although not the same as personality, they can convince people of a brand relationship's appeal. The U.S. military understands this. The Army conveys and operates by seven key values—loyalty, duty, respect, selfless service, honor, integrity and personal courage—and integrates them into many of its soldier training programs.

Track progress with measurement system

Graphic content

If you have held a Fortune 500 company's corporate identity and style manual, you can appreciate the degree to which it documents what one can and can't do to portray brand identity. These manuals are often up to 100 pages long and cover every visual element of materials, including shapes, colors and sizes. For nonprofits, graphic identity can also be complex. The University of Virginia Web site, for example, notes: "A significant factor in the success of the University's unified identity is adherence to a standard color palette."

Name

The name of a brand is central to its success. The principles that guide name development in the commercial sector also apply to nonprofits: The name should be memorable, distinctive, ownable, easy to pronounce, and relevant to the organization's mission and benefits. The Museum of Modern Art's name and logo is the perfect combination of these elements. The Manhattan museum's abbreviation had been MOMA for many years. One day the director had an epiphany: Why not use a lowercase "o"—portray it as MoMA? Today, everyone recognizes MoMA as the museum's graphic identity (and the sound of its name). It is the gold standard of what nonprofits can achieve.

Logo

Nonprofits need to exercise serious thought and reflection in developing a logo. The Carnegie Museum of Art's logo is a good representation. The golden-yellow "C" is for Carnegie, and its form of a brush stroke symbolizes the wonderful art at this Pittsburgh museum.

Tag line

The tag line completes the picture. Each telegraphs different impressions. More importantly, the tag line needs to communicate the USP. "Explore & Learn" (the Smithsonian), "Advance Humanity" (UNICEF), "Where the End of Poverty Begins" (CARE) and "Bringing the Real World to Kids" (Junior Achievement) are tag lines that provide additional relevance to brand objectives.

For Good Measure

The brand program is not complete until nonprofits create a system for measuring how well the brand is connecting with its target audience. Too often, they limit their evaluations to levels of donations or sales; focus exclusively on the number of members, volunteers or visitors; or simply note the quality and quantity of mentions in the media, or letters from the public. Although these measurements are important, they do not go far enough. To determine the nature of brand development progress, it is important to track the images, attitudes and perceptions of each target audience.

Common commercial sector tools can work quite well for nonprofits in conducting assessments. Strategic planning sessions among internal and external constituencies can unearth substantial guidance, market research can identify the brand-building elements a nonprofit should execute, and brand equity studies are now using measures that assess a nonprofit brand's financial worth. This can provide considerable insight into what nonprofits are accomplishing.

The best tools go a step further: They identify the drivers contributing most to a brand's success, and pinpoint the barriers nonprofits must remove to achieve higher and faster levels of progress in the brand's health. This allows brand managers to make the necessary adjustments—to attributes such as brand trust, credibility, responsiveness, competence and knowledge—to keep the brand strong and relevant.

Brand-Building Profits

A compelling brand image is more important to nonprofits than commercial sector companies for one fundamental reason: Nonprofits do not have the resources to send their messages to large numbers of people through the media.

They cannot solve awareness challenges with more advertising weight, but must define and execute their branding objectives right out of the gate. However, they also can't afford to do so by just delegating brand management responsibilities to a junior staffer, a well-intentioned but untrained volunteer or the person who recently mastered a graphic art software package.

There is so much depending on professional brand development and execution that it must be one of the nonprofit's key priorities. The potential impact on fundraising is substantial. Michael Hoffman, CEO of Changing Our World (a New York City philanthropic services company), puts it in perspective. "The brand tells the story. A strong brand is vital to long-term development and fundraising because it connects the mission with the organization and potential donors."

Professional brand development and execution must be one of the nonprofit's key priorities.

In fact, a strong brand may lead to profit-generating activities that can underwrite social programs. Many nonprofits are beginning to experiment with these initiatives and are experiencing success. Steve Case, co-founder of America Online, established a foundation to encourage entrepreneurial behavior among nonprofit managers—including development of professional skills integral to brand building. His view, stated in a May 2005 *Wall Street Journal* article, is that brand programs can contribute to "significant social change." I can't agree more, but would add this: These programs will drive social change that will endure.

LARRY CHIAGOURIS is associate professor of marketing at Pace University's Lubin School of Business in New York City and a senior partner at Brand Marketing Services Ltd. He may be reached at lchiagouris@pace.edu. This article originally appeared in the September/October 2005 issue of Marketing Management magazine and was edited for style and length before being reprinted. For more information on subscribing to Marketing Management, please call AMA at 800/262-1150.

Fidelity Factor

Ensure loyal customer relationships by infusing them with trust.

Jeff Hess and John W. Story

Until recently, marketers and academics were convinced that the ultimate goal of marketing was to satisfy customers. An entire generation of business students was sent forth with the conviction that all good things come from meeting or exceeding customers' expectations—that once they are satisfied, loyalty is inevitable.

On the contrary, more than 25 years of exhaustive investigation and simple observation have left us with an undeniable conclusion: Lasting profitability results more from enduring customer relationships than from a collection of satisfying transactions.

As a result, companies now are committed to customer relationships—building them, managing them, and asking marketing researchers to tell them how well they're doing. The belief that strong relationships are a significant market advantage has firms racing with competitors to bond with their customers.

But false starts, with promising new technologies such as those supporting customer relationship management (CRM), suggest we may have gotten ahead of ourselves.

To realize the promise of relationships, we first must understand them. What do they look like, where do they come from, what do we get out of them, and how are they different from the ongoing transactions we currently measure with loyalty programs? Once we learn the language of relationships, and formalize models and methods to build and track them, tools such as CRM can transform how marketing gets done.

The relationship framework has quickly emerged from a clever promotional differentiator to a competitive imperative, and is the dominant paradigm of marketing. In *Total Relationship Marketing* (Butterworth-Heinemann, 2002), Evert Gummesson writes that there's a built-in profitability to relationships, as they provide companies several bottom-line benefits not offered by customers participating in random transactions. From sales promotion to pricing, most marketing activities become more effective and less expensive when customers are on your side.

Professor Susan Fournier and Jeff Hess (one of the authors of this article) report the real secret behind the relationship

Executive Briefing

Although it is important to know the strength of customer bonds, it is absolutely essential to understand their nature. Just as personal relationships have many dimensions (friends, acquaintances, and romantic attachments), so do customer-brand relationships. To ignore these dimensions would be perilous. The trust-based commitment relationship model formalizes the processes by which multidimensional relationships develop—as well as the benefits that ensue.

revolution: Many customers form brand relationships similar to the bonds they form with other people, complete with personal and functional characteristics. And it is in this multidimensional relationship space that new classes of loyal behavior emerge, all of which can have a profound impact on the bottom line.

Figure 1 displays two views of how customers respond to their interactions with your brand. The traditional view represents the familiar process in which they evaluate your products and services on a set of performance attributes they deem important. The primary arbiter of return on investment (ROI) is whether customers are satisfied with performance, and whether overall satisfaction with your products and services leads to functional loyalty: "I stay with the brand because it does what it says it'll do, and because I get a good value for the money."

In the relationship view, trust resides in the center of the model, as a fundamental condition. Once the role of trust is recognized, a new world of diagnostics and benefits emerges, and the ultimate relationship disposition transforms from primarily functional to including personal dimensions. This model does not propose new types of relationships where none existed, but instead promotes a deeper understanding of previously studied behaviors and hidden motivations. Trust is the primary condition for personal connections, which (with functional connections)

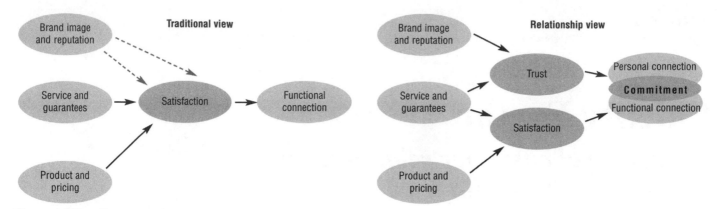

Figure 1 How Customers Interact with the Brand

translate into truly committed relationships. And committed relationships are profitable relationships. The trust-based commitment model described in Figure 2 formalizes the interaction among these relationship constructs.

Problematic Approaches

There are basic deficiencies with current configurations of loyalty, and little agreement on what loyalty is. Some companies portray it as behavioral (proportional or sequential behavior), some measure it as an attitude intended to predict behavior, and some build indices based on several behavioral and attitudinal measures. The problem with these approaches is that they take a narrow, purely revenue-based view of loyalty.

Certainly share and revenue are important business goals, but they often overlook customer behaviors that drive profitability. A typical functional loyalty model focuses on the revenue outcomes of functional connections. However, unless you take a multidimensional view of your customer interactions, a broad range of loyal behaviors remains behind a veil of conventional measures. A multidimensional commitment framework describes the personal connections leading to profitable behavior:

• Paying premium prices for the brand's products.
• Seeking a company's Web site to purchase products.
• Overcoming purchase barriers such as inconvenience or competitive offers.

• Forgiving the brand's minor failures.
• Trying the brand's new products.

Most companies agree that it makes good business sense to form bonds with customers, but the real epiphany is that customers enjoy being in relationships with their favorite companies. They are often willing and active partners in such connections. If you're looking at relationships from a purely functional perspective, there's a good chance you're missing significant opportunities to build partnerships of a personal nature—attachments yielding much more than repeat purchases and improved satisfaction scores.

Consider the customer ready to pay a higher price or endure inconvenient schedules to fly his or her favorite airline. Or think about the relatively unreliable, moderately performing, premium-priced auto brand known for its devoted long-term customer relationships. In various retail contexts where convenience and price competition dominate, many profitable brands rely on their customers driving past more convenient competitors to pay a premium at their locations. These events signify relational bonds not described by standard satisfaction and loyalty measures.

Beyond Satisfaction

Trust is at the center of customer relationship phenomena, and is the key to understanding relationships of a personal character. In fact, misunderstanding and misplacement of trust has

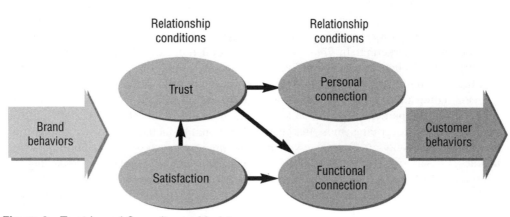

Figure 2 Trust-based Commitment Model

led to an anemic knowledge of customer-brand relationships, misapplication of investment, and the inability to accurately assess returns.

Although satisfaction is the indicator of perceived brand performance, trust is an acknowledgment of brand motivation. It's the powerful idea that a brand has its customers' best interests in mind, and that it'll do whatever it takes to make them happy. Trust lives in the dissatisfied customer happily marching into a favorite store, fully expecting a swift and peaceful resolution; it is absent in the dissatisfied customer anticipating conflict and aggravation.

When customers believe in your brand, they no longer worry you'll take advantage when their guards are down. Consequently, as in human relationships, they may engage in deeper commitment. Although customers may be skeptical that altruistic brand motivations exist, the idea becomes plausible when you implement actions and policies demonstrating your dedication to pleasing them.

Just like relationships with other people, customer relationships are built on trust—becoming more profound and expansive as trust endures. Introducing trust as the gateway to profitable relationships not only improves the precision with which you deploy precious resources, but also allows for a much more sophisticated assessment of customer-focused activities. But despite its essential role in building trust and personal relationships, many a customer-centered initiative has been erroneously marginalized because of the minimal impact on customer satisfaction. Until trust is defined and measured, important activities will continue to die on the vine with the relationships they support.

For instance, allowing customers to interact with people—rather than routing them through frustrating automated response systems—might seem a frivolous and inefficient use of resources. But person-to-person interaction is fundamental to forming trust. The surest way of undermining trust is to tell customers you're not interested in talking to them.

Trust as the key to enduring relationships is not a novel concept. Ad agencies have been using the language of trust and commitment for several years. But unlike satisfaction, which captured the imagination of marketing scholars and practitioners more than 25 years ago, trust has remained a chiefly intuitive application.

The Trust-Based Commitment Model

Many brands understand the importance of communicating their motivations through actions and promotions, but rarely do they formalize processes and measures for reliably planning and assessing relationship success. Marketers and academics have been slow to create a usable customer relationship model revolving around a rigorous understanding of trust. In this vacuum, they continue to rely on transactional satisfaction and traditional loyalty concepts.

Once the antecedents and implications of trust are elaborated, marketers can confidently invest in the next frontier:

customer-brand relationships. The promise of technologies such as CRM, data management, and the Internet will be realized only when their places in true relationship building and management are understood.

In the past, as relationship tools outpaced understanding of customer relationship development's social and psychological processes, marketers were quick to throw money at the problem of disconnected, random transactions. When first conceived, data management promised a rich, quantifiable understanding of individual customers and the ability to customize marketing activity to targeted customer segments. Although often increasing the efficiency with which brands promote to accessible customers, CRM activities and protocols rarely result in real customer relationships. These practices revealed hidden behaviors and patterns influencing the definition of customer-brand relationships, yet they could not reveal relational components of these behaviors. According to Atul Parvatiyar and Jag Sheth's article "Customer Relationship Management: Emerging Practice, Process, and Discipline" in the *Journal of Economic and Social Research,* it's possible that CRM systems may impede real relationship building; they've nearly become a mere surrogate for the technology applied to data management methods.

The trust-based commitment model in Figure 2 seeks to put "relationship" back into CRM by devising a formal structure of customer relationship concepts, upon which marketing can be built and assessed. This structure transcends behaviors and purchase patterns, to encompass relational components of attitudes and customer-brand interactions.

A relationship view doesn't aim to undermine the importance of classic marketing ideas (e.g., satisfaction, value, loyalty) or merely freshen up traditional models with new nomenclature. Rather, it reorganizes the basic customer process model so that satisfaction and related concepts take their places in a constellation of ideas, resulting in real relationships and relationship-specific benefits for customers and brands. This has significant financial implications.

Loyalty Redefined

In the relationship world, when we speak of loyalty we are ultimately speaking of commitment. Although it is tempting to define loyalty as simply repurchase, marketers often have little power over the variables and constraints directly controlling how customers pass through the purchase environment. In addition, repurchase is only one of several outcomes that can be described as loyal behaviors; some refer to sales volume and share, and some to profitability.

As Dave Aaker states in his recent *Planning Review* article "Managing the Most Important Asset: Brand Equity," strong brands certainly have loyal customers. But are such brands fully taking advantage of the benefits these customers offer? From customers' perspectives, loyalty is an intuitively adopted strategy, to maximize the value of their consuming skills and win the cost/utility game (reduce risk, increase information processing effectiveness, and gain tangible frequent-user benefits). However, it's also a way to take advantage of their customer status' hidden pleasures. Even more revolutionary than economic efficiency is that relationships allow customers to enjoy relational benefits alien to utility maximization (e.g., affiliation, association, value matching).

And the essence of how customer-brand relationship outcomes differ from those of more traditional loyalty models is that relationship connections significantly contribute to customer behaviors and result in increased profits.

STANDARD research methods are often ill-suited to describe a customer's disposition and resilience in the marketplace.

The assumption underpinning all loyalty and satisfaction models is that the measured customer processes reflect attitudes that determine behavior. The most expedient and common measures of attitudes and behavior assess repurchase intent or overall satisfaction, which extend to financial performance. This calculus often undermines the credibility of the research: Such models rarely yield accurate financial predictions, leaving decision makers to ponder the value of research data.

The heart of the dilemma is in the assumptions, and in the fact that standard research methods are often well removed from ultimate market behavior—or ill-suited to describe a customer's disposition and resilience in the marketplace. The best case: These assessments are an unreliable reflection of behavioral trends. The worst case: They mislead strategic planning regarding market share or volume superiority, by masking underlying relational weaknesses. It's important to remember that, by traditional criteria, customers repeatedly buying out of convenience appear loyal.

While competitors are content striving to meet expectations, the savvy brand moves beyond a transactional view—prizing relationships over unqualified repeat purchases. For instance, the fast-food market is often dominated by convenience and price considerations; relationship building in this environment might seem an exercise in futility with fleeting benefits. Competitive advantage can be gained in the face of transactional constraints, via customer relationship building. For example, restaurant brand A has nearly twice as many locations as restaurant brand B, with associated superiority in revenue. On a transactional basis, B's customers are slightly more satisfied; however, its customers have greater commitment. Consequently, they're more willing to pay premium prices and try the restaurant's new products. In this case, an assessment of relationship vs. transactional constructs will be much more revealing regarding B's potential emergence in the marketplace. B can use this information to capitalize on a potential competitive opportunity, whereas A is alerted to an emerging competitive threat.

As marketers, we are primarily managing the attitudes that customers take into the purchase environment. It is those attitudes that determine how they'll respond to competitive actions, inconvenience, pricing, and situational factors. Commitment is

a customer's ultimate relationship disposition—a fundamental and powerful concept carrying beliefs and attitudes that result in actions toward the brand, understood only when decomposed into its primary dimensions. It is the distinct personal and functional connections that separate commitment from standard loyalty and intention. And trust is the key to understanding how these connections develop.

At least as important as assessing customer bond strength is understanding its nature. Just as human relationships have many dimensions (friends, acquaintances, and romantic attachments), so do customer-brand relationships. And to ignore these dimensions is perilous; just ask The Coca-Cola Company. It may have underestimated the profound, personal nature of customers' bonds with Coke, and the betrayal felt from any change to the beloved brand. A negative response to a demonstrably superior product innovation can best be understood in a relationship light.

Connection Dimensions

The key to understanding and managing customer-brand relationships is the process by which trust and satisfaction evolve into commitment. Whether relationship partners are human or brands, trust is necessary for breaking down intellectual and emotional barriers to personal connection.

Satisfying transactions might continue indefinitely without transcending this interaction because customer-brand ties remain vulnerable to incident failure or competitive action and brand investment requirements proceed unabated. Trust can transform such repeated interactions into enduring relationships. Elena Delgado-Ballester and José Luis Munuera-Alemán—in their recent *European Journal of Marketing* article, "Brand Trust in the Context of Consumer Loyalty"—claim that all relationships, whether with people or brands, are built on trust. The point is that if you satisfy customers you are still vulnerable to competitive actions, but when trust develops, the relationship is more resilient. Trust allows customers to relax perpetual brand critiques and enjoy the benefits.

Marketers evaluate ROI more accurately when they understand that trust and satisfaction require different activities and that each communicates different motivations and competencies. The trust-based commitment model describes a process in which marketing activity investments have a specific and individual impact on trust and satisfaction. For example, in the retail category: Store environment, high-quality products, and easy-to-find merchandise lead to satisfaction; generous warranties and return policies, service guarantees, resolving problems with attentive and pleasant employees, and standing behind products lead to trust. Because such investments might not always be justified by short-term financial results, their real return is assessed only when trust is included as a central judge of ROI.

Just as relationship commitment is composed of functional and personal dimensions, satisfaction and trust uniquely contribute to each dimension of commitment. For instance, personal connections are primarily a function of high levels of trust. And customers who are habitually satisfied with the brand's products will form functional connections.

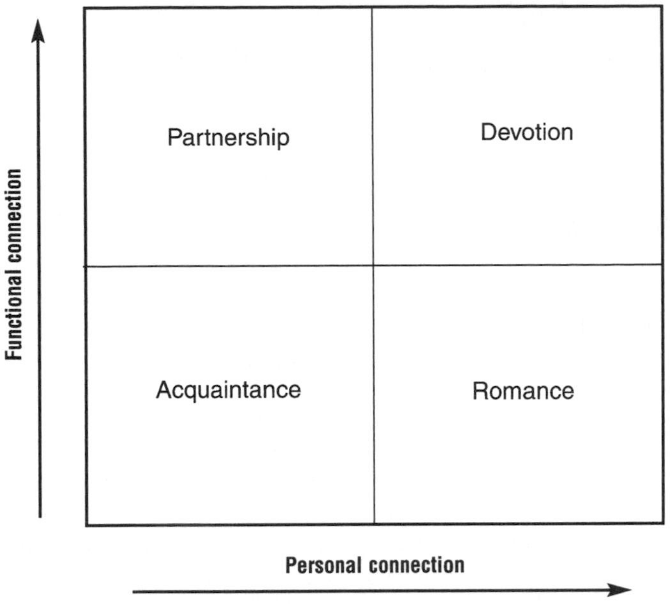

Figure 3   Relationship Types

Interpersonal allegories illuminate the nature of customer-brand relationships. Figure 3 suggests four types—based on the relative strength of functional and personal connections.

- Customers with strong functionally specific relationships may view them as partnerships, formed to achieve discrete functional outcomes free of personal investment.
- Customers with solid personal and functional connections offer a company many benefits associated with interpersonal devotion, such as immunity against failure and partner generosity.
- Personally connected customers invest in more emotive bonds, seeking to reap relational benefits. These bonds are more elaborately formed and regretfully severed, like romance.

- Disconnected customers are in relationships akin to acquaintances, in which interaction and benefits are incidental and fluid.

These four customers behave differently toward the brand and promotional efforts. Combining the trust-based commitment model with an understanding of the different classes allows a brand to manage customer relationships, and assess the value of investments in relationship development.

Ultimately, this permits firms to design strategies for developing committed relationships, map their brands relative to competitors by relationship type, and anticipate customer response to product introductions and promotional efforts (theirs and their competitors'). Placing trust in the center of customer-brand relationships—and expanding their conceptualization to multiple dimensions—opens the door to a new era of understanding, managing, and profiting from them.

Additional Reading

Armstrong, G. and P. Kotler (2002), *Principles of Marketing,* 9th ed. Englewood Cliffs, N.J.: Prentice Hall.

Fournier, S. (1998), "Consumers and Their Brands: Developing Relationship Theory in Consumer Research," *Journal of Consumer Research,* 24 (March), 343–373.

Garbarino, E. and M. S. Johnson (1999), "The Different Roles of Satisfaction, Trust, and Commitment in Customer Relationships," *Journal of Marketing,* 63 (April), 70–87.

Hess, J. (1995), "Construction and Assessment of a Scale to Measure Consumer Trust," in *Proceedings of the American Marketing Association Educators' Conference,* eds. B.B. Stern et G.M. Zinkhan, 6 (Summer), 20–25.

JEFF HESS is vice president and senior methodologist at Harris Interactive in Rochester, N.Y. He may be reached at jhess@harrisinteractive.com. **JOHN W. STORY** is assistant professor of marketing at Idaho State University in Pocatello. He may be reached at storjohn@isu.edu.

Trust in the Marketplace

JOHN E. RICHARDSON AND LINNEA BERNARD MCCORD

Traditionally, ethics is defined as a set of moral values or principles or a code of conduct.

. . . Ethics, as an expression of reality, is predicated upon the assumption that there are right and wrong motives, attitudes, traits of character, and actions that are exhibited in interpersonal relationships. Respectful social interaction is considered a norm by almost everyone.

. . . the overwhelming majority of people perceive others to be ethical when they observe what is considered to be their genuine kindness, consideration, politeness, empathy, and fairness in their interpersonal relationships. When these are absent, and unkindness, inconsideration, rudeness, hardness, and injustice are present, the people exhibiting such conduct are considered unethical. A genuine consideration of others is essential to an ethical life. (Chewning, pp. 175–176).

An essential concomitant of ethics is of trust. Webster's Dictionary defines trust as "assured reliance on the character, ability, strength or truth of someone or something." Businesses are built on a foundation of trust in our free-enterprise system. When there are violations of this trust between competitors, between employer and employees, or between businesses and consumers, our economic system ceases to run smoothly. From a moral viewpoint, ethical behavior should not exist because of economic pragmatism, governmental edict, or contemporary fashionability—it should exist because it is morally appropriate and right. From an economic point of view, ethical behavior should exist because it just makes good business sense to be ethical and operate in a manner that demonstrates trustworthiness.

Robert Bruce Shaw, in *Trust in the Balance*, makes some thoughtful observations about trust within an organization. Paraphrasing his observations and applying his ideas to the marketplace as a whole:

1. Trust requires consumers have confidence in organizational promises or claims made to them. This means that a consumer should be able to believe that a commitment made will be met.
2. Trust requires integrity and consistency in following a known set of values, beliefs, and practices.
3. Trust requires concern for the well-being of others. This does not mean that organizational needs are not given appropriate emphasis—but it suggests the importance of understanding the impact of decisions and actions on others—i.e. consumers. (Shaw, pp. 39–40)

Companies can lose the trust of their customers by portraying their products in a deceptive or inaccurate manner. In one recent example, a Nike advertisement exhorted golfers to buy the same golf balls used by Tiger Woods. However, since Tiger Woods was using custom-made Nike golf balls not yet available to the general golfing public, the ad was, in fact, deceptive. In one of its ads, Volvo represented that Volvo cars could withstand a physical impact that, in fact, was not possible. Once a company is "caught" giving inaccurate information, even if done innocently, trust in that company is eroded.

Companies can also lose the trust of their customers when they fail to act promptly and notify their customers of problems that the company has discovered, especially where deaths may be involved. This occurred when Chrysler dragged its feet in replacing a safety latch on its Minivan (Geyelin, pp. A1, A10). More recently, Firestone and Ford had been publicly brought to task for failing to expeditiously notify American consumers of tire defects in SUVs even though the problem had occurred years earlier in other countries. In cases like these, trust might not just be eroded, it might be destroyed. It could take years of painstaking effort to rebuild trust under these circumstances, and some companies might not have the economic ability to withstand such a rebuilding process with their consumers.

A *20/20* and *New York Times* investigation on a recent *ABC 20/20* program, entitled "The Car Dealer's Secret" revealed a sad example of the violation of trust in the marketplace. The investigation divulged that many unsuspecting consumers have had hidden charges tacked on by some car dealers when purchasing a new car. According to consumer attorney Gary Klein, "It's a dirty little secret that the auto lending industry has not owned up to." (*ABC News 20/20*)

The scheme worked in the following manner. Car dealers would send a prospective buyer's application to a number of lenders, who would report to the car dealer what interest rate the lender would give to the buyer for his or her car loan. This interest rate is referred to as the "buy rate." Legally a car dealer is not required to tell the buyer what the "buy rate" is or how much the dealer is marking up the loan. If dealers did most of the loans at the buy rate, they only get a small fee. However, if they were able to convince the buyer to pay a higher rate, they made considerably more money. Lenders encouraged car dealers to charge the buyer a higher rate than the "buy rate" by agreeing to split the extra income with the dealer.

David Robertson, head of the Association of Finance and Insurance Professionals—a trade group representing finance managers—defended the practice, reflecting that it was akin to a retail markup on loans. "The dealership provides a valuable service on behalf of the customer in negotiating these loans," he said. "Because of that, the dealership should be compensated for that work." (*ABC News 20/20*)

Careful examination of the entire report, however, makes one seriously question this apologetic. Even if this practice is deemed to be legal, the critical issue is what happens to trust when the buyers discover that they have been charged an additional 1–3% of the loan without their knowledge? In some cases, consumers were led to believe that they were getting the dealer's bank rate, and in other cases, they were told that the dealer had shopped around at several banks to secure the best loan rate they could get for the buyer. While this practice may be questionable from a legal standpoint, it is clearly in ethical breach of trust with the consumer. Once discovered, the companies doing this will have the same credibility and trustworthiness problems as the other examples mentioned above.

The untrustworthiness problems of the car companies was compounded by the fact that the investigation appeared to reveal statistics showing that black customers were twice as likely as whites to have their rate marked up—and at a higher level. That evidence—included in thousands of pages of confidential documents which *20/20* and *The New York Times* obtained from a Tennessee court—revealed that some Nissan and GM dealers in Tennessee routinely marked up rates for blacks, forcing them to pay between $300 and $400 more than whites. (*ABC News 20/20*)

This is a tragic example for everyone who was affected by this markup and was the victim of this secret policy. Not only is trust destroyed, there is a huge economic cost to the general public. It is estimated that in the last four years or so, Texas car dealers have received approximately $9 billion of kickbacks from lenders, affecting 5.2 million consumers. (*ABC News 20/20*)

Let's compare these unfortunate examples of untrustworthy corporate behavior with the landmark example of Johnson & Johnson which ultimately increased its trustworthiness with consumers by the way it handled the Tylenol incident. After seven individuals, who had consumed Tylenol capsules contaminated by a third party died, Johnson & Johnson instituted a total product recall within a week costing an estimated $50 million after taxes. The company did this, not because it was responsible for causing the problem, but because it was the right thing to do. In addition, Johnson & Johnson spearheaded the development of more effective tamper-proof containers for their industry. Because of the company's swift response, consumers once again were able to trust in the Johnson & Johnson name. Although Johnson & Johnson suffered a decrease in market share at the time because of the scare, over the long term it

has maintained its profitability in a highly competitive market. Certainly part of this profit success is attributable to consumers believing that Johnson & Johnson is a trustworthy company. (Robin and Reidenbach)

The e-commerce arena presents another example of the importance of marketers building a mutually valuable relationship with customers through a trust-based collaboration process. Recent research with 50 e-businesses reflects that companies which create and nurture trust find customers return to their sites repeatedly. (Dayal. . . . p. 64)

In the e-commerce world, six components of trust were found to be critical in developing trusting, satisfied customers:

- State-of-art reliable security measures on one's site
- Merchant legitimacy (e.g., ally one's product or service with an established brand)
- Order fulfillment (i.e. placing orders and getting merchandise efficiently and with minimal hassles)
- Tone and ambiance—handling consumers' personal information with sensitivity and iron-clad confidentiality
- Customers feeling that they are in control of the buying process
- Consumer collaboration—e.g., having chat groups to let consumers query each other about their purchases and experiences (Dayal. . . , pp. 64–67)

Additionally, one author noted recently that in the e-commerce world we've moved beyond brands and trademarks to "trustmarks." This author defined a trustmark as a

. . . (D)istinctive name or symbol that emotionally binds a company with the desires and aspirations of its customers. It's an emotional connection—and it's much bigger and more powerful than the uses that we traditionally associate with a trademark. . . . (Webber, p. 214)

Certainly if this is the case, trust—being an emotional link—is of supreme importance for a company that wants to succeed in doing business on the Internet.

It's unfortunate that while a plethora of examples of violation of trust easily come to mind, a paucity of examples "pop up" as noteworthy paradigms of organizational courage and trust in their relationship with consumers.

In conclusion, some key areas for companies to scrutinize and practice with regard to decisions that may affect trustworthiness in the marketplace might include:

- Does a company practice the Golden Rule with its customers? As a company insider, knowing what you know about the product, how willing would you be to purchase it for yourself or for a family member?
- How proud would you be if your marketing practices were made public. . . . shared with your friends. . . . or family? (Blanchard and Peale, p. 27)
- Are bottom-line concerns the sole component of your organizational decision-making process? What about human rights, the ecological/environmental impact, and other areas of social responsibility?

- Can a firm which engages in unethical business practices with customers be trusted to deal with its employees any differently? Unfortunately, frequently a willingness to violate standards of ethics is not an isolated phenomenon but permeates the culture. The result is erosion of integrity throughout a company. In such cases, trust is elusive at best. (Shaw, p. 75)
- Is your organization not only market driven, but also value-oriented? (Peters and Levering, Moskowitz, and Katz)
- Is there a strong commitment to a positive corporate culture and a clearly defined mission which is frequently and unambiguously voiced by upper-management?
- Does your organization exemplify trust by practicing a genuine relationship partnership with your customers— *before, during, and after* the initial purchase? (Strout, p. 69)

Companies which exemplify treating customers ethically are founded on a covenant of trust. There is a shared belief, confidence, and faith that the company and its people will be fair, reliable, and ethical in all its dealings. ***Total trust is the belief that a company and its people will never take opportunistic advantage of customer vulnerabilities.*** (Hart and Johnson, pp. 11–13)

References

ABC News 20/20, "The Car Dealer's Secret," October 27, 2000.

Blanchard, Kenneth, and Norman Vincent Peale, *The Power of Ethical Management,* New York: William Morrow and Company, Inc., 1988.

Chewning, Richard C., *Business Ethics in a Changing Culture* (Reston, Virginia: Reston Publishing, 1984).

Dayal, Sandeep, Landesberg, Helen, and Michael Zeissner, "How to Build Trust Online," *Marketing Management,* Fall 1999, pp. 64–69.

Geyelin, Milo, "Why One Jury Dealt a Big Blow to Chrysler in Minivan-Latch Case," *Wall Street Journal,* November 19, 1997, pp. A1, A10.

Hart, Christopher W. and Michael D. Johnson, "Growing the Trust Relationship," *Marketing Management,* Spring 1999, pp. 9–19.

Hosmer, La Rue Tone, *The Ethics of Management,* second edition (Homewood, Illinois: Irwin, 1991).

Kaydo, Chad, "A Position of Power," *Sales & Marketing Management,* June 2000, pp. 104–106, 108ff.

Levering, Robert; Moskowitz, Milton; and Michael Katz, *The 100 Best Companies to Work for in America* (Reading, Mass.: Addison-Wesley, 1984).

Magnet, Myron, "Meet the New Revolutionaries," *Fortune,* February 24, 1992, pp. 94–101.

Muoio, Anna, "The Experienced Customer," *Net Company,* Fall 1999, pp. 025–027.

Peters, Thomas J. and Robert H. Waterman Jr., *In Search of Excellence* (New York: Harper & Row, 1982).

Richardson, John (ed.), *Annual Editions: Business Ethics 00/01* (Guilford, CT: McGraw-Hill/Dushkin, 2000).

———, *Annual Editions: Marketing 00/01* (Guilford, CT: McGraw-Hill/Dushkin, 2000).

Robin, Donald P., and Erich Reidenbach, "Social Responsibility, Ethics, and Marketing Strategy: Closing the Gap Between Concept and Application," *Journal of Marketing,* Vol. 51 (January 1987), pp. 44–58.

Shaw, Robert Bruce, *Trust in the Balance,* (San Francisco: Jossey-Bass Publishers, 1997).

Strout, Erin, "Tough Customers," *Sales Marketing Management,* January 2000, pp. 63–69.

Webber, Alan M., "Trust in the Future," *Fast Company,* September 2000, pp. 209–212ff.

DR. JOHN E. RICHARDSON is Professor of Marketing in the Graziadio School of Business and Management at Pepperdine University, Malibu, California. **DR. LINNEA BERNARD MCCORD** is Associate Professor of Business Law in the Graziadio School of Business and Management at Pepperdine University, Malibu, California.

6 Strategies Marketers Use to Get Kids to Want Stuff *Bad*

In the next few weeks, marketers will try to nudge, prod and cajole kids into buying their stuff. Holiday hype has reached a point where parents need a tip sheet to know what to watch for to shield their kids, and themselves.

Bruce Horovitz

Every year at this time, visions of sugar-plum profits dance through the heads of toymakers and retailers.

Many take aim at the most susceptible target. kids.

Almost half of all kid-targeted toys, games and gadgets sold this year will be bought in the final three months. Kids through age 14 will influence $160 billion in spending in November and December, says James McNeal, author of *The Kids Market: Myths and Realities.*

That leaves marketers little time to make a Santa-size impression.

Meanwhile, slipping toy sales have raised the stakes. Last year, sales dipped 2% to $21.9 billion, reports market researcher NPD Group. Some categories dropped like a kid on a slide: plush toys by 14%, board games by 8%.

What's a toymaker to do? Advertise like mad.

Last year, marketers spent $1.4 billion per month marketing to children—15% more than the year before, McNeal says. "I call it 'surround selling.'"

Mattel Brands President Neil Friedman says Mattel will spend half its ad budget, estimated at $460 million by *Advertising Age,* in the fourth quarter.

Hasbro won't divulge its ad plans, but it is ramping up TV spots for hot toys such as its $299 life-size, interactive miniature pony: Butterscotch My FurReal Friends Pony. When making and placing ads, however, Chief Operating Officer Brian Goldner says, "We apply judgment as parents, not just as business people."

Critics don't buy that. The annual ad onslaught drives some crazy.

"It's greed," says Raffi Cavoukian, the kid-music singer turned child advocate intent on protecting kids from commercialism. "These companies want to turn America's kids into sales agents to nag Mom and Dad."

Marketer's goal: Get kids to nag Mom and Dad

In the next few weeks, marketers will try to nudge, prod and cajole kids into asking for their stuff. Some techniques that have worked for years are still effective, particularly, repetitive ads on kids shows. Among new ideas in 2006: a Wal-Mart website for toy picking that critics have panned for putting kids in control of e-mailed wish lists.

Holiday hype has reached a point where parents need a tip sheet to know what to watch for to shield their kids, and themselves.

Here it is: a list of six of the most effective techniques marketers are using this season to snatch the attention of youngsters.

Techie Wish Lists

Erin Willett wants Wal-Mart to kill its toy wish list website.

The mother of 4½-year-old Carter and 1½-year-old Nolan, recently wrote Wal-Mart's CEO that she'll do her shopping at Target until Wal-Mart dumps the site.

The site, www.walmart.com/toyland, features two elves who nudge kids to select toys by clicking on the word YES when a toy appears on the screen. Applause is played when YES is selected. But it's silent if NO is selected. "If you show us what you want on your wish list, we'll send it straight off to your parents," promises one elf.

Several consumer groups have asked Wal-Mart to close the site. "Wal-Mart is encouraging kids to nag for toys," says Susan Linn, co-founder of Campaign For a Commercial-Free Childhood.

"This site is the lowest of the low," says Gary Ruskin, founder of consumer group Commercial Alert.

The site "helps create a culture of nagging," says Diane Levin, co-founder of Teachers Resisting Unhealthy Children's Entertainment.

Even readers of ad industry trade journal *Advertising Age* find the site troubling. In a poll, 52% agreed that Wal-Mart "goes too far with its holiday website."

Wal-Mart says the site is a modern twist on an old tradition. "Making a Christmas wish list and sharing it with parents is a tradition that goes back as long as Santa," spokeswoman Jolanda Stewart says.

But some toys aren't on the site by accident. Some involve financial "sponsorships," says Stewart, though she declined to be specific. As for consumer complaints, she says, "We haven't received a significant number."

Repetitive TV Spots

Despite the hoopla over the Internet, the vast majority of kid-targeted ads for the holidays still will appear on one of seven TV networks: NBC, ABC, CBS, FOX, CW, Nickelodeon and Cartoon Network, says Paul Kurnit , founder of KidShop, a consulting firm.

"The best way to build brand awareness with kids is the 30-second TV commercial," Kurnit says.

TV viewing has leveled off, but the typical kid still watches 20 hours of TV weekly, he says.

The toy industry calls the eight weeks leading up to Christmas the "hard eight." That's when prices jump for slots on kids shows and when toy ads replace cereal ads.

Some makers of kids games spend their entire TV ad budget during the fourth quarter, he says.

Big-Screen Hype

Odds are, something with Johnny Depp's imprint is going to show up in your kid's Christmas stocking.

It won't be by accident.

On sale now are some 50 toys, from key chains to boats, linked to his hit film, *Pirates of the Caribbean: Dead Man's Chest.*

Never mind that the movie was rated PG-13. Toys for kids as young as 6 are flooding the market for the holidays. So, too, is the DVD to be released early next month.

Using movies as stepping stones for toy licensing is not new. But the sheer volume of *Pirates*-related toy and DVD marketing for Christmas 2006 raises concerns among some.

"Hollywood knows if you hook a kid's heart, the parent's wallet follows," Ruskin says. "Disney exploits children's love for *Pirates of the Caribbean* to get them to nag for toys."

For weeks, four different commercials promoting *Pirates* toys have appeared on Cartoon Network and Nickelodeon. Zizzle, the master toy licensee for *Pirates,* also hosted a look-alike contest at FAO Schwarz in New York for Jack Sparrow, the Depp character.

Toys include everything from $5.88 action figures to a plastic boat for $49.99. Most are geared for 7-to-12-year-olds, says Roger Shiffman, CEO of Zizzle and co-founder of Tiger Electronics.

Shiffman sees no conflict between the toys' target and a movie that's rated PG-13. "The toy line works with or without the movie. Boys love to be pirates."

Besides, the real connection isn't to the movie, but to the Pirate's rides at Disney theme parks, says Jessi Dunne, Disney consumer products chief.

Books as Toys

When is a book often a toy?

When it's sold by children's publisher Scholastic, Linn says. "Scholastic used to be about books, but now it's about toys, too,"
she says. "That can carry special weight before the holidays when children's antennae are up."

Over the past five years, the company has increasingly turned to toys and games to boost sales.

The toys or games are seldom sold alone, usually being packaged with books. Nearly half the books on the cover of its *2006 Holiday Gift Books* catalog are marketed with games, jewelry or plush toys.

The Care Bears Holiday Pack is advertised with a Cheer Bear plush. *The Animal Ark Spaniel in a Stocking Pack* has a charm bracelet. And *The Dog Happy Howliday Book* is sold with stickers and a dog charm.

"We are not a toy catalog by any means," says Judy Newman, president of Scholastic Book Clubs. "But the world is changing."

She won't say what the company makes in toy sales. "We need to make sure there's something for everyone," Newman says. "If you just have Shakespeare in there, kids won't participate."

Faux Toy Shortages

When is a toy shortage really a shortage and not just a stunt to build media hype and sales?

In the case of T.M.X. Elmo—an updated Elmo that keels over in laughter when tickled—that depends upon who you ask.

When the $39.99 plush doll was introduced Sept. 19, an estimated 250,000 units sold in one day, a record for the toy industry. This caused an immediate shortage.

Critics insist the shortage was set up by Mattel.

"Planned shortages are the perfect way to get kids to nag parents for presents," says Linn of Campaign for a Commercial-Free Childhood. "The buzz creates a sense of urgency to get the toy."

Executives at Mattel say that's nonsense.

"We're a public company. We don't plan shortages," insists Mattel's Friedman. "All that does is make for angry consumers and disappointed customers."

The shortage continues. "We're shipping every piece we can," Friedman says. "It's still tight."

Bus Radio

For many kids on school buses, the background noise is more than the drivers' pleas for quiet.

It could be a piped-in commercial, perhaps even for a holiday gift. About a month ago, Bus Radio began rolling out its student-targeted programming of music, news and commercials to about 800 school buses in 12 cities. Roughly eight minutes each hour are devoted to commercials. Ad revenue is shared with school districts.

Critics want it banned from the buses. "The school bus is one of the only places left in society where a child is free from a sales pitch," says Betsy Taylor, founder of New American Dream, a consumer group. "Let's leave it that way."

Who is advertising on Bus Radio?

The website Answers.com is. Beyond that, executives at Bus Radio won't name other sponsors.

"A lot of people blow it out of proportion," says Michael Yanoff, founder of Bus Radio. "Our shows are age-appropriate and designed for kids."

Wrestling with Ethics
Is Marketing Ethics an Oxymoron?

Every profession and business has to wrestle with ethical questions. The recent wave of business scandals over inaccurate reporting of sales and profits and excessive pay and privileges for top executives has brought questions of business ethics to the fore. And lawyers have been continuously accused of "ambulance chasing," jury manipulation, and inflated fees, leaving the plaintiffs with much less than called for in the judgment. Physicians have been known to recommend certain drugs as more effective while receiving support from pharmaceutical companies.

PHILIP KOTLER

Marketers are not immune from facing a whole set of ethical issues. For evidence, look to Howard Bowen's classic questions from his 1953 book, *Social Responsibilities of the Businessman:*

"Should he conduct selling in ways that intrude on the privacy of people, for example, by door-to-door selling? Should he use methods involving ballyhoo, chances, prizes, hawking, and other tactics which are at least of doubtful good taste? Should he employ 'high pressure' tactics in persuading people to buy? Should he try to hasten the obsolescence of goods by bringing out an endless succession of new models and new styles? Should he appeal to and attempt to strengthen the motives of materialism, invidious consumption, and keeping up with the Joneses?" (Also see Smith, N. Craig and Elizabeth Cooper-Martin (1997), "Ethics and Target Marketing: The Role of Product Harm and Consumer Vulnerability," *Journal of Marketing,* July, 1–20.)

The issues raised are complicated. Drawing a clear line between normal marketing practice and unethical behavior isn't easy. Yet it's important for marketing scholars and those interested in public policy to raise questions about practices that they may normally endorse but which may not coincide with the public interest.

We will examine the central axiom of marketing: Companies that satisfy their target customers will perform better than those that don't. Companies that satisfy customers can expect repeat business; those that don't will get only one-time sales. Steady profits come from holding onto customers, satisfying them, and selling them more goods and services.

This axiom is the essence of the well-known marketing concept. It reduces to the formula "Give the customer what he wants." This sounds reasonable on the surface. But notice that it carries an implied corollary: "Don't judge what the customer wants."

Marketers have been, or should be, a little uneasy about this corollary. It raises two public interest concerns: (1) What if the customer wants something that isn't good for him or her? (2) What if the product or service, while good for the customer, isn't good for society or other groups?

EXECUTIVE briefing

Marketers should be proud of their field. They have encouraged and promoted the development of many products and services that have benefited people worldwide. But this is all the more reason that they should carefully and thoughtfully consider where they stand on the ethical issues confronting them today and into the future. Marketers are able to take a stand and must make the effort to do so in order to help resolve these issues.

When it comes to the first question, what are some products that some customers desire that might not be good for them? These would be products that can potentially harm their health, safety, or well-being. Tobacco and hard drugs such as cocaine, LSD, or ecstasy immediately come to mind.

As for the second question, examples of products or services that some customers desire that may not be in the public's best interest include using asbestos as a building material or using lead paint indiscriminately. Other products and services where debates continue to rage as to whether they are in the public's interest include the right to own guns and other weapons, the right to have an abortion, the right to distribute hate literature, and the right to buy large gas guzzling and polluting automobiles.

We now turn to three questions of interest to marketers, businesses, and the public:

1. Given that expanding consumption is at the core of most businesses, what are the interests and behaviors of companies that make these products?
2. To what extent do these companies care about reducing the negative side effects of these products?
3. What steps can be taken to reduce the consumption of products that have questionable effects and is limited intervention warranted?

Expanding Consumption

Most companies will strive to enlarge their market as much as possible. A tobacco company, if unchecked, will try to get everyone who comes of age to start smoking cigarettes. Given that cigarettes are addictive, this promises the cigarette company "customers for life." Each new customer will create a 50-year profit stream for the cigarette company if the consumer continues to favor the same brand—and live long enough. Suppose a new smoker starts at the age of 13, smokes for 50 years, and dies at 63 from lung cancer. If he spends $500 a year on cigarettes, he will spend $25,000 over his lifetime. If the company's profit rate is 20%, that new customer is worth $5,000 to the company (undiscounted). It is hard to imagine a company that doesn't want to attract a customer who contributes $5,000 to its profits.

The same story describes the hard drug industry, whose products are addictive and even more expensive. The difference is that cigarette companies can operate legally but hard drug companies must operate illegally.

Other products, such as hamburgers, candy, soft drinks, and beer, are less harmful when consumed in moderation, but are addictive for some people. We hear a person saying she has a "sweet tooth." One person drinks three Coca-Colas a day, and another drinks five beers a day. Still another consumer is found who eats most of his meals at McDonald's. These are the "heavy users." Each company treasures the heavy users who account for a high proportion of the company's profits.

All said, every company has a natural drive to expand consumption of its products, leaving any negative consequences to be the result of the "free choice" of consumers. A high-level official working for Coca-Cola in Sweden said that her aim is to get people to start drinking Coca-Cola for breakfast (instead of orange juice). And McDonald's encourages customers to choose a larger hamburger, a larger order of French fries, and a larger cola drink. And these companies have some of the best marketers in the world working for them.

Reducing Side Effects

It would not be a natural act on the part of these companies to try to reduce or restrain consumption of their products. What company wants to reduce its profits? Usually some form of public pressure must bear on these companies before they will act.

The government has passed laws banning tobacco companies from advertising and glamorizing smoking on TV. But Philip Morris' Marlboro brand still will put out posters showing its mythical cowboy. And Marlboro will make sure that its name is mentioned in sports stadiums, art exhibits, and in labels for other products.

Tobacco companies today are treading carefully not to openly try to create smokers out of young people. They have stopped distributing free cigarettes to young people in the United States as they move their operations increasingly into China.

Beer companies have adopted a socially responsible attitude by telling people not to over-drink or drive during or after drinking. They cooperate with efforts to prevent underage people from buying beer. They are trying to behave in a socially responsible manner. They also know that, at the margin, the sales loss resulting from their "cooperation" is very slight.

McDonald's has struggled to find a way to reduce the ill effects (obesity, heart disease) of too much consumption of their products. It tried to offer a reduced-fat hamburger only to find consumers rejecting it. It has offered salads, but they weren't of good quality when originally introduced and they failed. Now it's making a second and better attempt.

Limited Intervention

Do public interest groups or the government have the right to intervene in the free choices of individuals? This question has been endlessly debated. On one side are people who resent any intervention in their choices of products and services. In the extreme, they go by such names as libertarians, vigilantes, and "freedom lovers." They have a legitimate concern about government power and its potential abuse. Some of their views include:

- The marketer's job is to "sell more stuff." It isn't the marketer's job to save the world or make society a better place.
- The marketer's job is to produce profits for the shareholders in any legally sanctioned way.
- A high-minded socially conscious person should not be in marketing. A company shouldn't hire such a person.

On the other side are people concerned with the personal and societal costs of "unregulated consumption." They are considered do-gooders and will document that Coca-Cola delivers six teaspoons of sugar in every bottle or can. They will cite statistics on the heavy health costs of obesity, heart disease, and liver damage that are caused by failing to reduce the consumption of some of these products. These costs fall on everyone through higher medical costs and taxes. Thus, those who don't consume questionable products are still harmed through the unenlightened behavior of others.

Ultimately, the problem is one of conflict among different ethical systems. Consider the following five:

Ethical Egoism

Your only obligation is to take care of yourself (Protagoras and Ayn Rand).

Government Requirements

The law represents the minimal moral standards of a society (Thomas Hobbes and John Locke).

Personal Virtues

Be honest, good, and caring (Plato and Aristotle).

Utilitarianism

Create the greatest good for the greatest number (Jeremy Bentham and John Stuart Mill).

Universal Rules

"Act only on that maxim through which you can at the same time will that it should become a universal law" (Immanuel Kant's categorical imperative).

Clearly, people embrace different ethical viewpoints, making marketing ethics and other business issues more complex to resolve.

Every company has a natural drive to expand consumption of its products, leaving any negative consequences to be the result of the "free choice" of consumers.

Let's consider the last two ethical systems insofar as they imply that some interventions are warranted. Aside from the weak gestures of companies toward self-regulation and appearing concerned, there are a range of measures that can be taken by those wishing to push their view of the public interest. They include the following six approaches:

1. Encouraging these companies to make products safer. Many companies have responded to public concern or social pressure to make their products safer. Tobacco companies developed filters that would reduce the chance of contracting emphysema or lung cancer. If a leaf without nicotine could give smokers the same satisfaction, they would be happy to replace the tobacco leaf. Some tobacco companies have even offered information or aids to help smokers limit their appetite for tobacco or curb it entirely.

Food and soft drink companies have reformulated many of their products to be "light," "nonfat," or "low in calories." Some beer companies have introduced non-alcoholic beer. These companies still offer their standard products but provide concerned consumers with alternatives that present less risk to their weight or health.

Auto companies have reluctantly incorporated devices designed to reduce pollution output into their automobiles. Some are even producing cars with hybrid fuel systems to further reduce harmful emissions to the air. But the auto companies still insist on putting out larger automobiles (such as Hummers) because the "public demands them."

What can we suggest to Coca-Cola and other soft drink competitors that are already offering "light" versions of their drinks? First, they should focus more on developing the bottled water side of their businesses because bottled water is healthier than sugared soft drinks. Further, they should be encouraged to add nutrients and vitamins in standard drinks so these drinks can at least deliver more health benefits, especially to those in undeveloped countries who are deprived of these nutrients and vitamins. (Coca-Cola has some brands doing this now.)

What can we suggest to McDonald's and its fast food competitors? The basic suggestion is to offer more variety in its menu. McDonald's seems to forget that, while parents bring their children to McDonald's, they themselves usually prefer to eat healthier food, not to mention want their children eating healthier foods. How about a first-class salad bar? How about moving more into the healthy sandwich business? Today more Americans are buying their meals at Subway and other sandwich shops where they feel they are getting healthier and tastier food for their dollar.

There seems to be a correlation between the amount of charity given by companies in some categories and the category's degree of "sin." Thus, McDonald's knows that overconsumption of its products can be harmful, but the company is very charitable. A cynic would say that McDonald's wants to build a bank of public goodwill to diffuse potential public criticism.

2. Banning or restricting the sale or use of the product or service. A community or nation will ban certain products where there is strong public support. Hard drugs are banned, although there is some debate about whether the ban should include marijuana and lighter hard drugs. There are even advocates who oppose banning hard drugs, believing that the cost of policing and criminality far exceed the cost of a moderate increase that might take place in hard drug usage. Many people today believe that the "war on drugs" can never be won and is creating more serious consequences than simply dropping the ban or helping drug addicts, as Holland and Switzerland have done.

Some products carry restrictions on their purchase or use. This is particularly true of drugs that require a doctor's prescription and certain poisons that can't be purchased without authorization. Persons buying guns must be free of a criminal record and register their gun ownership. And certain types of guns, such as machine guns, are banned or restricted.

3. Banning or limiting advertising or promotion of the product. Even when a product isn't banned or its purchase restricted, laws may be passed to prevent producers from advertising or promoting the product. Gun, alcohol, and tobacco manufacturers can't advertise on TV, although they can advertise in print media such as magazines and newspapers. They can also inform and possibly promote their products online.

Manufacturers get around this by mentioning their brand name in every possible venue: sports stadiums, music concerts, and feature articles. They don't want to be forgotten in the face of a ban on promoting their products overtly.

4. Increasing "sin" taxes to discourage consumption. One reasonable alternative to banning a product or its promotion is to place a "sin" tax on its consumption. Thus, smokers pay hefty government taxes for cigarettes. This is supposed to have three effects when done right. First, the higher price should discourage consumption. Second, the tax revenue could be used to finance the social costs to health and safety caused by the consumption of the product. Third, some of the tax revenue could be used to counter-advertise the use of the product or support public education against its use. The last effect was enacted by California when it taxed tobacco companies and used the money to "unsell" tobacco smoking.

5. Public education campaigns. In the 1960s, Sweden developed a social policy to use public education to raise a nation of non-smokers and non-drinkers. Children from the first grade up were educated to understand the ill effects of tobacco and alcohol. Other countries are doing this on a less systematic and intensive basis. U.S. public schools devote parts of occasional courses to educate students against certain temptations with mixed success. Girls, not boys, in the United States seem to be more prone to taking up smoking. The reason often given by girls is that smoking curbs their appetite for food and consequently helps them avoid becoming overweight, a problem they consider more serious than lung cancer taking place 40 years later.

Sex education has become a controversial issue, when it comes to public education campaigns. The ultra-conservative camp wants to encourage total abstinence until marriage. The more liberal camp believes that students should be taught the risks of early sex and have the necessary knowledge to protect themselves. The effectiveness of both types of sex education is under debate.

6. Social marketing campaigns. These campaigns describe a wide variety of efforts to communicate the ill effects of certain behaviors that can harm the person, other persons, or society as a whole. These campaigns use techniques of public education, advertising and promotion, incentives, and channel development to make it as easy and attractive as possible for people to change their behavior for the better. (See Kotler, Philip, Eduardo Roberto, and Nancy Lee (2002), *Social Marketing: Improving the Quality of Life,* 2nd ed. London: Sage Publications.) Social marketing uses the tools of commercial marketing—segmentation, targeting, and positioning, and the four Ps (product, price, place, and promotion)—to achieve voluntary compliance with publicly endorsed goals. Some social marketing campaigns, such as family planning and anti-littering, have achieved moderate to high success. Other campaigns including anti-smoking, anti-drugs ("say no to drugs"), and seat belt promotion have worked well when supplemented with legal action.

Social Responsibility and Profits

Each year *Business Ethics* magazine publishes the 100 best American companies out of 1,000 evaluated. The publication examines the degree to which the companies serve seven stakeholder groups: shareholders, communities, minorities and women, employees, environment, non-U.S. stakeholders, and customers. Information is gathered on lawsuits, regulatory problems, pollution emissions, charitable contributions, staff diversity counts, union relations, employee benefits, and awards. Companies are removed from the list if there are significant scandals or improprieties. The research is done by Kinder, Lydenberg, Domini (KLD), an independent rating service. (For more details see the Spring 2003 issue of *Business Ethics.*)

The 20 best-rated companies in 2003 were (in order): General Mills, Cummins Engine, Intel, Procter & Gamble, IBM,

Hewlett-Packard, Avon Products, Green Mountain Coffee, John Nuveen Co., St. Paul Companies, AT&T, Fannie Mae, Bank of America, Motorola, Herman Miller, Expedia, Autodesk, Cisco Systems, Wild Oats Markets, and Deluxe.

The earmarks of a socially responsible company include:

- Living out a deep set of company values that drive company purpose, goals, strategies, and tactics
- Treating customers with fairness, openness, and quick response to inquiries and complaints
- Treating employees, suppliers, and distributors fairly
- Caring about the environmental impact of its activities and supply chain
- Behaving in a consistently ethical fashion

The intriguing question is whether socially responsible companies are more profitable. Unfortunately, different research studies have come up with different results. The correlations between financial performance (FP) and social performance (SP) are sometimes positive, sometimes negative, and sometimes neutral, depending on the study. Even when FP and SP are positively related, which causes which? The most probable finding is that high FP firms invest slack resources in SP and then discover the SP leads to better FP, in a virtuous circle. (See Waddock, Sandra A. and Samuel B. Graves (1997), "The Corporate Social Performance-Financial Performance Link," *Strategic Management Journal,* 18 (4), 303–319.)

Marketers' Responsibilities

As professional marketers, we are hired by some of the aforementioned companies to use our marketing toolkit to help them sell more of their products and services. Through our research, we can discover which consumer groups are the most susceptible to increasing their consumption. We can use the research to assemble the best 30-second TV commercials, print ads, and sales incentives to persuade them that these products will deliver great satisfaction. And we can create price discounts to tempt them to consume even more of the product than would normally be healthy or safe to consume.

But, as professional marketers, we should have the same ambivalence as nuclear scientists who help build nuclear bombs or pilots who spray DDT over crops from the airplane. Some of us, in fact, are independent enough to tell these clients that we will not work for them to find ways to sell more of what hurts people. We can tell them that we're willing to use our marketing toolkit to help them build new businesses around substitute products that are much healthier and safer.

But, even if these companies moved toward these healthier and safer products, they'll probably continue to push their current "cash cows." At that point, marketers will have to decide whether to work for these companies, help them reshape their offerings, avoid these companies altogether, or even work to oppose these company offerings.

Remember Marketing's Contributions

Nothing said here should detract from the major contributions that marketing has made to raise the material standards of living around the world. One doesn't want to go back to the kitchen where the housewife cooked five hours a day, washed dishes by hand, put fresh ice in the ice box, and washed and dried clothes in the open air. We value refrigerators, electric stoves, dishwashers, washing machines, and dryers. We value the invention and diffusion of the radio, the television set, the computer, the Internet, the cellular phone, the automobile, the movies, and even frozen food. Marketing has played a major role in their instigation and diffusion. Granted, any of these are capable of abuse (bad movies or TV shows), but they promise and deliver much that is good and valued in modern life.

Marketers have a right to be proud of their field. They search for unmet needs, encourage the development of products and services addressing these needs, manage communications to inform people of these products and services, arrange for easy accessibility and availability, and price the goods in a way that represents superior value delivered vis-à-vis competitors' offerings. This is the true work of marketing.

PHILIP KOTLER is S.C. Johnson and Son Distinguished Professor of International Marketing, Kellogg School of Management, Northwestern University. He may be reached at pkotler@nwu.edu.

Author's note—The author wishes to thank Professor Evert Gummesson of the School of Business, Stockholm University, for earlier discussion of these issues.

UNIT 2

Research, Markets, and Consumer Behavior

Unit Selections

Key Points to Consider

- As marketing research techniques become more and more advanced, and as psychographic analysis leads to more and more sophisticated models of consumer behavior, do you believe marketing will become more capable of predicting consumer behavior? Explain.

- Where the target population lives, its age, and its ethnicity are demographic factors of importance to marketers. What other demographic factors must be taken into account in long-range market planning?

- Psychographic segmentation is the process whereby consumer markets are divided up into segments based upon similarities in lifestyles, attitudes, personality type, social class, and buying behavior. In what specific ways do you envision psychographic research and findings helping marketing planning and strategy in the next decade?

Student Web Site

www.mhcls.com/online

Internet References

Further information regarding these Web sites may be found in this book's preface or online.

Canadian Innovation Centre
http://www.innovationcentre.ca/
BizMiner—Industry Analysis and Trends
http://www.bizminer.com/market_research.asp
Small Business Center—Articles & Insights
http://www.bcentral.com/articles/krotz/123.asp
Maritz Marketing Research
http://www.maritzresearch.com
USADATA
http://www.usadata.com
WWW Virtual Library: Demography & Population Studies
http://demography.anu.edu.au/VirtualLibrary/

Creatas Images/Jupiter Images

If marketing activities were all we knew about an individual, we would know a great deal. By tracing these daily activities over only a short period of time, we could probably guess rather accurately that person's tastes, understand much of his or her system of personal values, and learn quite a bit about how he or she deals with the world.

In a sense, this is a key to successful marketing management: tracing a market's activities and understanding its behavior. However, in spite of the increasing sophistication of market research techniques, this task is not easy. Today a new society is evolving out of the changing lifestyles of Americans, and these divergent lifestyles have put great pressure on the marketer who hopes to identify and profitably reach a target market. At the same time, however, each change in consumer behavior leads to new marketing opportunities.

The writings in this unit were selected to provide information and insight into the effect that lifestyle changes and demographic

trends are having on American industry. The first unit article in the *Marketing Research* subsection describes how, as more companies are refocusing more squarely on the consumer, ethnography and its proponents have become star players. "Team Spirit" provides insight on how a company that creates collaborative teams can contribute to the success of brands as well as improve consumers' lives.

The articles in the *Markets and Demographics* subsection examine the importance of demographic and psychographic data, economic forces, and age considerations in making marketing decisions.

The articles in the final subsection examine how consumer behavior, social attitudes, cues, and quality considerations will have an impact on the evaluation and purchase of various products and services for different consumers.

The Science of Desire

As more companies refocus squarely on the consumer, ethnography and its proponents have become star players

SPENCER E. ANTE

The satellite-radio war can't be won by Howard Stern alone. So shortly after signing the shock jock to a $500 million contract in 2004, Sirius Satellite Radio called on a small Portland (Ore.) consulting firm to envision a device that would help it catch up with bigger rival XM Satellite Radio Holdings. Ziba Design dispatched a team of social scientists, designers, and ethnographers on a road trip to Nashville and Boston. For four weeks they shadowed 45 people, studying how they listen to music, watch TV, and even peruse gossip magazines. Their conclusion: A portable satellite-radio player that was easy to use and load with music for later playback could be a killer app in the competition against XM.

Last November, Sirius began selling the Sirius S50, a device the size of a slim cigarette pack that stores up to 50 hours of digital music and commentary. It features a color screen and handy buttons that let you easily pick your favorite song to listen to. Slip it into a docking station and it automatically gathers and refreshes programming from your favorite Sirius channels. Techies praised the device, declaring it better than XM's competing player, the MyFi, launched in October, 2004. The S50 became one of the holiday season's hottest sellers. Sirius says it has helped the company sign up more subscribers than XM has since last fall. "[Ziba's] research capabilities and innovative approach to design concepts were most impressive," says Sirius President James E. Meyer.

A portable satellite radio from Sirius. Hipper, more user-friendly lobbies at hotels owned by Marriott International Inc. A cheap PC from Intel Corp. designed to run in rural Indian villages on a truck battery in 113-degree temperatures. All these brainstorms happened with the guidance of ethnographers, a species of anthropologist who can, among other things, identify what's missing in people's lives—the perfect cell phone, home appliance, or piece of furniture—and work with designers and engineers to help dream up products and services to fill those needs.

Companies have been harnessing the social sciences, including ethnography, since the 1930s. Back then executives were mostly interested in figuring out how to make their employees more productive. But since the 1960s, when management gurus crowned the consumer king, companies have been tapping ethnographers to get a better handle on their customers. Now, as more and more businesses re-orient themselves to serve the consumer, ethnography has entered prime time.

The beauty of ethnography, say its proponents, is that it provides a richer understanding of consumers than does traditional research. Yes, companies are still using focus groups, surveys, and demographic data to glean insights into the consumer's mind. But closely observing people where they live and work, say executives, allows companies to zero in on their customers' unarticulated desires. "It used be that design features were tacked on to the end of a marketing strategy," says Timothy deWaal Malefyt, an anthropologist who runs "cultural discovery" at ad firm BBDO Worldwide. "Now what differentiates products has to be baked in from the beginning. This makes anthropology far more valuable."

Ethnography's rising prominence is creating unlikely stars within companies in retailing, manufacturing, and financial services, as well as at consulting firms such as IDEO, Jump Associates, and Doblin Group. Three years ago, IBM's research group had a handful of anthropologists on staff. Today it has a dozen. Furniture maker Steelcase Inc. relies heavily on in-house ethnographers to devise new products. Intel, in the midst of a wrenching transition from chipmaker to consumer-products company, has moved several of its senior social scientists out of the research lab and into leadership positions. "Technology is increasingly being designed from the outside in, putting the needs of people first and foremost," says Intel CEO Paul S. Otellini. "Intel's researchers are giving our designers a deeper understanding of what real people want to do with computers."

With more companies putting ethnographers front and center, schools around the country are ramping up social science programs or steering anthropology students toward jobs in the corporate world. In recent years, New York's Parsons School for Design and Illinois Institute of Technology's Institute of Design have put anthropologists on the faculty. Ditto for many business

Ethnography: Do It Right . . .

Anthropological research can be a potent tool—or a waste of time and money. Here's how to get the most bang for your buck:

Think Big Thoughts

Ethnography is **most effective when it's used to spot breakthrough innovations.** Don't use it for incremental improvements or to solve small problems. Ethnography works best when the questions are big and broad. "The good time to use it is with futuristic research," says Natalie Hanson, SAP's director for business operations.

Due Diligence

Many companies do not have the resources to hire their own anthropologists or social scientists. So **picking the right consultants can make or break a project.** With many poseurs jumping on the bandwagon, it's important to hire a firm with a track record, client references, and a staff with a mix of skills in social science, design, and business.

Start Early

Using ethnography at the beginning of the product development process is key because **it helps identify consumers' unmet needs.** It's those findings that can inspire a hit product or service. One danger of waiting too long to bring in social scientists is that you might end up with "feature creep," simply adding unnecessary bells and whistles.

Sell, Sell, Sell

Let's face it: Many executives think ethnography is bunk. So **managers must constantly educate others about its value.** Be clear that ethnography is not a cure-all but can spark innovation. "To get people to think about a softer approach is a challenge," says GE's marketing operations manager, Dominic McMahon.

Build a Culture

Organizations that have used ethnography to the greatest effect have usually made such research an integral part of their culture. "I don't believe it is one person's job to figure out user problems," says Alex Lee, president of OXO, a long-time user of ethnography. "What's important is the mindset of the people. Ideas come from every which way."

. . . and Reap the Rewards

Motorola A732

After observing how popular Chinese-character text messaging was in Shanghai, Motorola researchers developed a cell phone that lets you send messages by writing directly on the keypad using your finger.

TownePlace Suites

A team of ethnographers and designers from IDEO found that TownePlace guests often turn their bedrooms into work spaces. So it came up with a flexible modular wall unit where there had been only a dining table. Guests can use the unit either as an office or a place to eat.

OXO Hammer

To develop a line of professional-grade tools for consumers, OXO and Smart Design visited contractors and home renovators. One result: A hammer with a fiberglass core to cut vibration and a rubber bumper on top to avoid leaving marks when removing nails.

Citigroup PayPass

Citigroup teamed up with Doblin Group to brainstorm new payment services for consumers. This summer, Citi will launch a pilot project called PayPass that lets New York City subway riders pay with a special key chain tag that debits their checking accounts.

Sirius S50

Sirius and Ziba Design studied how people listen to music, read magazines, and watch TV. That led them to develop a portable satellite-radio player that is easily loaded with up to 50 hours of digital music for later playback.

---

schools. And going to work for The Man is no longer considered selling out. Says Marietta L. Baba, Michigan State University's dean of social sciences: "Ethnography [has] escaped from academia, where it had been held hostage."

Up Close and Personal

We know what you're thinking: Corporate ethnography can sound a little flaky. And a certain amount of skepticism is in order whenever consultants hype trendy new ways to reach the masses. Ethnographers' findings often don't lead to a product or service, only a generalized sense of what people want. Their research can also take a long time to bear fruit. Intel's India Community PC emerged only after ethnographer Tony Salvador spent two years traipsing around the developing world, including a memorable evening in the Ecuadorean Andes when the town healer conducted a ceremony that included spitting the local hooch on him.

Practitioners caution that all the attention ethnography is getting could lead to a backlash. Many ethnographers already complain about poseurs flooding the field. Others gripe that corporations are hiring anthropologists to rubber-stamp bone-headed business plans. Norman Stolzoff, founder of Ethnographic Insight Inc., a Bellingham (Wash.) consulting firm, says he has worked with several companies that insist on changing the line of questioning when they're not getting the answers

Eric Dishman

Title

General Manager & Global Director, Intel Health Research & Innovation Group

Education

Masters in communications from Southern Illinois University; PhD candidate in anthropology, University of Utah

Research

Dishman and his team are working with medical and engineering schools to help discover new technologies to improve health care for seniors. One innovation: A special PC that flashes the photo of a person calling, along with personal details, to help Alzheimer's sufferers remember whom they're talking to.

they need to justify a decision. "There's a lot of pressure to ratify decisions that are already being made," says Stolzoff, who holds a PhD from the University of California at Davis in cultural anthropology.

TRUE, ethnography can sound a bit flaky and take a while to bear fruit. But one B-school dean says "it could become a core competence" for executives

Still, in an accelerated global society where consumers are inundated with choices, markets are sliced into ever-thinner pieces, product cycles are measured not in years but in months

Jane Fulton Suri

Title

IDEO's Director for Human Factors Design & Research

Education

Masters in architecture from the University of Strathclyde, Glasgow

Research

Her 40 researchers help the likes of Procter & Gamble and Marriott detect unmet consumer needs and divine products to serve them. Suri's team came up with the idea for P&G's Magic Reach tool after watching people struggle to clean their bathrooms. The device's long handle and swivel head gets into those hard-to-reach places.

or weeks, and new ideas zip around the planet at the speed of light, getting up close and personal with Joe and Jane Consumer is increasingly important. Ethnography may be no silver bullet, says Roger Martin, dean of the University of Toronto's Rotman School of Business, but "it could become a core competence" in the executive tool kit. Here are three case studies that demonstrate how businesses are using it to spark innovation:

Refreshing a Product

While many companies embrace ethnography to create something new, others are using it to revitalize an existing product or service. In 2004, Marriott hired IDEO Inc. to rethink the hotel experience for an increasingly important customer: the young, tech-savvy road warrior. "This is all about looking freshly at business travel and how people behave and what they need," explains Michael E. Jannini, Marriott's executive vice-president for brand management.

To better understand Marriott's customers, IDEO dispatched a team of seven consultants, including a designer, anthropologist, writer, and architect, on a six-week trip. Covering 12 cities, the group hung out in hotel lobbies, cafés, and bars, and asked guests to graph what they were doing hour by hour.

What they learned: Hotels are generally good at serving large parties but not small groups of business travelers. Researchers noted that hotel lobbies tend to be dark and better suited to killing time than conducting casual business. Marriott lacked places where guests could comfortably combine work with pleasure outside their rooms. IDEO consultant and Marriott project manager Dana Cho recalls watching a female business traveler drinking wine in the lobby while trying not to spill it on papers spread out on a desk. "There are very few hotel services that address [such] problems," says Cho.

Having studied IDEO's findings, Marriott in January announced plans to reinvent the lobbies of its Marriott and Renaissance Hotels, creating for each a social zone, with small tables, brighter lights, and wireless Web access, that is better suited to meetings. Another area will allow solo travelers to work or unwind in larger, quiet, semiprivate spaces where they won't have to worry about spilling coffee on their laptops or papers. Guests would also like the option of checking themselves in, so Marriott is considering a new kiosk where they can swipe a credit card to do just that. Says Jannini: "We wanted something new but not gimmicky."

Cracking Markets

Breaking into a new market is a classic path to growth. But how do you infiltrate an industry about which you know next to nothing? For General Electric Co., ethnography was the answer. GE was already selling plastic materials to makers of cell phones and car parts. But executives wanted to get into the plastic-fiber business, which provides material for higher-value, higher-margin products such as fire-retardant jackets and bulletproof vests. So two years ago, GE Plastics Marketing Operations Manager Dominic McMahon hired Jump Associates. Says

McMahon: "We couldn't go to someone in the fiber world and say: 'Please tell us how to take your business.'"

GE discovered it was approaching its bid to break into the fibers biz all wrong: Instead of cheap commodities, customers want help developing advanced materials

In fact, it took many months to persuade a few manufacturers to participate in the study. They cooperated only because they figured GE would someday provide them with materials that would help their businesses. "The idea that GE could become a supplier to the industry was hugely exciting," says Jump researcher Lauren Osofsky. Customers refused to be videotaped, but they agreed to be tape-recorded. For a few months, GE execs and researchers from Jump interviewed presidents, managers, and engineers at textile makers, touring their offices and photographing their plants. An engineer told Jump he pulled off the highway one day to collect a bunch of milkweed so he could take it home and run it through a fiber-processing machine he keeps in his garage just to see what would happen. "It told us these people like to get their hands dirty," says Osofsky.

The yearlong study produced one profound insight that led GE to pull a strategic U-turn. GE thought the fibers industry was a commodity business focused on quickly obtaining the cheapest materials. What it found instead was an artisanal industry with customers who want to collaborate from the earliest stages to develop high-performance materials. As a result, GE now shares prototypes with customers. And instead of currying favor with executives, it works closely with engineers to solve technical problems. "That was a breakthrough and a huge opportunity," says McMahon. Before, GE was having a hard time even

getting meetings. Now, says McMahon, "we were suddenly welcomed wherever we went."

Transforming a Culture

For big corporations that don't market directly to consumers, ethnography has a singular appeal. This is especially true of Intel, which is facing tough competition from rival Advanced Micro Devices Inc. and believes it badly needs to branch out beyond its core chipmaking business. Since taking over a year ago, CEO Otellini has started to turn Intel into a company that is much more focused on consumer products: entertainment systems for the home; handheld computers for doctors; cheap, rugged PCs for emerging markets. Getting those gadgets right, Intel has concluded, requires closer relationships with customers. That means bringing in ethnographers at the highest levels of management.

INTEL has an ethnographer heading research for its new emerging-markets unit, with development centers in Bangalore, Cairo, São Paulo, and Shanghai

Intel has used them since the early 1990s. But it wasn't until the late '90s that their work began to influence the company's direction. One of the first breakthroughs came in 1997 when two Intel anthropologists, Tony Salvador and John Sherry, launched a project called "Anywhere at Work." The study took them to Alaska's Bristol Bay, where they realized that fishermen could use wireless technology to transmit the tally of their daily catch directly to the Alaska Fish & Game Dept. That observation, and others like it, helped persuade Intel to put its brainpower behind mobile computing and, eventually, into its popular wireless Centrino mobile technology.

Now, Salvador & Co. are studying the elderly to see how Intel can provide medical technology for the coming wave of retiring boomers, including a device to track and help ensure that patients take their meds. And, of course, Intel ethnographers helped devise the $500 Community India PC, which could turn into a big seller as hundreds of millions of rural Indians access the Web.

J. Wilton L. Agatstein Jr., who runs Intel's new emerging-markets unit, knows it's crucial to figure out the unique needs and aspirations of different cultures. That's why he hired Salvador to head research for the whole group. The pair have created a network of "platform-definition centers" in Bangalore, Cairo, São Paulo, and Shanghai. Agatstein describes the facilities—staffed by local engineers, designers, and marketers—as highly tuned antennae to help define and develop products for local markets. Agatstein is such a fervent believer in ethnography that he often tags along with Salvador on field trips: "He has taught me to look in ways I've never looked before."

Timothy deWaal Malefyt

Title
BBDO's Director for Cultural Discovery

Education
PhD in anthropology from Brown University

Research
Drawing on a network of anthropologists, Malefyt discovered that teens use e-mail for serious communication, instant messaging for informal chats, and text messaging to reach people they don't want to talk to. BBDO is talking with Frito-Lay and Campbell Soup about using this research to help them craft new marketing campaigns.

Not everyone at Intel shares their enthusiasm. This, after all, is a company that was founded and long run by data-driven engineers. Recently, Genevieve Bell, an ethnographer at Intel's Digital Home unit, asked engineers to identify experiences to categorize various technologies. Movies, music, and games were placed under the Escape rubric. Health and wellness were put in the Life & Spirituality basket.

The exercise elicited grumbles from a few Intel traditionalists. Says division chief Don McDonald: "We've had people say: 'Life and spirituality? What the !@#& are you talking about?'" But with anthropologists in ascendance, engineers—and everyone else—had better get used to it.

–With **Cliff Edwards,** San Mateo, Calif.

Team Spirit

Teamwork creates brands that change categories and improve lives.

ED BURGHARD AND LISA MACKAY

Just weeks before a new product was scheduled to hit test-market shelves, a team of Procter & Gamble (P&G) Feminine Care employees were gathered in a conference room, rethinking a critical element of their launch strategy.

This wasn't just any new product launch: It was the first new product in its category in more than 20 years. And this wasn't any marketing strategy team: It was a cross-functional team representing every organization that helped get the product to that point, including research and development, product safety and regulatory affairs, product and package design, market research, and, of course, brand management.

The challenge before the team was that the product's packaging, which was ready for production, wouldn't stand out from the competition the way every other aspect of the product would. The team debated the pros and cons and then made a unanimous decision: Rework the packaging fast and get it on the store shelves in a month or less.

Looking back, P&G's Tampax Pearl steering team describes that decision as "a revelation." Not only did it come to represent everything that was unique about the product, but it also symbolized how far the team had come in thinking and acting with a shared vision while developing and marketing one of the most successful new products in feminine care history.

The Tampax Pearl team is just one example. Across P&G, marketing, R&D (research and development), and other functions are collaborating in new ways to achieve the company's purpose, which is to provide products and services of superior quality and value that improve the lives of the world's consumers.

Principles of Teamwork

While every P&G organization approaches teamwork and collaboration a little differently, the Tampax Pearl example and the recent launches of several new pharmaceutical products showcase five important principles of successful teamwork:

1. Build the team before you build the product.
2. Balance product performance with consumer needs.
3. Innovation is not just for R&D.
4. Marketing isn't just for marketers.
5. Replicate success.

Build teams before products. The feminine care category is not known for innovation. In fact, it was this challenge that brought the Tampax Pearl team together in the first place. At the earliest stages of product development, R&D recognized the need for consumer insights that marketing could bring to the table. The goal was to develop the first tampon that meets both the functional and emotional needs of target consumers. The team also brought its understanding of safety and regulatory requirements into the product development efforts early, especially in light of health concerns associated with highly absorbent tampons that had been marketed in the early 1980s.

For P&G Pharmaceuticals, the need to incorporate marketing knowledge early in the product development cycle is simply a matter of return on investment (ROI). P&G Pharmaceuticals is a relatively new P&G organization, created with the acquisition of Norwich Eaton Pharmaceuticals Inc. in 1982. In its first few years, P&G Pharmaceuticals was driven by the need to build a strong research pipeline for compounds that showed promise of delivering important health outcomes to improve consumers' lives. The role of marketing in those early days was primarily focused on maximizing the success of Norwich Eaton's in-market brands and promising new drugs in development, such as Didronel, a prescription therapy for preventing and treating postmenopausal osteoporosis. Marketing's involvement in early stage drug development was limited to participation in quarterly review meetings with R&D management.

In one such quarterly review meeting, a team of P&G experts and physicians was reviewing the criteria of a promising new drug. Tom Finn, a P&G marketer who is now vice president of Worldwide Strategic Planning for P&G Pharmaceuticals, asked the team to rank the criteria in terms of which were most important to physicians who would prescribe such a product. His challenge sparked debate and uncovered the need to incorporate physician and consumer insights earlier in the process.

Balance performance with needs. Today, each potential new P&G pharmaceutical product must plug into a simple equation to move to the next stage of development: *consumer success = technical viability + consumer need*. Behind this equation is a formal process to assess the technical and commercial risk of a compound in development. This is where R&D and marketing really come together.

Areas for technical risk include efficacy, safety, side effects, dosage form, and amount. To understand consumer need, it's important to assess current consumer habits and practices, competitive activities and claims, and physicians' points of view. The next step is to reapply these criteria and reevaluate the potential for success or failure at each major stage in a new drug's development.

The key to success in this business is identifying the potential for failure earlier in the process—before the company has invested heavily.

To ensure it has the information needed to evaluate the potential for consumer success at the earliest stages of a drug's development, the team has established a team of marketers who are responsible for understanding how fledgling pharmaceutical products might meet the needs of consumers 10 or more years out. They have a very deep knowledge of the healthcare and pharmaceutical market and strong relationships with physicians. They help point out which technologies to study for future commercialization, and they identify the product claims that are critical to consumer acceptance.

These marketers work hand in hand with R&D to guide product development toward the most fertile consumer opportunities. Because R&D's goal is to develop drugs that will ultimately become P&G products, marketing guidance is crucial to ensure time and energy is being invested in the best projects.

On average, a new drug takes 10 to 12 years to develop from a core technology to a branded and packaged pharmaceutical product. Tufts University estimates that it costs $800 million to get a drug to market. Anyone in the pharmaceutical industry will tell you that more than 80% of all new drug compounds fail at some point during that lengthy gestation process. The key to success in this business is identifying the potential for failure earlier in the process—before the company has invested heavily. At P&G, this is called "failing fast and cheap."

In P&G Pharmaceuticals, the collaboration between marketing and R&D is fostered by a work environment that welcomes the opportunity to learn from bad news. If a potential product is determined to pose too much technical or commercial risk, the team quickly redirects efforts to projects with stronger potential.

Innovation beyond R&D. Collaboration between marketing and R&D sometimes results in more than a successful product. It can redefine a disease or a product category, resulting in significant new advancements for consumers.

The drug Actonel is a perfect example. Introduced in 1999, it was indicated for the treatment and prevention of postmenopausal and glucocorticoid-induced osteoporosis. In the years leading up to Actonel's release, however, P&G's marketing and R&D organizations were working closely together to better understand osteoporosis from the patient's point of view.

In clinical tests for Actonel, R&D learned that individuals who experience an osteoporosis-related fracture are much more likely to experience additional fractures within 12 months. This is called a "fracture cascade," and the science behind it has changed the way physicians treat this disease. Although Actonel was an effective treatment, the drug would not have been successful without insight into current treatment for osteoporosis. Marketing was able to leverage its strong relationship with physicians to help them understand the need for osteoporosis treatment at the earliest signs of a fracture cascade. As a result, roughly six million osteoporosis sufferers globally used Actonel therapy. Based on epidemiological estimates, this translates into saving approximately 5,000 consumer lives and nearly $1 billion in medical costs since the launch of Actonel.

On the Tampax Pearl team, marketing helped drive innovative product changes to every aspect of the product experience that became central to what made that product unique. For example, the Tampax Pearl's award-winning wrapper was designed to meet consumers' needs for an easier and quieter unwrapping experience. The tampon's design and even its fragrance were influenced by marketing and R&D's strong knowledge of the target consumer.

Marketing isn't just for marketers. As soon as early product prototypes were available, the Tampax Pearl team began a series of "Learning Connects" meetings with small groups of consumers. Both the timing and structure of these qualitative research efforts were unique, requiring the full team to participate earlier in the product development process. The technical members of the team reflect on these sessions as the first time they fully understood the impact of emotional needs associated with tampon use. Put simply, it changed the way they viewed the consumer's product experience. This advance research helped marketing and R&D shape a platform for bringing the product to market that would guide the rest of the commercialization process.

Later, when the team decided to scrap initial test-market packaging and start over, they were able to draw from the deep consumer insights they'd experienced together. The result was a package that may be Tampax Pearl's most important marketing tool, and it was not created by a marketing employee. The team's package and device designer led the team effort to create a box that defied category norms by displaying the product through a clear window. Its softer, prettier look was also designed to appeal to the target consumer.

Replicate success. On an average day at P&G, thousands of R&D and marketing professionals are collaborating to bring hundreds of potential new products one step closer to store shelves. Each time a new product is launched creates an opportunity to learn from the process and replicate its success.

P&G Pharmaceuticals, for example, is in the third phase of clinical trials for Intrinsa, a testosterone patch that shows promise in treating low sexual desire in menopausal women. This is a new-to-the-world market that is just beginning to be understood, thanks in part to a dedicated team of marketing and R&D professionals at P&G.

New Teamwork Tradition

Historically at P&G, once a product is developed and ready for consumer launch, marketing takes the lead. In truly collaborative teams, this is no longer the case. When P&G Pharmaceuticals prepares to launch a new drug, the collaboration between R&D and marketing continues to be critical. Together, the team agrees on labeling and other communications claims. Often, marketing will facilitate advance dissemination of R&D's pre-clinical data to begin building excitement in the marketplace. Marketing is also responsible for preparing P&G's market development organizations in key geographies to support a new product. This step requires a significant transfer of marketing and R&D knowledge to generate internal enthusiasm and momentum for the new product.

In addition, integrated in with marketing, P&G's External Relations organization leverages relationships with physician groups, professional nursing associations, and thought leaders who can provide crucial review of the safety profile and science behind the new product or drug. This is standard in P&G Pharmaceuticals and P&G Feminine Care and was applied by the Tampax Pearl team. The team sought feedback from a multi-disciplined board of well-respected scientists and health-care professionals before launching Tampax Pearl.

Finally, with input from the entire team, marketing developed and executed a strategic plan, often including television advertising, direct marketing, and public relations activities. The team reconvened at specific intervals to provide ongoing product guidance.

Around the world, more and more P&G teams are collaborating to ensure the success of the company's nearly 300 brands. As this collaboration becomes a way of life throughout the company, P&G will continue to build upon these principles of teamwork and streamline the process for bringing new brands to market that improve consumers' lives.

ED BURGHARD is marketing director and Harley Procter marketer with The Procter & Gamble Co. He may be reached at burghard.em@pg.com. **LISA MACKAY** is in product development with The Procter & Gamble Co. She may be reached at mackay.la@pg.com.

Eight Tips Offer Best Practices for Online MR

RICHARD KOTTLER

"You don't need a weatherman to know which way the wind blows."—Bob Dylan, 1965

Four decades ago, Bob Dylan's lyric was a call for dynamic individual thought. Today, it can be interpreted more literally: You really don't need a weatherman, you just need a Web browser. As we progress through the second decade of the Internet Age, the sheer ubiquity of the Internet as a consumer and business communications medium is absolute, and it is providing a dynamic means to get visibility into your customers' often-changing thoughts.

It has also altered the way we market and are marketed to, primarily by providing that same ubiquitous access to information and communication for marketers. In 2005, companies will spend more than $1.1 billion on online market research, a 16% increase over 2004, according to *Inside Research*.

The advantages of online research are self-evident: There's no need for data entry or interviews, and responses are collected automatically, saving time and money while eliminating coding errors and interviewer bias. Also, respondents may feel more comfortable in answering sensitive questions with their anonymity ensured.

With the increasing prevalence of online research, a handful of tips can begin to outline the best practices for maximizing the efficacy of conducting surveys via the Internet. Some of the tips outlined in this article, such as suggestions on planning, are equally relevant to offline and online research. Others are specific to the online realm.

No. 1: Planning—Real-World Common Sense for the Online Realm

If you are planning an online survey, do you know why you and your organization want to conduct it? If so, use these reasons to develop your survey's mission. Once developed, the mission should drive everything throughout the survey process to make sure that every action taken supports it. If you're uncertain as to why you are conducting your survey, or if your answer is, "We do it every year," dig deeper for the real reason before you begin plotting steps toward implementation. Once your survey is drafted, test it on a sample audience and include questions that elicit feedback on how the survey can be improved before it is put into play. And make certain your sample size maps to your budget and time constraints and the type of analysis to be conducted.

No. 2: Understand Your Population

Clearly, the population influences the entire research process—methodology, layout, content, incentives; everything is driven by their influence. The inability to properly define your population has serious ramifications.

If you're uncertain as to why you are conducting your survey, dig deeper for the real reason before plotting steps toward implementation.

No. 3: Use the Correct Medium to Contact Participants

Researchers can use a variety of media to invite participants to take part in online surveys, such as e-mail, Web links and popups:

- E-mail notifications work best for a well-defined audience, and a well-written missive provides a cost-effective means of reaching existing customers and prospects.
- Web links provide an easy means to elicit general feedback from Web site visitors. However, it is more difficult to target particular respondent profiles using Web links.
- Pop-ups have fallen out of favor, particularly as federal and state legislation are limiting such windows when they are triggered by adware and spyware. Broad consumer dissatisfaction, coupled with free blockers from

online properties such as Google and Yahoo!, has led to a veritable pop-up rebellion.

No. 4: Keep it Simple

Creating a short survey to answer a few questions is easy . . . and it's easy to create a long survey to answer many questions. The challenge is finding the balance between survey length and depth of questions and answers. The holy grail is the short survey that's long on answers. Here are some tips to make that happen:

- Keep questions and answer lists short and to the point.
- Use pre-existing questions when possible (the tried and true).
- Avoid using double negatives.
- Avoid double-barreled questions.
- Avoid leading questions.
- Avoid using loaded questions.
- Avoid vague quantifiers such as "few," "many" or "usually."
- Don't assume knowledge about specific topics or issues.
- Consider the location of open-ended questions.
- Remember the audience for each particular question, not just the overall survey.
- Always offer a "prefer not to answer" on sensitive questions and topics.
- Pretest whenever possible.
- Get feedback early in the process.

No. 5: Set Expectations—Then Reset Them

The top two respondents' questions are "How long will this take?" and "What will I get for doing this?" We'll answer the first question here and the second in No. 8.

- Briefly state the purpose of the survey and how long it should take to complete.
- Make sure the length of the survey is appropriate for your audience and purpose.
- Let your respondents know their progress throughout the survey using a bar or percentage section.

No. 6: Utilize the Power of Open-Ended Questions

Traditionally, researchers think of closed-ended questions when drafting a survey, meaning you provide response choices for participants. Traditionally, they provide two major benefits: They're easy for respondents to answer, and they're easier for surveyors to tabulate. However, they do limit the breadth of responses to predefined answers.

Now, new text mining technologies are emerging that make it possible to harvest data and knowledge from open-ended questions by exploring a greater breadth of respondent attitudes and preferences.

There are two types of open-ended questions: those with a predetermined set of answers and those with a nearly infinite range of potential answers. For example, "Which soft drinks have you enjoyed in the past month?" allows the respondent to answer the question without supplying a list, yet there are only a certain number of beverages on the market. However, "Are there additional features you'd like to see in our products?" will generate comments that are not as quickly classified as a simple list might be. However, it may uncover views or preferences that were heretofore unimagined.

Place open-ended questions at the end, as it gives you greater flexibility and more room to record verbatim responses. At the same time, be certain not to overuse open-ended questions. They do take more thought and time from the respondent and a slew of early open-ended questions may cause your respondent to quit.

No. 7: Monitor the Field

Be prepared to make changes, if necessary. Monitor for the following:

- If the completion rate is low, why?
- Is there a pattern to respondent dropout?
- Have the respondents been appropriately screened?
- If the survey is media-intensive, have you screened for connection speed?
- Is the survey taking longer than stated?

Offer respondents a chance to rate their survey experience in a closed- and open-ended question.

No. 8: Make It Worth Their While

Offering an incentive helps motivate people to take part in your survey. When choosing incentives, though, think about how these might influence the types of participants they could attract, or ultimately, deter. No one wants a cadre of survey respondents who are the online equivalent of the trade show swindlers who load up on shopping bags full of free vendor T-shirts, pins and hats, with no intention of becoming a customer any time soon. At the same time, it's important to match the relative value of an incentive to the effort required to complete the survey.

With the Internet, time is on your side. Data from a Web survey can be collected in a few days or a few weeks, while a survey via the mail adds at least a month to the process. By using online surveys, you'll save on postage, printing and wages for interviewers, and minimize the costs of data entry and data cleansing.

Ultimately, the Internet, if used properly, can provide the quickest path to valuable insight into your customers' minds.

RICHARD KOTTLER, based in the London office, is vice president of survey applications product management for SPSS Inc., a Chicago-based data analysis software provider.

A New Age for the Ad Biz

Marketers who once focused on youth are trying to entice the graying baby boom set.

JONATHAN PETERSON

Wailing guitars and psychedelic lava lamps were never the props for selling mutual funds. Youth-obsessed cosmetics vendors rarely featured makeup for women over 50, much less hyped that set's sex appeal.

And few ski resort operators dreamed of a day when they'd be courting middle-aged speedsters with gentler slopes and apres-ski wine tastings in the lodge.

Then again, the baby boom generation never got old before.

Across American industry, companies that traditionally ignored people over 40 are now actively seeking their business. Food makers are discovering gold in empty-nest households. Fitness salons and clothing retailers are targeting middle-aged women. A Toyota ad tells parents that life begins anew once they drop off their kids at college.

"All of a sudden corporate America is waking up to what's going on," said David Wolfe, a prominent marketing consultant and author who follows generational themes in advertising.

AARP, the advocacy group for people 50 and up, said it posted a 21% increase in advertising revenue for its AARP magazine for the first three months of the year, compared with an industry average of 0.4%. Among its new advertisers are cosmetics companies, including L'Oreal, Lancome, Vital Radiance and Aveeno.

"A couple years ago we had nobody advertising beauty products in the magazine," said Jim Fishman, group publisher for AARP publications.

Business, of course, has always been interested in baby boomers, the 78 million Americans born between 1946 and 1964. As children, boomers—the largest swath of the population—were the market for hula hoops and Hot Wheels. As adult yuppies, they snapped up BMWs and big-screen TVs.

What's different now is that the boomers are reaching an age at which the marketing world likes to write people off. The oldest boomers turned 60 in January. About half are now over 50.

In the long-held view of Madison Avenue, aging consumers are stuck in their habits, don't switch products and shy away from new experiences.

The boomer generation, as it has throughout its history, is changing the equation. They are healthier and more affluent than their predecessors. Many boomers cling to the view that they are still youthful. They have little loyalty to products, experts maintain, and thus are better targets for ad pitches.

Even in television, well-known for worshiping the 18-to-49 age group, there are signs of changing attitudes.

TV Land, the cable network that telecasts reruns of "The Brady Bunch," "Leave It to Beaver" and other shows boomers grew up with, has been adding original content aimed at expanding within that demographic base. This year, it plans a series of specials on the baby boom generation.

A 2005 reality show, "Chasing Farrah," focused on the daily life of Farrah Fawcett, "the ultimate boomer pin-up," in the words of TV Land President Larry W. Jones.

"More and more marketers are coming around to the fact that this is the biggest generation on Earth," Jones said. "They've got a ton of money and a ton of time. Why don't we target them?"

Few areas of American culture link youth and beauty more completely than cosmetics. Yet in January, Revlon Inc. introduced its first new brand in about five years—the Vital Radiance line aimed at women who have reached 50.

Notably, the products were not designed as an elixir against aging but to enhance beauty at a later stage of life. For example, the cosmetics contain more pigment to compensate for a loss of color in older skin. The packages have easy-to-read type. TV ads feature two female pals who do not conceal emerging wrinkles and graying hair.

Although the company won't give out numbers, some in the industry believe Revlon is hoping for Vital Radiance sales to top $100 million. Women over 45 buy more than half of the cosmetics sold by mass retailers, according to market research firm ACNielsen Co.

"It's a very important launch for the company," said Michele Johnson, senior vice president of marketing for Vital Radiance.

Such an initiative, she said, is "something you might see every five years, in terms of an entirely new brand."

Gap Inc., owner of the Gap, Banana Republic and Old Navy apparel chains, is also targeting boomer women, a group that may feel out of place in teenage-oriented mall stores that emphasize low-slung jeans and skimpy T-shirts.

To win them over, Gap launched in August a retail brand called Forth & Towne, with five stores in Chicago and New York. It plans about 10 more this year, in Los Angeles, San Francisco, San Jose and other cities.

"If you're us, you're looking at this fastest-growing demographic," said Gary Muto, president of Forth & Towne. "It spends the most on apparel, and we have very little market share over 35. Why wouldn't you go after it?"

In the new thinking, later adulthood can be a time of fun and self-indulgence. Consider the Toyota ad that features a young man in the foreground, standing outdoors on a college campus surrounded by his worldly possessions. In the background is the Toyota Highlander used by his parents to drive him there.

"5:15 P.M. Dropping the kid off at college," the text declares. "5:17 P.M. What kid?"

There are no authoritative data showing how marketing dollars are divided among age groups, according to ACNielsen. But a recent conference on marketing to boomers, sponsored by advertising agency J. Walter Thompson, was packed to standing room. Companies in the auto industry and other fields that historically have been aloof to aging consumers were well represented.

"Everybody all of a sudden feels like they need to get a boomer strategy," said Lori Bitter, a partner at the agency's mature market group.

Baby boomers have 'a ton of money and ton of time. Why don't we target them?'

Larry W. Jones, president of the TV Land network

Ski areas, having seen the data showing that 31% of skiers are over 45, are smoothing more slopes to make them friendlier to aging knees as well as putting on wine tastings and other events to win a mature crowd.

"These people represent a large portion of our business and a very important part of our business," said Christine Horvath of Squaw Valley USA.

Nowhere is the contest for boomer cash more spirited than in the field of money management, where firms are chasing an estimated bonanza of $30 trillion as boomers retire from their jobs and look to transfer their 401(k) nest eggs and other savings into new investments.

On top of that, a giant intergenerational transfer of wealth is underway. Boomers are in the process of inheriting $8 trillion as their parents pass away, according to Paul G. Schervish, director of the Center on Wealth and Philanthropy at Boston College.

For investment companies, "the window of opportunity is now," said Salim Ramji, an analyst with consulting firm McKinsey & Co.

Not long ago, ads for investment firms featured graying actors in formal, wood-paneled offices. To reach the new generation of retirees and near-retirees, advertisers are channeling Woodstock and other symbols of the bygone 1960s.

After American Express Co. spun off its financial advisory business into Ameriprise Financial Inc. last year, the new firm aired ads showcasing hippies, psychedelic vans, outdoor festivals, and guitars.

In one spot, a guy is shown as a long-haired youth and later as a graying adult—still wailing on the electric guitar.

Some accuse Ameriprise of pandering, but marketing expert Brent Green says the company is simply trying to show that it knows its customer base.

"The deeper message is that Ameriprise understands you as an aging baby boomer, that Ameriprise gets it," said Green, author of "Marketing to Leading-Edge Baby Boomers." "It's that Ameriprise knows where you're coming from."

A growing number of firms are betting that boomers will experience old age as a vital, extended period, transforming the prevailing view of life's later years—just as boomers left their imprint on America's visions of childhood, adolescence and adulthood.

This notion of life as a series of fresh chapters animates commercials for Fidelity Investments. One ad chronicles the life of Paul McCartney through his phases as a Beatle, a member of Wings, a poet and a father.

Said Fidelity marketing executive Claire Huang: "He fit perfectly our model that you don't really retire—you just keep doing something new."

JONATHAN PETERSON, *Los Angeles Times*, June 4, 2006.

The Halo Effect

Christian Consumers Are a Bloc That Matters to All Marketers

MICHAEL FIELDING

Politics. Sex. Religion.

Classic dinner-talk taboos, every one, although marketers for all kinds of products and services have largely capitalized on them—religion being a notable exception. For years it was a risk: "It's like being behind a political party," says Irene Dickey, lecturer in management and marketing at the School of Business Administration at the University of Dayton in Ohio. "Businesses just didn't go there."

Yet the United States has been getting religion. It was the talk of the presidential political campaign, enrollment in religiously based colleges is soaring, and some elements of religious pop culture, such as the ersatz rock group Creed and the "Left Behind" fiction series, have found fans among those who don't necessarily believe.

And some mainstream marketers have discovered an entrée to Christians' life style, in particular, that offers many earthly rewards. Major retailers, consumer products companies and marketing consultants have found that through Scriptures and sponsorship, viral marketing and targeting the right media, they can tap the secular benefits of the born-again Christian community. Those benefits include spending power, education, loyal buying habits—and a vocal culture that can spread good news far and wide, or trash an insincere company's empty efforts.

While it has yet to reach the status of a major targeted segment, the born-again Christian market has turned the heads of a few big-name companies, from Target to Disney.

"(Most) national brands have not targeted the segment because they don't understand it," posits Jeff Lambert, managing partner of 6-year-old public relations firm Lambert, Edwards & Associates Inc., based in Grand Rapids, Mich.

Born-again Christians are generally defined as those who follow literal interpretations of the Bible and acknowledge being born again through religious conversion. Theirs is among the fastest growing religious affiliations in the United States. (The born-again Christian community includes a subset, evangelicals, who generally believe that they have a personal responsibility to share their religious beliefs about Christ with

Christian Characteristics

32%
say they drank an alcoholic beverage in the last month

74%
of evangelicals are white and married

33%
are baby boomers

54%
live in the South

36%
of born-agains have volunteered to help with their church in the past week, compared with 24% of average adults

non-Christians. Although they are not the same—many born-again Christians are not evangelicals—the terms often are used interchangeably.)

According to Ventura, Calif.-based independent market research company Barna Research Group, about 72 million of the 235 million Christians in the United States, or 30.6%, say they are born-again. Some 14 million of that group, or 19.4%, consider themselves evangelical.

"(God and religion are) a part of their daily activities," Dickey says. "Their interests and opinions are often linked with their religion."

If any time is the right time to take a marketing message to the born-again segment, it is now.

"Religious Congregations and Membership," a 2000 study by the Nashville, Tenn.-based Glenmary Research Center, found that among the fastest-growing church denominations in America are many conservative Christian churches (numbering more than 100 evangelical denominations), some of which grew more than 20% over the 10-year period beginning in 1990, when the center conducted a previous survey. That surpassed the 16.2% growth rate of members of the Roman Catholic faith, the nation's largest denomination.

By comparison, more mainline Protestant denominations experienced some of the slowest growth rates, ranging from a high of 10.2% for the North American Baptist Conference for the decade to a drop of −51.4% among independent congregational churches not affiliated with the National Association of Congregational Christian Churches. The Jewish faith overall grew by 2.7%.

A marketer's message may be conveyed to born-again Christians in several ways—some inexpensive, some insightful.

First, a marketer may turn to the Scriptures. "If the company has a Christian founder or philosophy, it can communicate easily through Scriptures on its packaging," says John Nardini, vice president of marketing at Wayland, Mich.-based Denali Flavors. "It's really subtle, but Christians notice things like that."

While Denali is a company that follows Christian values, it does not play that fact up on its packaging, but other national companies do. Consider *Woman's Day* magazine, published by Hachette Filipacchi Media U.S. Inc.: A biblical verse runs along the top of the table of contents page in each issue. Recently, "Psalm 100: 5" greeted readers before leading them to stories about health and decorating.

Remember, though, that for born-again Christians, their religion is their life. They'll notice an empty marketing message. "With religion, it's a level higher than whether you like the Mets or whether you like the Yankees," warns Jonathan Jaffe, owner of Westfield, N.J.-based Jaffe Communications, a 3-year-old public relations consulting firm whose clients include a company catering to Christian consumers.

A separate step would be to consider sponsorship. A company could sponsor an event, as Target Corp. did in 2004, when the Minneapolis-based retailer sponsored a portion of a 2004–05 tour by Christian musical group the Newsboys. The retailer used in store positioning, promotion through local media outlets and the Newsboys' own Internet site. Separately, for more than two decades Walt Disney Co. has sponsored the "Night of Joy" at its Walt Disney World resort in Florida, featuring Christian music.

On a smaller scale, "Look beyond (big-scale ideas) to partner with an organization that reaches that audience," Lambert says, suggesting that prison ministries and youth organizations are ripe for sponsorship.

Indeed, Christian groups tend to be tremendously well organized at the grassroots level, which allows for effective and affordable marketing to small, highly involved groups of consumers.

Sponsorship also has a high ROI potential. "It is a terrific use of a company's marketing dollars," says Julie Fairchild, cofounder of Dallas-based public relations/marketing firm Lovell-Fairchild Communications, who considers herself a born-again Christian. At a 2004 Christian festival in Atlanta, for example, more than 100,000 attendees converged on downtown Atlanta

for several days—an infectious viral marketing opportunity, Fairchild points out.

For PR and advertising purposes, consider using Christian media as a vehicle for the marketing message. The right media don't even have to be particularly Christian: Jaffe alerts religion writers in the general media both locally and nationally of product updates by his clients that cater to Christian consumers.

'Grassroots marketing campaigns are the most effective because (Christian consumers) are connected. They really appreciate a company or product that does pay attention to their interests.'

Elsewhere, Denali owns lines of sub-branded premium ice creams and distributes them regionally. Among its products is Moose Tracks ice cream, which is produced by 85 dairies and distributed across the United States. The company has captured a solid Christian market by brokering on-air promotions for Moose Tracks with Christian radio stations. "Christian radio stations are personal fans of the ice cream, so they give it away," Nardini explains. "It's not 'Christian' ice cream, though. It's a national brand."

Nardini's home-run pitch to Moose Tracks' Christian consumers is that the company returns part of its profits to Christian causes.

As Jaffe says, "One of the biggest struggles of faith-based organizations is raising the money. When a for-profit company comes to them and says, 'We're willing to give you X amount of money,' that puts it at a higher level."

Finally, don't underestimate the impact of word-of mouth marketing. "Marketing to a Christian audience is no different from marketing to any other audience. It's just that they exercise choice based on a value system," Fairchild explains. "Grassroots marketing campaigns are the most effective because (Christian consumers) are connected, and they really appreciate a company or product that does pay attention to their interests. When they find something that lines up with that, they pass it along."

For example, Wal-Mart Stores Inc.'s charitable giving programs are secular and aimed at the local level. The company donates to religious organizations, among other groups, but only for programs that benefit the community in general. Still, in recent years, the stores have carried a broader selection of Christian books while continuing to refuse to carry what many conservative Christians consider offensive magazines. (Try finding laddie mags such as *Stuff*, *FHM* and *Maxim* on the shelves at the world's largest retailer.) So while Wal-Mart can disassociate itself from religious affiliation, company officials can boast that they're taking a moral stand. The word gets out—and viral marketing takes over.

Nardini touts the efficiencies of marketing to large numbers of consumers during gatherings of born-again Christians. Women of Faith and Promise Keepers confabs may draw up to

30,000 people per event, and the Billy Graham Crusades continue to fill stadiums nightly with three- and four-night stands.

And viral marketing has been a boon for One Christian Voice, one of Jaffe's clients, a Vancouver, Wash.-based long-distance telephone company. It has gained customers in 48 states in its first year of business.

'If they're interested in the values that are behind a company, they tend to stick with that company.'

A bonus for marketers: Born-again Christians are fiercely loyal once they've been effectively courted. "If you believe in something as fundamental (as religion), it pervades every single part of (your life)," Nardini says. "If there is a brand that supports those causes, they're going to support that 100%."

What marketers miss about Christians is that while they do all the things everyone else does, they're more passionate about certain things, Fairchild says. "If they're interested in the values that are behind a company, they tend to stick with that company," she says. "The values they're looking for are what everyone desires. It's peace and warmth and togetherness."

Finding these 72 million desirable consumers isn't difficult, marketers say.

- According to Barna:
  —just 32% of Christians say they drank an alcoholic beverage in the last month;
  —74% of evangelicals are white and married;
  —33% are baby boomers;
  —54% live in the South; and
  —36% of born-agains have volunteered to help with their church in the past week, compared with 24% of average adults.
- Born-again Christians are highly educated and intelligent. According to Barna, 29% of evangelical Christians have a college degree. That's higher than the national average of 26%. Furthermore, author Naomi Schaefer Riley reports in her latest book, *God on the Quad,* that enrollment at the 100 schools of the Council for Christian Colleges & Universities jumped 60% between 1990 and 2002—as attendance at colleges not affiliated with a religion remained flat.

- With the average lifetime cost to raise a child hovering above $200,000, and a marked preference for children among Christian couples, marketers infer there's no lack of spending power.
- Raleigh, N.C.-based construction consultancy FMI Corp. estimates the value of the religious building market at more than $8 billion, and expects it to grow 3.9% in 2005. That's much smaller than the $62.7 billion commercial building market or the $566 billion residential building market—but church construction is driven by individual giving, unlike other industry segments, so the theory is that booming church construction indicates Christian consumers with plenty of resources.

Prominent Christians include preacher Billy Graham, who continues to be listed as one of the 10 most admired men in the world, according to Gallup Polls; Rick Warren, author of *The Purpose Driven Life,* which has topped the *The New York Times* Bestseller list for nonfiction for nearly two years straight; and President Bush, whose wizard strategist Karl Rove stimulated a massive turnout among Christian voters to secure a second term for Bush in the 2004 general election. Speaker of the House Dennis Hastert, a Republican from Illinois, is a graduate of Wheaton College, an evangelical Christian school in Wheaton, Ill.

Yet despite their attractive demographics, marketers say, Christian consumers are often thought to be less discerning than others shoppers.

Wrong, Lambert says: "Don't assume the Christian consumer is less (savvy) than any other consumer. They're more educated than most other consumer audiences." Lambert's clients include the Colorado Spring, Colo.-based Christian Booksellers' Association, the world's largest Bible publisher, and Grand Rapids, Mich.-based Family Christian Stores, the nation's largest Christians retailer.

Part of the demystification of the segment is realizing that, just as other niche markets—Hispanics and African-Americans, for example—shop at all kinds of retail stores, so do born-again Christians. "It's about how they shop but also what they don't buy and where they don't want to shop," Lambert adds.

Dickey suggests that it's not difficult to send the right message to born-again Christians in order to raise their awareness of a product. "The elements there are pretty clear: Respect that this is a lifestyle and communicate with them with words and images . . . that are respectful of that target market."

Gen Y Sits on Top of Consumer Food Chain

They're savvy shoppers with money and influence

Jayne O'Donnell

Baby boomers have long been the most important generation to marketers because there are so many and they have so much money. Now, new research shows Generation Y—those born from 1982 to 2000—are showing clout with car, clothing and other retail sales that surpass all previous generations.

Retailing

Online marketing expert Kelly Mooney will release findings at a National Retail Federation conference today showing the 13- to 21-year-olds in the group influence 81% of their families' apparel purchases and 52% of car choices.

Mooney says that at 82 million people, Gen Y is the most influential generation for retailers because it is bigger than the baby boomers and its members have spending power and strong opinions at an earlier age.

Mooney's research into the habits of the teens and young adults, which included interviews and video diaries, shows slow websites, dismissive sales staff and free shipping that takes more than two days will turn them off to a brand.

These young people also either want merchandise that's cheap or elite, and retailers in the middle can get lost, Mooney says.

"They are more demanding and more savvy than they feel they're given credit for," says Mooney, who is speaking at the Shop.org conference in New York. "In some instances, they think they know more than the person selling them something."

Retail and apparel stock analyst Jennifer Black says the research tracks closely with the success of higher-end retailers such as Abercrombie & Fitch and J. Crew and lower-end ones such as Forever 21, which are all popular with young people.

"The moderate segment is getting more squeezed," says Black, president of Jennifer Black & Associates. "Girls want to buy something that's special vs. something that's kind of in the middle."

Black says her 18-year-old son, like a lot of kids his age, will occasionally shop at thrift stores, even though he doesn't have to.

"It's not because they don't have they money but because they want to save the money," Black says.

Mooney, co-author of the book *The Ten Demandments: Rules to Live By in the Age of the Demanding Customer,* studied 14- to 24-year-olds—the subset of Gen Y with the most money— and found a strong need for "instant gratification and immediacy."

These consumers will wait just three seconds for a page to download before they click away, Mooney says. They also process website information five times faster than older generations.

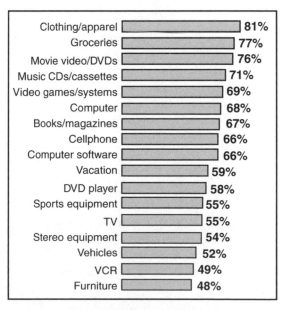

Figure 1 Gen Yers have more voice in purchases New research shows members of Generation Y—people born from 1982 to 2000—have greater say in household purchases. Percentages of children ages 13 to 21 who influence purchases, by category:

Source: Harris Interactive

"They don't distinguish between 'this is the store' and 'this is the website," Mooney says. "They don't have forgiveness that it's just the website.'"

Consumer psychologist Kit Yarrow says it shouldn't be surprising these young consumers have an "equal vote in the look and style of the family."

"Gen Y parents tend to be non-authoritarian and value their friendships with their kids," says Yarrow, a professor at San Francisco's Golden Gate University. "These parents also prize their own youthful, 'kid-like' qualities."

Mooney and her husband know firsthand what enterprising consumers kids can be. Their 7-year-old daughter tried to persuade her father to buy a Toyota Scion after seeing the car and then Googling it. After he told her it wasn't his first choice, she suggested a Porsche.

Gen Y's retail favorites can differ markedly from those of their elders. Jupiter Research surveyed consumers who bought products or services online in the past 12 months and found people ages 18 to 24 favored the websites for Best Buy, Circuit City and eBay more than consumers as a whole. And they were less likely to shop at the Macy's or J.C. Penney websites than other consumers.

They also like products that let them show some individuality.

Kenny Warren, a 20-year-old student at Southern Adventist University in Tennessee and a participant in Mooney's survey, says he got his 1993 Honda Accord in part because the brand had "credibility" but also because Honda makes it easy to accessorize cars. He's lowered the car, put on new rims and wheels and changed the exhaust, among other things. And though he has three computers and a webcam, Warren says he'll shop at thrift stores as long as it "makes me look good."

Not Micky Osterman, a 16-year-old high school student from Columbus, Ohio, and a survey participant. She likes high-end brands. "I want a . . . midnight blue Mustang convertible. I want to buy all my underwear at Victoria's Secret. I want to shop at Polo (and) The Limited. . . . I would love a pair of Dolce & Gabbana sunglasses. And a Coach purse."

You Choose, You Lose

Unrestrained customer choices can derail manufacturing productivity and profitability.

George H. Leon

"Have it your way" began as Burger King's declaration of customer freedom of choice in burger building, but quickly became the mantra of consumer marketing. Now there are a variety of categories that have climbed on the bandwagon. Dell Inc. offers online personal computer (PC) customization, and even humble Carmelite nuns provide online, interactive rosary bead configuration. The theory is that customer choice differentiates the brand, sells more product, and engenders customer loyalty.

But if customer freedom of choice has fully blossomed in consumer marketing, why is it being challenged in certain quarters of the B2B world? Specifically, manufacturers of heavy trucks—which historically have been built to customer specifications—are increasingly narrowing choices. Why do they seem to be moving opposite the rest of the world? Are they risking customer alienation in limiting choices? And how are they getting away with it—even positioning it as a benefit to customers?

Black or Black?

In the pioneering days of the automobile assembly line, the old joke that "a Model T Ford is available in any color, as long as it's black" implied that some degree of choice was sacrificed for the benefits of inexpensive mass production. More subtly and perhaps more importantly, the joke implied that customers should have a choice of color. Today, customers take for granted free choice of color when purchasing an automobile, whereas other options (such as a sunroof) add to the price. In other words, customer choice motivates customers not only to buy a particular brand, but also to spend more.

Of course, it's no coincidence that none of the available options requires the car to be reengineered. Assembly line production has evolved to where it can accommodate a certain level of customer choice—hence, the blanks on the

Executive Briefing

"Have it your way" quickly became the focus of consumer marketing in a variety of categories. The theory has been that customer choice differentiates the brand and engenders customer loyalty. However, in some segments of the B2B world, unconstrained customer choice translates into manufacturing platform complexity, maintenance of multiple supplier relationships, and higher engineering and development costs.

dashboard for controls of unselected options. One could say that automobile customer choice and production technology are in a state of equilibrium: The degree of customer choice offered is that which is economically supported by the production technology, and no more.

Big Macs. Mass production of fast food came much later than automobile assembly lines, in the 1950s. Initially, only a small variety of products was available, with no real choice of how each was configured; a hamburger was a hamburger. In fact, the uniformity of the customer experience initially served to differentiate McDonald's from the unpredictable mom-and-pop burger joints. It minimized customer risk of disappointment when exploring unknown territory. Later, Burger King tapped the latent customer need for choice when it declared: "Have it your way." Neither a quantum leap in production technology nor new-product development was required to withhold ingredients in burger hand-assembly. Competitors had to get on board, and fastfood production technology advanced to offer ever-increasing customer choice.

PCs. In contrast to the fast food industry, the early years of PC production presented customers with a chaotic environment of choices. In the late 1970s, buyers could decide from an array of architectures, associated processors, memory configurations, and disk-drive formats. It was easy to make a mistake, because software that ran on one brand might not run on another (it usually didn't). And no one knew for sure which standard, if any, would prevail. But as developers migrated to the IBM/MS-DOS standard in the early 1980s, owners of alternative architectures became increasingly marginalized, despite the alleged technological superiority of their machines over the somewhat bland IBM PC. IBM didn't attempt to build the "best" machine; it opted for a relatively plain "vanilla" box with open architecture and an operating system that would become the de facto world standard, accelerating technology adoption across the entire market. Although buyers still can choose from a variety of machine configurations, it's a lot more difficult for them to make a costly mistake than it was 25 years ago.

Dell pioneered customer choice by allowing customers to configure their PCs, but today one just as easily can configure an Apple iMac online: select a care plan and software, add an iPod, pay for the whole package, and have it delivered to his or her doorstep. Both Dell and Apple offer a number of desktop and laptop models, plus additional memory, hard-disk drives, wireless networking, and other configuration choices. Of course, this self-service approach assumes that customers know what will best meet their needs, and probably results in customers sometimes buying too much or too little. Because components essentially are "plug-in" or "bolt-on," the online customer interface nicely fits with the "pick-and-pack" production technology, where no reengineering of the basic product is required.

Rosary beads. Most of the world's 1 billion plus Catholics have at least one set of rosary beads, typically from their first Holy Communion. Although in 1961 there were black beads for boys, white beads for girls, and adult choices limited to wood or glass beads of various colors, today one can visit **www.sistersofcarmel.com** and build a fully customized rosary. More that 17 million combinations are possible online, with further options available by contacting the Carmelite nuns in Colorado Springs, Colo. Like burgers, rosaries are hand-assembled. And like PCs, the components are completely interchangeable, despite significant variations in value. Most importantly, the choices are completely in sync with the production technology, which is relatively primitive compared with the highly sophisticated customer interface.

Mack trucks. Heavy-truck buyers traditionally have been able to specify choice of engine, transmission, axles, tires, and other components. And they can select not only technical specifications (e.g., engine displacement, torque, horsepower, transmission gearing), but also component brands. For example, Freightliner Class 8 diesel trucks are available with a Detroit Diesel, Caterpillar, or Cummins engine, and with an Eaton Fuller, Meritor, or Allison transmission.

In contrast, Volvo Class 8 trucks come with only Volvo engines: the single-hood design of Volvo's top-of-the line

VT 880 melding "the traditional styling you want" with "the fuel-saving aerodynamics you need."

And although "a Mack truck can be spec'ed and customized to meet just about any requirement" (per Mack's Web site), don't ask for a Caterpillar engine. Instead, Mack offers an integrated drive train entirely consisting of Mack components. "Our engines, transmissions, and axles work better because they were designed to work together."

Self-service assumes that customers know what will best meet their needs, and might result in them buying too much or too little.

In fact, the overall trend in the market has been toward narrower choice sets and increasingly vertically integrated products. Even those manufacturers who've traditionally allowed customers to "spec a truck from the ground up" have significantly narrowed brand choices for major components (e.g., engines, transmissions, axles) and altogether eliminated them for minor components, in some cases.

The Nature of Choice

Automobile buyers have never experienced the array of choices traditionally afforded heavy-truck buyers, particularly when it comes to component brand. Don't ask your Toyota dealer for a Camry with a Ford engine or Honda transmission, for example. For wheels and tires, however, customers might have a choice of either standard wheels and tires or upgraded alloy wheels and high-performance tires. These choices increase the car's price and allow the dealer or manufacturer to make more on the sale. Typical "sport package" options that add value to the sale are engineered into the car, but in no way radically alter the design.

The bolt-on principle also applies to most PC configuration choices. For example, the Dell Web site recently offered six sizes of flat-screen and conventional display units (from 15 inches to 20 inches) for its Dimension 3000 PC. It also offered two sizes of hard-disk drive, three memory configurations, and two types of optical drive—but not the brand of these components. Commoditization of components allows manufacturers to get the best prices from suppliers while providing customers choice of technical specifications, but not component brand.

It is the simplicity of the Carmelite sisters' production technology, combined with a sophisticated customer interface, that allows them to present 17 million rosary choices. For a burger, though, pickles and lettuce are default options. No choices are available on how the burger is cooked, and don't even think about altering the 'technical specifications' of the components—asking for Vidalia onions and Jersey tomatoes.

The Value of Choice

In the heavy truck category, the trend toward narrower choices and integrated products is bringing it closer in options to other categories, with choices available in specification, not brand. Indeed, in the medium truck market, integrated products already are much more prevalent.

Truck buyers value choice of component brand primarily for functional reasons, but these reasons are often tinged with emotion. Functionally, customers select particular brands because they meet their technical specification requirements, have particular valued characteristics, and fit into their existing operations. Emotionally, customers might fear that alternative choices won't meet their requirements, doubt that other brands share characteristics of the preferred brand, and feel uncertain that an alternative brand will fit into their operations.

The bottom line is that customers might feel tied to specific brands to meet their technical specification requirements, depending on the demands of their applications. Moreover, even if an equivalent product is available, in terms of technical specifications, a customer might believe that one brand is better-constructed, more durable, easier to service, or simply superior in performance. Obviously, it is in the truck manufacturer's interest to understand how to get customers switching component brand rather than truck brand, and to know when a component switch would constitute a deal breaker (customers would change manufacturers to maintain the choices).

The Cost of Choice

When choices are interchangeable, bolt-on, or even commodity, they have four common elements.

- Customers typically can't pick the brand, and sometimes can't pick the type.
- Customers are offered fairly constrained technical specification choices.
- The options require little or no engineering modifications to the core product.
- In a commodity environment, the manufacturer can apply price pressure to suppliers of largely interchangeable parts and, by implication, maintain relatively simple supplier relationships.

Except for the simplest of components, none of these principles holds in the heavy-truck manufacturing industry. However:

- customers traditionally have been allowed to "spec a truck from the ground up," including choice of component brand.
- technical specifications are far more complex.
- particularly for major components, options might require a substantial amount of engineering effort on the manufacturer's part.

- because of the complexity of the technical specifications and engineering requirements, supplier relationships are far more complicated.

Not surprisingly, customer choice of components is considerably more costly in the truck category. Supply-chain management, inventory control, and contract management are especially complicated by multiple vendor relationships. In a nutshell, customer choice presents an expensive headache for manufacturers: It complicates day-to-day operations, potentially slows product development and launch, and creates uncertainty in forecasting earnings. The answer, of course, is rationalization: consolidation of suppliers, vertical integration of the product, simplified engineering, streamlined supply chain, reduced operations costs, and more certainty in forecasting. Life would be much simpler if manufacturers didn't need to accommodate customer choice. And that's the direction truck manufacturers seem to be taking.

Does this mean that truck manufacturers are increasingly insensitive to customer needs? Not at all. In fact, most would argue that they can better meet customer needs by providing an integrated product, or at least selecting components for customers. In other words, an integrated product—consisting of components that are designed to work together—should be better than a product consisting of different manufacturers' components. But even if the product is not fully integrated (the same brand components), one that's optimally assembled from various components should be better than one assembled from customer-selected components. Unlike the Dell self-service model, the assumption here is that customers might not be the best people to specify a truck.

In addition to improving the product, rationalization can enhance post-sale service and support. With fewer component brands for an organization to manage, technicians can be trained quicker and more thoroughly, service coverage can be more universal, and parts and supplies can be more readily available. The idea is a well-oiled machine of post-sale service and support. From a strictly rational/economic point of view, rationalization should command a price premium, which customers should be able to recover through improved product performance, less downtime, and reduced operating and maintenance costs. But customers must be convinced of the benefits, and possibly compensated for the loss of free choice.

The question, in the minds of customers and manufacturers, is how far can and will rationalization go? How much can customers' choices be narrowed, what will customers require in exchange, and what are the deal breakers?

Mistakes can be made in pricing and positioning rationalization. Insufficient rewards (e.g., price points, warranty terms) for fewer choices can result in share erosion. Conversely, excessive rewards can leave money on the table and substantially offset the financial gains realized through rationalization. So, despite the potential advantages, rationalization is a risky business in which bad decisions can spiral out of control. How can a manufacturer minimize the risks?

Customer Perspective

In an environment of increasingly constrained choices, customers face trade-offs between free choice in specifying a truck, the potential advantages of accepting a rationalized value proposition, and the risks of making changes. Customers might be willing to forgo some choices in exchange for the intrinsic benefits; this willingness probably is contingent on the importance of a particular feature, how well the product will meet their requirements, and the perceived value of the rewards.

The lesson is that when it comes to customer choice, more is not necessarily better.

Ideally, the manufacturer can anticipate and pre-engineer customers' requirements, and appropriately price and position the product. And it's understood that, at least for some customer segments, loss of a particular choice can be a deal breaker. In these instances, the manufacturer must decide between allowing that choice to continue or cutting loose the segment. To do so, the manufacturer must identify the deal breakers and understand customers' requirements, perceptions of benefits value, and willingness to trade choice for those benefits. Without this information, the manufacturer cannot make reasonable decisions about rationalization, and is in grave danger of presenting a suboptimal value proposition.

The manufacturer can get that information through market research. Typically some sort of conjoint design is the best approach toward understanding and quantifying customer trade-offs. When properly conducted, conjoint design not only identifies the deal breakers and informs the optimal configuration of the value proposition, but also estimates the share and revenue impacts of optimal and suboptimal solutions. Some examples of conjoint design guidelines:

- Most traditional discrete-choice conjoint design approaches are not up to the task. All except the smallest owner-operators among truck buyers do not pick a product, but rotate their fleet through a prescribed replacement cycle. Also, despite (or because of) frequent preferences for fleet uniformity, truck buyers tend to try new products a little at a time. To be realistic to customers, the conjoint design must accommodate their intentions to purchase multiple trucks in a given period, and allow them to try assorted value propositions in the exercise.
- Attributes of the conjoint design must not be fixed product features; they must represent realms of choices. Although traditional conjoint designs test

various product features and prices, this conjoint design would need to test various types of choices, prices, and benefits.

- The conjoint design should present customers with a realistic, multi-brand scenario. For example, truck buyers simultaneously consider multiple proposals, so the conjoint design should simultaneously present eight or more branded choices to represent the major suppliers.
- The conjoint design should incorporate and test positioning statements, such as "optimally engineered product," "higher quality and greater reliability," "faster, more responsive servicing," "lower operating costs," and "extended warranty."
- Qualitative research conducted with customers should precede and inform the conjoint design, to ensure identification and proper articulation of the conjoint design attributes.

When More Isn't Better

Examining the current relationships between production technology and customer choice in a category—and identifying emerging business models in the competitive landscape—foretells the challenges players are likely to encounter and offers insights on how to address them. The lesson is that when it comes to customer choice, more is not necessarily better. It's tempting to think that it is, given the ingrained ethos of choice in American culture, and the ease with which customers exercise free choice in the market. But close examination of customer choice, in any category, reveals that it's always constrained; there is no such thing as completely free choice. Of course, production technology will continue to evolve, and car manufacturers might someday offer complete choice of color or even an easy change of color. But that will mean production technology and customer choice have reached a different equilibrium in one corner of one category; it won't signal the advent of completely free choice.

Is completely free choice the ideal? The chaotic market of early personal computing is one free-choice scenario. But another scenario is complete commoditization. For example, if customers want to select not only the capacity of their PC's hard drive, but also the brand, all brands will need to be virtually interchangeable. And to a large degree, they are. But would that be desirable in all categories? The point is, the freer the choice, the more commoditized the elements must be; the production process isn't going to bend. Heavy-truck manufacturers could continue giving customers component brand choice if component suppliers agreed to build their products to the same specifications, eliminating the need for costly engineering by truck builders. But that's unlikely to happen, because component builders would lose their ability to differentiate, which is exactly what has happened with PC components: Although performance specifications might vary, all components essentially are plug-ins.

And what about pickles and lettuce? Today, it's hard to find a mom-and-pop joint that will serve a burger with a big, juicy slice of Jersey tomato. In fast-food establishments, customers can articulate only whether they want a topping—and tomato isn't always a choice. So is it really possible to have something our way? Who knows. Perhaps the demands of the growing "think globally, act locally" customer segment, along with evolving supply-chain technology, someday will enable us to get a Jersey tomato on our burgers. And maybe that's when the Carmelite sisters will open their fast-food restaurant.

GEORGE H. LEON is vice president of the technology practice at National Analysts, a market research and consulting firm in Philadelphia. He may reached at gleon@nationalanalysts.com.

From *Marketing Management,* January/February 2006, pp. 40, 42–45. Copyright © 2006 by American Marketing Association. Reprinted by permission.

Marketing: Consumers in the Mist

For real insights into your clients, hire an anthropologist

ALISON WELLNER

The way Ellen Moore saw it, the natives were getting restless. A professional ethnographer with 15 years experience, Moore was observing the negotiation rituals among a group native to the Eastern Seaboard of the United States. Most of the members were seated on humble and, judging by their pained expressions, rather uncomfortable seats. Only two males had secured more luxurious accommodations. This, Moore noted, created much tension in the room.

When one of these alpha males left to get some water, a competitor snatched his coveted position. When the first male returned, he was furious and spent the rest of the gathering on his feet. "He moves around a lot," Moore scribbled in her notebook. "His arms are crossed over his chest—he looks bored and irritated."

Moore wasn't in an exotic locale, observing a primitive tribe—that is, unless you consider the white-collar employees of a large federal government agency attending a meeting to be exotic. She was in a conference room at the Pier 5 Hotel, a boutique hotel in Baltimore's Inner Harbor. And she delivered her observations not to a conference of academics, but to Ken Conklin, general manager of the Pier 5 and two other hotels, who had hired Moore and another anthropologist to conduct a comprehensive ethnographic study of his guests.

Armed with their findings, Conklin knew what he needed to do: Order new chairs. That small change, as well as dozens of others, has helped bring about a 23% rise in meeting business since last spring. "Sometimes you don't want to hear what you need to hear," says the 45-year-old hotelier. "Ethnographic research opens up your eyes."

If the term *ethnographic research* conjures up sepia-tinged images from your Anthropology 101 textbook, you're on the right track. Look it up in an encyclopedia and you'll probably find a picture of its best-known practitioner, Margaret Mead, famous for her groundbreaking research among the people of Samoa. Traditionally, ethnographers have traveled to the world's distant corners seeking answers to some pretty big questions: What is society? What is culture? What do we, the members of the human family, share?

Today, of course, unknown primitive cultures are pretty scarce, and academic jobs are even scarcer. So more ethnographers are heading into boardrooms, bedrooms, and bathrooms, bringing new insights to a less exotic, but just as complex, tribe: consumers. And why not? The U.S. consumer market is made up of thousands of "individual little cliques, subcultures, really, that all have their unique way of looking at life," says Robbie Blinkoff, co-founder of Context-Based Research Group in Baltimore. An anthropologist who cut his teeth in Papua New Guinea, Blinkoff now studies consumers for clients like Kodak, Campbell's Soup, and Guinness beer. Consumer groups, he says, have their own language, rituals, symbols, and values. Crack the code, and you can develop new brands, products, and services that more effectively serve your unique tribe of customers.

That was Conklin's goal. Seeking to create a new identity for his hotels, he needed to know more than what his guests thought about things like customer service and the softness of the pillows. He already had stacks of comment cards for that. And traditional focus-group interviews struck him as stilted. "I needed to take a walk in my guests' shoes and see things from their point of view," he says.

Consumer groups have their own rituals and symbols. Crack the code, and you can create new, better products.

So he hired a small Baltimore outfit, Carton Donofrio Partners, to send ethnographers into the Pier 5, Brookshire Suites, and Admiral Fell Inn. The ethnographers painstakingly observed the myriad customs and rituals that characterize hotel life, keeping track of all that transpired—what people said and did, and also what they didn't say: the body language and small gestures. Moore and her partner also took some unusual steps. They gave guests disposable cameras, asking them to photograph things they considered "magical." The idea was to get a better understanding of exactly what guests did during their stay. "We met with them at the end of their stay and interviewed them about their experiences," Moore says. The pictures helped guests tell vivid stories about their experiences—stories that

Moore and her team combined with their own observations to provide dozens of specific recommendations for Conklin.

For example, while the hotels had long offered packages to families, the ethnography revealed that children were essentially ignored at the hotels. Now, when families arrive, the front desk ignores the parents and checks in the kids. That tiny gesture has been wildly popular, building lots of goodwill—and promises of return visits. Thanks to these kinds of changes, leisure business is up some $500,000, Conklin says. Not a bad return on the $45,000 he spent on the ethnography.

Most professional ethnographers have years of training. But that doesn't mean you can't do it yourself. Aspect Medical Systems, a 210-employee medical-device manufacturer in Newton, Mass., turned its own executives into ethnographers to redesign its signature product—a device that measures the degree of consciousness of a patient undergoing surgery to help an anesthesiologist deliver the appropriate dosage of knockout drugs.

Aspect employees put on surgical scrubs and headed into operating rooms, where they obsessively chronicled every detail of an anesthesiologist's activities. It became clear that their original big, bulky design simply would not work in actual hospitals. For one thing, doctors preferred to look at their equipment as little as possible and focus instead on the patient. They also realized the product had to be strong enough to withstand a lot of abuse.

Following hundreds of hours of observations, Aspect created the A-2000, a super-rugged device that requires minimal attention from the anesthesiologist. Since its launch in 1998, the A-2000 has sold 16,000 units (listed at $9,500 apiece) and is in use in more than 25% of the nation's operating rooms. "Ethnographic research isn't glamorous and it takes a lot of standing around, but when you get that 'ah-ha!' it's worth it," says John Shambroom, Aspect's director of engineering.

That "ah-ha" moment can be elusive. Even experienced ethnographers can find themselves buried by data, futilely hunting for the pattern that ties it all together. To avoid that fate, you have to make sure you're asking the right questions, says Anne Schorr, a partner at Conifer Research, an ethnographic research firm in Chicago. Among the things to look for: confusion, barriers, wear patterns, and what's known in the business as "user torture"—when a subject squeezes into a space or process that doesn't fit. Ethnographers also look for "duct-tape-and-string" solutions that customers have devised to solve problems you may not have anticipated.

But the most important element of a successful ethnography is an open mind. Consider SRAM, a Chicago-based bicycle component manufacturer. The company, which had a strong business designing shifters, chains, and the like, thought its next step was to create "a visionary product to lead the industry"—an ambition that included reinventing the bicycle itself, says Kent Solberg, SRAM's global industrial design manager. So the firm hired an anthropologist, who interviewed hundreds of bikers, put ethnographers on mountain bikes, and even mounted small "lipstick" cameras on handlebars.

SRAM learned a lot from the process. But the most important lesson was that changing the company's focus was a mistake. SRAM instead redoubled efforts to make better components for its bicycle manufacturer clients. "We realized that we're just a piece of the puzzle, not the whole puzzle," Solberg says. And so, it put ethnography in mothballs. But the investment was well worth it. Says Solberg: "We wouldn't have had the insight we had without the ethnographic research."

UNIT 3

Developing and Implementing Marketing Strategies

Unit Selections

Key Points to Consider

• Most ethical questions seem to arise in regard to the promotional component of the marketing mix. How fair is the general public's criticism of some forms of personal selling and advertising? Give some examples.

• What role, if any, do you think the quality of a product plays in making a business competitive in consumer markets? What role does price play? Would you rather market a higher-priced, better-quality product or one that was the lowest priced? Why?

• What do you envision will be the major problems or challenges retailers will face in the next decade? Explain.

• Given the rapidly increasing costs of personal selling, what role do you think it will play as a strategy in the marketing mix in the future? What other promotion strategies will play increased or decreased roles in the next decade?

Student Web Site
www.mhcls.com/online

Internet References
Further information regarding these Web sites may be found in this book's preface or online.

American Marketing Association Homepage
http://www.marketingpower.com
Consumer Buying Behavior
http://www.courses.psu.edu/mktg/mktg220_rso3/sls_cons.htm

"Marketing management objectives," the late Wroe Alderson once wrote, "are very simple in essence. The firm wants to expand its volume of sales, or it wants to handle the volume it has more efficiently." Although the essential objectives of marketing might be stated this simply, the development and implementation of strategies to accomplish them is considerably more complex. Many of these complexities are due to changes in the environment within which managers must operate. Strategies that fail to heed the social, political, and economic forces of society have little chance of success over the long run. The lead article in this section provides helpful insight suggesting a framework for developing a comprehensive marketing plan.

The selections in this unit provide a wide-ranging discussion of how marketing professionals and U.S. companies interpret and employ various marketing strategies today. The readings also include specific examples from industry to illustrate their points. The articles are grouped in four sections, each dealing with one of the main strategy areas: product, price, distribution (place), and promotion. Since each selection discusses more than one of these areas, it is important that you read them broadly. For example, many of the articles covered in the distribution section discuss important aspects of personal selling and advertising.

Product Strategy. The essence of the marketing concept is to begin with what consumers want and need. After determining a need, an enterprise must respond by providing the product or service demanded. Successful marketing managers recognize the need for continuous product improvement and/or new product introduction.

The articles in this subsection focus on various facets of product strategy. The first article in this subsection reveals how a phenomenal product is not necessarily embraced by the industry. The second article provides some thoughtful ideas about making and marketing remarkable products. The last article in this subsection analyzes the danger of some franchise stores having expanded too rapidly.

Pricing Strategy. Few elements of the total strategy of the "marketing mix" demand so much managerial and social attention as pricing. There is a good deal of public misunderstanding about the ability of marketing managers to control prices and even greater misunderstanding about how pricing policies are determined. New products present especially difficult problems in terms of both costs and pricing. The costs for developing a new product are usually very high, and if a product is truly new, it cannot be priced competitively, for it has no competitors.

"Making Cents of Pricing" stresses the importance of properly setting prices and measuring their impact on the entire organization in a manner that optimizes long-term market share and profitability. "Customer-Centric Pricing" delineates that while

The McGraw-Hill Companies, Inc./Jill Braaten, photographer

companies spend enormous amounts of energy and capital in creating value for customers, less regard is given to calculating the value they have created. "Boost Your Bottom Line by Taking the Guesswork Out of Pricing" examines the importance of starting your pricing analysis by asking potential customers what they believe your product is worth. "Pricing Gets Creative" examines why it takes more than absolute price levels to drive customer behaviors and perceptions.

Distribution Strategy. For many enterprises, the largest marketing costs result from closing the gap in space and time between producer and consumer. In no other area of marketing is efficiency so eagerly sought after. Physical distribution seems to be the one area where significant cost savings can be achieved. The costs of physical distribution are tied closely with decisions made about the number, the size, and the diversity of marketing intermediaries between producer and consumer. The articles in this subsection scrutinize ways retailers, Costco, and QVC can create value for their customers and be very competitive in the marketplace.

Promotion Strategy. The basic objectives of promotion are to inform, persuade, or remind the consumer to buy a firm's product or pay for the firm's service. Advertising is the most obvious promotional activity. However, in total dollars spent and in cost per person reached, advertising takes second place to personal selling. Sales promotion supports either personal selling and advertising, or both. Such media as point-of-purchase displays, catalogs, and direct mail place the sales promotion specialist closer to the advertising agency than to the salesperson.

The articles in this final unit subsection cover such topics as direct marketing, the Web's vital role in marketing promotions, and the sales secrets of successful salespeople.

The Very Model of a Modern Marketing Plan

Successful companies are rewriting their strategies to reflect customer input and internal coordination

SHELLY REESE

It's 1996. Do you know where your marketing plan is? In a world where competitors can observe and rapidly imitate each other's advancements in product development, pricing, packaging, and distribution, communication is more important than ever as a way of differentiating your business from those of your competitors.

The most successful companies are the ones that understand that, and are revamping their marketing plans to emphasize two points:

1. Marketing is a dialog between customer and supplier.
2. Companies have to prove they're listening to their customers by acting on their input.

What Is a Marketing Plan?

At its most basic level, a marketing plan defines a business's niche, summarizes its objectives, and presents its strategies for attaining and monitoring those goals. It's a road map for getting from point A to point B.

But road maps need constant updating to reflect the addition of new routes. Likewise, in a decade in which technology, international relations, and the competitive landscape are constantly changing, the concept of a static marketing plan has to be reassessed.

Two of the hottest buzz words for the 1990s are "interactive" and "integrated." A successful marketing plan has to be both.

"Interactive" means your marketing plan should be a conversation between your business and your customers by acting on their input. It's your chance to tell customers about your business and to listen and act on their responses.

"Integrated" means the message in your marketing is consistently reinforced by every department within your company. Marketing is as much a function of the finance and manufacturing divisions as it is the advertising and public relations departments.

Integrated also means each time a company reaches out to its customers through an advertisement, direct mailing, or promotion, it is sending the same message and encouraging customers to learn more about the product.

Why Is It Important?

The interaction between a company and its customers is a relationship. Relationships can't be reproduced. They can, however, be replaced. That's where a good marketing plan comes into play.

Think of your business as a suitor, your customers as the object of your affection, and your competitors as rivals. A marketing plan is your strategy for wooing customers. It's based on listening and reacting to what they say.

Because customers' priorities are constantly changing, a marketing plan should change with them. For years, conventional wisdom was 'prepare a five year marketing plan and review it every year.' But change happens a lot faster than it did 20 or even 10 years ago.

For that reason, Bob Dawson of The Business Group, a consulting firm in Freemont, California, recommends that his clients prepare a three year plan and review it every quarter. Frequent reviews enable companies to identify potential problems and opportunities before their competition, he explains.

"Preventative maintenance for your company is as important as putting oil in your car," Dawson says. "You don't wait a whole year to do it. You can't change history but you can anticipate what's going to happen."

Essential Components

Most marketing plans consist of three sections. The first section should identify the organization's goals. The second section should establish a method for attaining them. The third section focuses on creating a system for implementing the strategy.

Although some plans identify as many as six or eight goals, many experts suggest a company whittle its list to one or two key objectives and focus on them.

"One of the toughest things is sticking to one message," observes Mark Bilfield, account director for integrated marketing of Nissan and Infiniti cars at TBWA Chiat/Day in Los Angeles, which handles national advertising, direct marketing, public relations, and promotions for the automaker. Bilfield argues that a

Illustration by Kelly Kennedy

focused, consistent message is easier to communicate to the market place and to different disciplines within the corporation than a broad, encompassing one. Therefore, he advises, "unless there is something drastically wrong with the idea, stick with it."

Section I: Goals

The goals component of your plan is the most fundamental. Consider it a kind of thinking out loud: Why are you writing this plan? What do you want to accomplish? What do you want to achieve in the next quarter? The next year? The next three years?

Like taping your New Year's resolution to the refrigerator, the goals section is a constant reminder of what you want to achieve. The key difference between a New Year's resolution and your marketing goals, however, is you can't achieve the latter alone.

To achieve your marketing goals you've got to convince your customers to behave in a certain way. If you're a soft drink manufacturer you may want them to try your company's latest wild berry flavor. If you're a new bank in town, you need to familiarize people with your name and convince them to give your institution a try. Or perhaps you're a family-owned retailer who needs to remind customers of the importance of reliability and a proven track record in the face of new competition.

The goals in each of these cases differ with the audiences. The soft drink manufacturer is asking an existing customer to try something new; the bank is trying to attract new customers; the retailer wants to retain existing customers.

Each company wants to influence its customers' behavior. The company that is most likely to succeed is the one that understands its customers the best.

There's no substitute for knowledge. You need to understand the demographic and psychographic makeup of the customers you are trying to reach, as well as the best methods for getting their attention.

Do your research. Learn as much as possible about your audience. Trade associations, trade journals and government statistics and surveys are excellent resources, but chances are you have a lot of data within your own business that you haven't tapped. Look at what you know about your customer already and find ways to bolster that information. Companies should constantly be asking clients what they want and how they would use a new product.

"If you're not asking people that use your end product, then everything you're doing is an assumption," argues Dawson.

In addition, firms should ask customers how they perceive the products and services they receive. Too often, companies have an image of themselves that they broadcast but fail to live up to. That frustrates consumers and makes them feel deceived.

Companies that claim to offer superior service often appear to renege on their promises because their definition of 'service' doesn't mesh with their customers', says Bilfield.

"Airlines and banks are prime offenders," says Bilfield. "They tout service, and when the customers go into the airport or the bank, they have to wait in long lines."

The problem often lies in the company's assumptions about what customers really want. While an airline may feel it is living up to its claim of superior service because it distributes warm towels and mints after a meal, a business traveler will probably place a higher value on its competitor's on-time record and policy for returning lost luggage.

Section II: The Strategy

Unfortunately, after taking the time and conducting the research to determine who their audience is and what their message should be, companies often fail by zooming ahead with a plan. An attitude of, "OK, we know who we're after and we know what we want to say, so let's go!" seems to take over.

More often than not, that gung-ho way of thinking leads to disaster because companies have skipped a critical step: they haven't established and communicated an internal strategy for attaining their goals. They want to take their message to the public without pausing to get feedback from inside the company.

For a marketing plan to work, everyone within the company must understand the company's message and work cooperatively to establish a method for taking that message to the public.

For example, if you decide the goal of your plan is to promote the superior service your company offers, you'd better make sure all aspects of your business are on board. Your manufacturing process should meet the highest standards. Your financial department should develop credit and leasing programs that make it easier for customers to use your product. Finally, your customer relations personnel should be trained to respond to problems quickly and efficiently, and to use the contact as an opportunity to find out more about what customers want.

"I'm always amazed when I go into the shipping department of some company and say, 'What is your mission? What's the message you want to give to your end user?' and they say, 'I don't know. I just know I've got to get these shipments out on time,'" says Dawson.

Because the success of integrated marketing depends on a consistent, cohesive message, employees throughout the company need to understand the firm's marketing goals and their role in helping to fulfill them.

"It's very important to bring employees in on the process," says James Lowry, chairman of the marketing department at Ball State University. "Employees today are better than any we've had before. They want to know what's going on in the organization. They don't want to be left out."

Employees are ambassadors for your company. Every time they interact with a customer or vendor, they're marketing your company. The more knowledgeable and helpful they are, the better they reflect on your firm.

At Nordstrom, a Seattle-based retailer, sales associates are empowered to use their best judgment in all situations to make a customer happy.

"We think our sales associates are the best marketing department," said spokeswoman Amy Jones. "We think word of mouth is the best advertising you can have." As a result, although Nordstrom has stores in only 15 states, it has forged a national reputation.

If companies regard marketing as the exclusive province of the marketing department, they're destined to fail.

"Accounting and sales and other departments have to work together hand in hand," says Dawson. "If they don't, you're going to have a problem in the end."

For example, in devising an integrated marketing campaign for the Nissan 200SX, Chiat/Day marketers worked in strategic business units that included a variety of disciplines such as engineers, representatives from the parts and service department, and creative people. By taking a broad view of the business and building inter-related activities to support its goals, Chiat/Day was able to

Getting Started

A Nine-step Plan That Will Make the Difference Between Writing a Useful Plan and a Document That Gathers Dust On a Shelf

by Carole R. Hedden and the *Marketing Tools* editorial staff

In his 1986 book, *The Goal,* Eliyahu M. Goldratt writes that most of us forget the one true goal of our business. It's not to deliver products on time. It isn't even to manufacture the best widget in the world. The goal is to make money.

In the past, making money depended on selling a product or service. Today, that's changed as customers are, at times, willing to pay for what we stand for: better service, better support, more innovation, more partnership in developing new products.

This section of this article assumes that you believe a plan is needed, and that this plan should weave together your desires with those of your customers. We've reviewed a number of marketing plans and come up with a nine-step model. It is perhaps more than what your organization needs today, but none of the steps are unimportant.

Our model combines some of the basics of a conventional plan with some new threads that we believe will push your plan over the edge, from being satisfactory to being necessary. These include:

- Using and improving the former domain of public relations, image, as a marketing tool.
- Integrating all the business functions that touch your customers into a single, customer-focused strategic marketing plan.
- Borrowing from Total Quality theories to establish performance measures beyond the financial report to help you note customer trends.
- Making sure that the people needed to deliver your marketing objectives are part of your plan.
- "Selling" your plan to the people whose support is essential to its success.

Taking the Plan Off the Shelf

First, let's look at the model itself. Remember that one of the primary criticisms of any plan is that it becomes a binder on a shelf, never to be seen again until budget time next year. Planning should be an iterative process, feeding off itself and used to guide and measure.

Whether you're asked to create a marketing plan or write the marketing section of the strategic plan for your business, your document is going to include what the business is trying to achieve, a careful analysis of your market, the products and services you offer to that market, and how you will market and sell products or services to your customer.

1. Describe the Business

You are probably in one of two situations: either you need to write a description of your business or you can rely on an existing document found in your annual report, the strategic plan, or a capabilities brochure. The description should include, at minimum:

- Your company's purpose;
- Who you deliver products or services to; and
- What you deliver to those customers.

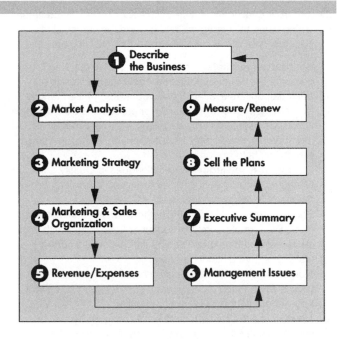

Too often, such descriptions omit a discussion about what you want your business to stand for— your image.

This is increasingly important as customers report they are looking for more than the product or service; they're in search of a partner. The only way to address image is to know who you want to be, who your customers think you are, and how you can bridge the gap between the two.

Part of defining your image is knowing where you are strong and where you are weak. For instance, if your current yield rate is 99.997 percent and customers rate you as the preferred supplier, then you might identify operations as a key to your company's image. Most companies tend to be their own worst critic, so start by listing all your strengths. Then identify weaknesses or the threats you face, either due to your own limitations or from the increased competency of a competitor.

The description also includes what your business delivers to its owners, be they shareholders, private owners, or employees. Usually this is stated in financial terms: revenue, return on investment or equity, economic value added, cash generated, operating margin or earnings per share. The other measures your organization uses to monitor its performance may be of interest to outsiders, but save them for the measurement section of your plan.

The result of all this describing and listing is that you should have a fairly good idea of where you are and where you want to be, which naturally leads to objectives for the coming 6, 12, or 18 months, if not longer.

2. Analyze the Market

This is the section you probably believe you own. *Marketing Tools* challenges you to look at this as a section jointly owned by most everyone working with you. In a smaller company, the lead managers may own various pieces of this section. In a larger organization, you may need to pull in the ideas and data available from

(continued)

other departments, such as logistics, competitor intelligence, research and development, and the function responsible for quality control or quality assurance. All have two things in common: delivering value to customers, and beating the competition.

Together, you can thoroughly cover the following areas:

- **Your target markets.** What markets do you currently compete in? What do you know about them in terms of potential, dollars available, and your share of the market? Something frequently prepared for products is a life cycle chart; you might want to do the same for your market. Is it embryonic, developing, mature or in decline? Are there new markets to exploit?
- **Customer Knowledge.** Your colleagues in Quality, Distribution, Engineering, or other organizations can be helpful in finding what you need.

  The customer's objectives. What threats do your customers face? What goals does the customer have? Work with your customer to define these so you can become a partner instead of a variable component.

  How is the customer addressing her or his markets? Do you know as much about your customer's position as you know about your own? If not, find out.

  How big is each customer, really? You may find you're spending more time on a less important customer than on the customers who can break you. Is your customer growing or in decline? What plans does the customer have to expand or acquire growth? What innovations are in development?

  What does your customer value? Price, product quality, service, innovation, delivery? The better you know what's driving your customer's purchasing decision, the better you'll be able to respond.
- **Clearly identify the alternatives your customer** has. As one customer told employees at a major supplier, "While you've been figuring out how to get by, we've been figuring out how to get by without you." Is backward integration—a situation in which the customer develops the capability in-house—possible? Is there an abundance of other suppliers? What is your business doing to avoid having your customers looking for alternatives?
- **Know your competition.** Your competitors are the obvious alternative for your customer, and thus represent your biggest threat. You can find what you need to know about your competitors through newspaper reports, public records, at trade shows, and from your customers: the size of expansions, the strengths that competitor has, its latest innovations. Do you know how your competition approaches your customers?
- **Describe the Environment.** What changes have occurred in the last 18 months? In the past year? What could change in the near future and over a longer period of time? This should include any kinds of laws or regulations that might affect you, the entry or deletion of competitors, and shifts in technology. Also, keep in mind that internal change does affect your customers. For instance, is a key leader in your business planning to retire? If so, decision making, operations or management style may change—and your customer may have obvious concerns. You can add some depth to this section, too, by portraying several different scenarios:

- What happens if we do nothing beyond last year?
- What happens if we capitalize on our strengths?
- What might happen if our image slips?
- What happens if we do less this year than last?

3. The Marketing Strategy

The marketing strategy consists of what you offer customers and the price you charge. Start by providing a complete description of each product or service and what it provides to your customers. Life cycle, again, is an important part of this. Is your technology or product developing, mature or in decline? Depending on how your company is organized, a variety of people are responsible for this information, right down to whoever is figuring out how to package the product and how it will be delivered. Find out who needs to be included and make sure their knowledge is used.

The marketing strategy is driven by everything you've done up to this point. Strategies define the approaches you will use to market the company. For instance, if you are competing on the basis of service and support rather than price, your strategy may consist of emphasizing relationships. You will then develop tactics that support that strategy: market the company vs. the product; increase sales per client; assure customer responsiveness. Now, what action or programs will you use to make sure that happens?

Note: strategy leads. No program, regardless of how good it is, should make the cut if it doesn't link to your business strategies and your customer.

The messages you must craft to support the strategies often are overlooked. Messages are the consistent themes you want your customer to know, to remember, to feel when he or she hears, reads, or views anything about your company or products. The method by which you deliver your messages comes under the heading of actions or programs.

Finally, you need to determine how you'll measure your own success, beyond meeting the sales forecast. How will you know if your image takes a beating? How will you know whether the customer is satisfied, or has just given up complaining? If you don't know, you'll be caught reacting to events, instead of planning for them.

Remember, your customer's measure of your success may be quite different from what you may think. Your proposed measures must be defined by what your customer values, and they have to be quantifiable. You may be surprised at how willing the customer is to cooperate with you in completing surveys, participating in third-party interviews, or taking part in a full-scale analysis of your company as a supplier. Use caution in assuming that winning awards means you have a measurable indicator. Your measures should be stated in terms of strategies, not plaques or trophies.

(continued)

4. The Marketing and Sales Organization

The most frequently overlooked element in business is something we usually relegate to the Personnel or Human Resources Office—people. They're what makes everything possible. Include them. Begin with a chart that shows the organization for both Marketing and Sales. You may wish to indicate any interdependent relationships that exist (for instance, with Quality).

Note which of the roles are critical, particularly in terms of customer contact. Just as important, include positions, capabilities, and numbers of people needed in the future. How will you gain these skills without impacting your cost per sale? Again, it's time to be creative and provide options.

5. Revenue and Expense

In this section, you're going to project the revenue your plan will produce. This is usually calculated by evaluating the value of your market(s) and determining the dollar value of your share of that market. You need to factor in any changes you believe will occur, and you'll need to identify the sources of revenue, by product or service. Use text to tell the story; use graphs to show the story.

After you've noted where the money is coming from, explain what money you need to deliver the projected return. This will include staff wages and benefits for your organization, as well as the cost for specific programs you plan to implement.

During this era of budget cuts, do yourself a favor by prioritizing these programs. For instance, if one of your key strategies is to expand to a new market via new technologies, products, or services, you will need to allocate appropriate dollars. What is the payback on the investment in marketing, and when will revenues fully pay back the investment? Also, provide an explanation of programs that will be deleted should a cut in funding be required. Again, combine text and spreadsheets to tell and to show.

6. Management Issues

This section represents your chance to let management know what keeps you awake at night. What might or could go wrong? What are the problems your company faces in customer relations? Are there technology needs that are going unattended? Again, this can be a collaborative effort that identifies your concerns. In addition, you may want to identify long-term issues, as well as those that are of immediate significance.

To keep this section as objective as possible, list the concerns and the business strategy or strategies they affect. What are the short-term and long-term risks? For instance, it is here that you might want to go into further detail about a customer's actions that look like the beginnings of backward integration.

7. Executive Summary

Since most senior leaders want a quick-look reference, it's best to include a one-page Executive Summary that covers these points:

- Your organization's objectives
- Budget requirements
- Revenue projections
- Critical management issues

When you're publishing the final plan document, you'll want the executive summary to be Page One.

8. Sell the Plan

This is one of the steps that often is overlooked. Selling your plan is as important as writing it. Otherwise, no one owns it, except you. The idea is to turn it into a rallying point that helps your company move forward. And to do that, you need to turn as many people as possible into ambassadors for your marketing efforts.

First, set up a time to present the plan to everyone who helped you with information and data. Make sure that they feel some sense of ownership, but that they also see how their piece ties into the whole. This is one of those instances where you need to say your plan, show your plan, discuss your plan. Only after all three steps are completed will they *hear* the plan.

After you've shared the information across the organization, reserve some time on the executive calendar. Have a couple of leaders review the plan first, giving you feedback on the parts where they have particular expertise. Then, present the plan at a staff meeting.

Is It Working?

You may think your job is finished. It's not. You need to convey the key parts of this plan to coworkers throughout the business. They need to know what the business is trying to achieve. Their livelihood, not just that of the owners, is at stake. From their phone-answering technique to the way they process an order, every step has meaning to the customer.

9. Measure/Renew

Once you've presented your plan and people understand it, you have to continuously work the plan and share information about it. The best way to help people see trends and respond appropriately is to have meaningful measures. In the language of Total Quality, these are the Key Result Indicators—the things that have importance to your customers and that are signals to your performance.

For instance, measure your ability to deliver on a customer request; the amount of time it takes to respond to a customer inquiry; your productivity per employee; cash flow; cycle time; yield rates. The idea is to identify a way to measure those things that are critical to you and to your customer.

Review those measurements. Share the information with the entire business and begin the process all over again. Seek new ideas and input to improve your performance. Go after more data and facts. And then renew your plan and share it with everyone—all over again.

It's an extensive process, but it's one that spreads the word—and spreads the ownership. It's the step that ensures that your plan will be constantly in use, and constantly at work for your business.

Carole Hedden is a writer and communication/planning consultant living in Elmira, New York.

create a seamless campaign for the 200SX that weaves advertising, in-store displays, and direct marketing together seamlessly.

"When everybody understands what the mission is, it's easier," asserts Bilfield. "It's easier to go upstream in the same direction than to go in different directions."

After bringing the different disciplines within your company on board, you're ready to design the external marketing program needed to support your goals. Again, the principle of integrated marketing comes into play: The message should be focused and consistent, and each step of the process should bring the consumer one step closer to buying your product.

In the case of Chiat/Day's campaign for the Nissan 200SX, the company used the same theme, graphics, type faces, and message to broadcast a consistent statement.

Introduced about the same time as the latest Batman movie, the campaign incorporates music and graphics from the television series. Magazine ads include an 800 number potential customers can call if they want to receive an information kit. Kits are personalized and include the name of a local Nissan dealer, a certificate for a test drive, and a voucher entitling test drivers to a free gift.

By linking each step of the process, Chiat/Day can chart the number of calls, test drives, and sales a particular ad elicits. Like a good one-two punch, the direct marketing picks up where the national advertising leaves off, leveraging the broad exposure and targeting it at the most likely buyers.

While the elaborate 200SX campaign may seem foolproof, a failure to integrate the process at any step along the way could result in a lost sale.

For example, if a potential client were to test drive the car and encounter a dealer who knew nothing about the free gift accompanying the test drive, the customer would feel justifiably annoyed. Conversely, a well-informed sales associate who can explain the gift will be mailed to the test driver in a few weeks will engender a positive response.

Help Is on the Way

Three Software Packages That Will Help You Get Started

Writing a marketing plan may be daunting, but there is a variety of software tools out there to help you get started. Found in electronics and book stores, the tools are in many ways like a Marketing 101 textbook. The difference lies in how they help.

Software tools have a distinct advantage: They actually force you to write, and that's the toughest part of any marketing plan. Sometimes called "MBA In a Box," these systems guide you through a planning process. Some even provide wording that you can copy into your own document and edit to fit your own business. Presto! A boiler plate plan! Others provide a system of interviewing and questioning that creates a custom plan for your operation. The more complex tools demand an integrated approach to planning, one that brings together the full force of your organization, not just Sales or Advertising.

1. Crush

Crush, a modestly named new product from a modestly named new company, HOT, takes a multimedia approach. (HOT stands for Hands-On Technology; *Crush* apparently stands for *Crushing the Competition*)

Just introduced a few months ago, *Crush* is a multimedia application for Macintosh or Windows PCs. It features the competitive analysis methods of Flegis McKenna, marketing guru to Apple, Intel and Genentech; and it features Mr. McKenna himself as your mentor, offering guidance via on-screen video. As you work through each section of a complete market analysis, McKenna provides germane comments; in addition, you can see video case studies of marketing success stories like Intuit software.

Crush provides worksheets and guidance for analyzing your products, customers, market trends and competitors, and helps you generate an action plan. The "mentor" approach makes it a

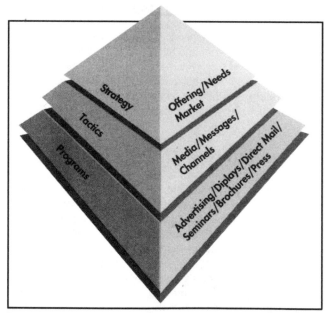

Pyramid Power: Plan Write's pyramid approach asks the user to define the messages for a business as part of the tactics.

useful tool for self-education; as you work through the examples and develop your company's marketing plan, you build your own expertise.

2. Marketing Plan Pro

Palo Alto's *Marketing Plan Pro* is a basic guide, useful for smaller businesses or ones in which the company leader wears

(continued)

a number of different hats, including marketing. It includes the standard spreadsheet capability, as well as the ability to chart numerical data. *Marketing Plan Pro* uses a pyramid process.

I liked the pyramid for a simple reason: It asks you to define messages for your business as part of your tactics. Without a message, it's easy to jump around, reacting to the marketplace instead of anticipating, leaving customers wondering what really is significant about your company or your product.

The step-by-step process is simple, and a sample plan shows how all the information works together. The customer-focus aspect of the plan seemed a little weak, demanding only sales potential and buying capacity of the customers. Targeted marketing is increasingly important, and the user may want to really expand how this section is used beyond what the software requires.

The package displays, at a glance, your strategy, the tactics you develop for each strategy, and the action plan or programs you choose to support the strategy. That could help when you're trying to prioritize creative ideas, eliminating those that really don't deliver what the strategy demands. Within each of three columns, you can click on a word and get help. Click on the heading program: a list of sample actions is displayed. They may not be what you're looking for, but if this is your first plan, they're lifesavers.

I also really liked *Marketing Plan Pro's* user's manual. It not only explains how the software works with your computer, it helps with business terms and provides a guide to planning, walking you through step-by-step.

3. Plan Write

Plan Write, created by Business Resource Software, Inc., is exponentially more powerful than *Marketing Plan Pro. Plan Write* brings together the breadth of the business, integrating information as far flung as distribution systems and image. And this software places your marketing strategy within the broader context of a business plan, the approach that tends to prove most effective.

As with *Marketing Plan Pro, Plan Write* provides a sample plan. The approach is traditional, incorporating a look at the business environment, the competition, the product or service mix you are offering, the way you will tell customers about that mix, pricing, delivery, and support.

Among the sections that were particularly strong was one on customer alternatives and people planning. Under the heading of customer alternatives, you're required to incorporate competitive information with customer information. If you don't meet the customer's needs, where could he or she go? Most often we look only at the competition, without trying to imagine how the customer is thinking. This exercise is particularly valuable to the company who leads the market.

The people part of planning too often is dumped on the personnel guy instead of being seen as a critical component of your organization's capabilities. *Plan Write* requires that you include how marketing is being handled, and how sales will be accomplished. In addition, it pushes you to define what skills will be needed in the future and where the gaps are between today and the future. People, in this plan, are viewed as a strategic component.

Plan Write offers a fully integrated spreadsheet that can import from or export to most of the popular spreadsheet programs you may already be using. Another neat feature allows you to enter numerical data and select from among 14 different graphing styles to display your information. You just click on the style you want to view, and the data is reconfigured.

Probably the biggest danger in dealing with software packages such as *Marketing Plan Pro* and *Plan Write* is to think the software is the answer. It's merely a guide.

—Carole Hedden

Section III: Execution

The final component of an integrated marketing plan is the implementation phase. This is where the budget comes in.

How much you'll need to spend depends on your goals. If a company wants to expand its market share or promote its products in a new region, it will probably have to spend more than it would to maintain its position in an existing market.

Again, you'll need to create a system for keeping your employees informed. You might consider adding an element to your company newsletter that features people from different departments talking about the marketing problems they encounter and how they overcome them. Or you might schedule a regular meeting for department heads to discuss marketing ideas so they can report back to their employees with news from around the company.

Finally, you'll need to devise a system for monitoring your marketing program. A database, similar to the one created from calls to the 200SX's 800 number, can be an invaluable tool for determining if your message is being well received.

It's important to establish time frames for achieving your goals early in the process. If you want to increase your market share, for instance, you should determine the rate at which you intend to add new customers. Failing to achieve that rate could signal a flaw in your plan or its execution, or an unrealistic goal.

"Remember, integrated marketing is a long-range way of thinking," warns Dawson. "Results are not going to be immediate."

Like any investment, marketing requires patience, perseverance, and commitment if it is to bear fruit. While not all companies are forward thinking enough to understand the manifold gains of integrated marketing, the ones that don't embrace it will ultimately pay a tremendous price.

SHELLY REESE is a freelance writer based in Cincinnati.

He Came.
He Sawed.
He Took on the Whole
Power-Tool Industry

Why wasn't anyone else interested in building a safer saw?

Melba Newsome

In February 2001, Stephen Gass strode to the podium in a conference room at Caesars Palace in Las Vegas and began the video presentation for SawStop, his new invention. The 75 attendees watched the screen closely as a woodworker fed a sheet of plywood into a power-saw blade spinning at 4,000 rpm. Then a hot dog was placed in the path of the blade. Miraculously, the instant the blade made contact with the wiener, the saw shut down and the blade retracted. The dog escaped with only a small nick—substitute a finger and it's the difference between a cut and an amputation.

Gass had given the same dog-and-pony show a dozen times, mostly for woodworkers, contractors, and a few industry executives. But this audience was different. It consisted of lawyers for the Defense Research Industry, a trade group for attorneys representing the power-tool industry. SawStop could help prevent thousands of serious injuries caused by power tools each year, Gass believed—if the industry would license it. He returned to his seat thinking he had made his case.

Then Dan Lanier, national coordinating counsel for Black & Decker, stepped to the podium. His topic: "Evidentiary Issues Relating to SawStop Technology for Power Saws." Lanier spent the next 30 minutes discussing a hypothetical lawsuit—in which a plaintiff suing a power-saw manufacturer contended the saw was defective because it did not incorporate SawStop's technology—and suggesting ways defense counsel might respond. Lanier recalls it as a rather dry exploration of legal issues. Gass heard something different. To his ears, Lanier's message was this: If we all stick together and don't license this product, the industry can argue that everybody rejected it so it obviously wasn't viable, thereby limiting any legal liability the industry might face as a result of the new technology. (Lanier denies this was his point.)

Gass was stunned. His tiny start-up, run by three guys out of a barn in Wilsonville, Oreg., had captured the attention of the entire power-tool industry. For months, he had been negotiating with major players such as Ryobi, Delta, Black & Decker, Emerson, and Craftsman about licensing his invention. Instead, they seemed intent on trying to make him and his product go away.

Some 32,000 Americans are rushed to emergency rooms with table-saw-related injuries each year, according to the Consumer Product Safety Commission; more than 3,000 of those visits result in amputations, usually of fingers or hands. The medical bill to reattach a severed finger runs from about $10,000 for a clean wound to more than $25,000 if there's nerve damage, infection, or other complications, according to lames W. Greer, president of the Association of Property and Casualty Claims Professionals, a trade group in Tampa. Factor in rehabilitation and lost time at work, and the cost per injury can easily reach six figures. Indeed, in 2002, the CPSC estimated the annual economic cost of table-saw injuries to be $2 billion. That's more than 10 times the size of the entire $175 million table-saw market. Clearly, this is an industry that could use a better mousetrap.

That's what Gass figured he had in the summer of 2000, when SawStop's technology made its debut. A year later, the Consumer Products Safety Commission awarded the device its Chairman's Commendation for product safety. *Popular Science* magazine named it one of 100 Best New Innovations. Tool industry bigwigs seemed impressed too. "It is probably one of the most major developments in the area of product safety applicable for table saws," said Peter Domeny, director of product safety for S-B Power Tool, which makes Skil and Bosch tools.

So, four years later, why isn't SawStop on every table saw on the market? That's the funny thing about better mousetraps. Build one, and the other mousetrap makers will probably hate your guts. They might even try to squeeze you out of the mousetrap business altogether. Just ask the inventors of air bags, safer cigarette lighters, and automatic shutoffs for electrical appliances—all of which encountered resistance from the status quo. Ultimately they prevailed and their innovations became standard. Gass still has a long way to go.

Gass didn't set out to take on the power-tool industry. Nor did he ever see himself as an entrepreneur. The amateur woodworker was standing in his workshop one day in 1999, staring at his idle table saw. "The idea came to me that it might be possible to stop the blade quickly enough to avoid serious injury," he says. A patent attorney who also holds a doctorate in physics, Gass loves nothing than solving complex technical problems. He got out pencil, paper, and calculator and got to work.

Stopping the blade, he figured, would require a two-part process. First, he needed a brake that would work quickly enough when it came into contact with a woodworker's hand. Next, he had to design a triggering system that could differentiate between finger and wood. Given the speed of the blade, it would have to stop in about 1/100 of a second—or at about an eighth of an inch of rotation after making contact. Any further, and the cut would be so deep that the device would be useless. To stop the blade this quickly would require about 1,000 pounds of force to decelerate the blade in 10 milliseconds. That calculation took Gass about 30 minutes. The trigger problem was a little more complicated, but Gass came up with the idea of running a small electrical charge through the blade. The system would sense when the blade hit flesh because the body would absorb some of the charge. The resulting drop in voltage would be enough to trigger the brake and stop the blade almost instantly.

Gass spent two weeks designing the technology and, using a $200 secondhand table saw, an additional week building a prototype. Then he began to experiment. With the blade whirring, he touched his hand to its smooth side. It stopped immediately. The same thing happened when he ran a hot dog into the blade's teeth. Gass repeated the experiment dozens of times—and each time the blade stopped immediately. Convinced his invention would be embraced by the industry, he videotaped a demonstration, registered the patent, and set out to convince manufacturers to license the technology, which he had dubbed SawStop. He sent a video demo to Delta Machinery in Jackson, Tenn., one of the largest table-saw manufacturers, and waited.

Gass was pleased with his results, but he also knew there was something else to be done: He had to test SawStop on a real finger. "There's not a lot of demand for a saw that's safe for hot dogs," he says with a laugh. And so, on a spring afternoon in 2000, Gass stood in his workshop and tried to summon the moxie to stick his left ring finger into the teeth of a whirring saw blade. He had rubbed the digit with Novocain cream, hoping to dull the pain of the cut. On the first try, his heart beating furiously, he eased in close but recoiled before making contact. A few minutes later, he tried again. This time, he rolled his finger close enough to get a faint red mark, but panicked and pulled back before the brake triggered. By now, his forearm

was cramping from the tension. It was difficult to keep his hand steady. Still, on his third attempt, he kept his nerve—and the blade stopped, just as he knew it would. "It hurt like the dickens and bled a lot," he says. But the finger remained intact.

Several months later, Gass finally heard back from Delta. "No, thanks. Safety doesn't sell," he says he was told over the phone. (Delta, now known as Delta Porter Cable, is now owned by Black & Decker. A Delta spokesperson who asked not to be identified denies that a Delta employee made the comment.) Gass could not believe his ears. "Everybody in woodworking knows somebody who's lost a finger or had an accident," he says. How could a major manufacturer not be interested?

Gass refused to give up. Working with three other lawyers from his Portland law firm, David Fanning, David Fulmer, and David D'asenzo, he raised $150,000, built a more sophisticated prototype, and signed up for the International Woodworking Fair in August 2000 in Atlanta. The reaction there was phenomenal. SawStop's booth was packed with spectators who stood riveted as Gass and his partners fed wiener after wiener into the table saw. "Afterward, these guys would walk up to us and say, 'I wanna shake your hand for doing this,'" recalls Fanning. "A lot of them were shaking with two or three fingers missing." It was all the validation the four men needed. A month later, Gass and Fanning walked away from law partnerships to pursue SawStop full-time. Fulmer, an associate at the firm, followed a few months later. D'asenzo invested in the venture but kept his day job.

"These guys would walk up to us and say 'I wanna shake your hand.' A lot of them were shaking with two or three fingers missing."

The fall of 2000 was hardly an auspicious time to launch a start-up. The Internet boom had just gone bust, the Nasdaq was in free fall, and investors were gun-shy. Yet SawStop was so practical and easy to understand, the trio had little trouble raising $1.2 million in angel funding from several different investors. They invested in more R&D, better prototypes, and small salaries for the three principals. "It was a no-brainer," says Grant Simmons, a New Orleans urologist who invested an undisclosed amount in SawStop after reading about the company and seeing a video demonstration in 2004. It was Simmons's first experience as an angel investor, and his interest was more than just financial: His father was a lifelong woodworker who had lost a finger in a table-saw accident. "This is revolutionary," Simmons says. "They are applying basic physics in a practical way to address a very important issue that people in the industry have totally ignored—safety." Gass, Fanning, and Fulmer, meanwhile, filed more than 50 patent applications to protect their invention.

The only thing they lacked was industry cooperation—but that seemed inevitable. After all, they believed, common sense and consumer demand ultimately would win out. What's more, the technology had implications far beyond table saws. It could potentially boost the safety of all power saws, including band saws and circular saws, as well as nail guns, lawn mowers, and other products. For the next two years, the partners engaged in what seemed to be promising talks with high-level executives at Emerson, Black & Decker, and Ryobi. In January 2002, they appeared to have turned the corner when Ryobi agreed to license SawStop's technology. Under the terms of the deal, there would be no up-front fee; Ryobi would pay a 3% royalty based on the wholesale price of all saws sold with SawStop's technology. The number would increase to 8% if the majority of the industry also licensed the technology. It was not a get-rich-quick deal, but Gass believed it was a vital first step.

When the contract arrived, Gass noticed a typo and called Ryobi's attorney, Bob Bugos, to make the correction. Gass says Bugos apologized and promised to take care of it right away. (Ryobi representatives declined to comment for this story.) When a week passed and the revised contract still had not arrived, Gass called back. He says Bugos was very apologetic and assured him the contract was on its way. Again, it didn't come. Gass says he called every two weeks and each time Bugos made the same promise. After about six months of going back and forth, it finally dawned on Gass that the Ryobi deal, like all the others, was going nowhere.

Indeed, the major power-tool manufacturers have professed to be somewhat less than impressed with SawStop. "The device has not been field-tested for results, durability, and reliability," said a representative from Delta Porter Cable. "It's an experimental system, not yet field-proven." According to Dan Lanier, the Defense Research Industry attorney, all of the manufacturers approached by Gass independently tested and evaluated the technology. And each one, Lanier said in an e-mail, encountered "significant problems." "The primary problem," he said, "was an unacceptably high rate of false trips of the braking device when cutting wet, green, or pressure-treated lumber." The industry, Lanier added, is also wary of the fact that even when the device works, the user still walks away with an injury. "Manufacturers discovered that, depending on the accident scenario and the type of blade used, a user even with a properly functioning SawStop-equipped table saw still could sustain a very severe injury," Lanier said. "Mr. Gass's hot dog demonstration simply is not representative of the way in which many table-saw accidents occur." Given those issues, manufacturers also felt that the 8% royalty sought by Gass was "exorbitant and unreasonable," Lanier said. (Representatives from Ryobi, S-B Power Tool, WHM Tool Group, and Emerson did not return repeated calls seeking comment.)

Gass counters that the industry tests were conducted on unrefined prototypes—models essentially built to demonstrate that the concept worked—and that many of the problems Lanier cites have since been addressed. On current models, most wood needs to dry for only an hour or two before being cut, he says. As for the fact that SawStop can result in an injury even when it works, Gass asks the following question: Isn't it better to walk away with a cut, even a deep one, than to lose a finger or a hand? "I think they were looking for reasons not to implement it," he says.

Gass sees the objections as a smoke screen for the industry's real concern: the increased risk of product-liability litigation. In most cases, when people sue power-tool manufacturers because they've lost a finger or hand in an accident, they're unsuccessful—because it's tough to prove that the manufacturer did anything wrong. Add SawStop to the mix, however, and the picture changes. Suddenly, the industry is promising an injury-proof saw. What if someone got hurt? "The manufacturer would be at a deeper risk and more vulnerable because it had made a promise of what the technology could do," says Jim O'Reilley, a product-liability expert at the University of Cincinnati. "Companies are going to be reluctant to expose themselves to that higher risk."

Indeed, precisely who would assume that risk turned out to be a major sticking point in SawStop's licensing negotiations. The manufacturers believed Gass should indemnify them against any lawsuit if SawStop malfunctioned. Gass, however, says that he could not possibly make such a guarantee since he would not actually be manufacturing the saws. And there is another facet to the liability issue. If SawStop did come to market and was proved effective in preventing accidents, it might be easier for plaintiffs to win lawsuits against manufacturers of traditional saws, because juries might be more likely to return a verdict against a manufacturer that chose not to implement SawStop. That's the main reason, Gass believes, that the big tool makers are refusing to deal with him. They want his product to go away.

After the deal with Ryobi fell apart in mid-2002, Gass, Fanning, and Fulmer faced a tough choice: Abandon the company and return to practicing law or build the saws themselves. None of the men had ever run a company, but they all understood that it's one thing to be an inventor and another to be an entrepreneur. They would be responsible for designing, manufacturing, marketing, and sales along with the day-to-day operations of a business. It was a tough prospect— but not a tough decision. All three agreed that if they didn't act, their technology would never see the light of day. "It seemed like the right thing to do," says Fanning. "There aren't very many opportunities to make money and do something good."

With wives and kids to support, Gass and his partners have found that the decision has not always been easy to stand by. Gass fondly recalls the six-figure salary he earned as a patent lawyer. At one point, he was so close to returning to his legal career that he got quotes for renewing the legal-malpractice insurance policy he dropped when he devoted himself to SawStop. "I never doubted my invention or wanted to give up, but I've wondered if we would be able to keep going," he says. "It's been touch-and-go several times with money, and we always manage to pull through at the last minute."

SawStop now operates with eight people out of a two-story barn Gass built himself. Filled with electronics, high-tech machinery, and every tool imaginable, the first floor is a handyman's paradise. In the corner is a large stack of woodworking timber left untouched since Gass launched his venture. Gass logs 12- to 14-hour days running the business upstairs. Desks, computers, and filing cabinets fill the second-floor office space.

A map of the United States hangs above the conference table. It's dotted with colored pushpins, each one representing a city where someone has purchased a SawStop table saw.

The first one rolled off the assembly line of a Taiwanese manufacturing plant in November 2004. SawStop has since sold about 600 and has 300 more on back order. A basic contractor saw retails for $799; the professional-level cabinet saw goes for $2,500. The company relies on trade shows, news stories, word of mouth, and ads in woodworking magazines for marketing. Selling online and direct-to-consumer is an acceptable way to get started, but Gass knows that to reach the larger market he will need to get into home improvement stores, where competition for shelf space is fierce. He's had discussions with Home Depot and Lowe's, but neither has committed to carrying the product.

So for now, Gass is banking on people like Sharon and Don Biers, owners of Collins Custom Cabinets. After one of the employees at their Lowell, Ark., shop lost a finger in a power-saw accident in February, the Biers bought a $2,500 SawStop cabinet saw and have since ordered two more. It didn't take long for the purchase to pay off. Within two weeks, another employee, John Stroud, inadvertently shifted his hand into the path of the blade and the saw shut down when it hit his fingernail. "We made the calculation that it's worth it for the safety of our guys," says Sharon Biers. "The accidents are usually caused by human error, but this saw grants you forgiveness." And not just for professionals. In May, Gass received an e-mail from a high school shop teacher in Princeton, Wis. "I have a sophomore who still has two thumbs thanks to your saw," the man wrote. The company knows of at least five other amputations that have been averted.

"Accidents are usually caused by human error, but this saw grants you forgiveness," says one contractor.

With the big tool companies declining to participate, Saw-Stop is seeking other ways to make sure its technology is adopted. In April 2003, the company filed a petition with the Consumer Product Safety Commission to make SawStop-like technology standard on all table saws. Six months later, the Power Tool Institute, a consortium of 17 power-tool makers, filed an opposing brief in which it argued that SawStop is a "speculative and untested technology. In addition, the cost to consumers and manufacturers of granting the petition would far outweigh any benefits that may be realized." The industry

also claims to be developing its own safety systems. The CPSC is expected to release its findings this summer. If it states, as Gass hopes and expects, that the technology is effective, it will be the first step in a long process of making SawStop—or a similar injury-prevention system—mandatory.

Meanwhile, the industry's product-liability fears appear to be coming to life. In 2003, a construction worker walked into the Wellesley, Mass., office of attorney Richard J. Sullivan. He was looking for someone to represent him in a case against Chicago-based S-B Power Tool. The worker had lost his thumb and four fingers while using a table saw. Doctors were able to reattach them, but even after six surgeries and $150,000 in medical bills, he still had no real functionality in the hand. Living on workers' comp, he fell behind financially and was forced to sell his home.

Sullivan turned the case down twice because he didn't see a way to hold the manufacturer accountable. Then a colleague told him about SawStop. "His injury occurred on a saw manufactured in April 2003 and sold in May 2003," Sullivan says. "The industry has known about this technology since 2001. That gave the manufacturer plenty of time to react." The lawsuit, filed in Massachusetts state court in the summer of 2004, alleges that the manufacturer was negligent for not implementing the technology and seeks compensation for lost wages, future lost wages, and pain and suffering. (Attorneys for S-B Power Tool responded in January, denying all claims.) "If Gass can figure this out by tinkering around in his backyard, what has this industry been doing for the past 20 years?" asks Sullivan, who has since taken on five similar cases. "They're like the auto industry, which had to be dragged kicking and screaming to install air bags."

Gass believes that Sullivan's cases are only the tip of the iceberg. "The legal standard says you have to make a product as safe as you reasonably can, and if you fail to do that, you're going to be responsible," he says. While Gass wants SawStop to be successful financially, he also admits that what began as an interesting physics problem in his workshop has become something of a crusade. "This is important to society and that responsibility weighs on me," he says. "It would have been so much easier if the manufacturers had just licensed this. Then, having SawStop would be just like having a stereo with Dolby or running shorts with Gore-Tex." Indeed, Gass still dreams of getting out of manufacturing altogether. He really doesn't want to make the power tools we buy. He just wants to make the power tools we buy better.

MELBA NEWSOME (melbanewsome@bellsouth.net) is a freelance writer in Charlotte, N.C.

In Praise of the Purple Cow

Remarkably honest ideas (and remarkably useful case studies) about making and marketing remarkable products. A manifesto for marketers

SETH GODIN

For years, marketers have talked about the "five Ps" (actually, there are more than five, but everyone picks their favorite handful): product, pricing, promotion, positioning, publicity, packaging, pass along, permission. Sound familiar? This has become the basic marketing checklist, a quick way to make sure that you've done your job. Nothing is guaranteed, of course, but it used to be that if you dotted your is and paid attention to your five Ps, then you were more likely than not to succeed.

No longer. It's time to add an exceptionally important new P to the list: Purple Cow. Weird? Let me explain.

While driving through France a few years ago, my family and I were enchanted by the hundreds of storybook cows grazing in lovely pastures right next to the road. For dozens of kilometers, we all gazed out the window, marveling at the beauty. Then, within a few minutes, we started ignoring the cows. The new cows were just like the old cows, and what was once amazing was now common. Worse than common: It was boring.

Cows, after you've seen them for a while, are boring. They may be well-bred cows, Six Sigma cows, cows lit by a beautiful light, but they are still boring. A Purple Cow, though: Now, that would really stand out. The essence of the Purple Cow—the reason it would shine among a crowd of perfectly competent, even undeniably excellent cows—is that it would be *remarkable*. Something remarkable is worth talking about, worth paying attention to. Boring stuff quickly becomes invisible.

The world is full of boring stuff—brown cows—which is why so few people pay attention. Remarkable marketing is the art of building things worth noticing right into your product or service. Not just slapping on the marketing function as a last-minute add-on, but also understanding from the outset that if your offering itself isn't remarkable, then it's invisible—no matter how much you spend on well-crafted advertising.

This is an essay about what it takes to create and sell something remarkable. It is a manifesto for marketers who want to make a difference at their company by helping create products and services that are worth marketing in the first place. It is a plea for originality, for passion, guts, and daring. Not just because going through life with passion and guts beats the alternative (which it does), but also because it's the only way to be

successful. Today, the one sure way to fail is to be boring. Your one chance for success is to be remarkable.

And that means you have to be a leader. You can't be remarkable by following someone else who's remarkable. One way to figure out a great theory is to look at what's working in the real world and determine what the successes have in common. With marketing, it's puzzling though. What could the Four Seasons and Motel 6 possibly have in common? Other than the fact that both companies have experienced extraordinary success and growth, they couldn't be more different. Or Neiman Marcus and Wal-Mart, both growing during the same decade? Or Nokia (bringing out new hardware every 30 days or so) and Nintendo (marketing the same Game Boy for 14 years in a row)?

It's like trying to drive looking in the rearview mirror. Sure, those things worked. But do they help us predict what will work tomorrow? The thing that all of those companies have in common is that they have *nothing* in common. They are outliers. They're on the fringes. Superfast or superslow. Very exclusive or very cheap. Extremely big or extremely small.

The reason it's so hard to follow the leader is this: The leader is the leader precisely because he did something remarkable. And that remarkable thing is now taken—so it's no longer remarkable when you decide to do it.

Stand Out from the Herd I: Going Up!

Elevators aren't a typical consumer product. They can easily cost more than a million dollars, they generally get installed when a building is first constructed, and they're not much use unless the building is more than three or four stories tall.

How, then, does an elevator company compete? Until recently, selling involved a lot of golf, dinners, and long-term relationships with key purchasing agents at major real-estate developers. No doubt that continues, but Otis Elevator Co. has radically changed the game by developing a remarkable Purple Cow.

Every elevator ride is basically a local one. The elevator stops 5, 10, 15 times on the way to your floor. This is a hassle for

Article 25. In Praise of the Purple Cow

NOW *THAT'S* REMARKABLE: OTIS ELEVATOR CO.

When is a bank of elevators more than a bank of elevators? When it's smart enough to tell you which elevator will provide the quickest ride to the floor you need to reach. A product *that* smart changes how people move, how buildings get designed—and how companies, in this case Otis Elevator Co., market their innovation.

NOW *THAT'S* REMARKABLE: TOMBSTONE PIZZA

It's good to be first with an innovation that the world is hungry for. Ron Simek learned that lesson when he launched the first successful line of frozen pizza. The product was a hit. Kraft bought it and advertised like mad. The rest is history. Of course, 40 years later, introducing another brand of frozen pizza seems less appetizing. Me-too products lead to also-ran companies.

you, but it's a huge, expensive problem for the building. While your elevator is busy stopping at every floor, the folks in the lobby are getting more and more frustrated. The building needs more elevators, but there's no money to buy them and no room to put them. Walk into the Times Square offices of Cap Gemini Ernst & Young, and you're faced with a fascinating solution to this problem.

Otis's insight? When you approach the elevators, you key in your floor on a centralized control panel. In return, the panel tells you which elevator is going to take you to your floor. With this simple presort, Otis has managed to turn every elevator into an express. Your elevator takes you immediately to the 12th floor and races back to the lobby. This means that buildings can be taller, they need fewer elevators for a given density of people, the wait is shorter, and the building can use precious space for people rather than for elevators. A huge win, implemented at a remarkably low cost.

Is there a significant real-estate developer in the world who is unaware of this breakthrough? Not likely. And it doesn't really matter how many ads or how many lunches the competition sponsors: Otis now gets the benefit of the doubt.

The Sad Truth About Marketing Just About Anything

Forty years ago, Ron Simek, owner of the Tombstone Tap (named for a nearby cemetery) in Medford, Wisconsin, decided to offer a frozen version of his pizza to his customers. It caught on, and before long, Tombstone Pizza was dominating your

grocer's freezer. Kraft eventually bought the brand, advertised it like crazy, and made serious dough. This was a great American success story: Invent a good product that everyone wants, advertise it to the masses, earn billions.

That strategy didn't just work for pizza. It worked for most everything in your house, including aspirin. Imagine how much fun it must have been to be the first person to market aspirin. Here's a product that just about every person on earth needed and wanted. A product that was inexpensive, easy to try, and promised huge immediate benefits. Obviously, it was a big hit.

Today, a quick visit to the drugstore turns up lots of aspirin and aspirinlike products: Advil, Aleve, Alka-Seltzer Morning Relief, Anacin, Ascriptin, Aspergum, Bayer, Bayer Children's, Bayer Regimen, Bayer Women's, BC Powder, Bufferin, Cope, Ecotrin, Excedrin Extra Strength, Goody's, Motrin, Nuprin, St. Joseph, Tylenol, and, of course, Vanquish. Within each of those brands, there are variations, sizes, and generics that add up to more than 100 different products to choose from.

Think it's still easy to be an analgesics marketer today? If you developed a new kind of pain reliever, even one that was a little bit better than the ones that I just listed, what would you do? The obvious answer, if you've got money and you believe in your product, is to spend everything you've got to buy tons of national TV and print advertising.

There are a few problems that you'll face, though. First, you need people who want to buy a pain reliever. While it's a huge market, it's not for everyone. Once you find people who buy pain relievers, then you need people who want to buy a *new kind* of pain reliever. After all, plenty of people want the "original"

10 Ways to Raise a Purple Cow

Making and marketing something remarkable means asking new questions—and trying new practices. Here are 10 suggestions.

1. Differentiate your customers. Find the group that's most profitable. Find the group that's most likely to influence other customers. Figure out how to develop for, advertise to, or reward either group. Ignore the rest. Cater to the customers you would choose if you could choose your customers.
2. If you could pick one underserved niche to target (and to dominate), what would it be? Why not launch a product to compete with your own that does nothing but appeal to that market?
3. Create two teams: the inventors and the milkers. Put them in separate buildings. Hold a formal ceremony when you move a product from one group to the other. Celebrate them both, and rotate people around.
4. Do you have the email addresses of the 20% of your customer base that loves what you do? If not, start getting them. If you do, what could you make for them that would be superspecial?
5. Remarkable isn't always about changing the biggest machine in your factory. It can be the way you answer the phone, launch a new brand, or price a revision to your software. Getting in the habit of doing the "unsafe" thing every time you have the opportunity is the best way to see what's working and what's not.
6. Explore the limits. What if you're the cheapest, the fastest, the slowest, the hottest, the coldest, the easiest, the most efficient, the loudest, the most hated, the copycat, the outsider, the hardest, the oldest, the newest, or just the most! If there's a limit, you should (must) test it.
7. Think small. One vestige of the TV-industrial complex is a need to think mass. If it doesn't appeal to everyone, the thinking goes, it's not worth it. No longer. Think of the smallest conceivable market and describe a product that overwhelms it with its remarkability. Go from there.
8. Find things that are "just not done" in your industry, and then go ahead and do them. For example, JetBlue Airways almost instituted a dress code—for its passengers! The company is still playing with the idea of giving a free airline ticket to the best-dressed person on the plane. A plastic surgeon could offer gift certificates. A book publisher could put a book on sale for a certain period of time. Stew Leonard's took the strawberries out of the little green plastic cages and let the customers pick their own. Sales doubled.
9. Ask, "Why not?" Almost everything you *don't* do has no good reason for it. Almost everything you don't do is the result of fear or inertia or a historical lack of someone asking, "Why not?"
10. What would happen if you simply told the truth inside your company and to your customers?

kind, the kind they grew up with. Finally, you need to find the people who are willing to listen to what you have to say about your new pain reliever. The vast majority of folks are just too busy and will ignore you, regardless of how many ads you buy. So you just went from an audience of everyone to an audience a fraction of that size. Not only are these folks hard to find, they're picky as well. Being first in the frozen-pizza category was a good idea.

Being first in pain relievers was an even better idea. Alas, they're both taken. Which brings me to the sad truth about marketing just about anything, whether it's a product or a service, whether it's marketed to consumers or corporations: Most people *can't* buy your product. Either they don't have the money, they don't have the time, or they don't want it.

And those are serious problems. An audience that doesn't have the money to buy what you're selling at the price you need to sell it for is not a market. An audience that doesn't have the time to listen to and understand your pitch treats you as if you and your product were invisible. And an audience that takes the time to hear your pitch and decides that they don't want it . . . well, you're not going to get very far.

The old rule was this: Create safe products and combine them with great marketing. Average products for average people. *That's broken.* The new rule is: Create remarkable products that the right people seek out.

As I write this, the top song in France, Germany, Italy, Spain, and a dozen other countries in Europe is about ketchup. It's called "Ketchup," and it's by two sisters you've never heard of. The number-two movie in America is a low-budget animated film in which talking vegetables act out Bible stories. Neither is the sort of product you'd expect to come from a lumbering media behemoth.

Sam Adams beer was remarkable, and it captured a huge slice of business from Budweiser. Hard Manufacturing introduced

NOW *THAT'S* REMARKABLE: U.S. POSTAL SERVICE

The runaway success of "zip+4" might give new meaning to the term "going postal." This simple innovation makes it quicker for the Postal Service to deliver mail, easier for marketers to target neighborhoods, and cheaper for marketers to send bulk mail. But the innovation would never have taken hold without savvy marketing by an organization not famous for its savviness.

a product that costs 10 times the average (the $9,945 Doernbecher crib) and opened up an entirely new segment of the hospital-crib market. The electric piano let Yamaha steal an increasingly larger share of the traditional piano market away from the entrenched leaders. Vanguard's remarkably low-cost mutual funds continue to whale away at Fidelity's market dominance. Bic lost tons of market share to Japanese competitors that had developed pens that were remarkably fun to write with, just as Bic had stolen the market away from fountain pens a generation or two earlier.

Stand Out from the Herd II: Mail Call

Very few organizations have as timid an audience as the United States Postal Service. Dominated by a conservative bureaucracy and conservative big customers, the USPS has an awfully hard time innovating. The big direct marketers are successful because they've figured out how to thrive under the current system, and they're in no mood to see that system change. Most individuals are in no hurry to change their mailing habits either.

The majority of new-policy initiatives at the USPS are either ignored or met with nothing but disdain. But "zip+4" was a huge success. Within a few years, the USPS was able to diffuse a new idea, making the change in billions of address records in thousands of computer databases.

How? First, it was a game-changing innovation. Zip+4 makes it far easier for marketers to target neighborhoods and much faster and easier to deliver the mail. The product was a true Purple Cow, completely changing the way customers and the USPS would deal with bulk mail. It offered both dramatically increased speed in delivery and significantly lower costs for bulk mailers. That made it worth the time it took for big mailers to pay attention. The cost of ignoring the innovation would be felt immediately on the bottom line.

Second, the USPS wisely singled out a few early adopters. These were organizations that were technically savvy and that were extremely sensitive to both pricing and speed issues. These early adopters were also in a position to sneeze the benefits to other, less astute, mailers.

The lesson here is simple: The more intransigent your market, the more crowded the marketplace, the busier your customers, the more you need a Purple Cow. Half-measures will fail. Overhauling the product with dramatic improvements in things that the right customers care about, on the other hand, can have an enormous payoff.

Why There Are So Few Purple Cows

If being a Purple Cow is such an effective way to break through the clutter, why doesn't everyone do it? One reason is that people think the opposite of remarkable is "bad" or "poorly done." They're wrong. Not many companies sell things today that are flat-out lousy. Most sell things that are good enough. That's why the opposite of remarkable is "very good." Very good is an everyday occurrence, hardly worth mentioning—certainly not the basis of breakthrough success. Are you making very good stuff? How fast can you stop?

Some people would like you to believe that there are too few great ideas, that their product or their industry or their company simply can't support a great idea. That, of course, is absolute nonsense. Another reason the Purple Cow is so rare is because people are so *afraid*.

If you're remarkable, then it's likely that some people won't like you. That's part of the definition of remarkable. Nobody gets unanimous praise—ever. The best the timid can hope for is to be unnoticed. Criticism comes to those who stand out.

Playing it safe. Following the rules. They seem like the best ways to avoid failure. Alas, that pattern is awfully dangerous. The current marketing "rules" will ultimately lead to failure. In a crowded marketplace, fitting in is failing. In a busy marketplace, not standing out is the same as being invisible.

In *Marketing Outrageously* (Bard Press, 2001), author Jon Spoelstra points out the catch-22 logic of the Purple Cow. If times are tough, your peers and your boss may very well point out that you can't afford to be remarkable. There's not enough room to innovate: We have to conserve, to play it safe. We don't have the money to make a mistake. In good times, however, those very same people will tell you to relax, take it easy. There's not enough need to innovate: We can afford to be conservative, to play it safe.

So it seems that we face two choices: Either be invisible, uncriticized, anonymous, and safe or take a chance at true greatness, uniqueness, and the Purple Cow. The point is simple, but it bears repeating: Boring always leads to failure. Boring is always the riskiest strategy. Smart businesspeople realize this and work to minimize (but not eliminate) the risk from the process. They know that sometimes it's not going to work, but they accept the fact that that's okay.

Stand Out from the Herd III: The Color of Money

How did Dutch Boy Paint stir up the paint business? It's so simple, it's scary. They changed the can.

Paint cans are heavy, hard to carry, hard to close, hard to open, hard to pour, and no fun. Yet they've been around for a long time, and most people assumed that there had to be a reason why they were so bad. Dutch Boy realized that *there was no reason*. They also realized that the can was an integral part of the product: People don't buy paint, they buy painted walls, and the can makes that process much easier.

Dutch Boy used that insight and introduced an easier-to-carry, easier-to-pour, easier-to-close paint jug. "Customers tell us that the new Twist & Pour paint container is a packaging innovation that was long overdue," says Dennis Eckols, group vice president of the home division for Fred Meyer stores. "People wonder why it took so long for someone to come up with the idea, and they love Dutch Boy for doing it."

It's an amazing innovation. Worth noticing. Not only did the new packaging increase sales, but it also got them more distribution (at a higher retail price!).

That is marketing done right. Marketing where the marketer changes the product, not the ads.

Why It Pays (Big) To Be a Purple Cow

As the ability to be remarkable continues to demonstrate its value in the marketplace, the rewards that follow the Purple Cow increase. Whether you develop a new insurance policy, make a hit record, or write a groundbreaking book, the money and satisfaction that follow are extraordinary. In exchange for taking the risk, creators of a Purple Cow get a huge upside when they get it right.

Even better, you don't have to be remarkable all the time to enjoy the upside. Starbucks was remarkable a few years ago. Now they're boring. But that burst of innovation and insight has allowed them to expand to thousands of stores around the world. Compare that growth in assets to Maxwell House. Ten years ago, all of the brand value in coffee resided with them, not with Starbucks. But Maxwell House played it safe (they thought), and now they remain stuck with not much more than they had a decade ago.

Once you've created something remarkable, the challenge is to do two things simultaneously: One, milk the Purple Cow for everything it's worth. Figure out how to extend it and profit from it for as long as possible. Two, build an environment where you are likely to invent an entirely new Purple Cow in time to replace the first one when its benefits inevitably trail off.

These are contradictory goals. The creator of a Purple Cow enjoys the profits, accolades, and feeling of omniscience that come with a success. None of those outcomes accompany a failed attempt at a new Cow. Thus, the tempting thing to do is to coast. Take no chances. Take profits. Fail to reinvest.

AOL, Marriott, Marvel Comics, Palm, Yahoo—the list goes on and on. Each company had a breakthrough, built an empire around it, and then failed to take another risk. It used to be easy to coast for a long time after a few remarkable successes. Disney coasted for decades. Milton Berle did too. It's too easy to decide to sit out the next round, rationalizing that you're spending the time and energy to build on what you've got instead of investing in the future. So here's one simple, tangible suggestion. Create two teams: the inventors and the milkers. Put them in separate buildings. Hold a formal ceremony when you move a product from one group to the other. Celebrate them both, and rotate people around.

Stand Out from the Herd IV: Chewing My Own Cud

So, how does an author get his new book to stand out from all of the other marketing books? By trying to create a remarkable way to market a book about remarkable marketing. How? By not selling it in stores. Instead, a copy of the book version of *Purple Cow* is available for free to anyone reading this article.

You pay for postage and handling ($5), and FAST COMPANY will send you one copy of the book-length version of this article for free (visit www.fastcompany.com/keyword/purplecow67 for details). How does this pay? Visit the site and I'll show you my entire marketing plan.

What It Means to Be a Marketer Today

If the Purple Cow is now one of the *Ps* of marketing, it has a series of big implications for the enterprise. In fact, it changes the definition of marketing. It used to be that engineering invented, manufacturing built, marketing marketed, sales sold, and the president managed the whole shebang. Marketing, better called "advertising," was about communicating the values of a product after it had been developed and manufactured.

That's clearly not a valid strategy in a world where product attributes (everything from service to design) are now at the heart of what it means to be a marketer. Marketing is the act of inventing the product. The effort of designing it. The craft of producing it. The art of pricing it. The technique of selling it. How can a Purple Cow company not be run by a marketer?

Companies that create Purple Cows, such as JetBlue Airways, Hasbro, Poland Spring, and Starbucks, *have* to be run by marketers. Turns out that the CEO of JetBlue made a critical decision on day one: He put the head of marketing in charge of product design and training as well. It shows. JetBlue sells a time-sensitive commodity just like American Airlines does, but somehow it manages to make a profit doing it. All of these companies are marketers at their very core.

The geniuses who managed to invent 1-800-COLLECT are true marketers. They didn't figure out how to market an existing service. Instead, the marketing is built into the product—from the easy-to-remember phone number to the very idea that MCI could steal the collect-call business from the pay-phone companies.

But isn't the same idea true for a local restaurant, a grinding-wheel company, and Citibank? In a world where anything we need is good enough and where just about all of the profit comes from the Purple Cow, we must all be marketers.

You've got a chance to reinvent who you are and what you do. Your company can reenergize itself around the idea of involving designers in marketing and marketers in design. You can stop fighting slow growth with mind-numbing grunt work and start investing in insight and innovation instead. If a company is failing, it's the fault of the most senior management, and the problem is probably this: They are just running a company, not marketing a product. And today, that's a remarkably ineffective way to compete.

Contributing editor **SETH GODIN** (sgodin@fastcompany.com) has written some of Fast Company's most influential articles, from "Permission Marketing" (April: May 1998) to "Unleash Your Idea Virus" (August 2000). This essay is adapted from his book, *Purple Cow: Transform Your Business by Becoming Remarkable* (Portfolio, May 8, 2003). The book is available at www.Apurplecow.com and other select locations.

Starbucks' 'Venti' Problem

Expanding Too Far Too Fast Can Turn Companies from Offbeat to Bland.

DANIEL GROSS

Coffee addicts were shaken, and stirred, recently when a memo written by Starbucks Corp. founder and Chairman Howard Schultz was posted on the Internet. Noting with a mixture of pride and horror that Starbucks has gone from 1,000 to 13,000 stores in 10 years, Schultz expressed regret over a "series of decisions that, in retrospect, have led to the watering down of the Starbucks experience and what some might call the commoditization of our brand."

"Some people," Schultz wrote, "even call our stores sterile, cookie cutter, no longer reflecting the passion our partners feel about our coffee."

The memo was seen as a rare example of brutal executive candor. Of course, to this Starbuck's habitué (doppio espresso, no sugar) it would have been more timely, say, five years ago, back when there was still a block in midtown Manhattan that didn't have a Starbucks.

But the Schultz memo is interesting and useful nonetheless, because it shows that even an iconic company that serves a highly addictive product can water down the immense value of its brand by expanding too far and too fast and in too many directions at once. Sadly, this is a fate that befalls many American companies. Time and again in recent years, we've seen small, cutting-edge and quirky brands gain critical mass—only to lose their charm and customer appeal after they engage in breakneck expansion.

Why does this happen? Companies can't help it, in part because the huge macroeconomic forces that dictate corporate behavior impel them to expand too fast and too wide. But at the same time, the powerful psychological forces that dictate consumer behavior can cause customers to recoil from the chains they once loved.

Many of America's best-known chains came of age in a period in which it was easy for companies to go public at a comparatively young age. And publicly held companies, whether they make turbines or tiramisu, are programmed to maximize efficiency and increase sales every quarter—no matter what. Inevitably, this mentality leads to the cutting of corners.

In his memo, Schultz noted that increasing the scale of Starbucks had led to a number of necessary corner-cuts: For instance, the introduction of "flavor-locked packaging" that has caused stores to lose their distinctive aroma, or the decision to install automatic espresso machines. "We solved a major problem in terms of speed of service and efficiency," Schultz noted, but "overlooked the fact that we would remove much of the romance and theatre that was in play with the use of the [La Marzocco] machines."

Consumers can quickly punish companies that water down their offerings too much for the sake of scale. Consider the sad case of Krispy Kreme. A beloved icon of the South, Krispy Kreme's chief selling point was a limited selection of sickly sweet doughnuts, made fresh on the premises. When the chain began to expand along the East Coast in the 1990s, exiled Southerners and salivating locals queued on the chilly sidewalks, waiting for the red light to signal fresh glazed gut-bombs.

But after Krispy Kreme went public in 2000, the company, eager to supercharge sales, started making doughnuts in central locations and distributing them, hours or even days later, for sale in convenience and grocery stores. Feh! The store-bought sugar rings quickly got stale. And so did Krispy Kreme. Soon after it was flogged on the cover of Fortune as "America's hottest brand" in July 2003, the stock collapsed.

In today's flat, borderless world, managers and investors now expect that a great business idea will—and can—instantly turn into a great global presence. These days, a suddenly hot company believes that it should be expanding in Canton, Ohio, at the same time it is expanding in Canton province in China. And that inevitably leads companies to engineer the individuality gene out of the company's DNA.

Schultz noted that the need to build so many outlets at once has resulted in "stores that no longer have the soul of the past and reflect a chain of stores vs. the warm feeling of a neighborhood store." In other words, in order to turn into a Fortune 500 company, Starbucks had to start thinking and acting like one. And nothing saps the essence out of a creative, quirky brand faster than a bunch of senior vice presidents at a Fortune 500 company.

Bigger isn't always better

Snapple, for instance, rode from obscurity to household name in the early 1990s based on its funky flavors and offbeat advertising campaign, which featured Wendy Kaufman, a heavyset employee of the company with a thick Long Island accent. The company's impressive growth attracted the attention of the conglomerate Quaker Oats Co., which paid a whopping $1.7 billion to buy Snapple in 1994.

Of course, the Quaker Oats crowd decided the suddenly big brand needed advertising that was more professional and high-concept. In 1996, when the company unceremoniously canned the Snapple Lady, the backlash in the marketplace was almost instantaneous. Sales plummeted, and in May 1997, Quaker Oats sold Snapple at a fire sale price of $300 million. One of the first acts of the acquirer, Triarc Companies, was to bring back Kaufman as a spokesperson.

The Snapple case illustrates how important consumer psychology is to the well-being of brands. Part of the original lure of Starbucks was that its arrival bestowed a certain cultural significance on one's town or neighborhood. No longer. When a chain becomes of *every* place, it's no longer of *any* place.

The first California Pizza Kitchen, which opened in Beverly Hills in 1985, with its then-exotic wood-burning ovens and Thai pizza, became part of the local, only-in-L.A. experience. But now that noshers can order mango tandoori chicken pizza at 180 outlets across the country, Angelenos no longer take pride in the chain. There's very little California in the California Pizza Kitchen any more.

One of the greatest traps into which rapidly growing chains fall is expanding beyond their natural habitat into inhospitable climes. The first Restoration Hardware was founded in 1980, in Eureka, Calif., and became a haven for yuppies interested in retro home furnishings. It grew slowly, mostly in California, and by 1998, the year it went public, it had 47 stores.

But then, pow! Within three years, the number of stores more than doubled as the company expanded into places such as Oklahoma, Mississippi and Missouri. This was like planting palm trees in Montana. It didn't take. Selling expensive retro light fixtures was a brilliant business model when it was confined to a few markets, but a failure when extended beyond the coasts. In recent years, Restoration Hardware has retrenched and closed stores.

Of course, not all offbeat brands succumb to the temptations of rapid growth and public capital. Several California-based firms have managed to expand at a reasonable pace without compromising their integrity or charm.

Trader Joe's, the quirky grocer whose first outlet opened in Pasadena in 1967, was acquired in 1979 by the family that owns the German grocer Aldi. Expanding methodically and slowly—there are now more than 250 outlets all over the country—Trader Joe's has maintained its combination of low prices, off-beat offerings and funky marketing materials.

In-N-Out Burger, which is privately held, has maintained a cult following, in large part because it has insisted on not turning burgers into an industrial process, all while expanding gingerly in California, Arizona and Nevada. As a result, it remains a destination, a privilege, a brand that is owned by the minority of Americans who have regular access to it.

The overriding imperative of American business is to give customers what they want, whenever and wherever they want it. That's precisely what Starbucks has done in recent years. And that's precisely what is causing the barista-in-chief so much angst.

DANIEL GROSS writes the Moneybox column for Slate.

Making Cents of Pricing

Build business cases to enhance the bottom line.

DAVID M. FELDMAN

Considering all the elements of the marketing mix, price has the most direct effect on profitability. Price is also the most easily controlled of the elements. Yet properly setting prices and measuring their impact on the entire organization is seldom done properly, or in a manner that optimizes long-term market share and profitability. Pricing strategy must focus on over all category profitability and consider the strategic implications of price changes on brand equity, product positioning, product cannibalization, and competitive response. In addition, the impact of price changes needs to be evaluated in the context of both return on marketing investment and impact on the remaining elements of the marketing mix.

Marketing departments traditionally provide insights into market acceptance of new offerings and prices but have had limited impact on building business cases for changing prices. At the 2004 AMA Research Conference, Sally Dancer, a senior practice expert at consulting firm McKinsey & Co., indicated that CEOs want marketing to become a full business partner. She then went on to challenge marketers to become more involved in developing business cases that directly link marketing initiatives with profits.

Based on what Dancer and others are saying, there is a big incentive for marketing departments to expand their traditional role of providing insights and become a more active partner in building a financial model, especially when it comes to developing pricing strategy. In order for marketing departments to make the transition from simply providing business insights to developing full-blown business cases, they need to redesign their research studies to reflect actual marketplace behavior, incorporating inputs for all items in the marketing mix.

Current Paradigms

Traditionally, the role of marketing in developing pricing strategy has been the ability to understand market acceptance of price changes to new and existing products and services. Through the use of conjoint experiments, market research-

ers have learned about the trade-offs between brands, prices, features, and channels for leveraging customer value propositions and developing pricing strategies. This is valuable information, but this type of research does not do a good job of replicating the complexity of current marketplaces and extracting the real impact of price and price sensitivity. For example, conjoint studies create an artificial marketplace that forces competitive offerings to contain similar features and prices when, in reality, many competitive offerings have features and prices that are unique to a single brand. In addition, conjoint experiments typically underestimate the impact of price and provide price sensitivity in aggregate, rather than by brand.

EXECUTIVE briefing
Marketing departments traditionally provide insights into market acceptance of new offerings and prices, but have limited impact on building business cases for changing prices. In order to make the transition from providing such insights into developing full-blown business cases, marketers need new business tools to enhance their positions in the organization.

Pricing research typically focuses on a customer's preference for specific offerings and reports findings in terms of percentages. Given the lack of a complete set of competitive offerings and prices in the marketplace, it's difficult to align preference measures with current market conditions and then accurately project how changes in the marketing mix will affect the marketplace, especially in financial terms. Furthermore, this process tends to lower the value of research because management can only make decisions on a relative "percentage" basis, rather than on an absolute "profit" basis. To develop a meaningful pricing strategy, marketers must integrate customer input on a complete competitive market-place with all the other business variables that affect pricing decisions.

Many organizations make pricing decisions based on secondary or syndicated data sources, internal costs, or competitive factors. Although each of these items needs to be considered, profit potential and brand equity can erode significantly with strategies based on these items alone. Some companies get input on customers' willingness to pay from measurements based on observed marketplace behavior. Such measurements are limited because they only reflect existing product and service characteristics. In addition, observational data doesn't involve controls, so it can be difficult to separate the trends and sensitivities in the observed data from external phenomena such as product availability, promotion, and advertising for both the company and competitors.

Because internal costs have a major impact on profitability, not linking them to market input on competitive pricing and customer willingness to pay can affect profits dramatically. It's unwise to develop a reactive pricing strategy based on customers leveraging one supplier over another to get the best possible price. It's equally unwise to develop a pricing strategy in reaction to competitive price changes, internal sales goals, or inventory levels. These factors need to be considered but basing pricing strategies only on such inputs can damage long-term profitability and product equity. Pricing strategy must also take into account long-term market response and impact on sales channels and profitability.

Business Case Development

Figure 1 shows a comprehensive approach to developing a financial model from market insight. The key is to be able to report the information collected from current and potential customers in the context of overall profitability. There are four key components to this approach:

- Determine the strategic and tactical issues to support the business case.
- Develop a competitive marketplace.
- Determine marketplace sensitivities.
- Determine the impact of changes to the marketing mix in terms of bottom line profitability.

Key Issues

The critical first step for marketing is to first understand the key issues. There is nothing more frustrating than to present the results of a study only to be asked: "Did you consider . . ." Therefore, it's extremely important to review with senior management all of the relevant marketing issues that affect costs and profitability before you design the study.

Following are examples of the types of questions that need to be considered when reviewing key issues with senior management. Note that most of the examples are strategic and need to be considered to keep a strategic focus on developing

business cases in concert with the myriad tactical issues that tend to overwhelm the planning process.

- How do I ensure that my pricing decisions will support the overall long-term positioning of my product?
- For a specific offering in a category, at what price will I maximize profitability for the entire company offering in the category?
- When introducing a new product, or an extension of an existing product, what will be the impact on existing products?
- How can I develop and price bundles of products/ services to enhance overall profitability?
- How do I tailor pricing and bundle offerings to meet the unique needs of my most valuable customers?
- For branded products, how can I effectively compete with value/generic offerings?
- How do I determine the specific benefits for which customers are willing to pay more?
- What will be the impact of competitive responses to my new offerings and how would that change my optimal offering/price?
- If market constraints force downward pressure on prices, how do I price my offerings to minimize the impact on overall positioning and long-term profitability?

Competitive Marketplace

Once the tactical and strategic issues are defined and prioritized, the research study needs to be carefully designed. When focusing on pricing strategy, the survey instrument must include actual market offerings and prices. The reason for this is twofold. First, it's important to be able to model what the respondents are currently purchasing based on current prices. This base case will be used to calibrate the model and to aid in determining cannibalization. Second, whenever new offerings or prices are considered, the respondent needs to react to them in the context of all the options currently available. Here's where a lot of research studies miss the mark by trying to measure response to new offerings and prices independent of the other alternatives available. By including all company and competitive offerings, the respondent's task of selecting new offerings or prices is more accurate and less subject to survey bias.

To accommodate these types of pricing studies, a custom-designed discrete choice experiment is highly recommended. A discrete choice experiment provides the best analytical methodology for developing pricing strategy. When properly executed, it allows the researcher to present a complete portfolio of products and services that parallels current marketplace offerings. In addition, combinations of new and existing products and services can be tested in and out of the current marketplace, as well as testing changing prices and specific features for any offering in the marketplace.

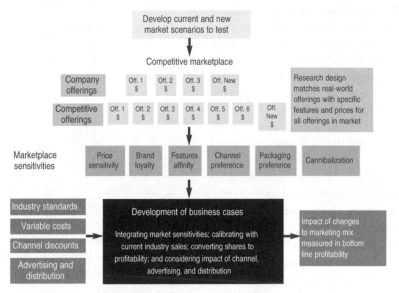

Figure 1 Developing Business Cases from Market Insight

In general, the key components of a discrete choice design involve multiple price levels for offerings from the company and key competitors, along with testing availability for certain offerings in the marketplace. In addition, offerings need to be tested in and out of the marketplace to determine which offerings will lose share when a new product or service is added and which offerings will gain share when a product or service is no longer in the market. Prices can be different for all products and services being tested and should reflect current market prices. The ranges of prices to be tested must be wide enough to allow proper sensitivity testing and future use of the market response tool.

It's important to understand how the market values the different components of an offering. For certain studies, part of the design needs to include options for de-bundling an offering, as well as for combining multiple products and services into a package offering. In both cases, multiple price levels would need to be tested for each de-bundling and package offering. Another consideration for the design is allowing respondent choices to be recorded in a way that matches how customers normally would purchase products and services. In addition, respondents should indicate not only which offering they would choose but also a volumetric measure, such as "how many" or "how often."

Marketplace Sensitivities

Once the survey has been properly designed and executed, market sensitivities need to be derived from customer input. The modeling of market input must analyze the choices the respondents gave to specific market conditions and convert them into measures of price sensitivity, brand loyalty, feature affinity, channel and packaging preference, and cannibalization. In addition to deriving these sensitivities, such detailed respondent-level choice data will also allow

development of segments. Grouping together segments of respondents who exhibit similar market sensitivities will provide a better understanding of the unique needs of target segments. A segment may be defined as customers who prefer a certain brand, feature, channel, or package option—or who have similar price sensitivity.

With these market sensitivities, market share estimates can be produced for new and existing offerings, and the effects of changing prices can be used to update market share estimates. Before these market sensitivities can be used to build a financial model, certain calibrations, conversions, and adjustments need to be made.

Profitability Model

The first step toward building a profitability model is in being able to link survey results to current market size and share. When linking to current market, a base case needs to be developed. The base case is defined as offerings currently in the marketplace, at current prices. The two functions of the base case are replicating known market shares and sizing the overall market in terms of total units sold. The linking is done by calibrating the model's base case with known market shares and market sizes at the same prices and availabilities. This is a very important step in bridging the richness of market input with the accuracy of known market information. No matter how good the sampling or how realistically the survey matches the actual buying experience, this step ensures all projections are based on an agreed-upon starting point. The key for the survey is in deriving sensitivities from market input, putting this information into a context that management can understand, and then using that to develop an effective pricing strategy.

Once the model has been calibrated and can produce share estimates for alternative scenarios, it needs to report results in profit or contribution. This involves integrating variable costs and relevant channel discounts. In most cases, subtracting the unit cost from the retail selling price will indicate the profit. But sometimes when a product or service is sold through different channels, a component of the business case involves examining the retail selling price minus the unit cost along with channel discounts. In this case, it would be important to break out the channel discounts so that assumptions on different channel discounts and their effects on channel volumes can be considered.

Before testing the financial impact of the various market scenarios, certain adjustments might need to be made. Advertising and distribution are the two main areas where adjustments need to be considered. Although there is a big advantage to collecting survey data from a carefully designed, controlled experiment, there also are biases associated with it. By nature of being survey driven, these types of market insights make the assumption that the entire marketplace has complete knowledge about new offerings and changes to prices, as well as 100% availability of any products or services being offered. To adjust for this, the marketing department, working with other departments, needs to set up a range of awareness levels and associated advertising costs, as well as a range of expected distribution levels. Typically these assumptions follow an "s" curve distribution as they track over time. Therefore, it's quite useful to give the financial model a time element so that assumptions for awareness and distribution levels can be tracked over a specified time period. Estimated costs to achieve these levels should also be included in the financial model.

Building Business Cases

To better understand how developing a financial model can improve marketing strategy, let's consider a case where a company is launching a new offering and wants to know the optimal price. The optimal price is defined as the price that provides the highest contribution for the entire company offering. After collecting and analyzing the market sensitivities, the model first produces market shares based only on existing products and current prices. These shares are calibrated against known market shares to adjust for any sample bias and to ensure that any projections are based on current market shares and sizes.

Next, using the market sensitivities derived from market input, a scenario of the new offering at a specific price is tested. Based on the market sensitivities, the model produces updated market share numbers. Knowing the potential of this new product is very important, but just as importantly, the model also tells us where that business will come from. For example, if the new offering gets a significant share but that new share cannibalizes your existing portfolio, your net gains may be very small. It will be much more important to study the effect that price has on the new offering to see if, by

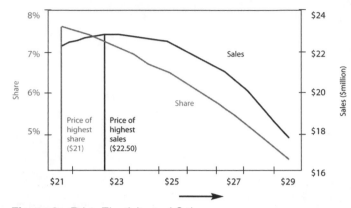

Figure 2 Price Elasticity and Sales

changing the price, you can better target the right customers and so minimize cannibalization and improve overall profitability for the company.

It's important to understand how the market values the different components of an offering.

In these types of studies, multiple price points are tested for the new offering as well as certain other offerings in the marketplace. Using these multiple price points, the model develops price elasticity curves that show the expected share at different price points.

Figure 2 shows two curves, with the gray curve representing share and the black one showing sales at different prices. Looking at the red share curve at a price of $21, projected share is 7.5%. If the price was raised to $29, share would drop to 4.5%. This does not tell us the optimal price, it only indicates that the lowest price provides the highest share. Figure 2 also indicates that the selling price that maximizes sales for the new offering is $22.50. But this is not the optimal price for the new offering either—it does not factor in the impact of the margin for the new offering.

Figure 3 shows a contribution curve (selling price less unit cost). This suggests that the optimum price to maximize contribution for the new offering is $25. It's interesting to note that even though share drops from 7.5% to 6.5% when price is raised from $21 to $25, contribution increased from $4.5 million to more than $7.5 million. But $25 is not the optimal price for the new offering either—we must still consider the impact of the new offering on the overall company contribution.

It's necessary to develop one final chart that allows the new offering's price to change, while also showing the effects on the overall company contribution. Figure 4 shows what the total company contribution will be at various price levels for the new offering. This chart indicates that the optimal selling price for the new offering should be at a higher price of $28.

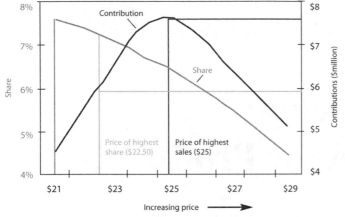

Figure 3 Optimum Price Based on Contribution

Figure 4 Optimum Priced Based on Overall Company Contribution

At this price, cannibalization is minimized, with the current offering and company contribution being maximized.

In terms of developing pricing strategy, marketing departments have a real opportunity to elevate themselves and become full business partners with the rest of the organization. This can be accomplished by enhancing their traditional marketing insights into complete business cases. The key

for research is to talk about profitability and to link pricing studies to business issues in the context of the relevant strategic environment. Success with pricing can only elevate research's positioning in the organization.

DAVID M. FELDMAN is a senior partner at SDR Consulting in Atlanta. He may be reached at dfeldman@sdr-consulting.com.

Customer-Centric Pricing:
The Surprising Secret for Profitability

Companies spend enormous amounts of energy and capital in creating value for customers, but less regard is given to actually capturing the value they have created. Segmentation based on buying behavior uncovers a tremendous differential in willingness to pay for subjective product attributes such as convenience, status, and quality. Purchase decisions are made through an assessment of a myriad of factors balancing perceptions of value components against price in a subtle, complex, and often sub-conscious decision matrix. Customer-centric pricing requires the simultaneous and continuous assessment of product attributes, customer perceptions, and the circumstances of time and place by listening to customers' actions. It is a means of assuring that companies assess the value they create for customers and extract that value from the marketplace.

ROBERT G. CROSS[a,b] AND ASHUTOSH DIXIT[c*]

1. In Search of Opportunity

Despite recent productivity gains, pressures on profitability persist. Due to an uncertain economy and fierce global competition, profits will continue to be inconsistent. Many companies have already cut costs and squeezed productivity to the extent that they are now cutting flesh, not fat. They need to find new ways to consistently grow the bottom line.

Companies spend billions on enhancing brand preference and product differentiation. However, when faced with the prospect of extracting the benefits of these efforts through price differentials, they often fail. Firms tend to respond to lower-priced competition in one of two ways: either by capitulation (cutting prices to meet competition), or by inaction (not responding and ultimately surrendering market share to competitors) (Porter, 1979). They do not often expend the effort to determine the appropriate price differential for their products in the marketplace, an oversight that results in billions of dollars of lost opportunity.

2. Back to the Future

Prior to the industrial revolution, all sales transactions were customer-centric, as each transaction was subject to individual bargaining and negotiation. After the industrial revolu-

tion tapped mass markets, however, face-to-face negotiations became impractical. Mass-market expansion led to standardized means of production and standardized sales terms. Accordingly, companies became more product-centric. This product centricity encompassed all aspect of the product, including product features, distribution, service, and price.

Currently, most pricing is still product-centric. Product managers focus on the cost of the product, its physical attributes (size, features, and functions), and the margins they seek from the product. Product positioning vis-à-vis the company's other offerings and competitive offerings may also play a role. This mostly internal focus often creates a disparity between what product managers and customers perceive a product's value to be. This disparity in value perception leads to lost profit opportunities from under-pricing (creating consumer surplus) or over-pricing (lost sales).

However, many businesses are becoming more conscious of the need to look externally, with greater frequency, at the customer perception of value when setting and revising prices. This phenomenon is a function of increased product differentiation and customer segmentation (Porter, 1979), as well as an increase in the knowledge and technology associated with predicting customer response (Cross, 1997).

---

[a] Revenue Analytics, Inc., USA
[b] Terry College of Business, University of Georgia, Athens, GA 30602, USA
[c] James J. Nance College of Business Administration, Cleveland State University, 2121 Euclid Avenue, BU 458, Cleveland, OH 44115-2214, USA
[*] Corresponding author. E-mail address: a.dixit1@csuohio.edu (A. Dixit).

3. The Customer-Centric Pricing Process

Successful companies go beyond the concept of value creation to the reality of value extraction. While value creation is about getting into the heads of the consumer, value extraction is about getting into their wallets. It is only when the customer agrees with the value proposition and pays for the goods or services that the efforts in value creation pay off. Key to this process is setting customer-centric prices that accurately reflect the perceived value of their products to each customer segment (Anderson & Narus, 2003; Cross, 1997; Dolan, 1995).

Price should be seen as a communicative device between buyer and seller which continually reflects constantly changing market variables such as brand preference, the availability of supply, substitutable alternatives, and a host of other factors (Hayek, 1945). Companies which understand this function and use a customer-centric approach to pricing will be able to extract more from their value-creation strategies.

The customer-centric pricing process is described in Fig. 1. Companies can take advantage of customer heterogeneity by careful attention to:

1. customer segmentation;
2. measuring customer value;
3. capturing the value created by pricing;
4. continual reassessment of the product's perceived value in the relevant market. (Fleischmann, Hall, & Pyke, 2004).

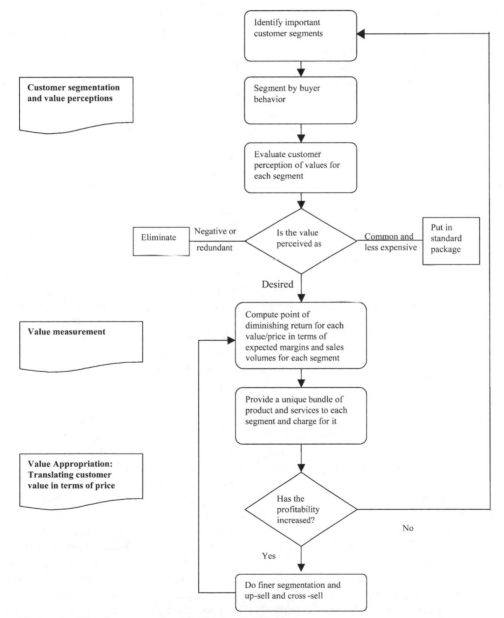

Figure 1 The Customer-Centric Pricing Process.

4. Segmentation Based on Value Perceptions and Buyer Behavior

Significant profit potential comes from understanding the value each customer segment places on individual products, then charging prices that accurately reflect that perceived value (Anderson & Narus, 2003, 2004; Nagle & Holden, 2002). Assessing and capturing the value that a firm creates for a specific market segment requires segmenting the customers into groups with similar perceptions of value and willingness to pay. Since customers define value by a wide variety of metrics, this is not an easy task. Conventional market segmentation techniques include demographic variables such as age, sex, race, income, marital status, education level, and geographical location, as well as psychographic variables such as activities, interests, opinions, and life-style (Assael & Roscoe, 1976; Wells, 1975).

These traditional methodologies have been able to effectively classify relatively homogeneous groups for purposes of product development, promotions, communications, advertising, and other marketing mix variables. (Smith, 1956; Haley, 1968; Frank, Massy, & Wind, 1972; Wansink & Park, 2000). They are not, however, necessarily effective in segmenting customers by willingness to pay, which varies based upon the customer's specific circumstances of time and place (Belk, 1975; Smith & Nagle, 2002). For example, demographic and psychographic segmentations do not adequately account for who will pay for the convenience of an ATM and when and where they will accept an additional fee.

To extract value from the marketplace through customer-centric pricing, we must answer the question: "What is this customer willing to pay at this point in time?" Segmentation by buying behavior is required to determine the answer. Unlike demographics and psychographics that attempt to define who the customers are, segmentation by buying behavior focuses on predicting how they will respond at the time of purchase. The hospitality industry has discovered that such customer-centric segmentation is a much better indicator of price sensitivity than either demographics or psychographics.

Take a sales executive for a pharmaceutical company, for example. She may be very specific about hotel location (proximate to the hospital she is calling on), but relatively indifferent to price if she is on an expense account. However, the same individual, whose demographics and psychographics remain the same, is likely to be more flexible about hotel location and significantly more price conscious if she is traveling with her family on a personal budget.

A customer's perception of the value of any product may change based on subjective factors, some related to the product itself, and others related to the individual's particular circumstances vis-à-vis the product. Factors that may tremendously influence the price a customer is willing to pay for a product include such seemingly difficult to isolate and quantify concepts as status, loyalty, convenience, urgency, and quality. In fact, these subjective, intangible factors may be more meaningful and valuable to the consumer than the product's tangible attributes.

4.1. The Surprising Secret to Profitability

Segmentation based on buying behavior uncovers a tremendous differential in willingness to pay for subjective product attributes such as convenience, status, quality, and need. These price differentials are far greater than most businesses assume, and they can be the basis for substantial profits. It is this price differential that companies could have or should have which is essential to incremental profit. For example, price increases which recognize value creation based on brand preference can reduce consumer surplus. If they do not reduce sales, the additional revenue drops directly to the bottom line. Similarly, discounts offered to micro-market segments of customers which have only a casual need for the product or who are brand indifferent might spark incremental sales. Both present profit-generating opportunities. Unfortunately, these opportunities are sometimes missed.

The desire for an edgy prestige among professionals has helped Harley Davidson leverage a relatively low-tech motorcycle into a premium-priced American icon. Accordingly, the value created by the brand image was captured. Comparable cravings were created when BMW launched its exotic Z8 sports car. However, many of the first buyers sold their cars for more than twice the sticker price to other eager customers who could not get on BMW's waiting list; thus, BMW did not extract all the value it had created. Similarly, extraordinary demand for Microsoft's Xbox game console (launched just prior to Christmas, 2001) caused many of the first units, bought at retail for $199, to be sold for over $1000 on auction sites. In each of these cases, the subjective value in status overwhelms the objective value of the item itself. Moreover, the consumer surplus sometimes shows up as profit to arbitrageurs, not as incremental profit to the entity that created the value in the first place.

Sporting events, concerts, and theaters often do not appreciate the vast differentials in perceived customer value they create. Super Bowl seats are often resold by "brokers" at prices that are generally five times what the NFL charges. When Mel Brooks' musical, "The Producers" first came out, the $35 Balcony seats were sold out for the next five months, and the $99 Orchestra seats were not available for another year, except from "brokers" who charged up to ten times the original price.

Customer-centric pricing aligns the price charged with the value created for the specific customer segment at the relevant time and place. This alignment reduces consumer surplus and significantly enhances profits as the incremental revenue from pricing precision becomes incremental profit. Accordingly, with customer-centric pricing, the company that creates the value captures the benefit of that value, not brokers or other resellers.

Not long ago, the Washington Opera was faced with a revenue shortfall. Rather than attempting to raise across-the-board ticket prices by 5% as they had always done in the past, they evaluated each seat based upon "customer experience" criteria. They found significant differences in the quality of the experience, even within the Orchestra section. The back row at the side of the Orchestra section was extremely different from the tenth row center, yet the price was the same. They also recognized that weekend performances were always sold out, but weekday performances invariably had empty seats. Previously, all seats were sold at one of three price levels: $47, $63, and $85. After customer-centric segmentation, they applied customer-centric prices that were aligned with the perception of value for each seat, for each day of the week. Nine different price levels were

---

Application of Principles

Miss Margaritte's Salon

   Margaritte Jackson owns a hair styling salon in a suburban office building. Her clients range from professional women working in the building to retirees living in the neighborhood. She has two stylists dedicated to "cut and style." She currently charges $50 for that service (which takes about one hour), and the two stylists perform, on average, 50 of these services per week, generating $2500 in revenue. This weekly revenue barely covers her costs. Her shop is extremely busy on Fridays and Saturdays, but virtually empty on Tuesdays and Wednesdays. To reduce her costs, she has considered asking each of her stylists to take one of those midweek days off with no pay.

   Margaritte was reluctant to ask her employees to take a cut in pay. Fortunately, she understood the concept of value creation. She renovated her shop and switched to an exclusive line of hair care products. She expected these actions to increase the perceived value of her services by 20 percent. Accordingly, she raised her price by 20 percent to $60 and maintained the same number of customers, generating a 20 percent increase in revenue to $3000.

   Despite this increase in revenue, she was still not netting much more income because of paying for the renovations and the increased cost of her supplies. Tuesdays and Wednesdays were still slow, and Fridays and Saturdays were still completely booked. She wished that she could spread the customers more evenly throughout the week, but she knew that most of them wanted their hair freshly done for the weekend. She decided to segment her customers by the perceived value they put on different days of the week. For Friday and Saturday cuts, she raised her price to $65. She gave a price incentive to customers who were willing to move to Tuesday and Wednesday, lowering the cost to $45. As it turns out, many of her retired customers were time-flexible and were glad to move to weekdays for a discount. Margaritte was still able to fill her Friday and Saturday schedules with those women who were less price conscious and more style conscious.

   To Margaritte's surprise and delight, by increasing her sales midweek and charging more on weekends, she increased her revenue another 20 percent. Only this time, it cost her nothing. The additional $600 per week was pure profit. It came from understanding that customers valued her services differently on different days of the week. This is customer-centric pricing.

---

installed with a broader dispersion of prices. Ticket prices were spread between $29 and $150, with midweek and weekend differentials. Seats in the balcony that would otherwise go unsold on weekdays were filled with people who could now afford the opera. Raising the price of the prime Orchestra seats closer to market value reduced the consumer surplus. As a result, the Washington Opera increased its revenues the next year by 9%, almost double what it could have only hoped for under a 5% across-the-board increase (Cross, 1997). These customer-centric pricing techniques are available to any business, irrespective of the level of sophistication, as illustrated by Miss Margaritte's Salon.

5. Customer Perceptions of Value Components

Customer-centric pricing requires the simultaneous and continuous assessment of product attributes, customer perceptions, and the circumstances of time and place. Customers' purchase decisions are made through an assessment of a myriad of factors balancing perceptions of value components against price using subtle, complex, and often sub-conscious decision variables.

   Customer-centric pricing requires understanding and utilizing these decision variables, in order to optimize revenue opportunities. For example, airlines have been adept at exploiting an urgency factor through revenue management to price-ration seats for last-minute, high-fare travelers while offering deeply discounted seats to advance purchase customers who have time to shop for the lowest fare (Cross, 1997).

   Brand loyalty is prized for fostering customer retention and raising competitive barriers. However, it also creates a significant opportunity for price premiums. Gillette has continued to invest in product improvement and promotion, and has created and leveraged brand loyalty successfully to raise razor prices, extracting very healthy margins from relatively ordinary shaving items. These profits enable Gillette to invest in R and D for new products, thus assuring market leadership.

   Customer-centric segmentation by buying behavior helps distinguish customers' decision patterns that are price-insensitive. Price-insensitive attributes identify where customer value is high and price premiums can be charged. Business managers frequently miss capturing the value they create. The Ritz Carlton hotel chain established an extraordinary reputation for luxury, quality, and customer service; however, it did not fully extract the value it created in the market, and was only marginally profitable for years. When Marriott International acquired the Ritz Carlton chain, it used sophisticated revenue optimization technology to understand when and where it could increase price. In its first five years of ownership of Ritz Carlton, Marriott was able to extract the value Ritz Carlton had created through its reputation for quality, consistency, and customer service. Marriott increased the average daily rate of the Ritz Carlton properties by 26%, compared to only a 6% increase in its other full service hotels.

   On the other hand, Marriott stays attuned to the desires of price-sensitive customer segments, as well. They introduced capacity-controlled discount rates with advance purchase restrictions. During the first summer these rates were offered, almost a quarter of a million room-nights were sold at this rate. Two-thirds of these room-nights represented incremental business (Hanks, Cross, & Noland, 1992).

6. Value Measurement: Listening to Customer Actions

Most firms that attempt to align product prices with customer value perceptions do so by gathering information through customer focus groups, surveys, or similar methods. Unfortunately, customers often say one thing, but do another. For example, Philips conducted a focus group of teenagers to assess their color preferences for boom boxes, and a majority of the participants listed "yellow" as their preferred color. However, at the end of the session, when participants were given their choice of picking a yellow or black boom box as they left the room, most took black boom boxes, even though they had marked "yellow" as their preferred color.

That actions speak louder than words should not come as a surprise. How many people would tell Coca-Cola, through a survey or traditional focus group, that they are willing to pay $4 for a 12 oz. can of Coke? Yet millions of $4 cans have been sold through hotel mini-bars. It is not that consumers would necessarily try to bias the results of the market research efforts; it is just that the consumers, themselves, may not be able to predict exactly what they would do, until faced with the decision. At that time, their decision will be influenced by the particulars of time and place. In this example, they may not be able to predict how thirsty they will be and whether there will be suitable alternatives.

At the critical point in the purchase decision, customers scan the immediate offerings in the marketplace and develop a consideration set based upon factors particular to their individual preferences. Within these factors, they develop a hierarchy based on their perceived values for different offerings (Zeithaml, 1988), and their purchase behavior is correlated to these perceptions of value at the instant of the decision.

The difficulties presented for customer-centric pricing are twofold. A consumer considering an automobile purchase will assign a wide range of values to each product attribute. Some will be relatively objective economic values such as fuel efficiency, maintenance, warranty, and resale value. Others will be subjective hedonic values such as design, safety, comfort, and status. Moreover, the consumer may not know in advance of making the purchase decision exactly how much weight he or she may give to each component in the value equation. Accordingly, adept companies must capture and analyze detailed customer transaction data to determine how typical members of the relevant micro-market respond to the offerings in similar circumstances. From this, they can model and predict future customer behavior.

Ford Motor Company has pioneered the application of these techniques in the automobile industry to determine what features the customers in each micro-market segment most desire

and what they are willing to pay for them. Understanding the wide range of customer preferences across a broad product line and expansive geographical market requires significant experimentation, data gathering, and analysis. Customers' perception of value will vary based on geography (trucks are more highly valued in the Southwest than the Northeast), vehicle type (truck buyers are more sensitive to cash rebates than car buyers), and product configuration (certain add-ons are much more valuable than their incremental cost).

How much rebates will affect market volume and profitability must be continually tested and analyzed. Through such market testing and analysis, Ford found that a $700 rebate for its Ranger Super Cab could encourage almost half of the customers considering the base model Ranger to upgrade to the more accommodating Super Cab. Despite the cash rebate, Ford still made thousands of dollars more profit on a Super Cab than a base model, since the customers' perception of incremental value is significantly more than the incremental cost to Ford in making the upgraded model. The automaker applied such "smarter pricing" techniques across its product lines, and Lloyd Hansen, Ford's Controller for Marketing and Sales, estimates that about $3 billion in pre-tax profits came from a series of such revenue management initiatives (Leibs, 2000).

7. From Value Creation to Value Appropriation

Customer-centric pricing involves identifying key customer segments, understanding what these customers value, creating customer value by offering unique bundles of products or services, and charging for it appropriately. Value creation is the basis for growth. The better a product is aligned with specific customers' preferences, the more it is valued. The more it is valued, the higher the probability that it will have competitive success. That is the premise behind customer focused value-creation strategies such as One-to-One Marketing and Mass Customization (Peppers & Rogers, 1993; Siminson, 2005; Zipkin, 2001).

These strategies understand the demise of the mass market and the rise of individualistic micro-market segments that demand products that address their specific needs, requirements, and desires. One-to-One Marketing and Mass Customization are successful to the extent they can differentiate both customers and products by recognizing enormous diversity in the global marketplace.

Most of these efforts at value creation focus on gaining market share or customer share in order to increase revenue and profitability. What they miss is the understanding that not only do customers want individualized products, they are often willing to pay a significant premium for them. The more differentiated a product, the less price-sensitive it will be.

Price should be a function of perceived value (Zeithaml, 1988). As companies engage in value-creation strategies and the perceived value increases to the specific customer set, the price should escalate. Often it does not. The result is what economists term a "consumer surplus," that is, a gap between what a customer is willing to pay, and what he or she actually pays.

There have been numerous predictions that the Internet would lower consumer search costs and enable software agents and shop-bots to drive costs down to the lowest common denominator. This phenomenon, however, has not occurred (Baker, Marn, & Zawada, 2001). Purchase decisions are still subjective. For the most part, they are not objectively driven by economically defined measures that can be incorporated into shop-bots. Consumers still place extraordinary value on their individual, subjective perceptions of the supplier related to factors such as reliability, convenience, and trust. These values are typically not predefined, and they vary based on circumstances of time and place. Accordingly, prices in the virtual world of commerce have exhibited the same degree of price dispersion as in the physical world.

One of the keys to customer-centric pricing is having a wide range of prices that address the relative values customers actually place on the products. As firms continue to attempt to differentiate themselves through customer value-add and more fully understand capturing the value they create through customer-centric pricing, the potential for even greater price differentiation exists.

Getting the optimal price has a salubrious effect on the bottom line. For companies with 8% profit margins, a 1% differential in price results in a 12.5% margin difference (Dolan, 1995). Through customer-centric pricing, firms set prices based on the perceived value of a product or service to specific customers or segments of customers. This strategy minimizes consumer surplus and maximizes profitability. Resourceful firms can use customer-centric pricing to leverage the value they have built in the marketplace and appreciably increase profits.

8. Sustaining Value

Building and sustaining customer value that generates a source of continual revenue requires long-term customer relations. Customer relationship management (CRM) processes and techniques have evolved to manage the effective interaction with customers over time (Lemon, White, & Winer, 2002; Sheth & Parvatiyaar, 1995). However, customer-centric prices are essential to complete the customer retention cycle.

Invariably, if the price is not right, the customer relationship is endangered. This is obvious if the price is too high, but it can also be true if the price is too low. Sports fans have always understood the tremendous difference in experience from one event to another. Unfortunately, during the highest demand times such as play-off games, often a majority of fans seeking to attend the games must resort to ticket brokers, thus bypassing the customer relationship process with the team altogether. The inability of the team to accurately assess the true value of the game and to price it accordingly causes awkwardness for the fan, who must seek out third party intermediaries. Not only does this error in pricing disrupt the customer relationship, it allows a third party arbitrageur to steal the financial premium that customers put on the event.

Major league baseball teams are just now discovering that fans are willing to pay significantly more for unique experiences such as big rivalries, or for big names such as Barry Bonds. On the other hand, these teams are also recognizing that ordinary games on weekdays against weak teams require significant discounts to fill the stands. The New York Yankees, despite setting a franchise attendance record in 2002, offered cheap $5 upper deck seats for weekday games in 2003 that would have otherwise gone unsold. A wide dispersion of prices can work to give different segments of fans the seats they desire, at the games they want, at prices they are willing to pay.

Let us revisit how Microsoft could have taken advantage of customer-centric pricing to create greater value for its customers and itself when it launched the Xbox in 2001. Microsoft knew the demand for the game console would far outstrip its ability to produce enough units to satisfy the pre-Christmas demand. Many of the most valuable gaming customers (the ones who wanted the latest product and were willing to pay a premium for it) were required to go to EBay and other auction sites and pay prices that were often five times the retail price. Microsoft could have simply raised the price to ration the early demand. That would have reduced the consumer surplus and kept the customers from going through third parties, but it would also have created the perception that the early purchasers were "ripped off" once productive capacity was brought in line with demand and prices dropped.

Following a customer-centric approach as outlined in Fig. 1, Microsoft could have created a "Collector's Edition" for the first few million units it was able to produce prior to the 2001 Christmas season. It could have included some free games, gold-tipped cables, a Collector's Edition box, and other features that were low in cost, but high in perceived value to the enthusiastic customer segment. Microsoft could have charged $499 (instead of $199) for the first few million units, kept its relationship with the most passionate gamers, and generated far greater profits. In addition to enhancing customer satisfaction for this group, Microsoft could have then created the perception of a bargain for the ordinary game console at a price of $199.

The innovative bundling of various product components with pricing aligned to the price sensitivities of each micro-market segment is the way to create sustainable value in the marketplace. A firm that optimizes revenue through customer-centric pricing not only increases profit, but is in a better position to offer price-sensitive customers lower-priced products with only attributes they value.

9. Economic Benefits

Understanding customer value creation and capturing that value through customer-centric pricing is a step toward a pareto optimal in the economy. A pareto optimal is a relationship in which all parties are better off, and no one is worse off (Pareto, 1906). Accordingly, both producers and consumers benefit.

Producers benefit from understanding customer willingness to pay for tangible product attributes such as product features, functions, warranties, and customer service. More importantly, using the feedback from customer-centric pricing, producers can assess the market value that various customer segments place on more subjective attributes such as brand preference, status, quality, and reliability.

Customer-centric pricing is more than just establishing price; it is a means of constantly communicating with consumers through the price mechanism and using that communication as a means to balance what the firm offers in terms of product attributes. For price-insensitive customers, that might mean a higher degree of reliability, or access to a product at the last minute. On the other hand, price-sensitive customers communicate their willingness to forgo certain product features or attributes for a lower price. Southwest Airlines, for example, has demonstrated that airline passengers do not want to pay a premium for a meal or assigned seating, but they will pay up to three times as much for a last-minute seat on certain flights at certain times. Accordingly, Southwest gives its customers what they want when they want, but not more, thereby increasing Southwest's profitability.

Finding these incremental revenue opportunities requires an accurate assessment of who will pay what amount at what time. These opportunities cannot be accurately predicted by surveys or focus groups. They require monitoring the real-time decision-making of millions of consumers in a dynamic marketplace and responding appropriately with a customer-centric focus. Missing these opportunities could result in missing a chance to extract a brand premium in certain market segments or undermine a competitor's advantage in others with precision discounting. These missed opportunities are a stealthy thief of profits. Money a firm could have had or should have had is hard to find, but extremely profitable if captured, as these revenues from existing assets fall right to the bottom line.

Profit-seeking companies must seize these opportunities. Once missed, they are gone forever. Customer-centric pricing is a means to assure that the value a firm creates is accurately assessed and captured through the price mechanism. This is the secret to profitability.

References

Anderson, J. C., & Narus, J. A. (2003). Selectively pursuing more of your customer's business. *Sloan Management Review, 44*(3), 42–49.

Anderson, J. C., & Narus, J. A. (2004). *Business market management: Understanding, creating, and delivering value.* Upper Saddle River, NJ: Prentice Hall.

Assael, H., & Roscoe Jr., A. M. (1976, October). Approaches to market segmentation analysis. *Journal of Marketing, 40,* 67–76.

Baker, W., Marn, M., & Zawada, C. (2001). Price smarter on the net. *Harvard Business Review, 79*(2), 122–127.

Belk, R. W. (1975). Situational variables and consumer behavior. *Journal of Consumer Research, 2*(3), 157–164.

Cross, R. G. (1997). *Revenue management: Hard-core tactics for market domination.* New York: Broadway Books.

Dolan, R. (1995). How do you know when the price is right? *Harvard Business Review, 73*(5), 174–183.

Fleischmann, M., Hall, J. M., & Pyke, D. F. (2004). Smart pricing. *Sloan Management Review, 45*(2), 9–13.

Frank, R. E., Massy, W. F., & Wind, Y. (1972). *Market segmentation.* Englewood Cliffs, NJ: Prentice Hall.

Haley, R. I. (1968, July). Benefit segmentation: A benefit oriented research tool. *Journal of Marketing, 32,* 30–35.

Hanks, R. D., Cross, R. G., & Noland, R. P. (1992). Discounting in the hotel industry: A new approach. *The Cornell H.R.A. Quarterly, 33*(1), 15–23.

Hayek, F. A. (1945). The use of knowledge in society. *American Economic Review, 35*(4), 519–530.

Leibs, S. (2000). Ford heeds the profits. *CFO Magazine, 16*(9), 33–35.

Lemon, K. N., White, T. B., & Winer, R. S. (2002). Dynamic customer relationship management: Incorporating future considerations into the service retention decision. *Journal of Marketing, 66*(1), 1–14.

Nagle, T. T., & Holden, R. K. (2002). *The strategy and tactics of pricing.* Englewood Cliffs, NJ: Prentice Hall.

Pareto, V. (1906). *Manuale d'economia politica.* Milan: Societ Editrice Libraria.

Peppers, D., & Rogers, M. (1993). *The one to one future.* New York: Currency Doubleday.

Porter, M. E. (1979). How competitive forces shape strategy. *Harvard Business Review, 57*(2), 137–145.

Sheth, J. N., & Parvatiyaar, A. (1995). Relationship marketing in consumer markets: Antecedents and consequences. *Journal of the Academy of Marketing Science, 23*(4), 255–271.

Siminson, I. (2005). Determinants of customers' responses to customized offers: Conceptual framework and research propositions. *Journal of Marketing, 69*(1), 32–45.

Smith, G. E., & Nagle, T. T. (2002). How much are your customers willing to pay? *Marketing Research, 14*(4), 20–25.

Smith, W. R. (1956, July). Product differentiation and market segmentation as alternative product strategies. *Journal of Marketing, 21,* 3–8.

Wansink, B., & Park, S. (2000). Comparison methods for identifying heavy users. *Journal of Advertising Research, 40*(4), 61–72.

Wells, W. D. (1975). Psychographics: A critical review. *Journal of Marketing Research, 12*(2), 196–213.

Zeithaml, V. A. (1988). Consumer perceptions of price, quality and value: A means–end model and synthesis of evidence. *Journal of Marketing, 52*(3), 2–22.

Zipkin, P. (2001). The limits of mass customization. *Sloan Management Review, 42*(3), 81–87.

Boost Your Bottom Line by Taking the Guesswork Out of Pricing

Do you know how much your product is *really* worth?

ALISON STEIN WELLNER

Every time he closed a sale, Kris Simmons kicked himself. That's because Simmons, president of Fire Eye Productions, a video production company based in Chattanooga, Tenn., knew he'd done it again: He'd set his price way too low. A client would ask for a quote, and Simmons would toss out a number based on some combination of his company's cash flow at the moment, his own fear of losing a customer, and what he'd begun charging when he founded Fire Eye four years earlier. "Basically, I'd throw a price out there and see what they'd take," he says.

From the outside, Fire Eye looked like a big success; Simmons was even nominated for the 2004 Young Entrepreneur of the Year Award given by Tennessee's small-business administration. But inside, the company was falling apart. Working 18-hour days to keep up with demand, Simmons had no time to make sales calls, which meant that cash flow was always erratic. He would hire employees, let them go when receivables dipped—and then hastily hire them back when the work flowed in again.

By August 2004, Simmons was fed up and exhausted. He knew what he had to do. He had to raise prices. A price hike would mean he could work fewer hours, earn more money, hire employees, and buy new equipment. On the other hand, if he raised his prices too high—and who knew how high was too high?—he would risk alienating his longtime customers. If he lost them, Simmons knew, Fire Eye would not survive. "These clients are my bread and butter," he thought. "If I make them mad and they leave, then I'm in a whole different kind of bad situation."

There's no more important number than the one on your price tag, and nothing provokes a case of the cold sweats like the thought of raising it. After years of almost no inflation, relentless downward pressure from places like China and India on the price of almost everything, and comparison shopping at the click of a mouse, it's more competitive than ever

out there. It's easy to see why fewer than one-third of business owners surveyed by the National Federation of Independent Business reported in February that they had increased their prices over the previous three months.

But that could be a big mistake—especially today, which might be the best opportunity companies have had to raise prices in some time. In March, the consumer-price index rose 3.1% over the previous year. If you're holding prices steady at a time when they are generally increasing nationwide, you may be surrendering more of your margin than you need to. "This is a very important time for everyone to review their prices," says Brent Lippman, CEO of Khimetrics, a pricing consultancy in Scottsdale, Ariz.

On the other hand, you can't raise prices if you haven't set them appropriately in the first place. Ask entrepreneurs how they arrived at their prices, and once you get past the usual stuff about optimization, segmentation, and market conditions, you'll often hear things like "it was pretty arbitrary" or "we go by our gut." Unfortunately, the gut often gets it wrong. "Entrepreneurs tend to keep prices too low," says Reed K. Holden, founder of Holden Advisors in Concord, Mass., and the co-author of *The Strategy and Tactics of Pricing,* a widely used text on the subject. Robert J. Dolan, dean of the Ross School of Business at the University of Michigan and co-author of *Power Pricing: How Managing Price Transforms the Bottom Line,* agrees. "You're likely leaving money on the table," Dolan says.

How do you make sure that money ends up in your pocket instead? Every industry has a dynamic of its own, and it would be hard to find two businesses that take the same approach to pricing. Still, there has been plenty of recent research into how consumers behave, examining how they assign value to goods and services and how smart managers can alter those perceptions. These insights can be valuable for any entrepreneur, in any industry.

But before we get to that, a quick primer on the wrong way to set prices: Many business owners base their prices on their costs, adding in a certain profit margin on top. "They say, 'Hey, if I could get my costs, plus 20%, that's not a bad business,'" says Dolan. Well, it could be a better business—if you could get a 40% margin. Others look at what their competitors charge and seek to bring their own prices in line or charge less. That may be your only option if your product or service is identical to that of the competition. But how do you know that your rivals know more about pricing than you do? And if you undercut them, you risk sparking a margin-killing price war. Then there are those who consult with customers before arriving at a price. But customers, obviously, have a powerful incentive to get you to keep your prices as low as possible. Setting prices based on what your salespeople report back can lead to similar problems. "Sales-people want to close deals, and they use price as a way of doing that," says Holden. "But that can be inconsistent with the real need of the business—profitability."

Of course, you can't make smart pricing decisions without taking your costs, competitors, customers, and sales-people into account. But nearly all experts agree that making any of those factors the primary basis for your decision is a big mistake. Instead, the right price for a product or service should rest on one thing—the value that a product or service provides.

When determining your prices, says John Gourville, a marketing professor at Harvard University who studies pricing, the first question to ask is this: How much would a rational consumer be willing to pay for your product, assuming the consumer had a perfect understanding of its actual worth? It sounds easy. But while most business owners spend a good chunk of their time touting the benefits of their products and services, "they haven't tried to monetize those benefits," says Brent Lippman. The first step toward creating a pricing strategy, then, is to do just that—think through the benefits of your product and make a rough calculation of what you think they're worth in dollar terms.

Marc Cenedella
The Ladders.com, New York City

Web-based job-search service
Price per month, 2004
$50
Price per month, 2005
$25
"From our point of view, we're charging only a fraction of the value we provide."

Marc Cenedella went through this process in 2003, when he was setting subscription rates for his start-up, TheLadders. com, an electronic job-search service that lists only positions paying more than $100,000. Most career sites allow job seekers to search for free and make money by charging employers. Cenedella's strategy is different: He charges job seekers and lets employers list their six-figure positions for free. After many meetings with "way too much pizza," Cenedella and his team arrived at their value figure: somewhere between $10,000

and $40,000. Their assumption was that a job seeker who used their site would find a position at least one month faster than one who didn't. Since that job would pay $100,000 or more, the value of the company's service translated to roughly one month's take-home pay, or somewhere between $10,000 and $40,000, depending on the job.

Fair enough. Of course, it's hard to imagine anyone coughing up tens of thousands of dollars for a weekly e-mail newsletter. And indeed, you'd be hard-pressed to find a pricing expert who would suggest that as an appropriate price.

That's because there are two kinds of value: objective value and perceived value. The former is what Cenedella came up with: the price of a product or service assuming the customer has a perfect understanding of its value—and understands it in the same way the seller does. Think of objective value as the most that you could rationally charge for a product. At the other end of the spectrum, the least you could rationally charge

---

Do You Offer Discounts?

(Maybe you shouldn't)

Nearly every company offers discounts, promotions, incentives, and giveaways. Such tactics are time-honored ways of keeping clients happy—and luring new ones into the store.

But you might be giving away the store if you're not careful. And you'd be surprised at how many savvy managers are anything but savvy when it comes to discounts, says Robert J. Dolan, dean of the University of Michigan's Ross School of Business and a business consultant. The problem, Dolan says, is that discounts are offered by different departments at different times for different reasons. Sales and marketing execs give breaks to help close deals, for example, while inventory managers cut rates to move excess stock. It adds up fast. The consulting firm McKinsey studied this phenomenon in 2003, dubbing it the "pocket-price waterfall"—that is, the amount of money you actually pocket per transaction drips away bit by bit until the small leak turns into a deluge.

How to avoid a soaking? First, get a handle on all of the discounts you offer. Next, think about the customer behavior you're trying to encourage—or discourage. Do you want people to pay by cash instead of credit? Settle accounts by the end of the month? Don't give away a penny without a clear understanding of what you're trying to accomplish. Another big mistake: grandfathering in discounts forever. Companies often offer discounts to close a particular deal, only to have the client insist on the same low price in the future. What was supposed to be a one-time incentive becomes official company policy. Let customers know when they're getting a special deal. After all, a discount that's expected isn't much of a perk.

—*Alison Stein Wellner*

for a product would be the incremental cost of producing it—a breakeven price. Somewhere between the two lies what is known as the perceived value of your product—that is, what a person actually is willing to spend. In a perfect world, your customer would see the value of your offering and be willing to fork over the full amount. But in many circumstances, there's a disconnect, and what people are willing to pay is very different from your product's objective value. (In those cases, you'll have to use marketing and other tricks to try to change your customer's perception of value. But more on that later.)

How do you determine what people are willing to pay? Study after study has demonstrated that when it comes to purchasing decisions, people are irrational. In one classic study, researchers asked consumers whether they would be willing to travel an additional 20 minutes to save $5 on a calculator that costs $15. Most said yes. Then they were asked the same question about a $125 jacket. Most answered no. Now, rationally, $5 is $5, whether you're buying a calculator or a jacket. But it's seldom that simple, according to Richard H. Thaler, a professor at the Graduate School of Business at the University of Chicago and author of "Mental Accounting Matters," an article published in 1999 in the *Journal of Behavioral Decision Making.* "People make [purchasing] decisions piecemeal, influenced by the context of the choice," writes Thaler, who won a Nobel Prize for his work in behavioral economics.

As it happens, the greatest influence on the context of a purchasing decision is whether the consumer believes the price is fair. Expectations play a big role in this. In a 1985 study conducted by Thaler, people were asked to consider the following hypothetical situation: You're lying on a beach on a hot day and you crave a cold beer. A friend offers to get one and wants to know what you're willing to spend. When she offers to go to a small grocery store, the median response is $1.50. But if the friend is buying the same beer at the bar of a fancy resort hotel, the price jumps to $2.65. Context and expectation drive the price up nearly 80%. Because we expect to pay more for a beer at a resort, we're willing to pay more.

The real trick in setting prices, then, is to understand—and try to shape—your customers' expectations. One of the key ways people set their expectations is to base them on what they've paid for similar products or services. Academics call this the "reference price," and it's one of the easiest pieces of competitive intelligence to gather. Simply shop your competitors.

Overcoming the power of the reference price is not an easy thing to do. At TheLadders.com, for example, the maximum objective value was $40,000. The product's reference price, however, was quite a bit lower: zero, since most job-listing services are free. There's a lot of room between nothing and $40,000, and free is the most difficult reference price to overcome. But it can be done. Satellite radio companies, for example, have been able to charge annual subscription fees of as much as $142—even though most listeners are accustomed to getting radio for free. How do they do that? Primarily through marketing, which in this context means taking the customers' reference price and making the case that they offer more value.

But starting at zero definitely limits how much you can charge. Cenedella priced a monthly subscription at $50—a number he admits to pulling out of thin air. Unsatisfied with the number of people signing up, he cut it to $35, and finally settled on $25. TheLadders.com now has nearly 300,000 subscribers, but Cenedella is far from satisfied. "From our point of view, we're charging only a fraction of the value we provide," he says. But he's stumped as to how to fix the situation.

Plenty of entrepreneurs are in the same boat. "The price you get for a product is a function of what it's truly worth—and how good a job you do communicating that value to the end user," says John Gourville. If Cenedella, for example, could guarantee customers that subscribing would shave a month off their job searches, he might be able to charge more. Or he could try to change his customers' reference price. E-mail newsletters may have a going rate of zero, but a good career counselor can cost hundreds, if not thousands, of dollars. If your marketing can convince people to put you into a different price category, it'll be a lot easier to charge more money for it. It's also important to remember that different customers have different expectations and reference prices. Cenedella might, for example, offer a special newsletter for investment bankers at a higher price than he would for, say, marketing executives.

Sam Calagione
Dogfish Head Craft Brewery Milton, Del.

**Premium microbrewed beer
Average price per case in 1999
$18
Average price per case in 2005
$24.60
"When we add new products, we always add them at higher prices. So while our median price level has increased significantly, we can honestly say that we've never raised prices."**

Sam Calagione, president of Dogfish Head Craft Brewery in Milton, Del., is a master at playing with pricing expectations. Dogfish Head's revenue grew 52%, to $8 million, in 2004—in large part because of Calagione's approach to pricing. Some Dogfish Head beers retail at about twice the price of most microbrews and four times that of most mass-market brands. How does Calagione do it? He encourages customers to use fine wine, rather than competing beers, as their reference price. "Wine customers," he says, "understand that an amazing bottle of pinot noir should command four times the price of an average bottle." He conveys this message, in part, with smart packaging. The company, for example, sells its premium Pangaea beer in 750 milliliter cork-finished wine bottles—at a cost of $14 a bottle. That's well above an average beer drinker's price expectation. But it's right in line with that of a wine connoisseur.

Calagione borrows more than the wine industry's packaging. He shuns the consumer advertising used by competing brands,

Get the Price You Want—and Avert the Dreaded Price War

Every salesperson has met one: the customer who cares only about price. High quality? Tell it to the other guy. Superior service? Forget it, the customer says. I won't pay a dime more than I have to.

Reed K. Holden, founder of Holden Advisors, a pricing strategy firm in Concord, Mass., calls them "price buyers," and they're particularly prevalent in the purchasing departments of large corporations—where they'll often release a request for proposal with a set of specs, pick the lowest bid, and call it a day. Such buyers are a huge pain to deal with. For one thing, they're not particularly loyal because they're always ready to drop you for a lower bidder. They're also not afraid to spark price wars. "These companies want their vendors to beat their brains out," says Holden.

If you have too many of these kinds of clients, you'll never have strong margins. But there are ways to cope. The key is to do business with a price buyer only when you can do it profitably—if you have excess inventory, for example, a price buyer might be exactly what you're looking for. (Case in point: Airlines often sell excess capacity to vacation-tour operators but don't create extra capacity to serve that market.) Another option with price buyers is to sell only what they're buying. "If people want a lower price, always be willing to give it to them," says Holden. "But be sure to take away some value."

An electronics company that Holden worked with, for example, gave one customer the price it demanded—but only on older technology. Newer, more innovative products were reserved for those willing to pay for them.

Whatever you do, don't tell yourself that you'll take a hit on one sale and make it up the next time. Price buyers rarely change. If you're in the grip of one, walk away. It may seem scary, but remember: If you must get a price buyer back, you can always do it by lowering your price.

—Alison Stein Wellner

was charging about one-third less than most of his rivals. That was good news. Because his customers' reference prices were a good deal higher than Fire Eye's, a price hike would not seem unreasonable.

Simmons acted immediately. Fire Eye's prices, he decided, would go up 25% across the board. Had he done more research—say, conducting an in-depth value calculation akin to what Cenedella did at TheLadders.com—he might have selected a gutsier number. But 25% was the most his nerves could take. "I didn't want to alienate myself from my customers," Simmons says. "And I thought it was a fair increase." His heart pounding, he began meeting with clients to break the news. He explained his company's situation. He argued that he could be a stronger vendor if he could invest in his infrastructure and hire new, experienced staffers. He also said he'd understand if clients wanted to take their business elsewhere. Simmons had made his play. How would his customers react?

Determining your new, higher price is one thing. Actually selling it to customers is something else. Simmons's approach—simply explaining the situation—is among the most effective. "People are actually very sensitive to what they think something costs to make," says Gourville. When costs increase, and a company cites that as a reason to justify a price hike, few customers react badly. Indeed, just as people appreciate a fair deal for themselves, they also tend to understand that a company has to stay in business as well.

Some customers may even urge you to raise prices: "We want you to be around."

In some cases, customers may even urge you to raise prices. That's what happened to Henk Keukenkamp, CEO of Scope It, a software company in El Dorado Hills, Calif. In 2003, Keukenkamp pegged the price of his project-costing software to that of a similar product offered by Microsoft: $795 per user, per year. When no one balked at the figure, he boosted it to $995. Even then, he found customers were shocked at the low price—so shocked that Keukenkamp began to feel foolish. "We thought the value we were providing was comparable to Microsoft," he says. "We were wrong. Our customers thought our value was nothing like Microsoft." A pricing theorist would call this a case of misperceived reference price. Finally, Keukenkamp recalls, a customer took him aside and said, "Look, $995 isn't very expensive. How are you going to make any money? We want you to be around to handle updates." Over the next 12 months, Keukenkamp raised the price of a license to $2,295 a year. "I still think we can push it higher," he says.

Keukenkamp's customers had a powerful motivation to keep him in business—they wanted him around to service the software. It's an enviable situation. But even if you're not as fortunate as Keukenkamp, you can still raise prices. You just have to do a better job explaining the reasons for the move. "It makes

instead hosting "beer dinners" attended by beer enthusiasts, early adopters who are likely to spread the word about new products that excite them. Calagione expected to host 18 such dinners in May alone. Taking another page from the wine industry, every time he launches a new product, he makes sure that there's not enough of it to satisfy demand. "We're not a commodity," he says. "By not satisfying demand initially, we create more demand for the future" People understand that a scarce product commands a higher price.

Calagione segmented his market by eschewing the typical American beer drinker and going after customers with high reference prices. Doing so enabled him to do something most businesses only dream about: align prices with objective value. And though he didn't think of it in those terms, that's precisely what Kris Simmons needed to do at his video production company, Fire Eye. His first step was to figure out what his competitors were charging—the reference price. He learned that he sense to try to justify why your prices are what they are," says Gourville. "It's better than having consumers feel like they're getting ripped off." And it's not necessary to raise prices across the board, all at once. Sometimes, a wise step is to test out new prices with small samplings of your customers.

If you don't trust your communication skills—or if you're reluctant to confront clients directly—you can slide a price hike in through the back door. One way is to eliminate discounts or change your terms and conditions. "People are more sensitive to list price than to discount terms," says Robert Dolan. Eliminating a discount of, say, 2% to clients who pay within 30 days, for example, is much easier to sell than a 2% increase in prices. (See "Do You Offer Discounts?") Or, conversely, you can raise prices but offer discounts to your most important customers.

You can also stop the gravy train and begin charging for add-on services you currently provide gratis. Another option is to keep prices constant but reduce the amount of product or service you're providing. If you're smart about it, according to Dolan, many customers won't notice the difference. Dogfish Head, for example, sells some of its beer in four-packs, rather than six-packs, which boost the price per bottle. Price hikes also can be masked by bundling an array of products or services together. Studies have shown that people think they're getting a better deal when they cannot determine the costs of the individual items they're purchasing.

Just keep in mind that psychology can also work against you. "People are going to use your past price as a reference point," says Dolan. There are two ways around this. You can convince customers that the new, higher price is accompanied by greater value. Or you can "destroy the reference point," Dolan says—through, say, a redesign or relaunch. If that's not pos-sible, introducing "premium" versions of your service can help raise reference prices across the board. Every time Calagione releases a new product, for example, he charges more than he has in the past, a move that increases Dogfish Head's average selling price while adding to his customers' reference prices.

Six months after his own price hike, Fire Eye's Simmons couldn't imagine why he didn't do it sooner. Apparently, he did a good job explaining the increase to his customers—not a single one jumped ship. "They were very understanding" Simmons says. He's invested his newfound profits into four new employees, freeing himself to pitch new customers. He's landed some large corporate clients, who, he's since learned, didn't take him seriously at his previous price. That's not the only change. In the past, Simmons routinely failed to charge for overtime. Now, if a project requires 10 more hours, it's added to the bill and those terms are explicitly spelled out in his contracts. He also altered his billing policies, asking for 50% payment up front rather than taking all of it upon a project's completion. This reduced the cost of his receivables, giving him a subtle increase in margin. "It's been rebirth, a new beginning," Simmons says.

Of course, there has been some fallout. Prior to the price hike, Fire Eye closed about 80% of the projects it bid on; today, the number is closer to 40%. On the other hand, today's deals are coming with far better margins, which is steadily improving the overall health of the company. "I'm only spending time with people who want to play my way," Simmons says. "I'll still work with clients on their budgets. But for the most part, I'm in business to make my life better. These prices are making life better for me"

Contributing editor **ALISON STEIN WELLNER** is a New York City-based freelance writer.

Pricing Gets Creative

It takes more than absolute price levels to drive customer behaviors and perceptions.

ERIC V. ROEGNER, MICHAEL V. MARN, AND CRAIG C. ZAWADA

Getting pricing right is among the most important jobs that marketers and sellers do. Too often, however, they labor under the assumption that price level (list price or net price) is the only pricing variable that makes a difference. In fact, a host of other pricing elements can be equally or even more important than price level. Together they comprise what we call pricing architecture.

The thoughtful "pricing architect" has countless design elements at his or her disposal, including the discounts and allowances to include in the pocket price waterfall, a tool that shows how much revenue companies really keep from each transaction. It enumerates discounts off of the list price that resellers and end customers pay, as well as other costs such as volume rebates, merchandising allowances, and freight charges that drive a wedge between invoice prices and the amount that the seller ultimately pockets.

Other design elements at the disposal of the pricing architect include the specific guidelines and policies for the discounts and allowances, the structure for differentiating list prices by customer segment, and even the way units of sales are structured and communicated. (For example, is it advisable to price telephone service on a per-minute or a fixed monthly basis?)

Companies that excel at pricing use these and other pricing design elements to create price architectures that most positively influence customer perception of price and induce customers to behave in ways that benefit those companies. In addition, special challenges and degrees of freedom arise in creating a pricing architecture for offerings that are packages of products and services, rather than just a single product.

Price Perception

Skillful pricers appreciate that price perception can be influenced as easily as benefit perceptions can be actively shaped, as the following examples illustrate.

To research the impact of price communication, a term life insurance provider that markets primarily by mail sent three sets of solicitations that were identical except for the price communicated in the brochure headline. In the first set, the price was

Executive Briefing

Price architecture can be more important than absolute price level in driving customer behaviors and perception. Whether selling goods or services, businesses that treat pricing as a source of competitive advantage set specific market and customer objectives for their price architecture. In addition, they regularly revisit their price structure to verify that it helps achieve those objectives. Companies that excel at pricing use various pricing design elements to create price architectures that most positively influence customer perception of price.

conveyed as $360 per year; in the second, $30 per month; and in the third, $1 per day. The annual price was, of course, basically identical in all three cases. And, in each case, the same payment of $180 was due twice a year. Amazingly, respondents were three times more likely to buy the policy when given the monthly quote compared with the annual quote, and almost 10 times more likely to buy when the price was quoted on a daily rather than an annual basis.

Or consider the retail bank that wanted to increase the price of an interest-bearing checking account it offered, while minimizing customer defections. The bank test marketed two price increase alternatives that, while different in form, resulted in the same monthly price increase for customers in a specific segment. In the first alternative tested, the monthly account service fee paid by the customer was increased by $3 and the interest rate paid on account balances stayed constant. In the second, the monthly service fee was only raised $1 but the interest paid on account balances was decreased by 0.2 percentage point. Although these two options generated an equal price increase, nearly four times as many customers defected when presented with the first price increase alternative vs. the second.

Pricing architecture can also influence the price perceptions of intermediaries. Figure 1 shows the pocket price waterfall for a microwave oven manufacturer selling to appliance retailers.

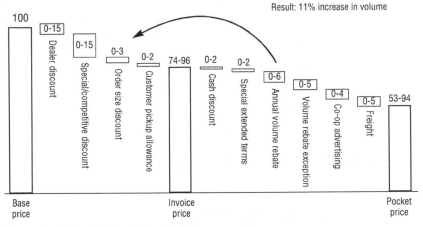

Figure 1 Pocket Price Waterfall–Microwave Oven

The price structure was complicated, with 10 on- and off-invoice discounts in play. Thinking that its price structure had grown too complex, the microwave oven company commissioned a market study to determine retailers' satisfaction with their price structure.

In interviews, retailers said they found the company's price structure somewhat complex, but no more so than that of most other appliance manufacturers. Retailers indicated that competitors' waterfalls were quite similar to the company's on the invoice. But off the invoice competitors' volume rebates, promotional programs, and payment terms had diverse attributes. Retailers said this off-invoice diversity made price comparison across microwave manufacturers difficult. So most retailers compared manufacturers' prices on an invoice price basis when choosing which microwave brands to carry; they assumed that the total of each competitor's off-invoice discounts were about the same.

Knowing now that retailers paid much more attention to on-invoice discounts, the microwave company moved its largest off-invoice discount, the annual volume rebate, onto the invoice. In other words, it estimated each account's annual sales volume, projected the account's year-end rebate, and then included this as a discount on each invoice. If account volume at the end of the year differed significantly from the estimate, a year-end adjustment to the rebate would be made. This reduced invoice price by up to 6% and left pocket price unchanged, but it increased sales volume to this category of retailers by 11%. This volume increase was not the result of lowering price. Rather, it came from changing pricing architecture and refining price structure to make the company's price look better against the yardstick that retailers used to compare competitive supplier prices.

As the examples here show, pricing architecture alternatives can be explored through market research, just like customer benefit perceptions. In fact, companies that excel at pricing regularly bundle price perception research with their general customer value research.

Influence on Customer Behavior

Beyond influencing customers' impression of price level, well-designed price architecture can drive a host of customer behaviors that may be crucial to a company's success. The first

principle of price architecture is that your pocket price waterfall should work for you. In other words, every element of your waterfall should be viewed as an investment designed to drive a specific customer behavior. To illustrate how this works, we explore how price architecture can affect the total volume that customers purchase, the product mix they select, and the resale price they pay. We also have seen companies successfully influence consumer behavior in areas that include the frequency with which they place orders and make payments, the size of their orders, and the nature of their promotions and stocking practices.

Total volume purchased. Some of the largest discounts along the pocket price waterfall can be the least effective. Annual volume bonuses are often large waterfall elements that just do not work for companies. They seldom stimulate as much sales volume and growth as expected.

An auto parts supplier's annual volume bonus program illustrates what so frequently goes wrong. This company sold its line of products to auto parts wholesalers and retailers. Accounts with annual purchases of between $100,000 and $200,000 would receive a bonus equal to 1% of their volume at the end of the year. The bonus rose to 2% for accounts buying between $200,000 and $500,000, to 3% for those purchasing $500,000 to $1 million, and so on.

Figure 2, which illustrates the distribution of this company's accounts based on annual volume, shows why the bonus structure wasn't working. Since the business was stable and mature, account growth greater than 20% was almost impossible. As a result, any account that had to increase its purchases by roughly 20% or more to reach the next bonus level was entirely unmotivated by the volume bonus structure. For example, if an account's volume was in the $300,000–$400,000 range, as was the case for 22% of the accounts, it would have to grow by 25% or more to reach the next volume bonus hurdle at $500,000. That was too large a volume jump for those accounts, which are shaded as "unmotivated accounts" in the figure. More than half of this company's accounts, representing nearly 75% of sales volume, fell into the unmotivated category. Each account gladly accepted its volume bonus check at the end of each year, but the bonus often had no impact on actual volume purchased. The company's obvious solution was to realign its volume bonus

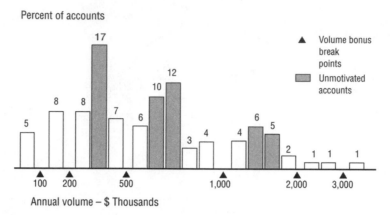

Figure 2 Auto Parts Company (Account Size Distribution)

break points to better match the distribution of account sales volumes.

Product mix. For companies that sell multiple product lines, large variations in profitability across lines are common. One company that manufactures hydraulic equipment sold six major product lines through industrial distributors. As Figure 3 shows, its most profitable lines (Mark I, Mark II, and Crestline) regularly generated pocket margins that were two to four times higher than its low-margin lines (Advent, C-Line, and Nova). The company was not aware of this extreme profit variability across lines until it created its first pocket margin transaction database. A host of factors, including which plant made the product, design efficiency, and the level of market competition, contributed to this wide average pocket margin variation by product line. In this situation, a mere 5% shift in product mix to high-margin products would increase total pocket margin dollars for this company by more than 8%. However, the company's price structure was blind to product mix, providing no incremental award to distributors who chose to purchase a richer mix of product lines. All discounts, allowances, rebates, terms, and conditions applied equally to all lines.

The company decided to rebalance its annual volume bonus program to pay a larger reward for Mark I, Mark II, and Crestline sales, and a lower reward for Advent, C-Line, and Nova purchases. It concentrated all of its cooperative

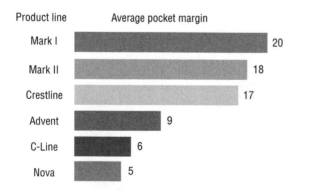

Figure 3 Hydraulic Equipment Company (Product Line Profitability)

A Mixed Bag

Pricing a packaged offer, whether as a bundle, an integrated offering, or a solution, becomes especially difficult when the components are fundamentally different in nature. This situation is commonly faced by high-tech suppliers, who must juggle a package that includes a physical component (the hardware), an intellectual property component (the software), and a human component (the service providers). But the challenges are relevant to anyone trying to price such a mixed bag. Whatever type of package is being offered, suppliers must carefully weigh the advantages and disadvantages of how they apportion the total price among the components. Even if the customers see just one price, this internal exercise can validate the price by constructing it from the bottom up. If the price is disaggregated, it can also ensure that minimum price levels are reached for each component.

One obstacle to allocating price effectively can be a company's tradition. For instance, a company founded as a hardware manufacturer may face internal resistance to a pricing architecture that highlights the value of software or services. A company can push forward, however, by understanding how the customer perceives the package's benefits and setting prices in line with that benefit perception. Benefit perceptions can shift dramatically from one market segment to another, so pricing policies for integrated packages should keep such differences in mind.

Another complication is that the economics of individual pieces could differ, with prices rising for some and falling for others. In this case, allocating an additional portion of the price to the component on an upward trend might make sense. Finally, if different components of the package are delivered at different times, the pricing architecture should probably be created to time payments as value is delivered. If, for instance, the hardware (usually the first component delivered) included in a package is not distinct, a buyer may be reluctant to make a large up-front payment, even if it reflects the value of the full package that will eventually be delivered.

advertising and promotional discount programs on the high-margin lines. It also allowed slightly longer payment terms on the three high-margin product lines, with 45 days to pay while still qualifying for a 1.5% cash discount, rather than the usual 30 days. These more generous terms caused distributors to stock greater inventory levels of the high-margin lines and ultimately to sell more as a result. While total dollars invested up and down the pocket waterfall remained virtually unchanged, the hydraulics company increased its high-margin product mix by 14% within one year and increased operating profits by 23%.

Resale price. The price at which a trade intermediary resells a supplier's product has strategic importance. If a retailer charges a price that is too high relative to competitive offerings, then sales volume may be insufficient. If the retail price is too low, the desired premium position and brand strength of the supplier's product may erode. A supplier's price architecture provides a powerful tool for influencing prices that resellers charge for its product.

Most trade intermediaries trigger their resale price off of the invoice price that they see from their suppliers—not the pocket price. In other words, they take the supplier's invoice price and add a specific margin to it to come up with the price to charge their customers. Thus, the lower the invoice price, the lower the resale price. By shifting discounting between on and off the invoice, a supplier can change invoice price without affecting its pocket price.

With that in mind, if you want to influence your resellers to sell your products at a higher price, you should shift discounting from "on invoice" to "off invoice." This will increase the invoice price that the reseller sees and, in most cases, engender higher resale prices. If, on the other hand, you want resellers to sell your products at a lower price, you should do the opposite and shift from off invoice to on invoice. This will lower the invoice price and usually result in lower resale prices as well. Care should be taken, however, to manage competitors' perceptions of this move.

In addition to the balance of on- and off-invoice discounting, consistently managing list prices can also help influence resale prices. Discounting that occurs between starting point list price and invoice price can often be large and vary widely. As a result, too many companies assert that "my list prices don't mean anything, since none of my direct customers buy at list price anyway." This attitude can result in list prices not being managed consistently and the loss of a potential opportunity to influence resale prices constructively.

Price-advantaged companies actively manage list price and use it to communicate price to the market. While list price may take on different meanings at different companies, it is a price level that has tangible meaning in the market and not just a random starting point for negotiation. When list prices are managed with consistency and diligence, changing them can deliver important and credible messages to the marketplace regarding industry price direction and the desired value repositioning of specific products.

Perception and Performance

Crafting a pricing architecture becomes an even more intricate challenge when a buying decision encompasses more than one product or service from an individual supplier. These packages can take several forms. In the most straightforward form, multiple products are bundled together and sold at the same time by a distributor. At the other extreme, a company may offer a carefully composed package of components that are engineered to work optimally together. Examples include a surround-sound entertainment system or a telecommunications infrastructure package comprising integrated hardware, software, and services.

Companies must apportion the overall package price among the offering elements to best communicate the benefits while also driving the desired buying behavior or performance of the customer. Even seemingly simple shifts in how price is allocated across a packaged offering can change the message buyers receive about the offering's benefits and the elements driving those benefits.

Perception. A supplier offering razors and razor blades to the market provides a familiar example of a common way to use pricing architecture to communicate price and extract optimal profits from a packaged offering. If a supplier prices its razors too high (despite real benefits) and its blades quite low, customers might hesitate to try the product because of the high perceived price driven by the initial price of the razor. Instead, razor makers tend to price the razor lower, expecting to recoup the missed revenue through blades that are priced slightly higher. This structure encourages potential users to try the product and experience its benefits.

Crafting a package's pricing architecture becomes more complex when different segments of the market have quite different perceptions of the relative benefits of its various elements, even if the final package is the same. As a result, a skillful pricer will not only look at the aggregate view of price allocation, but will seek ways to communicate these allocations that resonate among the specific segments.

The experience of a global data network systems provider shows how using price architecture to emphasize the benefits offered by portions of the package can cater to particular market segments. A leader in the high-end market for integrated networking systems, this supplier was being attacked in the mid-tier market. Traditionally, the company had placed a single price on its networking package to highlight the benefits offered by integration. But, as the market evolved, several competitors from the lower end of the market began to attack the mid-range market using lower price as their primary weapon. The attackers only offered portions of the total package, but they compared their hardware and software prices to the aggregate price the incumbent supplier charged for the full package (in essence comparing their apples to the incumbent's orange), creating a large gap in price perception. Since mid-tier customers didn't always appreciate the full suite of benefits included in the integrated offering, they would often see the competing systems as operationally similar. As a result, the attackers rapidly began growing share.

Realizing the problem was price perception and not an inherent flaw in the actual offering, the networking supplier explicitly assigned prices to the hardware and software operating system that could be compared directly with the attackers' offerings. The incumbent also differentiated the pricing of the remaining, more advanced feature functionality so that these benefits could be articulated separately. This allowed customers to compare apples to apples, removed the perceived price gap, and halted the company's share loss.

Performance. Just as packaged offerings provide new opportunities for influencing price perception, they also open up unique opportunities to use pricing architecture to drive customer buying behavior, as well as the supplier's revenue capture. From being a one-stop source for all MRO (maintenance, repair, and operations) items to offering outsourced IT services, packaged offerings integrate to varying degrees directly into a customer's business system. Consequently, they can allow suppliers to use more robust pricing mechanisms that share business risk, increase the formal tie between supplier and customer, and close the door to competitors.

Pricing mechanisms tend to fall into one of two categories.

1. Pay-per-use arrangements. A pay-per-use approach is a common way to share business risk with payments escalating as the buyer increases use of the offering (e.g., a software application installed on multiple PCs). This approach is effective when it's hard to quantify the direct benefits of a product, such as increased IT security; when the benefits offered by the product are realized as part of a greater whole; or when the customer has principal control over whether the benefits are captured.

Related to pay-per-use agreements, pay-as-you-grow deals link payments to increases in sales, unit volume, or some other clear growth measurement. Many software companies have turned to this method, which would commonly allow company shrinks. Pay-as-you-grow plans could be more appropriate if it's difficult to identify or count individual uses of a product or if the benefits delivered are delayed.

2. Pay-by-performance arrangements. Performance-based pricing is more complex. A customer and supplier must agree to a set of performance metrics and then link payments to the achievement of specific targets. The best candidates for this structure offer benefits that are clearly measurable, such as revenue directly tied to the package installed. Performance-based pricing should be considered only if the supplier significantly influences or actually controls delivery of the offerings' benefits. This is the most common architecture used when a true "outsourced" solution is offered.

The building industry offers another good example of how performance-based pricing can work. One contractor offered to retrofit its customers' infrastructure with a building automation system at no initial cost. Instead, payments were based on the energy savings generated by the integrated offering. The customer and supplier agreed to a baseline of energy costs. As the energy costs went below this baseline, the supplier was paid the difference. The more energy that was saved, the more money the supplier made.

Milking Your Waterfall

There is an architecture to pricing that can be more important than absolute price level in driving customer behaviors and perception. Whether selling goods or services individually or in packages, businesses that treat pricing as a source of competitive advantage set specific market and customer objectives for their price architecture choices to achieve. They regularly reassess those objectives and always make sure that their price structure is working for them and that their waterfall elements are not just entitlements to customers, but also efficiently drive desired customer behaviors.

All of the authors are with McKinsey & Company's marketing and sales practice. ERIC V. ROEGNER and MICHAEL V. MARN are partners in McKinsey & Company's Cleveland office. CRAIG C. ZAWADA is a partner in the firm's Pittsburgh office. They may be reached at mckinsey_marketing_practice@mckinsey.com.

Editor's Note—This article is based on a chapter in *The Price Advantage* written by Michael V. Marn, Eric V. Roegner, and Craig C. Zawada (John Wiley & Sons, 2004).

The Old Pillars of New Retailing

**Looking for the silver bullet that will solve your retailing woes?
It doesn't exist. The best retailers lay a foundation for success
by creating customer value in a handful of fundamental ways.**

LEONARD L. BERRY

Everyone who glances at a newspaper knows that the retailing world is brutally competitive. The demise of Montgomery Ward in the realm of bricks and mortar as well as the struggles of eToys on-line—to choose only two recent examples—make it clear that no retailer can afford to be complacent because of previous successes or rosy predictions about the future of commerce.

Despite the harsh realities of retailing, the illusion persists that magical tools, like Harry Potter's wand, can help companies overcome the problems of fickle consumers, price-slashing competitors, and mood swings in the economy. The wishful thinking holds that retailers will thrive if only they communicate better with customers through e-mail, employ hidden cameras to learn how customers make purchase decisions, and analyze scanner data to tailor special offers and manage inventory.

But the truth of the matter is, there are no quick fixes. Yes, technology can help any business operate more effectively, but many new advances are still poorly understood—and in any case, retailing can't be reduced to tools and techniques. Over the past eight years, I've analyzed dozens of retail companies to understand the underlying differences between outstanding and mediocre performers. My research includes interviews with senior and middle managers and frontline employees, observations of store operations, and extensive reviews of published and internal company materials. I've found that the best retailers create value for their customers in five interlocking ways. Doing a good job in just three or four of the ways won't cut it; competitors will rush to exploit weakness in any of the five areas. If one of the pillars of a successful retailing operation is missing, the whole edifice is weakened.

The key is focusing on the total customer experience. Whether you're running physical stores, a catalog business, an e-commerce site, or a combination of the three, you have to offer customers superior solutions to their needs, treat them with real respect, and connect with them on an emotional level. You also have to set prices fairly and make it easy for people to find what they need, pay for it, and move on. These pillars sound simple on paper, but they are difficult to implement in the real world. Taking each one in turn, we'll see how some retailers have built successful operations by attending to these commonsense ways of dealing with customers, and how others have failed to pay them the attention they require.

Pillar 1: Solve Your Customers' Problems

It has become commonplace for companies to talk about selling solutions rather than products or services. But what does this really mean for retailers? Put simply, it means that customers usually shop for a reason: they have a problem—a need—and the retailer hopes to provide the solution. It's not enough, for example, just to sell high-quality apparel—many retailers do that. Focusing on solutions means employing salespeople who know how to help customers find clothing that fits and flatters, having tailors on staff and at the ready, offering home delivery, and happily placing special orders. Every retailer hopes to meet its customers' pressing needs; some do it much better than others.

The Container Store provides its customers with superior solutions. The 22-store chain, based in Dallas, averages double-digit annual sales growth by selling something that absolutely everyone needs: storage and organization products. From boxes and trunks to hangers, trays, and shelving systems, each store carries up to 12,000 different products.

The Container Store's core strategy is the same today as it was in 1978, when the company was founded: to improve customers' lives by giving them more time and space. The company accomplishes this mission well. It starts with the selection of merchandise, which must meet criteria for visibility, accessibility, and versatility. The company's philosophy is that its products should allow people to see what they've stored and get at it easily. The merchandise must also be versatile enough to accommodate customers' particular requirements.

Store organization is another key ingredient of superior solutions at the Container Store. The merchandise is organized in sections such as kitchen, closet, laundry, office, and so on. Many products are displayed in several sections because they can solve a variety of problems. A sweater box, for example, can also store office supplies. Plastic trash cans can also be used for dog food and recyclables. Individual products are often combined and sold as a system—thus, parents in the store who want to equip their children for summer camp may find a trunk filled with a laundry bag, a toothbrush case, a first-aid pouch, leakproof bottles, a "critter catcher," and other items.

Great service is another component of the Container Store's ability to solve its customers' storage problems. The company is very careful about hiring; it patiently waits until it finds just the right person for a position. Container Store employees are well trained to demonstrate how products work and to propose solutions to complex home organizational problems. They are also treated very well, both in terms of pay and in less tangible ways. In fact, the Container Store was ranked the best place to work in the country in 1999 and 2000 by *Fortune* magazine.

A relentless focus on solutions may sound simple, but it's not. The Container Store has many imitators, but none have matched it. Many businesses have only the fuzziest concept of selling solutions. Department store chains, for example, have stumbled in recent years. They lost their one-stop shopping advantage by eliminating many merchandise categories outside of apparel and housewares. And even as they focused on apparel, they lost ground both to specialty retailers that have larger category selections and to discounters that have lower prices. Finally, they lost their customer service advantage by employing salespeople who often are little more than poorly trained order takers. As a result, these stores do a relatively poor job of solving customers' problems. That's probably why only 72% of consumers shopped in department stores in 2000 compared with 85% in 1996.

Clearly, the lesson here is that you must understand what people need and how you're going to fill that need better than your competitors. The Container Store has figured this out; many department stores and other struggling retailers must go back to the beginning and answer these basic questions.

Pillar 2: Treat Customers with R-e-s-p-e-c-t

The best retailers show their customers what Aretha Franklin sang about: respect. Again, this is absolutely basic, and most retail executives would say that of course they treat customers with respect. But it just isn't so.

Everyone has stories to tell about disrespectful retailing. You're in an electronics store, looking for assistance to buy a DVD player or a laptop computer. You spot a couple of employees by their uniforms and badges, but they're deep in conversation. They glance in your direction but continue to ignore you. After awhile, you walk out, never to return.

Or you're in a discount store, looking for planters that have been advertised at a low price. You go to the store's garden center but cannot find the planters. This time, you succeed in flagging down an employee. You ask about the planters, but she just mumbles "I dunno" and walks away. Frustrated, you go to the customer service desk and ask the clerk where you might find the advertised planters. He suggests that you try the garden center. Once again, you head for the exit.

It's easy to go on. Stories about women trying to buy cars, as everyone knows, are enough to make your hair curl. The fact is, disrespectful retailing is pervasive. In the 2000 Yankelovich Monitor study of 2,500 consumers, 68% of those surveyed agreed with the statement that "Most of the time, the service people that I deal with for the products and services that I buy don't care much about me or my needs."

Disrespectful retailing isn't just about bored, rude, and unmotivated service workers. Cluttered, poorly organized stores, lack of signage, and confusing prices all show lack of respect for customers.

The best retailers translate the basic concept of respect into a set of practices built around people, policies, and place:

- They select, prepare, and manage their people to exhibit competence, courtesy, and energy when dealing with customers.
- They institute policies that emphasize fair treatment of customers—regardless of their age, gender, race, appearance, or size of purchase or account. Likewise, their prices, returns policy, and advertising are transparent.
- They create a physical space, both inside and outside the store, that is carefully designed to value customers' time.

In 1971, a 30-year-old entrepreneur named Len Riggio bought a floundering Manhattan bookshop called Barnes & Noble. Today, Barnes & Noble is the nation's largest bookseller, with fiscal 1999 sales of $3.3 billion. Respect for the customer has been at the heart of the company's rise.

Riggio's biggest idea was that books appeal to most everyone, not just to intellectuals, writers, and students in cosmopolitan cities. Riggio listened to prospective customers who wanted bigger selections of books, more convenient locations, and less intimidating environments. He put superstores in all types of communities, from big cities like Atlanta and Chicago, to smaller cities like Midland, Texas, and Reno, Nevada. His respect for the customer led him to create stores with spacious and comfortable interiors, easy chairs for relaxing with a book, and Starbucks coffee bars. To this day, he considers his best decision the installation of easy-to-find public restrooms in the stores. As he said in a recent speech, "You work so hard and invest so much to get people to visit your store, why would you want them to have to leave?"

Besides the large selection of books, the stores also have an active calendar of author signings, poetry readings, children's events, and book discussion groups. Many Barnes & Noble superstores have become a social arena in which busy consumers—who normally rush in and out of other stores—linger.

Riggio sees the Internet as much more than a way to deliver books to customers; it's another opportunity to listen to them and thus show respect for them. He views the store network and Barnesandnoble.com as portals to each other. Customers can ask salespeople at Internet service counters to search Barnesandnoble.com for out-of-stock books, for customer reviews of titles that interest them, and for information about authors, such as other books they've published. Customers in a superstore can order the books they want on-line and have them shipped either to that store or to any other address. If a return is necessary, customers can bring their on-line purchase back to the store.

The value of respect often gets little more than lip service from retailers. Some companies wait until it's too late to put words into action.

Pillar 3: Connect with Your Customers' Emotions

Most retailers understand in principle that they need to connect emotionally with consumers; a good many don't know how to (or don't try to) put the principle into practice. Instead, they neglect the opportunity to make emotional connections and put too much emphasis on prices. The promise of low prices may appeal to customers' sense of reason, but it does not speak to their passions.

Many U.S. furniture retailers are guilty of ignoring consumers' emotions. Although the average size of new homes in the country has grown by 25% since 1980, furniture accounts for a lower percentage of total U.S. consumer spending today (1%) than it did in 1980 (1.2%). Making consumers wait up to two months to receive their furniture contributes to these poor results. How can consumers get emotionally involved in products they know they won't see for weeks?

Poor marketing also hurts the industry. Most furniture stores focus strictly on price appeals, emphasizing cost savings rather than the emotional lift that can come from a new look in the home. "We don't talk about how easy it can be to make your home more attractive," says Jerry Epperson, an investment banker who specializes in the furniture industry. "All we talk about is 'sale, sale, sale' and credit terms."

Great retailers reach beyond the model of the rational consumer and strive to establish feelings of closeness, affection, and trust. The opportunity to establish such feelings is open to any retailer, regardless of the type of business or the merchandise being sold. Everyone is emotionally connected to some retailers—from local businesses such as the wine merchant who always remembers what you like; to national companies like Harley-Davidson, which connects people through its Harley Owners Group; to catalog retailer Coldwater Creek, which ships a substitute item to customers who need to make returns before the original item is sent back.

One retailer that has connected especially well with its target market in recent years is Journeys, a Nashville, Tennessee-based chain of shoe stores located primarily in shopping malls. The chain focuses on selling footwear to young men and women between the ages of 15 and 25. Started in 1987, Journeys didn't take off until 1995 when new management took over. The chain has achieved double-digit comparable-store sales increases in

five of the six years since then and is now expanding by as many as 100 new stores per year.

Journeys has penetrated the skepticism and fickleness that are characteristic of many teens. By keeping a finger on the pulse of its target market, the company consistently has the right brands available for this especially brand-conscious group of consumers. Equally important, it creates the right store atmosphere—the stores pulsate with music, video, color, and brand merchandising.

A Journeys store is both welcoming and authentic to young people; it is simultaneously energetic and laid-back. Journeys' employees are typically young—the average age of a store manager is about 25—and they dress as they please. Customers frequently visit a store in groups just to hang out; salespeople exert no pressure to buy. And everyone, whether they've made a purchase or not, usually leaves with a giveaway—for instance, a key chain, a compact-disc case, a promotional T-shirt, or one of the 10 million or so stickers the stores give out over the course of a year. The stickers, which usually feature one of the brands Journeys sells, often end up on backpacks, skateboards, school lockers, or bathroom mirrors. Journeys also publishes a bimonthly magazine, *Dig,* that is available in the stores, and it runs a Web site that seeks to replicate the atmosphere of its stores. The number of site visits explodes whenever the company's commercials appear on MTV.

Journeys works in large part because it has created an atmosphere that connects emotionally with the young people it serves. Other retailers should bear in mind that it takes more than a room full of products with price tags on them to draw people in.

Pillar 4: Set the Fairest (Not the Lowest) Prices

Prices are about more than the actual dollars involved. If customers suspect that the retailer isn't playing fair, prices can also carry a psychological cost. Potential buyers will not feel comfortable making purchases if they fear that prices might be 30% lower next week, or if certain charges have only been estimated, or if they are unsure whether an advertised sale price represents a genuine markdown.

Consider some of the pricing tactics commonly used by certain home improvement retailers. One well-known company advertises products as "special buys" even though it has not lowered the regular prices. Another purposely misrepresents a competitor's prices on price-comparison signs within its stores. Still another company promotes lower-grade merchandise implying that it is top quality. One retailer puts a disclaimer in its ads that reads: "Prices in this ad may be different from the actual price at time of purchase. We adjust our prices daily to the lumber commodity market." The disclaimer paves the way for the retailer to raise its prices regardless of the advertised price.

Excellent retailers seek to minimize or eliminate the psychological costs associated with manipulative pricing. Most of these retailers follow the principles of "everyday fair pricing"

Are Your Retailing Pillars Solid—or Crumbling?

	Inferior Retailers . . .	Superior Retailers . . .
Solutions	gather products, stack them on shelves, put price tags on them, and wonder where their customers are.	consider what people really need and how they can meet that particular need better than competitors can.
Respect	are staffed by people who don't know what customers want and aren't about to interrupt their conversations to find out.	actually train and manage the salespeople they hire so that they are courteous, energetic, and helpful to customers.
Emotions	act as if their customers are Spock-like Vulcans who make purchases solely according to cold logic.	recognize that everything about a retail experience sends a message to customers that goes to the heart, not just the brain.
Pricing	focus exclusively on their supposed low prices, often because they have nothing else of value to offer customers.	focus on having fair prices instead of playing mind games with "special offers," fine print, and bogus sales.
Convenience	are open for business when it's convenient for them, close checkout lanes when it's convenient for them, deliver products when it's convenient for them, and so on.	understand that people's most precious commodity in the modern world is time and do everything they can to save as much of it as possible for their customers.

instead of "everyday low pricing." A fact of retail life is that no retailer, not even Wal-Mart, can truthfully promise customers that it will always have the lowest prices. An uncomfortable truth for many retailers is that their "lowest price anywhere" positioning is a crutch for the lack of value-adding innovation. Price is the only reason they give customers to care.

Retailers can implement a fair-pricing strategy by clearing two hurdles. First, they must make the cultural and strategic transition from thinking value equals price to realizing that value is the total customer experience. Second, they must understand the principles of fair pricing and muster the courage needed to put them into practice. Retailers who price fairly sell most goods at regular but competitive prices and hold legitimate sales promotions. They make it easy to compare their prices with those of competitors, and they avoid hidden charges. They don't raise prices to take advantage of temporary blips in demand, and they stand behind the products they sell.

Zane's Cycles in Branford, Connecticut, is one of the most successful independent bicycle retailers in the United States. Zane's has grown its one-store business at least 20% every year since it was founded in 1981, selling 4,250 bicycles in 2000 along with a full array of accessories. The company's success illustrates the appeal of fair pricing.

Zane's sells better bike brands with prices starting at $250. It stands behind what it sells with a 30-day test-drive offer (customers can return a bike within 30 days and exchange it for another) and a 90-day price protection guarantee (if a buyer finds the same bike in Connecticut at a lower price within 90 days, Zane's will refund the difference plus 10%). Zane's also offers free lifetime service on all new bicycles it sells; it was likely the first bicycle retailer in the United States to take this step. The promise of lifetime service includes annual tune-ups, brake and gear adjustments, wheel straightening and more.

Zane's holds only one promotional sale a year, a three-day spring weekend event featuring discounts on all products.

Vendors and former employees come to work at the huge event—some even fly in to participate. Customers who purchase a bicycle at Zane's within 90 days before the sale are encouraged to return during the event for a refund based on the discounted price of their bike. The company refunded about $3,000 during the 2000 sale, but most of that money remained in the store because customers bought more gear. Zane's sold 560 bicycles during the 2000 sale—that's more than the typical one-store U.S. bicycle retailer sells in an entire year. And yet the limited duration of the sale means that Zane's sells about 85% of its bicycles at the regular price.

When Connecticut passed a bike-helmet law in 1992, Zane's sold helmets to kids at cost rather than take advantage of legislated demand. Owner Chris Zane convinced area school administrators to distribute flyers to students under 12 announcing that policy. "We sold a ton of helmets and made a lot of new friends for the store," Zane says. "Our customers trust us. They come in and say, 'I am here to get a bike. What do I need?' They have confidence in our ability to find them just the right bike at a fair price and to stand behind what we sell."

Constant sales, markdowns on over-inflated prices, and other forms of pressure pricing may boost sales in the short term. Winning customers' trust through fair pricing will pay off in the long term.

Pillar 5: Save Your Customers' Time

Many consumers are poor in at least one respect: they lack time. Retailers often contribute to the problem by wasting consumers' time and energy in myriad ways, from confusing store layouts to inefficient checkout operations to inconvenient hours of business. When shopping is inconvenient, the value of a retailer's offerings plummets.

Slow checkout is particularly annoying to busy people. Managers usually know how much money they are saving by closing a checkout lane; but they may not realize how many customers they've lost in the process. For a food shopper waiting behind six other customers in the "10 Items or Fewer" lane to buy a carton of milk, the time invested in the purchase may outweigh the value of the milk. The shopper may follow through this time but find another store next time. Studies by America's Research Group, a consumer research company based in Charleston, South Carolina, indicate that 83% of women and 91% of men have ceased shopping at a particular store because of long checkout lines.

To compete most effectively, retailers must offer convenience in four ways. They must offer convenient retail locations and operating hours and be easily available by telephone and the Internet (access convenience). They must make it easy for consumers to identify and select desired products (search convenience). They need to make it possible for people to get the products they want by maintaining a high rate of in-stock items and by delivering store, Internet, or catalog orders swiftly (possession convenience). And they need to let consumers complete or amend transactions quickly and easily (transaction convenience).

ShopKo, a discount chain based in Green Bay, Wisconsin, illustrates how shopping speed and ease can create value. ShopKo's more than 160 large discount stores operate in 19 midwestern, mountain, and northwestern states; 80% of the customer base is working women. With fiscal 1999 sales of $3.9 billion (including its small-market subsidiary, Pamida), ShopKo is much smaller than Wal-Mart, Kmart, or Target, yet it competes successfully against all three. Since 1995, following the arrival of new management a year earlier, ShopKo has more than doubled sales and achieved record earnings growth.

ShopKo takes possession convenience seriously and is in-stock 98% of the time on advertised and basic merchandise. Search convenience is another strength. ShopKo stores are remarkably clean and neat. Major traffic aisles are free of passage-blocking displays. Customers near the front of the store have clear sight lines to the back. Navigational signs handing from the ceiling and on the ends of the aisles help point shoppers in the right direction. Clothing on a hanger has a size tag on the hanger neck; folded apparel has an adhesive strip indicating the size on the front of the garment. Children's garments have "simple sizing"—extra small, small, medium, and large—with posted signs educating shoppers on how to select the proper size.

ShopKo has a "one-plus-one" checkout policy of opening another checkout lane whenever two customers are waiting in any lane. Ready-to-assemble furniture is sold on a pull-tag system. The customer presents a coded tag at checkout and within three minutes the boxed merchandise is ready to be delivered to the customer's car. These ways of operating give ShopKo an edge in transaction convenience.

ShopKo is succeeding in the fiercely competitive discount sector by focusing on the total shopping experience rather than on having the lowest prices. Shopping speed and ease combined with a pleasant store atmosphere, a well-trained staff, and a carefully selected range of merchandise creates a strong mix of customer value.

While ShopKo creates real convenience for its customers, the term is often used carelessly in retailing. Consider that Internet shopping is commonly referred to as convenient. The Internet does indeed offer superior convenience for some stages of the shopping experience; it is inferior for other stages. On-line shoppers who save a trip to a physical store must wait for delivery. Christmas shoppers who receive gifts ordered on-line *after* the holiday learn a lesson about possession inconvenience. This is one reason that the most promising path for most retailers is a strategy that combines physical and virtual stores. Increasingly, the best-managed retailers will enable customers to take advantage of the most effective features of physical and virtual shopping, even for the same transaction.

Retail competition has never been more intense or more diverse than it is today. Yet the companies featured in this article, and hundreds of other excellent retailers, are thriving. They understand that neither technology nor promises of "the lowest prices anywhere" can substitute for a passionate focus on the total customer experience. These retailers enable customers to solve important problems, capitalize on the power of respectfulness, connect with customers' emotions, emphasize fair pricing, and save customers time and energy. In an age that demands instant solutions, it's not possible to combine those ingredients with Redi-Mix, crank out a concrete-block building, and hope the structure will stand. But retailers who thoughtfully and painstakingly erect these pillars will have a solid operation that is capable of earning customers' business, trust, and loyalty.

LEONARD L. BERRY is Distinguished Professor of Marketing and holds the M.B. Zale Chair in Retailing and Marketing Leadership at Texas A&M University in College Station, Texas. He founded Texas A&M's Center for Retailing Studies and directed it from 1982 to 2000. He is the author of *Discovering the Soul of Service* (Free Press, 1999).

Why Costco Is So Damn Addictive

A day with Jim Sinegal, the MERCHANDISING MAESTRO who gets shoppers to buy 2,250-count packs of Q-Tips and mayo by the drum.

MATTHEW BOYLE

A man who looks like Wilford Brimley moseys into the Costco warehouse store in the Seattle suburb of Issaquah, Wash., on a bright Columbus Day morning, easily blending into the throngs of shoppers picking up Cheerios, toilet paper, and cashmere sweaters.

But as soon as Costco CEO Jim Sinegal crosses the threshold of this vast, 150,000-square-foot theater of retail, it's abundantly clear that he's not just a spectator—he's the executive producer, director, and critic. "Jim's in the building!" crackles over the walkie-talkie of warehouse manager Louie Silveira. In the apparel section, Silveira's infectious grin morphs into a look of slight panic.

A sudden hop in his step, Silveira, who can log 15 miles a day walking the aisles, scurries over to Sinegal. Unsmiling, hands in his pockets, a coffee stain on his $12.99 Costco shirt, Sinegal turns out to be a no-nonsense connoisseur of detail. He greets his manager with a barrage of questions: "What's new today?"

"We just moved this $800 espresso machine to an end-cap," Silveira responds, meaning he moved it out from the middle of the aisle to a more prominent location at the end.

"How are in-stocks?"

"We're good there."

"What did we do in produce last week?"

"$220,000."

Wielding a bar-code scanner like a six-shooter, Silveira answers each query to Sinegal's satisfaction, but evidently that's not often the case. "When he starts looking at an item too long," Silveira confides later, "I say, 'Oh, shit.'"

Sinegal makes a beeline for a table full of $29.99 Italian-made Hathaway men's dress shirts, located just off the "racetrack," which is retail lingo for the U-shaped path along the perimeter—down one side, across, and back up the other side—that most shoppers follow upon entering the warehouse. He takes a shirt out of the box, fingers it, ponders a moment, then puts it back. He walks away, but soon returns to the table. He looks concerned.

In keeping with Costco's low-price, limited-selection philosophy, the Hathaway shirts are all the same size—a 34/35-inch sleeve. Today, at least, if you want a more precise length, you're out of luck. "I'm anxious to see how it does," says Sinegal, bending to pick up a bit of trash off the floor.

Sinegal needn't worry. The shirts, like everything else at Costco, will no doubt sell out within days, to be replaced by another item in the company's carousel of ridiculously priced high-quality inventory. With $59 billion in sales from 488 warehouse locations, Costco, No. 28 in the FORTUNE 500, is the fourth-largest retailer in the country and the seventh-largest in the world. In the 23 years since Sinegal co-founded Costco with Jeff Brotman (now chairman), it has never reported a negative monthly same-store sales result. Yet he's modestly compensated—Sinegal earned $450,000 in salary and bonus last year, chump change by CEO standards. Add in his stockholdings and he's worth $151 million. (One note on that: On Oct. 12, Costco disclosed that an internal review of stock-option granting identified one grant to Sinegal that was "subject to imprecision" and "may have benefited [Sinegal] by up to $200,000." Sinegal says he takes "full responsibility.")

The company counts nearly 48 million people as members, and those customers are not only slavishly devoted (averaging 22 trips per year, according to UBS analyst Neil Currie), but surprisingly affluent as well (more than a third have household incomes over $75,000). While Wal-Mart stands for low prices and Target embodies cheap chic, Costco is a retail treasure hunt, where one's shopping cart could contain a $50,000 diamond ring resting on top of a 64-ounce vat of mayonnaise. Despite having 82 fewer outlets than its nearest rival, Wal-Mart's Sam's Club, Costco generates about $20 billion more in sales.

Clearly, Costco is doing something right—but what? And how? To figure that out, we shadowed Sinegal, who has spent 52 of his 70 years in the retail business. He got his start working for Sol Price, who created the warehouse-club format, and left Price to launch Costco in 1983. Over the years, he's become a merchandising grand master, an exceedingly shrewd practitioner of the unglamorous but elusive art of getting the right product in the right place at the right time for the right price.

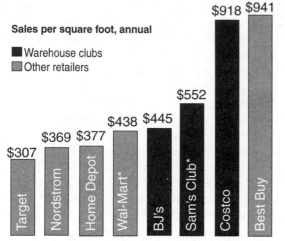

Sales per square foot, annual

■ Warehouse clubs
▨ Other retailers

$307 Target
$369 Nordstrom
$377 Home Depot
$438 Wal-Mart*
$445 BJ's
$552 Sam's Club*
$918 Costco
$941 Best Buy

*Estimate.

Big Box, Big Bucks Costco sells more efficiently than its low-margin peers. It even outdoes plusher names like Nordstrom, and holds its own against higher-markup "category killers" like Best Buy.

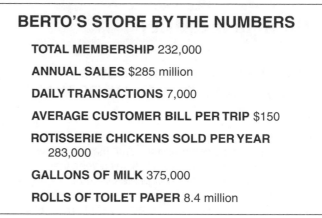

BERTO'S STORE BY THE NUMBERS

TOTAL MEMBERSHIP 232,000

ANNUAL SALES $285 million

DAILY TRANSACTIONS 7,000

AVERAGE CUSTOMER BILL PER TRIP $150

ROTISSERIE CHICKENS SOLD PER YEAR 283,000

GALLONS OF MILK 375,000

ROLLS OF TOILET PAPER 8.4 million

When Jim Sinegal told Sol Price that he was launching a warehouse club to compete with Price's own Price Club, "Sol was pissed," recalls Sinegal, sipping Starbucks coffee (black) in his modestly appointed office at Costco headquarters in Issaquah. Price had a point: His erstwhile protégé was now his top rival in the fast-growing warehouse-club business. Wal-Mart launched Sam's Club that same year; Price Club and Costco later merged, in 1993.

And what a strange business it is. Costco refuses to mark up any item more than 14%, in contrast to supermarkets and department stores, which often carry markups of 25% and 50%, respectively. "We always look to see how much of a gulf we can create between ourselves and the competition," Sinegal says. "So that the competitors eventually say, 'Fuck 'em, these guys are crazy. We'll compete somewhere else."

To illustrate, Sinegal recounts a story about denim. "Some years ago we were selling a hot brand of jeans for $29.99. They were $50 in a department store. We got a great deal on them and could have sold them for a higher price, but we went down to $29.99. Why? We knew it would create a riot." Low markups may create excitement, but they also mean lower profits: Costco ekes out pretax margins of around 3%. Despite the microscopic margins, Costco earned $1.1 billion last fiscal year through its membership fees—$50 per year of pure profit—and its spartan approach to costs. The company doesn't use pricey ad agencies. Products move right from the delivery truck to the charm-free concrete sales floor. Signage looks like it was made with a cheap laser printer. There are no commissioned salespeople. There aren't even any shopping bags. The only cost that Costco doesn't skimp on is wages and benefits, which are the envy of big-box employees nationwide.

And yet Costco's card-carrying legions come in droves, waiting anxiously in fancy foreign cars on Saturday mornings for the store to open. Carts in hand, they display a fervor not usually seen outside of houses of worship. Why? Because we all love a bargain, and Lord help us if we miss one. "We only carry about 4,000 items," says Sinegal, "compared with 40,000 in a typical supermarket and 150,000 in a Wal-Mart supercenter. Of that 4,000, about 3,000 can be found on the floor all the time. The other 1,000 are the treasure-hunt stuff that's always changing. It's the type of item a customer knows they'd better buy because it will not be there next time, like Waterford crystal. We try to get that sense of urgency in our customers." (It should be mentioned that showing up on the sales floor of a discount emporium doesn't necessarily fit the marketing strategies of your Waterfords and Calvin Kleins and other high-end brands. Whatever those companies think, Costco wants to sell their products and makes a practice of acquiring them—legally—on the gray market.)

The limited-variety approach isn't for everyone, though. Sinegal explains: "We carry a 325-count bottle of Advil for $15.25," he says. "Lots of customers don't want to buy 325. If you had ten customers come in to buy Advil, how many are not going to buy any because you just have one size? Maybe one or two. We refer to that as the intelligent loss of sales: We are prepared to give up that one customer. But if we had four or five sizes of Advil, as grocery stores do, it would make our business more difficult to manage. Our business can only succeed if we are efficient. You can't go on selling at these margins if you are not."

The more efficient the product sourcing, the more latitude Sinegal can give his store managers in how they lay out those big bottles of Advil. "There are certain merchandise displays that all warehouses do," he says. "TVs are always in the front, for example. But the intent is not to tell these guys how to run their places. Our managers are entrepreneurs, not somebody who just comes in and unlocks the doors." Indeed, with some locations doing upwards of $300 million in sales a year, each warehouse is a mini-corporation, and each manager a de facto CEO. (See "Down In the Aisles.")

Costco differs from other retailers in many ways, but it's not as if Sinegal feels he has nothing to learn from them. "Whole Foods has a lot of theater to it," he says. "It's difficult to walk in there and not buy something." He also learned a lot from

ANNUAL EDITIONS

Down in the Aisles

How to be great at Costco? Know WHAT CUSTOMERS WANT before they do.

If Jim Sinegal is Costco's general, his 488 warehouse managers are field commanders. With the average warehouse generating $128 million in sales a year, they effectively run their own small companies. Humberto "Berto" Yniguez heads the 139,000-square-foot warehouse in Marina Del Rey, Calif., which employs about 500 people and moves $285 million of product a year—the highest-grossing store in the U.S. (Actually it's No. 2; No. 1 is in Honolulu, where everything's so expensive you'd have to pay shoppers to stay away from Costco. So we're sticking with Berto.) "His store hums," says Sinegal.

That hum does not happen by chance. Yniguez is a model student of Sinegal's approach to retailing. Superstars at Costco have the usual skills recruiters look for: people skills, smarts. A yen for crisis management is a plus. Yniguez has that down: A brief stint as a police officer in his early 20s taught him how to settle disputes quickly, which comes in handy when you're dealing with wild-eyed coupon clippers all day.

But Sinegal looks for something else in his employees too: that rare ability to know just what item will sell best in a given spot at a given time. It's more than just pushing candy near Halloween or air conditioners during a heat wave. "Berto's a great merchant," says Sinegal. "When you walk into his warehouse, you feel like you are enveloped in merchandise. It's all around you." And you have to know your customers: "A lot of our members are affluent, and they have higher expectations," Yniguez says. "I could sell a $45,000 diamond in this building, but it would not sell elsewhere."

Yniguez's merchandising ideas often take root elsewhere, like when he started selling large plants to local real estate developers at up to $350 a pop. To keep the plants from cluttering the sales floor, Yniguez leaves them in the parking lot for same-day pickup. Now a handful of other Costcos are doing the same—not surprising, given that seven of his former assistants are running their own warehouses. The student, in turn, becomes the teacher. "Without folks like Berto, we fail," Sinegal says. "It's that simple." —M.B.

Stew Leonard's, a supermarket chain in the Northeast: "When we did our fresh foods, we studied them closely." And Target: "They have high standards, but they do that without being boring. That's the trick."

Sinegal has taken Costco where no warehouse club had gone before—pharmacy, fresh bakery and meat, store brands one could be proud to serve in the home, and international expansion. Sinegal's son Michael is currently heading Costco's Japanese operations. Will he run the company someday? Sinegal won't go there.

Being a CEO was the last thing on 18-year-old Jim Sinegal's mind when he took a job unloading mattresses at Fed-Mart, Sol Price's precursor to Price Club. "It wasn't that great a job," Sinegal recalls. "I was getting a buck and a quarter an hour. But it was exciting. Sol was a major part of that excitement. He was not big on compliments, but you never doubted what was on his mind. Ever. He was always able to discover everything we were doing wrong. He just had a knack for it."

Price saw that the young Sinegal had the knack too, and chose him to overhaul Fed-Mart's flagship store. "When I was 26," Sinegal continues, "Sol made me the manager in the original San Diego store, which had become unprofitable. I was supposed to narrow down the selection and get out of troublesome categories like apparel. We had way too much apparel. So here I was, this kid, and I was given a tremendous responsibility. As a result of simplifying the process, we were able to get it back into the black."

If Wal-Mart is low prices and Target is cheap chic, Costco is a treasure hunt.

Sinegal embraced Price's iconoclastic approach. "An awful lot of what we did at Fed-Mart was counterintuitive to people who were in the merchandising business at that time," Sinegal says. "We didn't advertise or accept major credit cards. It was all self-service. Also, you had to be a member of the club. People paid us to shop there."

Most counterintuitive of all was Price's stubborn refusal to wring an extra buck from his customers. "Many retailers look at an item and say, 'I'm selling this for ten bucks. How can I sell it for 11?' We look at it and say, How can we get it to nine bucks? And then, How can we get it to eight? It is contrary to the thinking of a retailer, which is to see how much more profit you can get out of it. But once you start doing that, it's like heroin."

Sinegal works diligently to prevent that addiction from entering Costco's bloodstream. Now that he's in Price's role—retail sage—how does he impart what he's learned, and how does he know who his best students are? Step one is obvious: Hire smart young workers. "One of the first places we recruit is at the local university," Sinegal says. "These people are smarter than the average person, hard-working, and they haven't made a career choice." Those who demonstrate smarts and strong people skills move up the ranks. But without merchandising savvy—that ability to know what product would sell best on an end-cap on any given Saturday—an employee has no chance to become warehouse manager. "People who have the feel for it just start to get it," says Sinegal. "Others, you look at them and it's like they are staring at a blank canvas. I'm not trying to be unduly harsh, but that's the way it works. They are not going to become a Louie."

Back in his warehouse, Louie Silveira is perhaps wishing he'd become someone else. He's still facing an Issaquah inquisition from Sinegal, who's convinced he saw a digital piano—

140

$1,999 at the Issaquah warehouse—priced lower in one of his Florida locations the week before. He's not sure which, but tells Silveira to track it down. Silveira checks on a few, but they are all priced the same as his. Sinegal isn't satisfied.

The following day, after hours of boring budget meetings, Sinegal finds, to his delight, that the piano was indeed marked down to $1,499 in the Kendall, Fla., outlet. No victory is too small. "Every time you go someplace, you see something that excites you," Sinegal says. "I was just in the South of France, and there was this gelato stand. I could not believe the excitement it created. I haven't figured out how we will do it at Costco, but it's in my noodle."

A Sales Channel They Can't Resist

Home-shopping giant QVC is becoming one of the most powerful forces in retail. Here's the secret to its surprising success.

ELIZABETH ESFAHANI

"She's one of the sweetest ladies you'll ever meet," announces QVC host David Venable. "Bea Toms, let's start with your signature ham biscuits." Hailing from the Virginia foothills of the Blue Ridge Mountains, Toms is one of 10 new merchants selected by QVC for "Decade of Discoveries," a two-hour special broadcast live from Philadelphia's Franklin Institute museum. Forced to leave home at age 13, she began her culinary career by earning her keep on a Maryland dairy farm. After 50 years as a caterer, the 91-year-old great-great-grandmother finally decided to share her gastronomic secrets with the world and penned *Recipes From a Country Cook.* Her QVC-fanatic daughter persuaded her to bring the book to one of the network's nationwide product searches.

As Toms discusses her applesauce bread, Venabie cuts in. "Bea," he says, "we're almost sold out," Toms's jaw drops. "No!" she says incredulously. "In fact," Venable continues, "we are sold out." Toms shrieks in amazement. "That's wonderful," she says, as tears begin to well in her eyes. Her entire inventory—1,413 books—is gone. More precisely, she has done $37,535 in sales in three and a half minutes.

As amazing as that is for an unknown merchant hawking an unknown product, the feat is repeated over and over again during the show. In less than six minutes, Louie Sorrentino takes orders for $39,018 worth of Potpourri Glo, an illuminated fragrance jar. Nicholas Woodman sells more than 3,200 units of GoPro Hero, a $17.73 wearable waterproof camera, in nine minutes and 12 seconds. And in less than five minutes, Sherre McMahon moves $37,128 worth of Shooks—a product she invented that extends the length of any necklace.

Of course, these entrepreneurs are hoping that this is just the beginning, and that QVC can do for them what it did for Jeanne Bice, who makes a special appearance at the end of the show. Bice was discovered 10 years ago on a similar search; today her Quacker Factory apparel line rakes in nearly $100 million a year, exclusively on QVC. "Everyone asks me," she says, "'Can you remember what your first time on air was like?' And I say, 'Oh, Honey, I remember it like it was yesterday. QVC promised they could take us to glory, and they've done that and so much more.'" Bice's limited-edition Decade of Discoveries sweatshirts sell out so quickly that she has to switch to a backup item for the show's final minutes.

Newbie merchants do little to upgrade the lowbrow image of home shopping, once described by *Wired* magazine as "trailer-park housewives frantically phoning for another ceramic clown." But look past its reputation for costume jewelry and collectibles and you'll find that QVC is earning a place in the pantheon of the world's most successful and innovative retailers. Last year QVC rang up $5.7 billion in sales and $760 million in operating profit, making the Liberty Media subsidiary nearly as big and roughly twice as profitable as Amazon.com. Its 13 percent operating margin beats those of brick-and-mortar heavyweights such as Federated Department Stores, Target, and Wal-Mart. The quarter ending in August was another blockbuster, with sales up 15 percent over the same period in 2004. Although QVC sells no advertising, it is the third-largest U.S. broadcaster in terms of revenue (behind NBC and ABC), and its sales and profits are larger than those of all other TV-based retailers combined. "I don't think people realize the actual size and strength of their business," says Cathay Financial media analyst Andy Baker. "They continue to get it right and are throwing off tons of cash."

And if you stay tuned for a few hours, you'll see that the same QVC formula that turned Toms and her co-stars into retail celebrities is also moving merchandise for an increasing number of well-known upscale brands. In the past few years, prominent manufacturers such as Estée Lauder, Nextel, and Tourneau have begun selling through QVC The network's $80 million single-day sales record happened on Dec. 2, 2001, when Dell sold $65 million worth of PCs. (One month later Michael Dell went on QVC, doing $48,000 in sales every minute he chatted on air.) Even couture designers like John Bartlett and Marc Bauer, who wouldn't have been caught dead on a home-shopping network in the past, now sell lines on QVC.

QVC makes its money the same way other retailers do—by buying merchandise from suppliers and selling it at a markup. (Its gross margin hovers around 38 percent, on par with that of department stores.) But instead of leasing retail space, QVC pays cable operators 5 percent of sales, a kind of rent that not only secures coveted low-number channels but also motivates cable companies to promote QVC on other stations. The resulting boost in viewership begets volume: Last year 7.2 million people, 90 percent of them women, made a QVC purchase in the United States. And the network has developed intense loyalty among its clients, with

QVC's Revenue Has Grown an Average of 14 Percent Annually Since 1996 and Its Operating Profit Margin Tops Those of Most Major Players in 21st-Century Retail

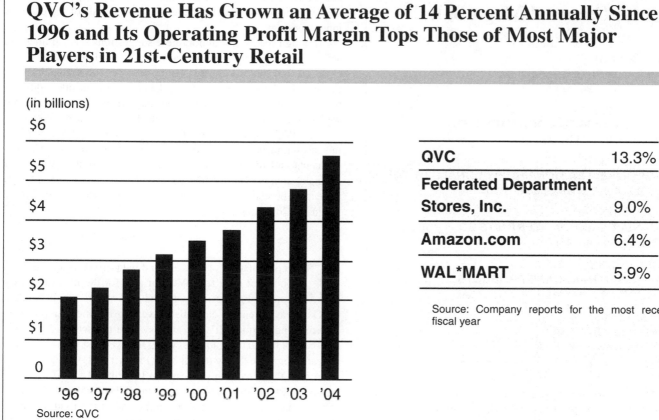

(in billions)

Source: QVC

QVC	13.3%
Federated Department Stores, Inc.	9.0%
Amazon.com	6.4%
WAL*MART	5.9%

Source: Company reports for the most recent fiscal year

93 percent of its annual revenue coming from repeat customers. A decade ago many predicted a bleak future for home shopping—retail consultant Alan Millslein told the *New York Times* in 1996 that the format was "a vehicle for broken-down movie stars . . . a soufflé that never rose"—but QVC has proven skeptics wrong, growing sales about 14 percent annually since 1996.

The secret to QVC's continued expansion has been honing the art and science of TV retailing to a point where it is every bit as powerful—and profitable—as Internet-only e-commerce. While Web retailers analyze data to make the most of each mouse-click. QVC line producers also react in real time, adjusting camera angles, lighting, and dialogue to maximize sales and profits. Remarkably, the company's website, QVC.com, is already the nation's sixth-largest general merchandise Internet retailer, and thanks to shrewd coordination with TV programming that drives buyers online, its sales grew 30 percent in the first half of this year. And with more and more retailers realizing that they can't compete solely on price, QVC is attracting attention as the gold standard of "entertainment"—the blend of entertainment and retailing. "We aren't really in the business of selling," says Darlene Daggett, QVC's president for U.S. commerce, whose comment is particularly ironic given that she, more than anyone, is credited with turning the company into a dynamic merchandiser. Explains Jeffrey Rayport, a former Harvard Business School professor and author of *Best Face Forward,* a book on customer service that uses QVC as a case study, "Daggett has transformed QVC into a company that uses products to build relationships with customers."

Daggett has perfected QVC's folksy but analytical style over a 16-year career at the company. She arrived in 1989, just three years after QVC (which stands for quality, value, and convenience)

was launched by Joseph Segel, founder of collectibles marketer the Franklin Mint. In those days QVC—like many of the home-shopping channels launched within a year of the cable debut of Home Shopping Network (HSN)—was all about jewelry, which made up 50 percent of the network's sales. But in contrast to HSN's aggressive sell, Segel fostered a softer approach intended to nurture loyal viewers. As director (and later head) of merchandising, Daggett steadily moved the business away from dependence on bangles and studs (jewelry is now just 22 percent of sales), and in 2002, QVC CEO Doug Briggs tapped her to oversee the company's $4.1 billion U.S. operation, where she has continued to shift the mix toward home decor, beauty, and fashion. She believes that the ideal QVC product is what she calls a "deep" brand—one that makes an emotional connection with viewers. "We will never be good at selling commodities," she says. "This is a business about want, not need."

That approach to selling is evident almost everywhere on a recent afternoon at QVC's 20,000-square-foot studios in West Chester, Pa. At 3 P.M. host Rick Domeier is a whirlwind of energy as he roams about the studio looking for his "guest experts"—manufacturers' representatives who will appear on air with him to sell their products, Backstage, he greets Cathie Marie Georges, who will be presenting a decorative wall rack. "So what's your QVC story?" Domeier asks.

A 10-year QVC veteran and former star of *The Young and the Restless,* Domeier says he's looking for a story line that will resonate with viewers. Often it's an elevator pitch conveying what's unique about a product, plus an inspiring tale of how it came to be. Georges says that she and her husband wanted to turn a functional item into a piece of art. "I love that you designed this," Domeier says. "Feel free to play that up on air."

Lights! Camera! Mega-Sales!

DEC. 2, 2001
DELL COMPUTER
$65 million in 24 hours

MARCH 30, 2004
ROCCO DISPIRITO COOKWARE SETS
$1.1 million in 24 hours

SEPT. 28, 2004
THINK LIKE A BILLIONAIRE, BY DONALD TRUMP
62,000 copies in less than an hour

NOV. 8, 2004
SHANIA TWAIN *GREATEST HITS* CD
$600,000 in one hour

JULY 15, 2005
JONATHAN HAIR-CARE PRODUCTS
$85,104 in 13 minutes

AUG. 7, 2005
NFL MEMORABILIA
7,400 orders in two hours

Part of why such stories connect so powerfully with viewers is that the network always broadcasts live. There are no scripts or prompters; hosts rely on live demonstrations, impromptu banter, and call-in testimonials to build trust. It's reality TV from before the term existed: Watch long enough and you'll catch hosts dropping products, setting off fire alarms, and tripping down stairs. "The element of not knowing what's going to happen next is key," Domeier says. QVC folks call it the "backyard fence" sell—the feeling that the merchants are neighbors visiting from next door.

Live broadcasts also allow the company to respond quickly to sales trends to stoke demand. High above Domeier in an off-camera nook, line producer Alan Massaro's eyes dart among six flat-screen TVs displaying images and graphs. As Domeier talks up a 114-piece Reed & Barton flatware set, Massaro reminds him to emphasize the number of pieces in the set. Six minutes into the pitch, Massaro patches through a call from a viewer named Pat, who says she is buying one for her son. During the testimonial, call volume doubles. Three minutes after Pat hangs up, Massaro tells Domeier that only 100 sets remain, and Domeier relays the information to viewers. In another two minutes, all 977 of the $117 flatware sets have sold out.

The network s most rigorous analysis, however, is reserved for the product chosen each day as "today's special value," or TSV. These items are QVCs all-stars: They've already proven that they can generate high dollars-per-minute activity. QVC buys the TSV in bulk, offers it at a rock-bottom price, and promotes it eight times during a 24-hour period. A TSV can generate as much as 20 percent of a day's sales.

"So what did you guys think?" asks Jack Comstock, VP for TV sales strategy. Every day at 9 A.M., Comstock leads a meeting of QVC execs to analyze results from TSV footage recorded hours earlier. This time the TSV is a battery-powered scented candle that flickers like a real flame without the risk of accidental fire. The candle fared well, and everyone agreed that the host made an effective presentation. However, the group decided that the product could have been displayed on a hutch in the background and that viewers might have reacted better to more visuals of the candle's inner workings.

Although seemingly minor, these suggestions spark immediate action. First the candle is rushed to QVC's online studio, where close-ups are shot and posted on the website 10 minutes later. In the next TSV spot, the host turns the candle on its side, allowing the camera to zoom in. The changes pay off. While the candle did well in the early segments, it flat-out kills later in the day, selling out QVC's inventory of 61,620 units—a total of $1.7 million in sales—four hours ahead of schedule. A summary of the TSV's segments and results is stored on the QVC intranet, where, for instance, analysis shows that the candle sold better when lights were at 80 percent strength than at 45 percent. "Too dark to see the product," Comstock concludes.

The combination of soft sell and data-driven rigor has been a boon not only for QVC but also for the many formerly unknown brands it has turned into superstars. In a sense QVC acts as a venture capitalist, investing airtime in a portfolio of promising startups. It's not an easy path to success: Less than 4 percent of the 20,000 inquiries QVC received last year resulted in appearances. (See "How to Get Your Product on QVC.")

In fact, the screening process can be brutal. Even if a vendor makes it past quality-control tests (many fail several times), a lackluster initial performance can mean the end of the road. Products that generate customer complaints totaling more than 1 percent of shipped units land on a list circulated weekly to QVC execs. ("You don't want to be on that list," says John Hunter, QVC's senior VP for customer services.) There's also a continuous weeding out of underachievers: During the morning analysis meeting, Comstock and his crew identify the poorest performer of the day, Tranquility Yoga Wear. Everyone agrees that the host did a great job pitching the brand, but the hour-long segment missed its $350.000 sales target by more than $100,000. There is discussion about the price point being too high. No matter: The line will be liquidated at a discount on QVC.com.

But for products that can demonstrate demand in their initial eight minutes of fame, it's the chance of a lifetime. Take Leslie Blodgett, CEO of cosmetics company Bare Escentuals. When Blodgett pitched QVC on a line of natural cosmetics in 1997, her company had sales of less than $10 million and about a dozen stores concentrated on the West Coast. After months of waiting, she got eight minutes of airtime and promptly sold out. On her third appearance, she racked up $400,000 in sales in 20 minutes, about as much business as one of her stores did in a year. Today, Bare Escentuals is QVC's No. 1 cosmetics brand, having sold $212 million in the past eight years. On her TSV day in June, Blodgett's 24-hour sales total hit $9.3 million. The exposure has allowed her to expand to 23 stores nationwide, with another six opening by the end of the year. "Suddenly I had a customer base that spread from Hawaii to New York," she says.

QVC has also found success with its own brands. In the past few years, the company has ramped up development of private-label products, which now constitute a third of its sales. A bedding line called Northern Nights brings in more than $50 million a year, and Dialogue, QVC's sportswear brand, is among the network's top sellers in apparel. After noticing customer interest in Dialogue's Modal natural-fabric items, Daggett spun off Freelance—a clothing line made entirely of that fabric.

How to Get Your Product on QVC

1. Develop Your Story

Ask yourself, Will your product shine on TV? Does it solve a problem or make life easier? QVC looks for high-margin items that cost more than $15. Watch the network and surf QVC.com to see if your product fits in.

2. Apply to Become a Vendor

Do it online at www.qvcproductsearch.com or mail an application and product samples to: *QVC Studio Park Vendor Relations 1200 Wilson Drive Mail Stop #128 West Chester, PA 19380-4262*

3. Put Your Product Through Its Paces

If QVC is interested, you'll know within three weeks. Be prepared to fail quality tests and rework your packaging. When you eventually pass, a QVC buyer will help to create a sales strategy.

4. Bulk Up Those Inventories

The network will likely require you to deliver a minimum of $20,000 worth of your product (at wholesale prices) before your first segment.

5. Practice Your Pitch

QVC provides an online course in sales strategies for new merchants. A month before debuting, vendors travel to QVC headquarters for a half-day class to practice on camera with a host, who offers tips on what works and what doesn't.

Skeptics point out that QVC is nearing full U.S. penetration—it now reaches 90 million of America's 92 million households with pay TV—implying that future growth is limited. Daggett counters that, with less than 10 percent of households that get QVC currently making purchases, there are plenty of potential new customers. The key. she says, will be to offer a wider array of merchandise and more well-known brands. "We've been on the cusp of being a very sexy place to shop for a long time," Daggett says. "National brands make us easier to trust."

Nevertheless, she admits that luring big-name companies has not been easy. Many believe that an association with home shopping will taint their brands: Dean Factor, grandson of makeup mogul Max Factor, reportedly said that Saks and Neiman Marcus refused to carry his Smashbox cosmetics line because it appeared on QVC in the 1990s. Others fear that QVC will cannibalize traditional sales channels. "I've been politely told 'no' more times than I care to count," Daggett says.

But thanks to a growing library of case studies illustrating QVCs positive impact, the tide seems to be turning. Since Michael Dell's 2002 on-air debut, his company has been doing $100 million in sales on QVC annually. And Daggett scored a major coup in 2003, when, after years of pursuit, Estée Lauder agreed to test its high-end Prescriptives cosmetics brand on QVC. Of the first 50,000 viewers who purchased Prescriptives products, 76 percent were new customers for Lauder. In addition, traffic to Prescriptives counters in stores jumped 5 percent in the week after the brand's QVC airing.

In fact, what may be most attractive to national brands is QVC's value as a marketing tool to increase sales through traditional channels. It provides a forum for product demos, and QVC estimates that for every 10,000 orders it receives, 1.5 million people are watching. In 2004 the network gave away $1,000 rebate coupons for GM's Saturn division, driving $60 million in new car purchases. Birkenstock, which first appeared on QVC in 1996. estimates that its QVC airtime is worth at least $8 million in traditional advertising. The shoemaker even alerts its brick-and-mortar stores in advance of on-air appearances to allow them to stock up: Some stores have seen demand jump as much as 5 percent the following week.

Daggett has also pursued a host of branding partnerships to lure those who might otherwise flip past QVC. In June, QVC introduced the Antiques Road Show collection, an exclusive line of vintage jewelry inspired by the eponymous public-TV program, and in August, Condé Nast's *Lucky* magazine shipped a special "Lucky Shops QVC" edition to 80.000 viewers who bought subscriptions. Daggett made an appearance last October on *The Apprentice,* in which the hit TV shows two teams tried to sell products on the air. More recently, in a tie-in with the Bravo reality show *Blow Out,* celebrity hairdresser Jonathan Antin sold more than 35,000 units of his hair-care line, making his the most successful hair product launch in QVC's history.

Of course, Daggett recognizes that it will take time to shed home shopping's historical baggage. She says the challenge will be to attract new shoppers while not alienating the current clientele. "The last thing we want to do." she says, "is to change the brand and not have our customers travel along with us."

If the live audience for "Decade of Discoveries" is any indication, QVC's loyal fans seem ready for Daggett's ride. As the show ends, 64-year-old Becky Lawson of Newark, Del., pops out of her seat to have her picture taken with any QVC employee she can find. Known to her friends jokingly as the "QVC queen," she says virtually everything she owns—clothes, furniture, cookware—was bought from QVC vendors. "I almost never go to the store anymore except for groceries." she says. "It's entertaining. They're like friends."

ELIZABETH ESFAHANI (eesfahani@business2.com) is a writer-reporter at *Business 2.0.*

Direct Mail Still Has Its Place

Marketers find it works best as part of integrated campaigns

MICHAEL FIELDING

Long pegged as the wallflower at the direct marketing disco, direct mail has been enjoying a full dance card in the last five years with the heavy push toward integration of all media channels, from Internet to telemarketing. Capitalizing on a combination of technological developments and its unique place in the marketing mix, direct mail is leading the way.

"People always associated direct mail with junk mail," explains Beth Ann Kilberg-Walsh, manager for marketing communications at Xerox Corp.'s Rochester, N.Y.-based Production Systems Group, which works with production publishing, transaction printing and enterprisewide printing clients. She began her career with Advo Inc., the nation's largest direct mail company. "But direct mail is not dead."

In fact, with more than three-quarters of marketers using it, direct mail is the most popular method of direct marketing (compared with 64% who use e-mail), according to the Direct Marketing Association; 69% of consumers prefer traditional mail over e-mail for direct marketing, according to Weymouth, Mass.-based consulting firm InfoTrends.

Direct mail brings several distinct qualities to the marketing mix. For one thing, digital printing technologies enable a level of personalization and segmentation unavailable until recent years, at a reasonable cost. For another, direct mail is uniquely tactile among direct marketing options—something that no other direct marketing method offers. Finally, direct mail completes an integrated marketing campaign, pulling in offline prospects to online destinations, and improving response rates and ROI across the board.

"Direct mail is becoming more and more relevant," says Diane Quinlisk, senior manager of market development at Kodak Graphics Communications Group, also based in Rochester. "It used to be the stepchild of the ad vehicles because it was sent en masse and wasn't very sexy. Today, though, digital technologies allow for quality and color and a variety of personalized images."

In fact, it allows for personalization of messages that are almost unique to each individual customers' needs and interests.

"The new technologies allow for more color and varied text than ever before, making even the most mundane mail, such as a credit card solicitation, an intriguing marketing vehicle," explains Quinlisk, who promotes the company's newest print technologies that allow for both personalized variable data campaigns and mass printing. Kodak's NexPress, for example, is designed for four-color, short-run personalized pieces in variable data campaigns. "Direct mail has stepped into a new phase," she says.

In addition to being highly targeted, direct mail's three-dimensional qualities and tangibility offer endless potential to deliver creative, highly unique marketing messages.

"People will get annoyed at incoming commercial e-mail a lot more quickly than they will at junk mail," argues Peter Fader, Frances and Pei-Yuan Chia Professor of Marketing at The Wharton School of the University of Pennsylvania in Philadelphia. "The process of going through mail—real versus virtual—is still enjoyable."

Chicago-based Arc Worldwide understood that, and leveraged it to an exponential degree, in November 2005 when it launched its "Verb Yellowball" campaign for the Atlanta-based Centers for Disease Control and Prevention. The campaign encouraged youths ages 9 to 13 to incorporate physical activity into their everyday lives.

Verbatim:
'Direct mail makes money, and as long as it does that, it will still be used.'

Following a prequalified stage to gauge interest by educators, Arc sent complete kits that included posters, teacher materials and 500,000 yellow balls. Each ball bore a unique tracking code, and was designed to be played with and passed on to friends and siblings. "The message was: Play with it, tell us about it on our Web site and pass it on to another kid," explains Stella Kusner, account director. "People get so much junk mail these days that the only way to break through is to add some other dimension."

The campaign worked: It generated more than 13,000 Web log entries and 100,000 videos on the campaign's Internet site.

Being tangible and three-dimensional also has fringe benefits such as staying power. "It is not only about a response but about how you're branding your product," explains Andy Wright, executive vice president of sales and marketing services at Plymouth, Minn.-based Carlson Marketing Group. "Direct mail has amazing staying power. There's a persistence within the home."

Finally, direct mail provides a highly efficient environment in which to measure return on investment. "Marketers are not stupid," Wright adds. "They have budgets. If something works, they use it. Direct mail makes money, and as long as it does that, it will still be used."

Despite its high costs (compared with more cost-effective and widely popular Internet campaigns), direct mail campaigns can still be deployed with fiscal responsibility.

Wright suggests segmenting an audience to get the best results at an acceptable price from a campaign that includes direct mail. Send unique but often costly direct mail pieces to the premium customers and prospects, he suggests, while sending more cost-effective pieces to the other segments of a target audience. For example, in a recent campaign for a large multinational packaged goods client's campaign for one of its personal care lines, Carlson designed its premium direct mail pieces to be sent to the top 15% of 200 million of the company's customers. The middle-tier recipients—55% of the total—received flat mail (as opposed to dimensional mail such as a uniquely shaped package) with coupons or discounts, while the remainder of the audience received e-mails.

While remaining cost-effective, that approach also allows for more efficient ROI measurement. "Direct mail has the ability for us to understand how each piece performs if you're doing it properly," adds Doug Rozen, vice president of interactive marketing at Carlson.

Many forms of direct mail are, in fact, cost-effective. Companies typically find that their revenue from several forms of direct mail—including catalogs and flat mail—are double the initial costs, according to the U.S. Postal Service.

Direct mail also produces higher overall response rates than those of e-mail, newspapers and magazines combined, and its response rates rank just below those of catalogs, according to the U.S. Postal Service. While telemarketing produces among the highest response rates, it is limited by the national Do-Not-Call registry and a reputation as being intrusive. Similarly, e-mail campaigns—while highly trackable and famously affordable—are limited by spam and junk filters and are viewed as equally intrusive.

Quinlisk says that she has noticed marketing budgets shift in their focus from traditional broadcast media to the interactive and direct world, proving that executives have placed their faith in the proven ROI of direct mail.

She cautions, though, that marketers must ensure that a direct mail campaign is done correctly. "The only reason you want to go into the mail is that you want to have some call to action such as a URL, phone number or a coupon to bring to the nearest retail location," she explains. "Response isn't as important as conversion" to a sale.

Nevertheless, while particular methods of direct marketing—such as direct mail, e-mail, telemarketing—will always have contingents of supporters and detractors, most marketers agree that the best campaigns are those that are integrated. Witness Xerox's transition from sending individual mass mailings for each campaign just four years ago to entirely integrated campaigns.

The new method begins with a personalized dimensional mailer with a call to action sent to targeted audiences in a variety of industries. Clients then electronically confirm receipt of the mailer on an Internet site. While there, they complete a short survey, the results of which are sent to a database of other clients. If they don't respond to the initial mailer, Xerox sends a personalized piece of flat mail (such as a postcard) four to six weeks later, again directing them to the site. Once they are registered, they are invited to opt into personalized portals that contain relevant industry information for other clients like them, such as commercial printers, direct marketers and publishers.

The results speak for themselves: Xerox's new campaigns now enjoy response rates of 6% to 15%, compared with previous rates that hovered at 1%.

Says Kusner: "A random direct mail piece that's not connected to another channel won't mean anything if it's not part of a larger story."

The Online Ad Surge

Brand advertising online has taken off—and it's shaking up Madison Ave.

STEPHEN BAKER

In the golden age of TV, they called them roadblocks. Advertisers mounted such visual barricades by placing the same spot at the same minute on the three big networks. That way, the ad would blanket the entire medium, collaring viewers whether they were tuned to Lawrence Welk, *Dragnet,* or Uncle Miltie. The roadblock was a simple but powerful approach—and near impossible to pull off in today's fractured TV market.

But who said a roadblock had to be on TV? A year ago, Ford Motor Co. executives unveiled a roadblock on the Internet to promote their F-150 truck. On the day of the launch, Ford placed bold banner ads for 24 hours on the three leading portals—AOL, MSN, and Yahoo! Some 50 million Web surfers saw Ford's banner. And millions of them clicked on it, pouring onto Ford's Web site at a rate that reached 3,000 per second. The company says the traffic led to a 6% jump in sales over the first three months of the campaign. Naturally, more Internet roadblocks have followed, most recently with the Oct. 25 launch of the F-500 sedan. Says Rich Stoddart, Ford's marketing communications manager: "We've proved we can leverage the Web for the mass market."

Ford and everyone else. Advertisers are seeing that the top few Web properties now reach true mass audiences. Each of the three biggest portals attracts 70% of the Americans online to its properties monthly, according to comScore Networks, a traffic-tracking organization. Demand for this prime real estate is so strong that there isn't enough to go around, and prices to advertise are soaring. A year ago, media buyers could land discounted space on the home pages of major portals for between $100,000 and $180,000 per 24 hours, say buyers. Now, the cost is reaching $300,000. Forget about discounts. If advertisers are lucky enough to land the space, they often must agree to spend an equal amount elsewhere on the portal. Facing this traffic jam at the top sites, advertisers are jostling for spots throughout the Net. "A few years ago, it was kids with green hair selling ads," says Gary Stein, an analyst at Jupiter Research. "Now Internet ads are mainstream, and part of every company's media buy."

Why the change? The Internet is growing up. Broadband connections now reach more than half of American households, including the lion's share of the prosperous ones. Although the Internet still takes in only 4.3% of U.S. advertising revenue, surveys indicate that it accounts for 14% of America's media time. And that's not including those who are Web-surfing at work—a major audience for advertisers. Smitten by the growing reach and power of the Net, blue-chip advertisers are stretching far beyond the cramped text ads on search engines that have turned Google Inc. into a global sensation. Now advertisers are packing online ads with music and color video, just like those on TV. They're looking to the Web to build brands.

The result is a surge in growth that's extending from Madison Ave. to the West Coast campuses of Yahoo! and MSN. While the overall ad industry grows at a respectable 7.7% a year, Internet ads are galloping ahead at a 28.8% clip. New York consulting firm eMarketer predicts online advertising will reach $9.3 billion this year—$5.4 billion of it in brand ads. "It's a great time to be alive in this industry," enthuses David J. Moore, chief executive of 24/7 Real Media Inc., an ad agency.

For anyone who recalls the soaring expectations that preceded the Net advertising crash earlier in the decade, even a touch of euphoria is grounds for serious heebie-jeebies. Last time around, many of the most enthusiastic advertisers—the cash-happy dot-coms themselves—dropped dead. From 2000 to 2002, Internet advertising plummeted 25%. But something is decidedly different this time. Since the bust, the industry has pieced together the technology—from video delivery to customer tracking—to make good on the shining predictions of the boom. The Net is winning over mainstream advertisers with its computational precision. It delivers hard, quantifiable results measured in clicks and sales—down to the penny. In the process, it's turning advertising from an art into a science.

Does this mean the Internet is going to vacuum up the world's advertising dollars? No, but it'll angle for its fair share. Some of the Net's market grab will come from easy pickings, such as Yellow Pages and direct-response mail—fields where Internet search delivers unmatched efficiency. Brand advertising, meanwhile, will probably come straight from the hide of TV, billboards, and print media. Ford, in line with other auto makers, has moved 10% of its ad budget online, and the number is on the rise. Joanne Bradford, MSN's chief media revenue officer, expects other industries to follow suit, with online accounting for 8% to 12% of the advertising outlay by decade's end. Within two years, online advertising is projected to reach $13.8 billion, motoring past the slower-growing magazine industry, according to Kagan Research LLC in Monterey, Calif.

Tangle of Complexity

The importance of internet advertising extends far beyond the numbers. Now that advertisers have their hands on a tool that measures an ad's effectiveness, they're starting to press other media for similar accountability. It's a process sure to cause disruptions. Take TV. For decades, Nielsen Media Research has been providing reports on how many customers watch a specific program. But in a nation full of TiVo Inc. zappers and channel surfers, how many are actually seeing the ads? Nielsen is now rolling out technology that measures precise minute-by-minute data in local markets. And it's also working with TiVo to survey ad viewership among TiVo users. These steps bring TV a step closer to Internet-style accountability. But if the results show that viewers are skipping ads, TV's economics could take a beating. "It starts to shift the playing field," says Douglas McCormick, CEO of iVillage Inc. and a former cable-TV exec. "Internet [costs per thousand viewers] are going to start looking a lot more attractive."

In fact, the Net is helping break down walls that traditionally divide different media. More and more, publishers are delivering selected customers to advertisers, and reaching customers across a host of media, including the Net. Instead of appearing in a certain show or time slot, their ads are coupled with subject areas, such as health or sports. ABC News, for example, delivers subject-specific ads to TV, the Net, and cell phones. Advertisers want "to reach consumers, wherever they are," says Alan Ives, vice-president for sales at ABC Interactive.

This new world of advertising is bubbling with innovations, many of them blending advertising with content or other goodies. Weather.com, for one, urges the public to download a free weather bar that links up to a host of advertisers, from Scotts, the lawn-care company, to American Express. And on Nov. 9, Amazon.com and J.P. Morgan Chase announced a venture to produce short films on the Amazon site. Customers who use an Amazon Visa card to buy items advertised in the movies will get a 5% discount.

All of this innovation creates a tangle of complexity—and simplifying it represents a growing challenge for the industry. While ad agencies can snap up 30-second spots on *Monday Night Football,* the Internet offers almost infinite options. First, advertisers have to pick from a fast-growing number of formats, from skyscrapers that crawl up a page to rollovers—ads that expand as the mouse runs across them. Then they have to figure out on which of the thousands of commercial sites to run the ad. And they must decide whether to orchestrate the campaign to hit people with different ads at work and at home—or maybe arrange a succession of ads, so that a customer's first viewing introduces a product, and the second provides details. "The complexity can be a barrier," says Yahoo's chief sales officer, Wenda Harris Millard. She says Yahoo offered 700 different ad forms when she arrived three years ago. It's down to a fraction of that now, but it remains a lot more complicated than old-fashioned TV or magazine buys.

Here the big players have an outsize advantage. They can sell Internet ads as part of a bigger package. CNN, for example, sold pricey sponsorships for Election Day coverage to companies, such as Samsung and DHL. The condition? Sponsors had to advertise on TV and the Web. While CNN's TV coverage was swamped by rival Fox News, the exposure on the Web page more than made up for it. Over that 24-hour period, CNN.com bested the competition with a dizzying 650 million visits.

Already, advertisers are busy linking their Net promotions to offline campaigns, from newspapers to TV. In the most recent Super Bowl, for example, Mitsubishi Motors bought a 30-second ad. It enticed viewers to visit its Web site to see what happened when a Mitsubishi Galant faced off against a Toyota Camry in a crash test. In the following six hours, some 11 million people visited the site. Many of them provided their e-mail addresses, watched the 50-second video, and clicked the tires in the car company's virtual lot. Such visits are critical, especially for the auto industry. Why? Studies show that shoppers, punching away at search engines, spend an average of five hours researching cars online before setting foot in a showroom.

'Toe in the Water'

It was the success of search-based advertising that breathed life back into the industry following the dot-com collapse. Led by Overture Services—now a unit of Yahoo—and later by Google, the search engines delivered a breakthrough innovation. They interpreted the key words typed in by customers as requests for products and services. And they auctioned the rights to place text ads alongside search results to any company or individual that was interested. The offer has been irresistible: Advertisers paid their bid, be it a penny or a dollar, only when a customer clicked on their ad. Paid search grew from a mere cipher in 1999 into a $3.9 billion business, according to eMarketer. "Search became a way for marketers of all stripes to dip their toe in the water," says Ted Meisel, president of Yahoo's Overture Division.

The question is whether the search industry will continue to pace the growth of Internet advertising. eMarketer predicts that growth of such search ads in the U.S. could slow from 55% this year to 19% in 2005. This poses little problem for Yahoo, a powerhouse in both arenas. But Google risks missing out on growth in brand ads. The reason? Advertisers and agencies traditionally separate the direct-marketing teams, which feed into search, from the creative and brand teams that oversee display ads. For now, Google is attempting to bridge the gap by developing ads with images and pictures to accompany search results.

The rush toward display advertising online is similar to the rise of cable TV a generation ago. Until the early 1980s, advertisers saw cable mostly as a direct-marketing tool for niche products, from miraculous vegetable choppers to belly-busting exercise machines, all of them accompanied by a prominent 1–800 number. But in 1982 an advertising executive named Ted Bates proposed a so-called 5% solution. He noted that with half of America's homes cabled, the industry was reaching the scale of a mass market. Advertisers would see substantial gains, he predicted, if they shifted just a nickel from every budgeted dollar to cable from the networks. It paid off. Cable stormed into brand advertising—and is positioned to overtake the broadcast networks within two years, according to eMarketer.

Now Net publishers and ad agencies are pushing their own 10% solution. And they have the ammo to make their appeal. Recent case studies by the industry's trade group, the Interactive Advertising Bureau, showed that while TV spreads the word, the Net can drive home the particulars. One case covered Universal Studios' 2002 DVD release of *ET, the Extraterrestrial.* The studio spent 94% of the budget on TV, nearly 6% on banner ads, and less than 1% on animated ads that floated at the top of Web pages. The result? While most viewers learned of the offering on TV, the animated ads reinforced a key message. Among pure TV viewers, 39.4% learned that the DVD contained never-before-seen footage. But of those who saw TV and the animated ad, the number rose to 48.1%. The study's conclusion: Universal would have fared better by reducing TV by about a quarter and lifting the animated component to 25%. Universal declines to comment on the study.

Video is the latest rage in Net advertising. It represents 11% of online spending, says Jupiter Research. And advertisers are budgeting for more. Take brokerage TD Waterhouse Group. In addition to search and banner ads, the company is running 30-second online videos with *Law & Order's* Sam Waterston. This will contribute to a 42% hike in the company's Internet spending in the next year, says Senior Vice-President Stuart Rubinstein. "Full-motion video is the perfect vehicle," he says.

Tight Squeeze

The biggest trouble with online video is a shortage of slots for it. While demand grows, much of it is focused on the Net's biggest sites, the home pages of the major portals, along with their finance, sports, e-mail, and auto sites. It adds up to perhaps two dozen pages, all of them run by the giants of the Web. While smaller targeted sites reach niche audiences, most of the crush for branding campaigns is for megasites—and many advertisers get crowded out. "We called MSN to run some video for Adidas," says Sarah Fay, president of Carat Interactive Inc., a Boston media buyer. "They gave us one day in November, and it was on a weekend." The squeeze is so severe that advertisers in the hottest segments of the market—autos, finance, and entertainment—are gobbling up prime video slots months in advance. Within a year or two, industry insiders expect this buying to evolve into an Internet version of the TV industry's annual up-front sales.

The portals are taking advantage of the hot video market to funnel advertisers toward thousands of their less-trafficked pages. Increasingly, they're bundling prime spots into package deals, which include more obscure placements—on pages for foreign-language studies or artisanal cheesemaking. MSN is even offering advertisers who venture into these digital hinterlands a hand in developing new and innovative advertisements.

MSN's Bradford says varied locations have different uses. The home page serves a message to 20 million users a day, while placements in back pages reach niche audiences, sometimes numbering only in the tens of thousands.

Advertisers have plenty of room for video on their own home pages. And much of their ad effort, on and offline, is focused on getting Web surfers to drop by. Many TV watchers these days sit close enough to a computer to type in a Web address or "Google" a site without moving from the couch. During golf's U.S. Open in June, TaylorMade-Adidas Golf ran TV ads promoting its new R7 driver. Traffic on the site jumped 22% in the hour after each ad, says Jason Woodmansee, the company's director of global eMarketing. Once visitors came to the site, they not only clicked through videos showing the club in action but also located nearby stores and signed up for e-mails. That way, the company used the Net to turn a broad TV audience into a vast collection of individual relationships.

But how to reach customers with just the right message? Increasingly, advertisers are tracking them down. With a technology called behavioral targeting, a Who's Who of publishers, from NYTimes.com to BusinessWeek.com, use systems that quietly map the click path of registered visitors to their site or network. These programs do not accumulate personal data on the user. But using digital cookies dropped into each visitor's browser, they focus on behavior. For example, the system knows which site an anonymous Web surfer comes from. It also keeps tabs on how much time that reader spends looking at a particular article, and which ads he or she clicks on. Instead of asking consumers loads of questions about themselves, says Eric Christensen, general manager of Belo Interactive in Dallas, "we can now infer from their behavior on the site. That has been a big change in the last year."

Publishers follow their customers gingerly, knowing they run the risk of inciting a privacy backlash. Web surfers, under siege from spam and torrents of pop-up ads, are primed to fend off bothersome ads. And previous attempts to track customers have run into legal tangles. Aggressive consumer profiling by DoubleClick, a once high-flying Net ad company, sparked a lawsuit four years ago by 10 state attorneys including New York's Eliot Spitzer. DoubleClick, which set out to build databases combining personal info with Web-surfing habits, retreated on its plans and settled the lawsuit. It failed to recover its market leadership, though, and now is up for sale.

But while DoubleClick fades, scores of companies are storming into the growing world of online advertising. They range from tech outfits that create new forms of banners and skyscrapers to advertising startups that tie together vast networks of publishers, from fishing sites to political blogs. "Net advertising is only nine years old, and everybody's just now getting started," says Gurbaksh Chahal, CEO of BlueLithium, a San Jose (Calif.) advertising company. Those who manage to climb atop the Internet's advertising wave are in for a wild ride.

Behind the Magic

How do stellar sellers work their magic? From the first cold call to closing the deal, discover the top sales secrets of some seriously successful salespeople.

CHRIS PENTTILA

How to sell more, better and faster: It's what keeps salespeople awake at night, no matter what they sell. And in an economy that's still soft around the edges, selling well is more important than it's ever been.

So how can you and your sales team excel in turning prospects into long-term customers? Here are 17 how-to secrets and words of wisdom from sales experts and entrepreneurs for mastering the entire sales process.

How to Make a Cold Call

A cold call is not a time to make a sale. It's [a time] to *give* something. The first question is, "Is it OK if I share with you what we do and why people use us? Then, we can decide whether it makes sense to go further." Be as discerning of the prospect as they are of you. No one's going to do business with a beggar. —*Bill Caskey, author of* Same Game, New Rules: 23 Timeless Principles for Selling and Negotiating *and founder of Caskey Achievement Strategies, a BzB sales training and consulting firm in Indianapolis*

How to Get Past the Gatekeeper

Voice mail is today's gatekeeper. The [most important] part of an effective voice mail is establishing your credibility by referencing a referral, your research or some newsworthy event in their company. The secret is to not talk about your product or service; focus on results. Talk like a businessperson, not a salesperson. —*Jill Konrath, founder of Selling to Big Companies, a St. Paul, Minnesota, sales training firm*

How to Write a Sales Letter

The secret to a successful sales letter is making it look just like a typical business letter. You want to position yourself as a peer who has a great idea and a helpful offer. In working with sales consultants at IBM, we coach them to start where the last conversation left off—something like, "After your comment to me on the phone last month, I've been thinking about a way to X." Your opening shot can't be a misfire. —*Dianna Booher, author*

of E-Writing: 21st Century Tools for Effective Communication *and CEO of Booher Consultants Inc., a Dallas/Fort Worth-area communication training firm*

How to Generate Repeat Business

Our customers aren't customers: our customers are owners. That sets a certain bar. If one of our owners is going to take a flight, a sales vice president may be helping with the luggage and the catering. We feel like if we get in from of our customers and we hustle, at the end of the day, it will be translated into repeat business. —*Kenny Dichter, founder of New York City-based Marquis Jet, an 80-employee global leader in private jet cards whose Marquis Jet Card Program has a 90 percent customer renewal rate*

How to Upset Your Current Clients

I asked a client if they were thinking about redoing their website. They said, "No." I didn't tell them, but I was going to work on something because I had a vision for it. I presented it to them, and they loved it. I had a $10,000 sale for that website. The biggest secret is just taking the time to think, "What does my client need that he's not asking for?" —*Paula Yakubik, founder of MassMedia, a 7-year-old Las Vegas PR and advertising firm with 18 employees and $3.5 million in annual sales*

How to Hire a Good Sales Manager

Successfully hiring a strong sales manager is a balance between science and art. All strong sales-manager candidates exhibit three behavioral traits: a high energy level, tenacity and competitiveness. The biggest mistake companies make is that they try to find someone who will change the process because sales are not at the desired level. The majority of the time, the process isn't broken; what they didn't find was someone who has sold in that process before. Finding a manager compatible with the process is crucial. —*Jim Kasper, author of* Creating the #1 Sales Force: What It Takes to Transform Your Sales Culture

How to Offer Great Customer Service

The big secret is to passionately believe in your people. It's easy to say and difficult to execute unless you're in a culture that supports and encourages great customer service. Everyone's going that extra mile. Behind every transaction is a personal relationship. —*Jack Mitchell, author of* Hug Your Customers: The Proven Way to Personalize Sales and Achieve Astounding Results *and CEO of Mitchells/Richards, a high-end Connecticut clothing retailer with $70 million in annual sales*

How to Close a Sale

At the end of a sales conversation, the customer knows everything [he or she] needs to know to make a decision. The key is to ask the customer to take action. Simply ask, "Why don't you give it a try?" Don't sit there hoping that somehow, sometime, somewhere, the customer will take action on his own. Like a dentist's job is to pull the tooth, the salesperson's job is to ask for the order at the end of the presentation. —*Brian Tracy, author of* The Psychology of Selling: Increase Your Sales Faster and Easier Than You Ever Thought Possible *and founder of Brian Tracy International, a Solana Beach, California, sales consulting firm*

How to Sell When Price Is the Determining Factor

If you're selling something on price, you'd better start learning how to declare Chapter 11, because you're on your way. Look at what's going on with the airlines and department stores. Everyone gets confused thinking it's all about price, but it's about relevance. Get away from price, and get to value. —*Sergio Zyman, founder, chairman and CEO of the Zyman Group, an Atlanta management consulting firm*

How to Meet a Prospect in Person

This is your big chance to make an impression. Don't have your cell phone and your pager on, and don't have anything in your notebook that doesn't have to do with that customer. Ask follow-up questions, clarify that you understand what they're saying, and give them feedback that you're listening. You don't want an hour to go by where [the prospect] didn't feel it was valuable spending time with you. —*Seleste Lunsford, co-author of* Strategies That Win Sales; Best Practices of the World's Leading Organizations

How to Give a Great Sales Presentation in Five Minutes or Less

Whether you have six minutes or 60 minutes to make a presentation, always organize your content, adapt to the moment, and dialogue with your audience. Reveal your core statement early and clearly, and support it with no more than three main points. If pressed for time, leave anecdotes and stories on the sidelines. —*Bob Lipp, president of Better Business Presentations, a Great Neck, New York, firm that helps executives improve their presentation and public speaking skills*

How to Surpass a Sales Quota

People sit back and relax when they've made their quota. But that's when you really pour it on. At 5 o'clock, make 15 more calls. When you have a lot of business coming in and you're doing well, that's the best time to make calls to surpass your quota. Your actions are much more powerful when you're doing well than when you're trying to get started. —*Barry Farber,* Entrepreneur's *"Sales Success" columnist and president of Farber Training Systems, a Livingston, New Jersey, sales management and motivational company*

How to Schedule Your Week Most Effectively

Every weeknight I would complete my Day-Timer with contacts I needed to make and proposals I needed to present the next day. I always had a complete plan written down. Map out your sales calls so you minimize drive time. Log all details about each appointment, tracking all steps of the sale until it's closed. This prevents redoing or forgetting scheduled items and will keep your day on task. —*Henry A. Penix, author of* Unwrap Your Gift *and a former salesperson who ranked in the upper 2 percent of all salespeople for The Pitney Bowes Corp.*

How to Create Customer Loyalty

The hardest thing is getting somebody to trust you. After you build a relationship, the trust comes. Going the extra mile, being a good communicator, letting them know if there are problems—that makes people feel good. Be consistent. Do what you say you're going to do. When I see a parent with one child bring a second child to me, that's when I know I've created customer loyalty. —*Kara Vample Turner, president and CEO of 7-year-old Primary Colors Daycare Center in Durham, North Carolina*

How to Relate Better to Your Prospect

Ninety-five percent of what's sold in the world isn't an end unto itself, it's a means to an end. Nobody wants to buy computers; what they want is the ability to transfer information more quickly and accurately so groups can work together better, so they can put products out to market faster, so they can capture more market share. What does the client want to achieve? When you ask that question, it changes everything. —*Bill Stinnett, author of* Think Like Your Customer *and president of Sales Excellence Inc., an Evergreen, Colorado, sales training and consulting firm*

How to Follow Up with a Prospect

I learned the importance of follow-up early on. I probably lost several projects because I was shy. [Now], we look for reasons to callback. If we get a sense of what they want, we'll sketch something, call them and try to get them back in. If you

don't care enough to [take the initative and] call, I can't imagine people wanting you to build their dream home. —*Lambert Arceneaux, owner of Allegro Builders, an 8-year-old Houston home builder with eight employees and projections of $12 million in sales for 2005*

How to Reduce the Sales Cycle

There is little magic to this, but a lot of work. Reps are loath to ask tough questions. [Does the prospect] have a committed budget? What's the process for releasing funds, and who has final authority to do so? What is the event driving this initiative? [If you] want to reduce the sales cycle, target prospects better, and qualify them rigorously. —*Barry Trailer, partner with CSO Insights, a Carte Madera, California, sales effectiveness research and benchmarking firm*

Got Advertising That Works?

How the "Got Milk?" campaign shook consumers out of their milk malaise.

JEFF MANNING AND KEVIN LANE KELLER

The 10-year-old "Got Milk?" campaign—considered one of the most popular ad campaigns of the 1990s—was borne of necessity. In February 1993, the California Milk Processor Board (CMPB) was reviewing reports on per capita U.S. consumption of milk over the last 15 years. To anyone involved in the production and sales of milk, the numbers painted a disturbing picture. Not only had there been a steady decline in milk consumption over the previous two decades, but the decline was now accelerating. The CMPB's ad budget paled in comparison to the big beverage marketers like Coca-Cola and Pepsi. With almost $2 billion in media spending annually in beverages as a category, CMPB had to make the most of its $23 million budget to have milk's message heard among the noise.

To revitalize sales of a product in seemingly perpetual decline, CMPB and its ad agency Goodby, Silverstein & Partners developed the "Got Milk?" campaign. The campaign was based on a milk deprivation strategy that reminded consumers how inconvenient it was to be without milk when eating certain foods such as cereal, brownies, or chocolate chip cookies. The "Got Milk?" campaign was launched in November 1993. Although focus groups indicated that consumers liked the ads, the actual launch exceeded all expectations. The campaign zoomed to a 60% aided-recall level in only three months, enjoyed 70% awareness within 6 months, and surpassed the long-running "It Does a Body Good" campaign in top-of-mind awareness in less than a year. The "Got Milk?" campaign quickly became a consumer favorite, prompting a *Los Angeles Times* reporter to comment, "Since the ad campaign began, it has reached a near-cult following."

Not only did the campaign get consumers talking, it also exceeded initial expectations of merely stemming the sales decline by increasing actual milk consumption. The number of consumers who reported consuming milk at least "several times a week" jumped from 72% at the start of the campaign to 78% a year later. California household consumption of milk increased every month in the first year after the launch except for the first two months that the campaign began. This performance was in sharp contrast to the rest of the country where consumption actually declined over the same period. In the year prior to the campaign's launch, California milk processors experienced a decline in sales volume of 1.67% or $18 million. A year after the launch, sales volume increased 1.07% or $13 million, for a total turnaround of $31 million. On a month-to-month comparison, sales volume had increased every month to rise 6.8% by the end of the first year.

"Got Milk?" is now deeply entrenched in the American vernacular. The campaign has virtually universal awareness, won just about every marketing and creative competition around, spawned more than 100 rip-offs, led to an unprecedented licensing program, been used in thousands of newspaper articles, justified a book, appeared on hundreds of celebrity moustache ads, and has been mentioned in popular TV shows. Not to mention the fact that it also helped stem the long-term decline in milk sales.

A number of key lessons emerged that help to shed light on arguably one of the most successful ad campaigns of the last decade and, more importantly, provide guidance to advertising and communication efforts for virtually any brand. On the tenth anniversary of the launch of the program, here are 10 of the most important lessons.

1. Target the right consumers. When sales slide, some firms mistakenly and frantically attempt to attract new users to turn things around. The first step in stopping a sales decline, however, is making sure no other customers leave the brand franchise, especially those most loyal customers who generate much of the brand volume and profit. These customers typically will be most receptive to brand communications and, in fact, may actually be the best short-term source of sales growth. Once brand sales are stabilized, additional sources of growth via new market segments can be targeted.

Accordingly, in order to generate quick results, CMPB decided to target "regular" users of milk who used the product several times a week or more. Regular users constituted 70% of the California market and already had favorable attitudes toward drinking milk and presumably could be influenced in the short term. In contrast, non-users or light users typically refrained from milk for actual or perceived health reasons, which probably could not be changed very quickly.

Consumers could relate to the plight of the poor protagonist and, more important, got the message—running out of milk was no fun.

2. Thoroughly study your target market to find fresh insights. Consumer immersion is critical, and creative research invariably is needed to uncover fresh insights that will yield a stronger brand positioning. Qualitative and quantitative research are increasingly being supplemented by more experiential research where consumers are studied in more naturalistic settings.

To more fully understand their consumers, "Got Milk?" research efforts went beyond traditional focus groups and surveys. Goodby, Silverstein & Partners employed a series of creative, more experiential research studies. For example, to learn how consumers responded to running out of milk, they placed small video cameras in the refrigerators in the agency and took out all the milk to see how employees would react when they found out. One of the most productive research studies involved having a group of consumers go without milk for a week and return to the agency to share their experiences. Consumers' tales of woe and despair made it clear that milk was an integral part of consumers lives, and their anecdotes and recollections even provided inspiration for later advertising creative.

3. Unearth a deeply competitive strategy and stay with it. The challenge in brand building these days is to find competitively unique, but also consumer-relevant, market positions. Because so many potential points of differences between brands have been competed away, it's often difficult to find any viable opportunities in the marketplace. Uncovering those opportunities requires leaving no stone unturned.

The key consumer insight that emerged from CMPB research was almost frighteningly simple and obvious: Sell milk with food. And yet, as CMPB reviewed milk advertising from around the country (and the world), it found that food was almost totally absent. Perhaps in an attempt to compete against soft drinks, the dairy industry had lost contact with its roots. Consumers hadn't, though. They said time and time again that certain foods drive their milk decision.

Nobody doubted that previous milk campaigns successfully achieved positive shifts in consumer attitudes toward milk. What was missing, however, was a corresponding change in consumer behavior. Consumers knew milk was good and thought they should drink more of it, but they never thought enough about milk to be motivated to change their consumption habits. The typical milk campaign, emphasizing calcium and other vitamins, caused consumers to tune out. A new campaign had to break the mold for milk advertising, grab attention, and shake consumers out of their "milk malaise."

Although so many people drank milk every day, milk suffered from a complete lack of consumer mind share. People just didn't think about milk often enough at home, and they almost never thought about milk outside of the home. In order

for any campaign to be successful, this lack of mind share had to change. One way to implement the change was to get consumers to stop taking milk for granted, to take them by surprise by creating a new and different image for milk.

Based on the consumer insight, the CMPB and Goodby, Silverstein & Partners decided to reach out to the regular users with a "deprivation strategy." The most effective way to capitalize on milk's relationship with food was to create an advertising campaign that paired the two together. Each ad in the campaign highlighted one of milk's perfect complements: cereal, chocolate chip cookies, peanut butter and jelly sandwiches, and so on. The clever creative twist, however, was to deprive the main character of milk. The end result was delicious food *without milk*—the deprivation strategy. Certain foods without milk represented "cruel and unusual punishment" to most people, and the advertising campaign would set out to drive this message home. In each of the ads, a meal or snack would be essentially ruined because of the absence of milk.

Milk deprivation essentially redefined beverage marketing so that milk won and Coke and Snapple lost. It also spoke directly to an incredibly wide range of consumers: Running out of milk is a pain in the butt regardless of one's age or income or lifestyle!

4. Entertain . . . but sell. The right positioning and message is necessary but not sufficient to create a successful ad campaign—there must also be the right creative. In other words, great advertising comes from knowing what to say, as well as how to say it.

The CMPB knew that other beverages had successfully built up strong brand images over the last decade and believed milk could do the same by taking a more lighthearted approach that talked directly to consumers. The dairy industry had taken itself too seriously. Eating is the most popular form of entertainment in California, the United States, and the world. Get people smiling at your advertising and they would look, listen, and consume more milk.

The television ads gradually built the tension that was so critical to the deprivation strategy. Each television ad began with a close-up of one of the food complements such as the peanut butter and jelly sandwich. Once the desire for the food was established, the protagonist took a big bite. While joyfully chewing the food, the protagonist casually reached for a glass of milk. Unfortunately, there was no more milk left in the container. A desperate search for even a single drop ensued, but all efforts were in vain. At the height of anguish, the voice-over pronounced, "Got Milk?"

The ads were funny, but relevant. Consumers could relate to the plight of the poor protagonist and, more important, got the message—running out of milk was no fun. The solution was obvious—be sure to always stock enough milk.

5. Treat the consumer with respect. Advertising doesn't have to aim for the lowest common denominator. In fact, the highest common denominator can be a breath of fresh air to consumers. By not considering what consumers would really like to see, advertisers fail to adopt the right consumer "voice" and thus use a completely wrong approach.

"Got Milk?" is an inherently humble idea. Rather than lecturing (a la Mom), it asks a simple, thought-provoking question: "Do you have enough milk?" It displays a genuine interest in the consumer's opinion that was unheard of in 1993. Think of how much difference one letter would have made—"Get Milk!" instead of "Got Milk?"

6. Adopt a memorable and inspiring brand slogan and signature. Too often, consumers fail to grasp the meaning of ad campaigns or, even worse, draw the wrong conclusions. In such cases, help the consumer out. Devise a few words or a short phrase as a brand slogan or ad tag line that captures the essence of the ad campaign and what it intends to say about the brand. Then use the brand slogan to the fullest extent possible.

For example, the brand slogan can be a vital part of the brand signature—the way the brand is identified at the conclusion of a TV or radio ad or displayed within a print ad. The brand signature must creatively engage the consumer and cause him or her to pay more attention to the brand itself and, as a consequence, increase the strength of brand associations created by the ad. An effective brand signature can dynamically and stylistically provide a seamless connection to the ad as a whole, improving recall and motivating purchase.

"Got Milk?" was a powerful call to action and distilled the brand positioning and message of the ad down to two simple words. Effectively, it functioned as a hook or handle to the intent and main message of the campaign. It was shorthand to consumers that boiled down the key take-away that CMPB wanted to have happen. Moreover, the synonymous brand name and slogan was often used in a manner fitting the ad (e.g., in flames for the "yuppie in hell" ad or in primary school print for the "school lunchroom bully" ad), further enhancing its ability to function as a hook to the brand message.

7. Integrate, integrate, integrate. The days when it was the case that "if you build a great ad, they will come" are long gone. Ad campaigns must incorporate multiple media, taking advantage of the unique characteristics of each and blending them together so that the whole is greater than the sum of the parts.

In order to maximize the impact on consumer behavior, the media strategy for "Got Milk?" focused on consumers in the place where they typically used milk (in the home) and where they typically bought milk (in the supermarket). According to CMPB, there were three ideal times to communicate the milk message: on the way to the store, in the store, and at home where milk could be immediately consumed. The media strategy complemented the overall communications strategy to reach this goal. The advertising creative strategy motivated consumers to crave the featured food and/or check their refrigerators for the availability of milk. The media strategy focused primarily on television as the medium, thereby catching consumers in their homes where 90% of total milk is consumed. Furthermore, the media buy for the ads typically concentrated on those times of day when consumers drank the most milk (i.e., mornings during breakfast, late evening snacks, and so on). It was thought that timing ads in this manner—given the "call to action" nature of the campaign—could potentially lead to more impulse usage of milk. Each usage occasion was further broken down into the type of user in order to purchase television advertising time.

Children were targeted in the early morning hours as well as late afternoons, while adults were targeted at prime time and late night snack times.

It was the magic of TV, outdoor billboards, publicity, cross promotions, and licensing that took "Got Milk?" from an ad to an icon.

To capitalize on the remaining communications expenditures within the store, the "Got Milk?" billboards were located near supermarkets as a reminder to consumers before they entered the store. Billboards and signs at bus shelters reinforced the television campaign and featured the same foods as the television ads with one bite taken out. Of course, each billboard prominently displayed the key question: "Got Milk?" The intention was to get consumers thinking about milk before they entered the store so they would buy milk once they were inside. Other promotions included milk coupons on many recognizable brands of complementary foods located throughout the supermarket, point of purchase displays, shelf talkers at the complementary food locations, and "Got Milk?" check-out dividers.

It could be strongly argued that "Got Milk?" would have failed if it had only been a TV campaign. It was the magic of TV, outdoor billboards, publicity, cross promotions, and licensing that took "Got Milk?" from an ad to an icon.

8. Don't try to make it alone. Increasingly, brands are being built with the assistance and help of other brands. Co-branding, ingredient branding, brand alliances, and joint promotions are all ways to partner with other brands in an attempt to find "win-win" solutions that lead to greater brand equity and better profitability than would have otherwise been possible.

Breaking with the past milk campaigns, CMPB decided to leverage milk's relationship with food by partnering with those foods instead of relying on pulling consumers over to the dairy case. The complementary television, radio, print, and billboard campaigns all leveraged this relationship and capitalized on the advertising budgets of several major brands of cereals and cookies. "Got Milk?" could not have gone far without its host of "co-dependent" brands: Nesquik, Oreos, Cheerios, Girl Scout cookies, even Cookie Monster and Snap! Crackle! & Pop! These alliances helped elevate "Got Milk?" to an unchallenged position in the minds of consumers, the media, and the retail trade.

9. Keep campaigns . . . but keep them fresh. One common mistake in advertising is that successful campaigns are dropped too soon because marketers and their agencies tire of the campaign sooner than consumers actually do. Unfortunately, more often that not, there is no "Plan B" and an updated, rejuvenated version of the old ad campaign would have had a much greater likelihood of success than an unknown or untested new ad campaign. When your board of directors starts to get bored with your campaign, run it another five years.

Sure we get tired of our own campaigns. We think about them and watch them and talk about them all the time. It would have been easy to drop "Got Milk?" after four or five years, when

The "Got Milk?" Advertising Campaign Has Also Met With Critical Acclaim.

In 1995, the ads won an Effie Award, as well as top honors from several other major advertising award committees. In September of that same year, "Got Milk?" joined the familiar "milk moustache" program as a national campaign, and the Goodby, Silverstein & Partners ads began receiving national exposure in television, print, and outdoor media.

Though the only commonly shared element of the two commercial series was the prominence of milk, consumers assumed that the two series originated from the same source. In fact, the dairy farmers group, Dairy Management Inc. (DMI), controlled the national "Got Milk?" campaign while the National Milk Processors Education Program (MilkPEP) funded the milk moustache campaign. DMI had approached the CMPB to purchase the licensing rights to "Got Milk?" to replace its own campaign. In California, the CMPB continued to govern the "Got Milk?" campaign, employing Goodby, Silverstein & Partners to develop the ads. Leo Burnett USA handled the national "Got Milk?" creative after Goodby, Silverstein & Partners licensed its work, while Bozell Worldwide did the milk moustache ad work. Perhaps in an effort to consolidate the equity achieved by the separate campaigns, MilkPEP obtained licensing rights to the slogan in 1998 and replaced the milk moustache ads tag line "Milk. What a Surprise" with Dairy Management's "Got Milk?" That same year, the two milk groups forged a partnership that combined their considerable advertising budgets, pooling DMI's $70 million TV and outdoor budget and MilkPEP's $110 million milk moustache budget.

"The Got Milk?" campaign continues to be strong and pay dividends. For 2002 and the first half of 2003, milk sales in California, where the ad campaign is centered, increased roughly 1.5%, whereas sales in the rest of the country remained flat.

10. Treat agencies as partners and keep the focus on great work. Adversarial relationships rarely work, and the most successful and longest running ad campaigns often come from establishing a high degree of trust between a core group of decision-makers for the client and agency. Less can be more, and getting the right people involved (no more or no less) is critical. Therefore, streamline, prune, and then cut some more people out of the marketing department. There is a basic, nearly immutable rule: Advertising gets more fractured, self-serving, and plain old dumb with each person that passes judgment on it.

"Got Milk?" creative has been approved (or disapproved) by the same person since day one. At the same time, advertising is often the single largest discretionary expense on the spreadsheet. Yet the CEO is often completely removed from strategic development and the work that goes on the air. The CMPB CEO viewed every single focus group (more than 150).

It's also important to build pliant, trusting, enduring relationships with agency principals. In 1993, the CMPB's stated goal was to become Goodby, Silverstein & Partners best client. Despite his agency having more than quadrupled in size, Jeff Goodby, the agency founder and creative talent, still works on "Got Milk?" Importantly, he doesn't just glance at finished TV spots. Rather, he actually pencils and doodles layouts.

A *New Yorker* cartoon from the early '70s still rings true. It depicts two white-haired, executive types fishing from a rowboat. One says; "We haven't caught a fish all day." The other replies; "Right, let's fire the agency." Client management must take full responsibility for the results of the advertising it approves. Changing CMOs and firing agencies doesn't get rid of mediocre advertising. It only amplifies it.

The principles applied in developing and running the landmark "Got Milk?" ad campaign are relevant to virtually any brand. Ensuring that brand advertising adheres to these principles can be an important means of enhancing the productivity and longevity of any ad campaign.

Jeff Manning is executive director of the California Milk Processor Board. He may be reached at manning@gotmilk.com. **Kevin Lane Keller** is E.B. Osborn professor of marketing, Amos Tuck School of Business, Dartmouth College. He may be reached at kevin.keller@dartmouth.edu.

Authors' Note—The authors would like to thank Keith Richey for his research assistance. It is gratefully appreciated.

the first "God, can't we do something new?" remark surfaced. Thankfully, that didn't happen and the tag line is conservatively valued at more than $1 billion and an irreplaceable asset to the milk industry.

UNIT 4
Global Marketing

Unit Selections

Key Points to Consider

- What economic, cultural, and political obstacles must an organization consider that seeks to market globally?

- Do you believe that an adherence to the "marketing concept" is the right way to approach international markets? Why, or why not?

- What trends are taking place today that would suggest whether particular global markets would grow or decline? Which countries do you believe will see the most growth in the next decade? Why?

- In what ways can the Internet be used to extend a market outside the United States?

Student Web Site
www.mhcls.com/online

Internet References
Further information regarding these Web sites may be found in this book's preface or online.

International Trade Administration
   http://www.ita.doc.gov
World Chambers Network
   http://www.worldchambers.net
World Trade Center Association On Line
   http://iserve.wtca.org

It is certain that marketing with a global perspective will continue to be a strategic element of U.S. business well into the next decade. The United States is both the world's largest exporter and largest importer. In 1987, U.S. exports totaled just over $250 billion—about 10 percent of total world exports. During the same period, U.S. imports were nearly $450 billion—just under 10 percent of total world imports. By 1995 exports had risen to $513 billion and imports to $664 billion—roughly the same percentage of total world trade.

Whether or not they wish to be, all marketers are now part of the international marketing system. For some, the end of the era of domestic markets may have come too soon, but that era is over. Today it is necessary to recognize the strengths and weaknesses of our own marketing practices as compared to those abroad. The multinational corporations have long recognized this need, but now all marketers must acknowledge it.

International marketing differs from domestic marketing in that the parties to its transactions live in different political units. It is the "international" element of international marketing that distinguishes it from domestic marketing—not differences in managerial techniques. The growth of global business among multinational corporations has raised new questions about the role of their headquarters. It has even caused some to speculate whether marketing operations should be performed abroad rather than in the United States.

The key to applying the marketing concept is understanding the consumer. Increasing levels of consumer sophistication is evident in all of the world's most profitable markets. Managers are required to adopt new points of view in order to accommodate increasingly complex consumer wants and needs. The markets in the new millennium will show further integration on a worldwide scale. In these emerging markets, conventional textbook approaches can cause numerous problems. The new marketing perspective called for by future circumstances will require a long-range view that considers basics of exchange and their applications in new settings.

Digital Vision/Getty Images

The selections presented here were chosen to provide an overview of world economic factors, competitive positioning, and increasing globalization of markets—issues to which each and every marketer must become sensitive. "Managing Differences: The Central Challenge of Global Strategy" presents a new framework—called the AAA Triangle—that encompasses all three of the major challenges of globalization. "Segmenting Global Markets: Look Before You Leap" reveals the significance of having an understanding of both local and global issues. "How China Will Change Your Business" describes the ever-increasing presence and influence China has in our lives. "Three Dimensional" shows how the markets of Japan, Korea, and China are far from homogeneous. The fifth article reveals the significant impact that technology will have globally. "The Great Wal-Mart of China" reveals Wal-Mart's strategy for making its presence known in the Chinese market. The last article reflects the importance of marketing to the world's 4 billion poor people.

Managing Differences

The Central Challenge of Global Strategy

With the globalization of production as well as markets, you need to evaluate your international strategy. Here's a framework to help you think through your options.

PANKAJ GHEMAWAT

When it comes to global strategy, most business leaders and academics make two assumptions: first, that the central challenge is to strike the right balance between economies of scale and responsiveness to local conditions, and second, that the more emphasis companies place on scale economies in their worldwide operations, the more global their strategies will be.

These assumptions are problematic. The main goal of any global strategy must be to manage the large differences that arise at borders, whether those borders are defined geographically or otherwise. (Strategies of standardization and those of local responsiveness are both conceivably valid responses to that challenge—both, in other words, are global strategies.) Moreover, assuming that the principal tension in global strategy is between scale economies and local responsiveness encourages companies to ignore another functional response to the challenge of cross-border integration: arbitrage. Some companies are finding large opportunities for value creation in exploiting, rather than simply adjusting to or overcoming, the differences they encounter at the borders of their various markets. As a result, we increasingly see value chains spanning multiple countries. IBM's CEO, Sam Palmisano, noted in a recent *Foreign Affairs* article that an estimated 60,000 manufacturing plants were built by foreign firms in China alone between 2000 and 2003. And trade in IT-enabled services—with India accounting for more than half of IT and business-process offshoring in 2005—is finally starting to have a measurable effect on international trade in services overall.

In this article, I present a new framework for approaching global integration that gets around the problems outlined above. I call it the AAA Triangle. The three A's stand for the three distinct types of global strategy. *Adaptation* seeks to boost revenues and market share by maximizing a firm's local relevance. One extreme example is simply creating local units in each national market that do a pretty good job of carrying out all the steps in the supply chain; many companies use this strategy as they start expanding beyond their home markets. *Aggregation* attempts to deliver economies of scale by creating regional or sometimes global operations; it involves standardizing the product or service offering and grouping together the development and production processes. *Arbitrage* is the exploitation of differences between national or regional markets, often by locating separate parts of the supply chain in different places—for instance, call centers in India, factories in China, and retail shops in Western Europe.

Because most border-crossing enterprises will draw from all three A's to some extent, the framework can be used to develop a summary scorecard indicating how well the company is globalizing. However, because of the significant tensions within and among the approaches, it's not enough to tick off the boxes corresponding to all three. Strategic choice requires some degree of prioritization—and the framework can help with that as well.

Understanding the AAA Triangle

Underlying the AAA Triangle is the premise that companies growing their businesses outside the home market must choose one or more of three basic strategic options: adaptation, aggregation, and arbitrage. These types of strategy differ in a number of important ways, as summarized in the exhibit "What Are Your Globalization Options?"

The three A's are associated with different organizational types. If a company is emphasizing adaptation, it probably has a country-centered organization. If aggregation is the primary objective, cross-border groupings of various

What Are Your Globalization Options?

When managers first hear about the broad strategies (adaptation, aggregation, and arbitrage) that make up the AAA Triangle framework for globalization, their most common response by far is "Let's do all three." But it's not that simple. A close look at the three strategies reveals the differences—and tensions—among them. Business leaders must figure out which elements will meet their companies' needs and prioritize accordingly.

	ADAPTATION	AGGREGATION	ARBITRAGE
Competitive Advantage Why should we globalize at all?	To achieve local relevance through national focus while exploiting some economies of scale	To achieve scale and scope economies through international standardization	To achieve absolute economies through international specialization
Configuration Where should we locate operations overseas?	Mainly in foreign countries that are similar to the home base, to limit the effects of cultural, administrative, geographic, and economic distance		In a more diverse set of countries, to exploit some elements of distance
Coordination How should we connect international operations?	By country, with emphasis on achieving local presence within borders	By business, region, or customer, with emphasis on horizontal relationships for cross-border economies of scale	By function, with emphasis on vertical relationships, even across organizational boundaries
Controls What types of extremes should we watch for?	Excessive variety or complexity	Excessive standardization, with emphasis on scale	Narrowing spreads
Change Blockers Whom should we watch out for internally?	Entrenched country chiefs	All-powerful unit, regional, or account heads	Heads of key functions
Corporate Diplomacy How should we approach corporate diplomacy?	Address issues of concern, but proceed with discretion, given the emphasis on cultivating local presence	Avoid the appearance of homogenization or hegemonism (especially for U.S. companies); be sensitive to any backlash	Address the exploitation or displacement of suppliers, channels, or intermediaries, which are potentially most prone to political disruption
Corporate Strategy What strategic levers do we have?	Scope selection Variation Decentralization Partitioning Modularization Flexibility Partnership Recombination Innovation	Regions and other country groupings Product or business Function Platform Competence Client industry	Cultural (country-of-origin effects) Administrative (taxes, regulations, security) Geographic (distance, climate differences) Economic (differences in prices, resources, knowledge)

sorts—global business units or product divisions, regional structures, global accounts, and so on—make sense. An emphasis on arbitrage is often best pursued by a vertical, or functional, organization that pays explicit attention to the balancing of supply and demand within and across organizational boundaries. Clearly, not all three modes of organizing can take precedence in one organization at the same time. And although some approaches to corporate organization (such as the matrix) can combine elements of more than one pure mode, they carry costs in terms of managerial complexity.

Most companies will emphasize different A's at different points in their evolution as global enterprises, and some will run through all three. IBM is a case in point. (This characterization of IBM and those of the firms that follow are informed by interviews with the CEOs and other executives.) For most of its history, IBM pursued an adaptation strategy, serving overseas markets by setting up a mini-IBM in each target country. Every one of these companies performed a largely complete set of activities (apart from R&D and resource allocation) and adapted to local differences as necessary. In the 1980s and 1990s, dissatisfaction with the extent to which country-by-country adaptation curtailed opportunities to gain international scale economies led to the overlay of a regional structure on the mini-IBMs. IBM aggregated the countries into regions in order to improve coordination and thus generate more scale economies at the regional and global levels. More recently, however, IBM has also begun to exploit differences across countries. The most visible signs of this new emphasis on arbitrage (not a term the company's leadership uses) are IBM's efforts to exploit wage differentials by increasing the number of employees in India from 9,000 in 2004 to 43,000 by mid-2006 and by planning for massive additional growth. Most of these employees are in IBM Global Services, the part of the company that is growing fastest but has the lowest margins—which they are supposed to help improve, presumably by reducing costs rather than raising prices.

Procter & Gamble started out like IBM, with mini-P&Gs that tried to fit into local markets, but it has evolved differently. The company's global business units now sell through market development organizations that are aggregated up to the regional level. CEO A.G. Lafley explains that while P&G remains willing to adapt to important markets, it ultimately aims to beat competitors—country-centered multinationals as well as local companies—through aggregation. He also makes it clear that arbitrage is important to P&G (mostly through outsourcing) but takes a backseat to both adaptation and aggregation: "If it touches the customer, we don't outsource it." One obvious reason is that the scope for labor arbitrage in the fast-moving consumer goods industry may be increasing but is still much less substantial overall than in, say, IT services. As these examples show, industries vary in terms of the headroom they offer for each of the three A strategies.

Even within the same industry, firms can differ sharply in their global strategic profiles. For a paired example that takes us beyond behemoths from advanced countries, consider two of the leading IT services companies that develop software in India: Tata Consultancy Services, or TCS, and Cognizant Technology Solutions. TCS, the largest such firm, started exporting software services from India more than 30 years ago and has long stressed arbitrage. Over the past four years, though, I have closely watched and even been involved in its development of a network delivery model to aggregate within and across regions. Cognizant, the fourth largest, also started out with arbitrage and still considers that to be its main strategy but has begun to invest more heavily in adaptation to achieve local presence in the U.S. market in particular. (Although the company is headquartered in the United States, most of its software development centers and employees are in India.)

The AAA Triangle allows managers to see which of the three strategies—or which combination—is likely to afford the most leverage for their companies or in their industries overall. Expense items from businesses' income statements provide rough-and-ready proxies for the importance of each of the three A's. Companies that do a lot of advertising will need to adapt to the local market. Those that do a lot of R&D may want to aggregate to improve economies of scale, since many R&D outlays are fixed costs. For firms whose operations are labor intensive, arbitrage will be of particular concern because labor costs vary greatly from country to country. By calculating these three types of expenses as percentages of sales, a company can get a picture of how intensely it is pursuing each course. Those that score in the top decile of companies along any of the three dimensions—advertising intensity, R&D intensity, or labor intensity—should be on alert. (See the "The AAA Triangle" for more detail on the framework.)

How do the companies I've already mentioned look when their expenditures are mapped on the AAA Triangle? At

The AAA Triangle

The AAA Triangle serves as a kind of strategy map for managers. The percentage of sales spent on advertising indicates how important adaptation is likely to be for the company; the percentage spent on R&D is a proxy for the importance of aggregation; and the percentage spent on labor helps gauge the importance of arbitrage. Managers should pay attention to any scores above the median because, most likely, those are areas that merit strategic focus. Scores above the 90th percentile may be perilous to ignore.

Note: Median and top-decile scores are based on U.S. manufacturing data from Compustar's Global Vantage database and the U.S. Census Bureau. Since the ratios of advertising and R&D to sales rarely exceed 10%, those are given a maximum value of 10% in the chart.

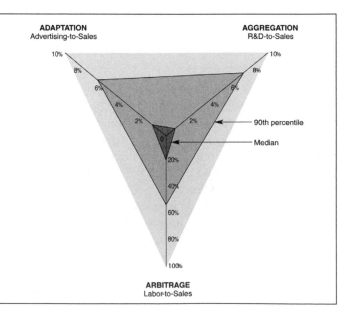

Procter & Gamble, businesses tend to cluster in the top quartile for advertising intensity, indicating the appropriateness of an adaptation strategy. TCS, Cognizant, and IBM Global Services are distinguished by their labor intensity, indicating arbitrage potential. But IBM Systems ranks significantly higher in R&D intensity than in labor intensity and, by implication, has greater potential for aggregation than for arbitrage.

From A to AA

Although many companies will (and should) follow a strategy that involves the focused pursuit of just one of the three A's, some leading-edge companies—IBM, P&G, TCS, and Cognizant among them—are attempting to perform two A's particularly well. Success in "AA strategies" takes two forms. In some cases, a company wins because it actually beats competitors along both dimensions at once. More commonly, however, a company wins because it manages the tensions between two A's better than its competitors do.

The pursuit of AA strategies requires considerable organizational and material innovation. Companies must do more than just allocate resources and monitor national operations from headquarters. They need to deploy a broad array of integrative devices, ranging from the hard (for instance, structures and systems) to the soft (for instance, style and socialization). Let's look at some examples.

Adaptation and aggregation. As I noted above, Procter & Gamble started out with an adaptation strategy. Halting attempts at aggregation across Europe, in particular, led to a drawn-out, function-by-function installation of a matrix structure throughout the 1980s, but the matrix proved unwieldy. So in 1999, the new CEO, Durk Jager, announced the reorganization mentioned earlier, whereby global business units (GBUs) retained ultimate profit responsibility but were complemented by geographic market development organizations (MDOs) that actually ran the sales force (shared across GBUs) and went to market.

The result? All hell broke loose in multiple areas, including at the key GBU/MDO interfaces. Jager departed after less than a year. Under his successor, Lafley, P&G has enjoyed much more success, with an approach that strikes more of a balance between adaptation and aggregation and allows room for differences across general business units and markets. Thus, its pharmaceuticals division, with distinct distribution channels, has been left out of the MDO structure; in emerging markets, where market development challenges loom large, profit responsibility continues to be vested with country managers. Also important are the company's decision grids, which are devised after months of negotiation. These define protocols for how different decisions are to be made, and by whom—the general business units or the market development organizations—while still generally reserving responsibility for profits (and the right to make decisions not covered by the grids) for the GBUs. Common IT systems help with integration as well. This structure is animated by an elaborate cycle of reviews at multiple levels.

Such structures and systems are supplemented with other, softer tools, which promote mutual understanding and collaboration. Thus, the GBUs' regional headquarters are often collocated with the headquarters of regional MDOs. Promotion to the director level or beyond generally requires experience on both the GBU and the MDO sides of the house. The implied crisscrossing of career paths reinforces the message that people within the two realms are equal citizens. As another safeguard against the MDOs' feeling marginalized by a lack of profit responsibility, P&G created a structure—initially anchored by the vice chairman of global operations, Robert McDonald—to focus on their perspectives and concerns.

Aggregation and arbitrage. In contrast to Procter & Gamble, TCS is targeting a balance between aggregation and arbitrage. To obtain the benefits of aggregation without losing its traditional arbitrage-based competitive advantage, it has placed great emphasis on its global network delivery model, which aims to build a coherent delivery structure that consists of three kinds of software development centers:

- The global centers serve large customers and have breadth and depth of skill, very high scales, and mature coding and quality control processes. These centers are located in India, but some are under development in China, where TCS was the first Indian software firm to set up shop.
- The regional centers (such as those in Uruguay, Brazil, and Hungary) have medium scales, select capabilities, and an emphasis on addressing language and cultural challenges. These centers offer some arbitrage economies, although not yet as sizable as those created by the global centers in India.
- The nearshore centers (such as those in Boston and Phoenix) have small scales and focus on building customer comfort through proximity.

In addition to helping improve TCS's economics in a number of ways, a coherent global delivery structure also seems to hold potential for significant international revenue gains. For example, in September 2005, TCS announced the signing of a five-year, multinational contract with the Dutch bank ABN AMRO that's expected to generate more than €200 million. IBM won a much bigger deal from ABN AMRO, but TCS's deal did represent the largest such contract ever for an Indian software firm and is regarded by the company's management as a breakthrough in its attempts to compete with IBM Global Services and Accenture. According to CEO S. Ramadorai, TCS managed to beat out its Indian competitors, including one that was already established at ABN AMRO, largely because it was the only Indian vendor positioned to deploy several hundred professionals to meet the application development and maintenance needs of ABN AMRO's Brazilian operations.

Arbitrage and adaptation. Cognizant has taken another approach and emphasized arbitrage and adaptation by investing heavily in a local presence in its key market, the United States, to the point where it can pass itself off as either Indian or U.S.-based, depending on the occasion.

Cognizant began life in 1994 as a captive of Dun & Bradstreet, with a more balanced distribution of power than purely Indian firms have. When Cognizant spun off from D&B a couple of years later, founder Kumar Mahadeva dealt with customers in the United States, while Lakshmi Narayanan (then COO, now vice chairman) oversaw delivery out of India. The company soon set up a two-in-a-box structure, in which there were always two global leads for each project—one in India and one in the United States— who were held jointly accountable and were compensated in the same way. Francisco D'Souza, Cognizant's CEO, recalls that it took two years to implement this structure and even longer to change mind-sets—at a time when there were fewer than 600 employees (compared with more than 24,000 now). As the exhibit "Cognizant's AA Strategy" shows, two-in-a-box is just one element, albeit an important one, of a broad, cross-functional effort to get past what management sees as the key integration challenge in global offshoring: poor coordination between delivery and marketing that leads to "tossing stuff over the wall."

Even within the same industry, firms can differ sharply in their global strategic profiles.

Not all of the innovations that enable AA strategies are structural. At the heart of IBM's recent arbitrage initiatives (which have been added to the company's aggregation strategy) is a sophisticated matching algorithm that can dynamically optimize people's assignments across all of IBM's locations—a critical capability because of the speed with which "hot" and "cold" skills can change. Krisha Nathan, the director of IBM's Zurich Research Lab, describes some of the reasons why such a people delivery model involves much more rocket science than, for example, a parts delivery model. First, a person's services usually can't be stored. Second, a person's functionality can't be summarized in the same standardized way as a part's, with a serial number and a description of technical characteristics. Third, in allocating people to teams, attention must be paid to personality and chemistry, which can make the team either more or less than the sum of its parts; not so with machines. Fourth, for that reason and others (employee development, for instance), assignment durations and sequencing are additionally constrained. Nathan describes the resultant assignment patterns as "75% global and 25% local." While this may be more aspirational than actual, it is clear that to the extent such matching devices are being used more effectively for arbitrage, they represent a massive power shift in a company that has hitherto eschewed arbitrage.

The Elusive Trifecta

There are serious constraints on the ability of any one organization to use all three A's simultaneously with great effectiveness. First, the complexity of doing so collides with limited managerial bandwidth. Second, many people think an organization should have only one culture, and that can get in the way of hitting multiple strategic targets. Third, capable competitors can force a company to choose which dimension it is going to try to beat them on. Finally, external relationships may have a focusing effect as well. For instance, several private-label manufacturers whose businesses were built around arbitrage have run into trouble because of their efforts to aggregate as well as arbitrage by building up their own brands in their customers' markets.

Cognizant's AA Strategy

Cognizant is experimenting with changes in staffing, delivery, and marketing in its pursuit of a strategy that emphasizes both adaptation and arbitrage.

STAFFING
- Relatively stringent recruiting process
- More MBAs and consultants
- More non-Indians
- Training programs in India for acculturation

DELIVERY
- Two global leads—one in the U.S., one in India—for each project
- All proposals done jointly (between India and the U.S.)
- More proximity to customers
- On-site kickoff teams
- Intensive travel, use of technology

MARKETING
- Joint Indian–U.S. positioning
- Use of U.S. nationals in key marketing positions
- Very senior relationship managers
- Focus on selling to a small number of large customers

To even contemplate a AAA strategy, a company must be operating in an environment in which the tensions among adaptation, aggregation, and arbitrage are weak or can be overridden by large scale economies or structural advantages, or in which competitors are otherwise constrained.

Consider GE Healthcare (GEH). The diagnostic-imaging industry has been growing rapidly and has concentrated globally in the hands of three large firms, which together command an estimated 75% of revenues in the business worldwide: GEH, with 30%; Siemens Medical Solutions (SMS), with 25%; and Philips Medical Systems (PMS), with 20%.[1] This high degree of concentration is probably related to the fact that the industry ranks in the 90th percentile in terms of R&D intensity. R&D expenditures are greater than 10% of sales for the "big three" competitors and even higher for smaller rivals, many of whom face profit squeezes. All of this suggests that the aggregation-related challenge of building global scale has proven particularly important in the industry in recent years.

GEH, the largest of the three firms, has also consistently been the most profitable. This reflects its success at aggregation, as indicated by the following:

Economies of scale. GEH has higher total R&D spending than SMS or PMS, greater total sales, and a larger service force (constituting half of GEH's total employee head count)—but its R&D-to-sales ratio is lower, its other expense ratios are comparable, and it has fewer major production sites.

Acquisition capabilities. Through experience, GEH has become more efficient at acquiring. It made nearly 100 acquisitions under Jeffrey Immelt (before he became GE's CEO); since then, it has continued to do a lot of acquiring, including the $9.5 billion Amersham deal in 2004, which moved the company beyond metal boxes and into medicine.

Economies of scope. The company strives, through Amersham, to integrate its biochemistry skills with its traditional base of physics and engineering skills; it finances equipment purchases through GE Capital.

GEH has even more clearly outpaced its competitors through arbitrage. Under Immelt, but especially more recently, it has moved to become a global product company by migrating rapidly to low-cost production bases. Moves have been facilitated by a "pitcher-catcher" concept originally developed elsewhere in GE: A "pitching team" at the existing site works closely with a "catching team" at the new site until the latter's performance is at least as strong as the former's. By 2005, GEH was reportedly more than halfway to its goals of purchasing 50% of its materials directly from low-cost countries and locating 60% of its manufacturing in such countries.

In terms of adaptation, GEH has invested heavily in country-focused marketing organizations, coupling such investments relatively loosely with the integrated development- and manufacturing back end, with objectives that one executive characterizes as being "more German than the Germans." It also boosts customer appeal with its emphasis

on providing services as well as equipment—for example, by training radiologists and providing consulting advice on post-image processing. Such customer intimacy obviously has to be tailored by country. And recently, GEH has cautiously engaged in some "in China, for China" manufacture of stripped-down, cheaper equipment aimed at increasing penetration there.

GEH has managed to use the three A's to the extent that it has partly by separating the three and, paradoxically, by downplaying the pursuit of one of them: adaptation. This is one example of how companies can get around the problem of limited managerial bandwidth. Others range from outsourcing to the use of more market or marketlike mechanisms, such as internal markets. GEH's success has also depended on competitors' weaknesses. In addition to facing a variety of size-related and other structural disadvantages relative to GEH, SMS and particularly PMS have been slow in some respects—for instance, in shifting production to low-cost countries. For all these reasons, the temptation to treat the GEH example as an open invitation for everyone to pursue all three A's should be stubbornly resisted.

Besides, the jury is still out on GEH. Adapting to the exceptional requirements of potentially large but low-income markets such as China and India while trying to integrate globally is likely to be an ongoing tension for the company. What's more, GEH isn't clearly ahead on all performance dimensions: SMS has focused more on core imaging, where it is seen as the technological leader.

Developing a AAA Strategy

Let's now consider how a company might use the AAA Triangle to put together a globally competitive strategy. The example I'll use here will be PMS, the smallest of the big three diagnostic-imaging firms.

At a corporate level, Philips had long followed a highly decentralized strategy that concentrated significant power in the hands of country managers and emphasized adaptation. Under pressure from more aggregation-oriented Japanese competitors in areas such as consumer electronics, efforts began in the 1970s to transfer more power to and aggregate more around global product divisions. These were blocked by country chiefs until 1996, when the new CEO abolished the geographic leg of the geography-product matrix. It is sometimes suggested that Philips's traditional focus on adaptation has persisted and remains a source of competitive advantage. While that's true about the parent company, it isn't the case for PMS. Any adaptation advantage for PMS is limited by SMS's technological edge and GEH's service-quality edge. These can be seen as global attributes of the two competitors' offerings, but they also create customer lock-in at the local level.

More generally, any adaptation advantage at PMS is more than offset by its aggregation disadvantages. PMS's absolute

R&D expenditures are one-third lower than those of GEH and one-quarter lower than those of SMS, and PMS is a much larger part of a much smaller corporation than its rivals are. (Philips's total acquisition war chest at the corporate level was recently reported to be not much larger than the amount that GEH put down for the Amersham acquisition alone.) In addition, PMS was stitched together out of six separate companies in a series of acquisitions made over three years to improve the original and aging X-ray technology. It is somewhat surprising that this attempt has worked as well as it has in a corporation without much acquisition experience to fall back on—but there have also clearly been negative aftereffects. Most dramatically, PMS paid more than €700 million in 2004 related to past acquisition attempts—one consummated, another considered—nearly wiping out its reported earnings for that year, although profitability did recover nicely in 2005.

PMS's preoccupation (until recently) with connecting its disparate parts is also somewhat to blame for the company's lack of progress on the arbitrage front. PMS has trailed not only its rivals but also other Philips divisions in moving manufacturing to low-cost areas, particularly China. Although

Philips claims to be the largest Western multinational in China, PMS did not start a manufacturing joint venture there until September 2004, with the first output for the Chinese market becoming available in 2005 and the first supplies for export in 2006. Overall, PMS's sourcing levels from low-cost countries in 2005 were comparable to levels GEH achieved back in 2001, and they lagged SMS's as well.

Insights on positioning relative to the three A's can be pulled together into a single map, as shown in "AAA Competitive Map for Diagnostic Imaging." Assessments along these lines, while always approximate, call attention to where competitors are actually located in strategy space; they also help companies visualize trade-offs across different A's. Both factors are important in thinking through where and where not to focus the organization's efforts.

How might this representation be used to articulate an action agenda for PMS? The two most obvious strategy alternatives for PMS are AA strategies: adaptation-aggregation and adaptation-arbitrage.

Adaptation-aggregation comes closest to the strategy currently in place. However, it is unlikely to solve the aggregation-related challenges facing PMS, so it had better offer some meaningful extras in terms of local responsiveness. PMS could also give up on the idea of creating a competitive advantage and simply be content with achieving average industry profitability, which is high: The big three diagnostic-imaging companies (which also account for another profitable global triopoly, in light bulbs) are described as "gentlemanly" in setting prices. Either way, imitation of bigger rivals' large-scale moves into entirely new areas seems likely to magnify, rather than minimize, this source of disadvantage. PMS does appear to be exercising some discipline in this regard, preferring to engage in joint ventures and other relatively small-scale moves rather than any Amersham-sized acquisitions.

The adaptation-arbitrage alternative would aim not just at producing in low-cost locations but also at radically reengineering and simplifying the product to slash costs for large emerging markets in China, India, and so forth. However, this option does not fit with Philips's heritage, which is not one of competing through low costs. And PMS has less room to follow a strategy of this sort because of GEH's "in China, for China" product, which is supposed to cut costs by 50%. PMS, in contrast, is talking of cost reductions of 20% for its first line of Chinese offerings.

If PMS found neither of these alternatives appealing—and frankly, neither seems likely to lead to a competitive advantage for the company—it could try to change the game entirely. Although PMS seems stuck with structural disadvantages in core diagnostic imaging compared with GEH and SMS, it could look for related fields in which its adaptation profile might have more advantages and fewer disadvantages. In terms of the AAA Triangle, this would be best thought of as a lateral shift to a new area of business, where the organization would have more of a

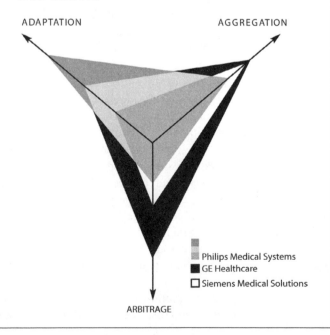

AAA Competitive Map for Diagnostic Imaging

Philips Medical Systems, the smallest of the big three diagnostic-imaging firms, historically emphasized adaptation but has recently placed some focus on aggregation. Siemens Medical Solutions emphasizes aggregation and uses some arbitrage. The most successful of the three, GE Healthcare, beats each of its rivals on two out of the three A's.

ADAPTATION

AGGREGATION

Philips Medical Systems
GE Healthcare
Siemens Medical Solutions

ARBITRAGE

competitive advantage. PMS does seem to be attempting something along these lines—albeit slowly—with its recent emphasis on medical devices for people to use at home. As former Philips CFO Jan Hommen puts it, the company has an advantage here over both Siemens and GE: "With our consumer electronics and domestic appliances businesses, we have gained a lot of experience and knowledge." The flip side, though, is that PMS starts competing with large companies such as Johnson & Johnson. PMS's first product of this sort—launched in the United States and retailing for around $1,500—is a home-use defibrillator. Note also that the resources emphasized in this strategy—that is, brand and distribution—operate at the local (national) level. So the new strategy can be seen as focusing on adaptation in a new market.

Not all the integration that is required to add value across borders needs to occur within a single organization.

What do these strategic considerations imply for integration at PMS? The company needs to continue streamlining operations and speed up attempts at arbitrage, possibly considering tools such as the pitcher-catcher concept. It needs to think about geographic variation, probably at the regional level, given the variation in industry attractiveness as well as PMS's average market share across regions. Finally, it needs to enable its at-home devices business to tap Philips's consumer electronics division for resources and capabilities. This last item is especially important because, in light of its track record thus far, PMS will have to make some early wins if it is to generate any excitement around a relaunch.

Broader Lessons

The danger in discussions about integration is that they can float off into the realm of the ethereal. That's why I went into specifics about the integration challenges facing PMS—and it's why it seems like a good idea to wrap this article up by recapitulating the general points outlined.

Focus on one or two of the A's. While it is possible to make progress on all three A's—especially for a firm that is coming from behind—companies (or, often more to the point, businesses or divisions) usually have to focus on one or at most two A's in trying to build competitive advantage. Can your organization agree on what they are? It may have to shift its focus across the A's as the company's needs change. IBM is just one example of a general shift toward arbitrage. But the examples of IBM, P&G, and, in particular, PMS illustrate how long such shifts can take—and the importance, therefore, of looking ahead when deciding what to focus on.

Make sure the new elements of a strategy are a good fit organizationally. While this isn't a fixed rule, if your strategy does embody nontrivially new elements, you should pay particular attention to how well they work with other things the organization is doing. IBM has grown its staff in India much faster than other international competitors (such as Accenture) that have begun to emphasize India-based arbitrage. But quickly molding this workforce into an efficient organization with high delivery standards and a sense of connection to the parent company is a critical challenge: Failure in this regard might even be fatal to the arbitrage initiative.

Employ multiple integration mechanisms. Pursuit of more than one of the A's requires creativity and breadth in thinking about integration mechanisms. Given the stakes, these factors can't be left to chance. In addition to IBM's algorithm for matching people to opportunities, the company has demonstrated creativity in devising "deal hubs" to aggregate across its hardware, software, and services businesses. It has also reconsidered its previous assumption that global functional headquarters should be centralized (recently, IBM relocated its procurement office from Somers, New York, to Shenzhen, China). Of course, such creativity must be reinforced by organizational structures, systems, incentives, and norms conducive to integration, as at P&G. Also essential to making such integration work is an adequate supply of leaders and succession candidates of the right stripe.

Think about externalizing integration. Not all the integration that is required to add value across borders needs to occur within a single organization. IBM and other firms illustrate that some externalization is a key part of most ambitious global strategies. It takes a diversity of forms: joint ventures in advanced semiconductor research, development, and manufacturing; links to and support of Linux and other efforts at open innovation; (some) outsourcing of hardware to contract manufacturers and services to business partners; IBM's relationship with Lenovo in personal computers; customer relationships governed by memoranda of understanding rather than detailed contracts. Reflecting this increased range of possibilities, reported levels of international joint ventures are running only one-quarter as high as they were in the mid-1990s, even though more companies are externalizing operations. Externalization offers advantages not just for outsourcing noncore services but also for obtaining ideas from the outside for core areas: for instance, Procter & Gamble's connect-and-develop program, IBM's innovation jams, and TCS's investments in involving customers in quality measurement and improvement.

Know when not to integrate. Some integration is always a good idea, but that is not to say that more integration is always better. First of all, very tightly coupled systems are not particularly flexible. Second, domain selection—in other words, knowing what not to do as well as what to do—is usually considered an essential part of strategy. Third, even when many diverse activities are housed within one organization, keeping them apart may be a better overall approach than forcing them together in, say, the bear hug of a matrix structure. As Lafley explains, the reason P&G is able to pursue arbitrage up to a point as well as adaptation and aggregation is that the company has deliberately separated these functions into three kinds of subunits (global business units, market development organizations, and global business shared services) and imposed a structure that minimizes points of contact and, thereby, friction.

For most of the past 25 years, the rhetoric of globalization has been concentrated on markets. Only recently has the spotlight turned to production, as firms have become aware of the arbitrage opportunities available through offshoring. This phenomenon appears to have outpaced strategic thinking about it. Many academic writings remain focused on the globalization (or nonglobalization) of markets. And only a tiny fraction of the many companies that engage in offshoring appear to think about it strategically: Only 1% of the respondents to a recent survey conducted by Arie Lewin at Duke University say that their company has a corporate-wide strategy in this regard. The AAA framework provides a basis for considering global strategies that encompasses all three effective responses to the large differences that arise at national borders. Clearer thinking about the full range of strategy options should broaden the perceived opportunities, sharpen strategic choices, and enhance global performance.

Note

1. Figures are for 2005. Otherwise, the account is largely based on Tarun Khanna and Elizabeth A. Raabe, "General Electric Healthcare, 2006" (HBS case no. 9-706-478); D. Quinn Mills and Julian Kurz, "Siemens Medical Solutions: Strategic Turnaround" (HBS case no. 9-703-494); and Pankaj Ghemawat, "Philips Medical Systems in 2005" (HBS case no. 9-706-488).

PANKAJ GHEMAWAT is the Anselmo Rubiralta Professor of Global Strategy at IESE Business School in Barcelona, Spain, and the Jaime and Josefina Chua Tiampo Professor of Business Administration at Harvard Business School in Boston. He is the author of "Regional Strategies for Global Leadership" (HBR December 2005) and the forthcoming book *Redefining Global Strategy: Crossing Borders in a World Where Differences Still Matter*, which will be published in September 2007 by Harvard Business School Press. For a supplemental list of publications on globalization and strategy, go to www.hbr.org and click on the link to this article.

Segmenting Global Markets: Look Before You Leap

Before implementing a global market segmentation strategy, it's critical to understand both local and global issues.

V. KUMAR AND ANISH NAGPAL

"I am a citizen, not of Athens or Greece, but of the world."

Today we live in a global marketplace that makes Socrates' famous words more valid than ever before. As you read this article, you may be sitting on a chair from Paris, wearing a shirt made in Britain, and using a computer, without which you are handicapped, that probably was made in Taiwan. Have you ever wondered why and how this happens?

Global marketing refers to marketing activities of companies that emphasize four activities: (1) cost efficiencies resulting from reduced duplication of efforts; (2) opportunities to transfer products, brands, and ideas across subsidiaries in different countries; (3) emergence of global customers, such as global teenagers or the global elite; and (4) better links between national marketing infrastructures, which paves the way for a global marketing infrastructure that results in better management and reduced costs.

As the business world becomes more globalized, global market segmentation (GMS) has emerged as an important issue in developing, positioning, and selling products across national boundaries. Consider the global segment based on demographics, global teenagers. The sharing of universal needs and desires for branded, entertaining, trendy, and image-oriented products makes it possible to reach the global teen segment with a unified marketing program. For example, Reebok used a global advertisement campaign to launch its Instapump line of sneakers in the United States, Germany, Japan, and 137 other countries worldwide.

What Is GMS?

Global market segmentation can be defined as the process of identifying specific segments—country groups or individual consumer groups across countries—of potential customers with homogeneous attributes who are likely to exhibit similar buying behavior.

The study of GMS is interesting and important for three reasons. First of all, considering the world as a market, different products are in different stages of the product life cycle at any given time. Researchers can segment the market based on this information, but the membership of the countries in each segment is fleeting. This makes it difficult to re-evaluate and update the membership of each segment.

Second, with the advent of the Internet, product information is disseminated very rapidly and in unequal proportions across different countries. The dynamic nature of this environment warrants a continuous examination of the stability of the segment membership. Third, the goal of GMS is to break down the world market for a product or a service into different groups of countries/consumers that differ in their response to the firm's marketing mix program. That way, the firm can tailor its marketing mix to each individual segment.

Targeted segments in GMS should possess some of the following properties:

Measurability. The segments should be easy to define and measure. Objective country traits such as socioeconomic variables (e.g., per capita income) can easily be gauged, but the size of the segments based on culture or lifestyles is much harder to measure. Thus, a larger scale survey may be required for segmenting global markets depending upon the basis of GMS.

Size. Segments should be large enough to be worth going after. Britain and Hong Kong can be grouped together in the same segment, because of previous British supremacy in Hong Kong, but their population sizes differ.

Accessibility. The segments should be easy to reach via the media. Because of its sheer size, China seems to be an attractive market. However, because of its largely rural population, it has less access to technology.

Executive Summary

The primary purpose of this article is to shed more light on the more complex challenges of global market segmentation (GMS). To provide a complete understanding, we discuss some of the well-known issues in segmenting foreign markets and move on to state the various properties of global target markets. We conclude that companies can implement GMS most effectively by first gaining a full understanding of both local and global concerns.

Actionability. Effective marketing programs (the four Ps) should be easy to develop. If segments do not respond differently to the firm's marketing mix, there is no need to segment the markets. Certain legal issues need to be considered before implementing an advertisement campaign. For example, many countries, such as India, do not allow direct slandering of the competitor's products.

Competitive Intensity. The segments should not be preempted by the firm's competition. In fact, in global marketing, small companies often prefer entry of less competitive markets and use this as one of the segmentation criteria when assessing international markets.

Growth Potential. A high return on investment should be attainable. Typically, marketers face a trade-off between competitive intensity and growth potential. Currently, Latin American markets have good growth potential, but the instability of local currencies causes major problems.

Companies typically employ the following six-step process for implementing GMS:

- Identify purpose (by introducing a new or existing product and choosing appropriate marketing mix programs in groups of countries)
- Select segmentation criteria (traditional vs. emerging)
- Collect relevant information
- Segment the countries/consumers according to criteria
- Reevaluate the fit of the segment after implementation of the intended program
- Update/reassign segment membership

An interesting aspect of the GMS process is the need to constantly reevaluate segment membership. The process of assigning membership to countries into a segment could be done using traditional procedures, or by evaluating the countries by using emerging techniques.

Traditional Segmentation Bases

The choice of the segmentation basis is the most crucial factor in an international segmentation study. That a segmentation approach is essential in international markets is no longer questioned. Rather, the basis for segmentation becomes the focus. For example, for its Lexus brand, Toyota would segment the market based upon household income. On the other hand, if Marlboro were planning to introduce a new brand of cigarettes, it would segment the market based on population.

Individual- and country-based segmentation includes the following categories:

Demographics. This includes measurable characteristics of population such as age, gender, income, education, and occupation. A number of global demographic trends, such as changing roles of women, and higher incomes and living standards, are driving the emergence of global segments. Sony, Reebok, Nike, Swatch, and Benetton are some firms that cater to the needs of global teenagers.

Culture. This covers a broad range of factors such as religion, education, and language, which are easy to measure, and aesthetic preferences of the society that are much harder to comprehend. Hofstede's classification scheme proposes five cultural dimensions for classifying countries: Individualism vs. Collectivism, Power Distance (PD), Uncertainty Avoidance (UA), Masculinity vs. Femininity, and Strategic Orientation (long-term vs. short-term). For example, Austria, Germany, Switzerland, Italy, Great Britain, and Ireland form one cluster that is medium-high on Individualism and high on Masculinity. These cultural characteristics signify the preference for "high performance" products and a "successful achiever" theme in advertising.

Geography. This is based upon the world region, economic stage of development, nation, city, city size and population density, climate, altitude, and sometimes, even the ZIP code. It is easy to form country segments using regional blocks such as NAFTA, European Union, MERCOSUR, or Asia-Pacific. However, the value of such segments may vary depending on the need. These groupings are viable for developing trade policies, but not for marketing products/services given tremendous variation in other factors.

Environment. GMS is further complicated by different political, legal, and business environments in each country. Economic indicators such as Gross Domestic Product (GDP) may be used. However, it may not be relevant to refer to country segments based on this criterion because a country can move from one level of GDP to another, making this criterion obsolete.

Behavior-based segmentation includes three categories, which are shown in Table 1.

Emerging Segmentation Bases

Countries also can be segmented by means of product *diffusion patterns* and *response elasticities*. Some countries are fast adopters of the product, whereas some countries require a lag period to adopt the product. With this in mind, a firm could introduce its products in countries that are innovators (fast adopters) and later in those countries that are imitators (lag countries).

Rather than using macro-level variables to classify countries, a firm might consider segmenting markets on the basis of

Table 1   Traditional Segmentation Basis (Behavior-Based)

Segmentation Basis	Brief Description	Example
Psychographics	This segment groups people in terms of their attitudes, values, and lifestyles and helps predict consumer preferences in products, services, and media.	Porsche AG divided its buyers into five distinct categories: Top Guns, Elitists, Proud Patrons, Bon Vivants, and Fantasists—each group having a particular characteristic.
Benefit	This approach focuses on the problem a product solves, regardless of location. It attempts to measure consumer value systems and perceptions of various brands in a product class.	Toothpaste consumers can be segmented into Sensory, Sociable, Worrier, and Independent segments. Sociable consumers seek bright teeth; Worriers seek healthy teeth. Aqua packaging could indicate fluoride for the Worrier segment, and white (for a white smile) for the Sociable segent.
Behavior	This examines whether or not people buy and use a product, as well as how often and how much. Consumers can be categorized in terms of usage rates (heavy, medium, and light).	ABB classifies customers according to their switchability criterion—loyal customers, those loyal to competitors, and those who can be lost to or won from the competition.

new-product diffusion patterns. As Table 2 indicates, country segments formed on the basis of diffusion patterns may differ by product.

This type of segmentation allows the global marketer to segment countries on the basis of actual purchase patterns. Having knowledge of purchase patterns can help marketers make mode-of-entry decisions and help determine the sequence of countries in which the product should be introduced.

Consumers in lag countries can learn about the benefits of the product from the experience of adopters in the lead country, and this learning can result in a faster diffusion rate in the lag markets. Thus, countries can be grouped according to the degree of learning they exhibit for a given lead country. Lag countries that exhibit strong learning ties are potential candidates for sequential entry (using a waterfall strategy). Entry into countries that exhibit weak learning effect can be accelerated since there is not much to gain by waiting. Here, a sprinkler strategy (simultaneous entry into the relevant markets) would work well.

If a firm wants to introduce its innovation into a new country, it must be aware that the diffusion rate depends upon the kind of innovation. The diffusion pattern of a continuous innovation (one that has a majority of features in common with earlier products plus some new features that improve performance or add value) is very different from a discontinuous innovation (which is new or drastically different from earlier forms in several relevant features or attributes).

In the case of continuous innovations, such as home computers, the introduction of a successive generation will influence not only its diffusion but also the diffusion of the earlier generations. In such cases, diffusion will occur more quickly since consumers have some related knowledge. Hence, when a new generation of the product is introduced in the lead market while the lag markets are still adopting the existing (older) generation, information on the added benefits of the new generation travels faster from the lead market to potential adopters in the lag markets. The users in the lag markets will be familiar with the innovation and can easily absorb the benefits of the next generation.

Another interesting way to group countries is according to their response elasticities. Consumers across countries respond in different ways when the price of the product changes. Grocerystore scanner systems store a wealth of information that can then be used to find customer buying patterns. If the data shows the customers are price sensitive toward a particular product, couponing strategies can help target that segment, where legal.

Table 2   Segments Based Upon Diffusion Patterns

Segment	Product Categories				
	VCRs	Cellular phones	Home computers	Microwave ovens	CD players
1	Germany, UK, France, Sweden	Denmark, Norway	Belgium, UK, Netherlands	Germany, Italy, Denmark, Austria	Belgium, Netherlands, Sweden, Austria, Finland
2	Belgium, Denmark, Spain, Austria, Finland	Finland, France	France, Italy, Sweden, Norway, Austria, Germany	Belgium, UK, Netherlands, France, Spain	Spain, Denmark, Germany
3	Italy, Portugal	Germany, UK, Italy, Switzerland	Spain, Portugal	Norway	Switzerland, Italy

Source: Kumar, V., Jaishankar Ganesh, and Raj Echambadi, "Cross-National Diffusion Research: What Do We Know and How Certain Are We?" *Journal of Product Innovation Management,* 15, 1998.

Implementing GMS

It is important to consider some of the conceptual and methodological issues so GMS can fulfill its high potential. Table 3 gives a brief description of the four critical types of equivalencies that should be taken into account when implementing GMS.

Construct equivalence refers to whether the segmentation basis has the same meaning and is expressed similarly in different countries and cultures. Different countries under study must have the same perception or use for the product being researched. Otherwise, comparison of data becomes meaningless. If, for example, a firm is studying the bicycle market, it must realize that, in the United States, bicycles are classified under the recreational-sports industry, whereas in India and China they are considered a basic means of transportation.

Similar activities also may have different functions in different countries. For example, for many U.S. families, grocery shopping is a chore to be accomplished as efficiently as possible. However, in India and many other countries interaction with vendors and local shopkeepers plays a very important social function.

Construct equivalence is easier to establish for the general bases, such as geographic variables. However, for bases such as values and lifestyles, construct equivalence is much harder to achieve. VALS-2 identifies eight segments based on two main dimensions: self-orientation and resources. Another VALS system was developed for Japan, presumably because the U.S.-based VALS-2 system was not appropriate for that country. Instead it identifies 10 segments based on two key dimensions: life orientation and attitudes toward social change.

Scalar equivalence means that scores from different countries should have the same meaning and interpretation. The first aspect used to determine scalar equivalence concerns the specific scale or scoring procedure used to establish the measure. The standard format of scales used in survey research differs across countries. For example, in the United States a 5- or 7-point scale is most common. However, 20-point scales are used in France.

The second aspect concerns the response to a score obtained in a measure. Here the question arises as to whether a score obtained in one research context has the same meaning and interpretation in another context. For example, on an intention-to-purchase scale, does the proportion of likely buyers indicate a similar likelihood of purchase from one country to another, or does a position on the Likert scale have the same meaning in all cultures?

Differences in response styles often result in a lack of scalar equivalence. Some of these response styles include "extreme" responding and "social desirability" responding. Research shows Chinese respondents show a "marked degree of agreeability," while Americans show a "marked willingness to dissent." These differences can cause problems in the data-collection process, which can lead to erroneous grouping of countries.

Measurement equivalence refers to whether the measures used to operationalize the segmentation basis are comparable across countries. For example, consider the level of education. The United States uses one educational scale while in Europe the educational system is quite different, and the term

Table 3 Types of Equivalence

Equivalence			
Construct	**Scalar**	**Measurement**	**Sampling**
Are we studying the same phenomena in Brazil, India, and Britain?	Do the scores on consumers in the U.S., Argentina, and Japan have the same meaning?	Are the phenomena in France, Singapore and South Africa measured in the same way?	Are the samples used in Hong Kong, China, and Romania equivalent?

"college" is not appropriate. Also, household income is difficult to compare across countries owing to differences in the tax structure and purchasing power.

Some items of a segmentation basis have measurement equivalence, but the others do not. For example, research shows that in the U.S. consumer innovativeness is expressed both in terms of purchase of new products and in social communication about new products. In France, however, the latter does not apply. Hence, only items pertaining to the person's tendency to purchase new products have measurement equivalence across the two countries. The researcher thus faces the dilemma of either using the same set of items in each country (etic scale) or adapting the set of items to each country (emic-scale). A compromise would be a combined emic-etic scale with some core items common to all countries and some country-specific items.

Sampling equivalence deals with problems in identifying and operationalizing comparable populations and selecting samples that are simultaneously representative of other populations and comparable across countries. One aspect of sampling equivalence deals with the decision-making process, which varies across countries. For example, in the United States, office supplies are often purchased by the office secretary, whereas this decision is made by a middle-level manager or CEO in some countries.

It is also important to consider whether the sample is representative of the population. In most developed countries, information on potential markets and sampling frames is easily available. However, in Japan, the most popular residential list for sample studies was made inaccessible to researchers. Developing countries do not have extensive databases and so obtaining the sampling frame to suit the needs of the research could be difficult.

Equivalence presents a dilemma in the minds of managers. On one end, it would be wise to develop scales specifically for each culture; on the other, responses collected in this manner may not mean the same thing. This issue can be resolved to some extent by using a combination of items in the scale.

Think Globally, Act Locally

Used effectively, segmentation allows global marketers to take advantage of the benefits of standardization (such as economies of scale and consistency in positioning) while addressing the needs and expectations of a specific target group. This approach means looking at markets on a global or regional basis, thereby ignoring the political boundaries that define markets in many cases.

The greatest challenge for the global marketer is the choice of an appropriate base for segmentation. Pitfalls that handicap global marketing programs and contribute to their suboptimal performance include market-related reasons, such as insufficient research and overstandardization, as well as internal reasons, such as inflexibility in planning and implementation. If a product is launched on a broad scale without formally researching regional or local differences, it may fail.

The successful global marketers will be those who can achieve a balance between the local and the regional/global concerns. Procter and Gamble's Pampers brand suffered a major setback in the 1980s in Japan when customers favored the purchase of diapers of rival brands. The diapers were made and sold according to a formula imposed by Cincinnati headquarters, and Japanese consumers found the company's hard-sell techniques alienating. Globalization by design requires a balance between sensitivity to local needs and global deployment of technologies and concepts.

GMS offers a solution to the standardization vs. adaptation issue because it creates the conceptual framework for offering standardized products and marketing programs in multiple countries by targeting the same consumer segments in different countries. The formulation of a global strategy by a firm may result in the choice of one particular segment across markets or multiple segments. However, in implementing the marketing mix for maximum effect, the principle "Think globally, act locally" becomes a critical rule for guiding marketing efforts.

V. KUMAR (VK) is Marvin Hurley Professor of Business Administration, Melcher Faculty Scholar, Director of Marketing Research Studies and Director of International Business Programs at the University of Houston, Bauer College of Business, Department of Marketing. He may be reached at vkumar@uh.edu. **ANISH NAGPAL** is a doctoral student at the University of Houston, Bauer College of Business, Department of Marketing.

From *Marketing Research,* Spring 2001, pp. 8–13. Copyright © 2001 by American Marketing Association. Reprinted by permission.

How China Will Change Your Business

TED C. FISHMAN

China's miracle economy can come at you in a lot of ways, from all directions.

- Mention an interest in China to your old friend who owns an industrial toolmaking shop and he confides that his factory, which was started by his father and has bought a comfortable suburban life for three generations of his family as well as good wages to hundreds of workers, "is getting killed by the people over there."
- Stop at the auto supply store for windshield-wiper fluid. Half the store is now a showroom for small Chinese motor scooters, some of which look like half-Harleys, others like Ducatis. Most cost less than $300.
- Decide at last to plunge into digital photography. Photo magazines all rave about a small new camera from Nikon, an engineering wonder that can shoot fast, captures dimly lit scenes, and costs half the price of similar machines a year ago. Nikon is one of Japan's marquee brands, but when you bring the camera home from the store you spot the words in small print on the product itself: "Made in China."
- Wake up in Santa Barbara, Calif., one morning to a sky that looks as though it is painted a shiny white. The morning's newspaper reports that the sunlight is playing tricks on something known as the Asian Brown Cloud, a mass of dust that has drifted over the Pacific from China. The cloud contains particles of loose earth from deforested land mixed with arsenic and other industrial pollutants from the country's factories.

Powered by the world's most rapidly changing large economy, China is an ever increasing presence and influence in our lives, connected to us by the world's shipping lanes, financial markets, telecommunications, and above all, by the globalization of appetites. China sews more clothes and stitches more shoes and assembles more toys than any other nation. It has become the world's largest maker of consumer electronics, pumping out more TVs, DVD players, and cell phones than any other country. And more recently, it has ascended the economic development ladder higher still, moving quickly and expertly into biotech and computer manufacturing. It is building cars (there are more than 120 automakers in China), making parts for Boeing 757s, and exploring space with its own domestically built rockets.

Americans tend to focus on the huge inequality in trade between the two countries. It is a worry Americans help to create by buying ever more from China's humming factories. In 2004, the Chinese sold the United States $160 billion more in goods than they bought. Contrary to common wisdom, however, the trade deficit with China does not mean that Americans are spending down the national wealth at a faster pace than ever before. So far, most of China's gains with American buyers have come at the expense of the other countries that once lured American dollars, especially other Asian economies. Americans—and the world—get more stuff in the bargain.

Ever since China started on the capitalist road, opinions about its prospects have figuratively, and literally, been all over the map. The present mood is a combustible mix of euphoria, fear, admiration, and cynicism. On those emotions ride great tides of capital, the strategic plans of businesses great and small, and the gravest political calculations in the world's capitals and city halls.

Yet few working Americans have a full awareness of China's rise. How could they? Nothing like this has ever happened before, and it's occurring on the other side of the globe. Yet Americans—particularly anyone involved in running a business—need to know what is happening today in China and to understand how China's fate has become inextricably bound with our own. Conceding China's rise does not mean conceding to China. But it does require acknowledging some important truths:

1. China's economy is much larger than the official numbers show. In 2003, China's official GDP was $1.4 trillion. By that measure, it was the seventh-largest economy in the world. As with nearly all economic statistics from China, however, that measure is suspect. One reason the real number may be much higher is that, in competition for development funds, local Chinese authorities have considerable incentive to underreport their growth rates to the nation's central planners. Another reason is that the government measures only China's legal economy. Its underground economy, made up of both unsavory businesses and more mundane ones that lack a government stamp (and tax bill), is enormous but uncountable.

Economists also note that China's official GDP underplays the true size of its economy because China uses the massive power of its foreign currency reserves to keep the world price of the yuan marching in lockstep with the dollar. If the dollar had not dropped against the euro and other world currencies over the past few years, China's ranking would be a notch or two bigger. Critics of China's currency policies, including American domestic manufacturers such as steel mills, casters, plastics molders, and machine-tool makers, argue that China artificially depresses the value of its currency against the dollar by as much as 40%.

A dollar spent in China buys almost five times more goods and services than a dollar spent in a typical American city like Indianapolis. Taking purchasing-power parity into account, the U.S. Central Intelligence Agency estimates that China's economy looks more like one with a GDP of $6.6 trillion. Put another way, it makes more sense to think of China's economy as closer to two-thirds the size of the U.S. economy than to one-seventh.

2. The growth of China's economy has no equal in modern history.

China's economy has grown so fast that it has taken on the mythic qualities of one of Mao's showcase farms. Since China set about reforming its economy a generation ago, its GDP has expanded at an annual rate of 9.5%. Countries in the early stages of economic reform often come up fast, but not like China. The country is closing in on a 30-year run during which its economy has doubled nearly three times. Neither Japan's nor South Korea's postwar boom comes anywhere close. Nicholas Lardy, an economist at the Institute for International Economics, notes that China grew mightily even during the worldwide economic doldrums of 2001–02.

China is so committed to economic growth that the Chinese often talk as though they can will it to happen. It is a necessary optimism that pervades official Chinese communication. Orville Schell, the author of *Virtual Tibet* and the dean of the school of journalism at the University of California, Berkeley, draws a parallel between the unity of focus the Chinese demonstrated for anti-capitalism and their focus now on capitalism. Schell argues that in both instances there is a willingness to suspend logic and see only bright tomorrows. Both lead to excess. In its capitalist present, China has been willing to overlook the dark side of modernization, seeing economic progress as the solution to all the country's challenges. Even so, every time the worst is predicted for China's economy, it seems to grow faster, create stronger industries, import more, and export more.

3. China is winning the global competition for investment capital.

One reason China's economy is growing so fast is that the world keeps feeding it capital. According to Japan's Research Institute of Economy, Trade and Industry, one-third of China's industrial production was put in place by the half-trillion dollars of foreign money that has flowed into the country since 1978. In 2003, foreigners invested more in building businesses in China than they spent anywhere else in the world. The U.S. used to attract the most foreign money, but in 2003 China took a strong lead, pulling in $53 billion to the U.S.'s $40 billion.

With money comes knowledge. The catalytic role of foreigners in the country is still growing quickly; every day China receives a river of European, Asian, and American experts in manufacturing, banking, computing, advertising, and engineering. In 2003, the exports and imports by foreign companies operating in China rose by over 40%. More than half of China's trade is now controlled by foreign firms. Many of these import goods into the country that they then manufacture into exports. Foreign companies have pumped up China's trade volume enough to make it the third-largest trading country in the world, behind the U.S. and Germany and now ahead of Japan.

4. China can be a bully.

China can spend, it can hire and dictate wages, it can throw old-line competitors out of work. In just a three-year period from 2000 to late 2003, for example, China's exports to the U.S. of wooden bedroom furniture climbed from $360 million to nearly $1.2 billion. During that time, the work force at America's wooden-furniture factories dropped by 35,000, or one of every three workers in the trade. China now makes 40% of all furniture sold in the U.S., and that number is sure to climb.

5. China's economy is an entrepreneurial economy.

China's industrial competitors, including the U.S., often misapprehend the source of China's productive strength. They fear that another centrally governed, well-planned assault on strategic industries is being plotted in Beijing. The world has already seen how effective the Japanese, Koreans, and Taiwanese can be when they focus on sectors they mean to conquer. Even Chinese government planners like to talk as though they are aping the centrally coordinated, government-financed assaults on strategic global industries that their Asian neighbors have pulled off over the past 40 years. However, in looking at how Chinese businesses really take shape—locally and opportunistically—Kellee Tsai, a political scientist at Johns Hopkins University and a former analyst at Morgan Stanley, argues that nothing could be further from the truth. For a world fretting over Chinese economic competition, the entities to fear are not government planners but enterprises that spring on the scene lean and mean, planned and financed by investors who want to make money quickly.

An emblem of the Zhejiang province in China is Hong Dongyang, an entrepreneur whose story is now well-known throughout the country. Hong was once a schoolteacher. She began making socks in the 1970s on a home sewing machine. At first Hong sold them along the roads near her home. She opened a stand and christened her embryonic enterprise Zhejiang Stocking Company. Hong's sock company was predictably copied en masse by others. Today, the province is the Chinese sock capital, with more than 8,000 companies spinning out eight billion pairs a year, one-third of the world's supply. In 2001, the Chinese makers produced 1% of the socks on U.S. feet. In just two years, sock imports from China to the U.S. jumped two-hundred-fold and now make up 7% of the U.S. market, James J. Jochum, assistant secretary for export administration at the U.S. Department of Commerce, has noted that the Chinese manufacturers cut their prices by more than half in 2003 and helped drive one in four U.S. sock makers out of business.

6. The most daunting thing about China is not its ability to make cheap consumer goods.

The American economy won't crater just because the Chinese can produce sofas and socks for less than we can. The Japanese, for their part, have lost the television business. The Italians are losing the fine-silk business. Consumer goods trade on the surface of the world's economy and their movement is easy for the public to watch. The far bigger shift, just now picking up steam, is occurring among the products that manufacturers and marketers trade with each other: the infinite number and variety of components that make up everything else that is made, whether it is the hundreds of parts in a washing machine or computer or the hundreds of thousands of parts in an airplane.

THE CYCLE OF CODEPENDENCY
China is at one moment our greatest threat, the next our friend. It is siphoning off American jobs; it is essential to our competitive edge. China exports deflation; it stokes soaring prices.

Given how quickly China is climbing the industrial ladder, perhaps the next question is whether any commercial technology is beyond an imminent challenge from China. Gal Dymant, an American Israeli venture capitalist in Beijing, believes the answer is that few will be. One of the companies Dymant works with, a database publisher named Asia Direct, produces an annual China Hi-Tech Directory. Tracking the directory's updates year to year gives Dymant an informal measure of the shifts in Chinese industry.

The first thing one notices about the directories, he says, is how much thicker they grow every year, particularly in industries where there have been large foreign investments. In 2003, Asia Direct's volume grew considerably fatter in the sections devoted to China's domestic mobile-phone manufacturers and suppliers, broadband communications, and in companies establishing themselves in cities outside of China's eastern powerhouses. The manufacture and sale of integrated chips is also soaring, along with healthy gains in China's software and information-services markets. Then again, every section in the directory has grown, including biotechnology, semiconductors, and Internet development, areas in which Chinese firms have newly established themselves, many now in partnership with the world's leading technology-driven companies.

For his part, Dymant is putting together an investor group to Build a Chinese version of one of the world's most advanced and costly medical devices, the magnetic resonance imaging (MRI) machine. "The talent is here to build anything," Dymant says. "We think we can develop MRIs for about 60% of the price they are built for in the U.S."

7. China is closing the research and development gap—fast.
The ability of American industry to stay ahead of its international competition rests on the national gifts and resources that the U.S. devotes to innovation. The research gap between the U.S. and China remains vast. In December, Washington authorized $3.7 billion to finance nanotechnology research, a sum the Chinese government cannot easily match within a scientific infrastructure that would itself take many more billions (and years) to build.

Yet when it comes to more mainstream applied industrial development and innovation, the separation among Chinese, American, and other multinational firms is beginning to narrow. Last year, China spent $60 billion on research and development. The only countries that spent more were the U.S. and Japan, which spent $282 billion and $104 billion, respectively. But again, China forces you to do the math: China's engineers and scientists usually make between one-sixth and one-tenth what Americans do, which means that the wide gaps in financing do not necessarily result in equally wide gaps in manpower or results. The U.S. spent nearly five times what China did but had less than two times as many researchers (1.3 million to 743,000). China's universities and vocational schools will produce 325,000 engineers this year—five times as many as the U.S.

For now, the emphasis in Chinese labs is weighted overwhelmingly toward the "D" side—meaning training for technical employees and managers. Nevertheless, foreign companies are moving quickly to integrate their China-based labs into their global research operations. Motorola alone has 19 research labs in China that develop technology for both the local and global markets. Several of the company's most innovative recent phones were developed there for the Chinese market.

8. China now sets the global benchmark for prices.
Big news can be found in little places. In its November 2003 circular, a dryly written four-page publication, the Chicago Federal Reserve Bank noted complaints from American makers of automotive parts that "automakers had been asking suppliers for the 'China price' on their purchases." The bank's analysts observed that U.S. suppliers had also been asked by their big customers to move their factories to China or to find subcontractors there.

Over much of the business world, the term China price has since become interchangeable with lowest price possible. The China price is part of the new conventional wisdom that companies can move nearly any kind of work to China and find huge savings. It holds that any job transferred there will be done cheaper, and possibly better.

It is plainly understood that asking suppliers to lower prices is merely another way of telling them they ought to be prepared to meet the best price out of China, even if they are making their products in Japan or Germany. General Motors, which buys more than $80 billion worth of parts a year, now has a clause in its supply contracts that gives its supplier 30 days to meet the best price the company can find worldwide or risk immediate termination.

In fact, in the U.S. between 1998 and 2004, prices fell in nearly every product category in which China was the top exporter. "The manufactured goods that have dropped in price the most are those made by China," says W. Michael Cox, chief economist for the Federal Reserve Bank of Dallas, citing figures assembled by the bank for its 2003 annual report, published in 2004. Personal computers, the most outstanding example, fell by 28%, televisions by nearly 12%, cameras and toys by around 8%, while other electronics, clothing of all sorts, shoes, and tableware also dropped in price.

9. China's growth is making raw materials more expensive.
Even as China puts pressure on U.S. manufacturers to lower prices, it's squeezing them from a different direction. Its voracious demand for raw materials has caused prices to spike. Copper prices jumped 37% last year, aluminum and zinc both rose about 25%, and oil was up 33%. In 2003, according to the calculations of Stephen Roach, chief economist at Morgan Stanley, the Chinese bought 7% of the world's oil, a quarter of all aluminum and steel, nearly a third of the world's iron ore and coal, and 40% of the world's cement. The trend is for bigger amounts yet to come.

The squeeze is leaving U.S. manufacturers with no alternative but to become more productive. Better machines, software, and advanced management techniques, for instance, now mean that U.S. companies on average produce far more per worker than they did a quarter of a century ago when manufacturing employment was high. From 1977 to 2002, productivity throughout the U.S. economy grew by half, but in manufacturing it more than doubled. Surprisingly, despite losing huge numbers of workers, U.S. manufacturers actually finished 2003 making more stuff than they did in 2001. Output was up, if only by half a percent.

10. No company has embraced China's potential more vigorously than Wal-Mart. And no company has been a bigger catalyst in pushing manufacturers to China. Estimates of how much of Wal-Mart's merchandise comes from abroad today range from 50% to 85%. Chinese factories are, by far, the most important and fastest-growing sources for the company. In 2003, Wal-Mart purchased $15 billion worth of goods from Chinese suppliers. A whopping portion of between 10% and 13% of everything China has sent to the U.S. winds up on Wal-Mart's shelves. Writing in *The Washington Post,* Peter Goodman and Phillip Pan reported in February 2004 that "more than 80% of the 6,000 factories in Wal-Mart's worldwide database of suppliers are in China." The company has 560 people on the ground in the country to negotiate and make purchases.

Wal-Mart is often demonized for its part in shipping U.S. manufacturing jobs overseas. It is difficult, however, to separate the role of Wal-Mart's thousands of suppliers in the migration of manufacturing out of the U.S. from the larger global trends realigning how and where the world makes things. If Wal-Mart has a unique part in the trend, it is in how expertly the company has managed that trend and, in so doing, accelerated it. China's low-cost manufacturing machine feeds Wal-Mart's critical mass by allowing companies to build assembly lines that are so huge that they achieve ever-greater economies of scale and drive prices downward all the more.

The next question is whether any commercial technology is beyond an imminent challenge from China.

Wal-Mart's Chinese suppliers can achieve startling, market-shaking price cuts. By selling portable DVD players with seven-inch LCD screens from China for less than $160, for instance, Wal-Mart recently helped cut the price of these trendy devices in half. Even with superlow prices, Chinese factories can sell in such giant quantities that they willingly oblige. To get ready for its big Thanksgiving sale in 2002, Wal-Mart picked Sichuan Changhong Electric, one of the world's largest makers of televisions, to supply sets under the Apex Digital brand. Changhong makes 15 million TVs a year, most of them for export. Eight of 10 shipped overseas go to the U.S. In 2002, its sets at Wal-Mart sold for far less than comparable models from other makers, sometimes undercutting the competition by $100 or more. The models the company delivered for the sale helped the event net $1.4 billion.

In late December, state-owned Changhong reported nearly half a billion dollars in losses, purportedly linked to unpaid bills owed by Apex. The scandal, though mired in murky details, nevertheless highlights both the ability of China's big firms to sustain losses and keep running and their willingness to satisfy American retailers' demands for ever-lower prices.

11. There are hidden costs associated with doing business in China. Companies that engage with China must expect pressure to transfer their technology and thus create their own competition in the country. The Chinese use the carrot of their vast market to extract concessions from foreign firms that will help build China's industrial might. It is a policy worthy of grudging admiration. When viewed from the Chinese side, it has a long record of success.

Motorola virtually invented China's mobile-phone market. Its corporate archives show that the company knew that eventually the transfer of technology to China would sow formidable rivals. Nevertheless, Motorola decided its best strategy was to get into China early and to bring its best technology. The proof today is in the size and efficacy of the country's mobile communications network: Calls get through to phones in high-rises, subway cars, and distant hamlets—connections that would stymie mobile phones in the U.S.

What no one at Motorola anticipated was how crowded the Chinese market would become. Nokia and Motorola now battle for market share in the Chinese handset business. German, Korean, and Taiwanese makers figure strongly. And all these foreign brands are now facing intense competition from indigenous Chinese phone makers. More than 40% of the Chinese domestic handset market now belongs to local companies such as Ningbo Bird, Nanjing Panda Electronics, Haier, and TCL Mobile. The domestic makers have become so strong that when Siemens found its mobile handset business in China wanting, it joined with Ningbo Bird to gain both low-cost manufacturing and a developed distribution channel. Yet Motorola can't exit the Chinese market. If it did, says Jim Gradoville, Motorola's vice president of Asia Pacific government relations, the Chinese companies that emerged would be the leanest and most aggressive in the world, and a company like his would have no idea what hit it. So Motorola stays. Already the largest foreign investor in China's electronics industry, Motorola plans to triple its stake there to more than $10 billion by 2006.

12. Piracy is a problem. Foreign companies have little defense against even outright theft of their technology in China. China's failure to police intellectual property, in effect, creates a massive global subsidy worth hundreds of billions of dollars to its businesses and people. By investing in the country's manufacturing infrastructure, by providing the expertise, machines, and software China needs to produce world-class products, the world is also helping assemble the biggest, most sophisticated, and most successful "illegal" manufacturing complex in the world.

Seen another way, China's loose intellectual property rules turn the tables on the Western colonial powers and the Japanese who throughout the nineteenth and early twentieth centuries violated China's land and people. As China grows into a great power, the wealth transferred into the country by expropriating intellectual property will propel it forward.

13. China's heavy buying of U.S. debt has lowered the cost of money in the U.S. In the first half of 2004, China's total foreign exchange reserves topped $460 billion. In size, that puts China's cumulative dollar account at roughly equal to a third of its gross domestic product. If China simply spent its dollars, it would flood the world market with American currency and drive the dollar down. But China, no fool, is not interested in pushing the dollar down. So instead of selling its dollars, it lends them back to the U.S.

China keeps tight wraps on the value, composition, and trading of its portfolio, but Wall Street commonly assumes that the country owns a large amount of high-grade U.S. corporate bonds, intertwining its national fortunes with America's blue chips (many of them the same corporations reaping fortunes in China itself).

China also has almost certainly built a large stake in the market for bonds issued by Fannie Mae and Freddie Mac, the companies that buy home mortgages from banks and thrift institutions and resell them as bundled securities. This means that billions of dollars' worth of investments belonging to the Chinese are plowed indirectly into the American real estate market, and that an ever-increasing share of Americans' mortgage payments pour into the coffers of the government of China.

As long as China is an aggressive lender, Americans—whether borrowing for their own private purchases or acting in the roles of taxpayers—can borrow money at lower rates than they would otherwise have to pay. Much of the recent boom in real estate prices in America, especially in the East and West Coast markets, is attributable to these low rates.

14. Americans and Chinese have become reliant on each other's most controversial habits. The Chinese need a low-priced currency to keep their export machine going and create jobs. But maintaining the yuan's low price also means that Chinese consumers are stuck with a currency that would otherwise buy more for them on the world market. China's diligent savers suffer too since their bank deposits are tied up in accounts that earn low government-mandated rates of return, as the government, in effect, siphons off money from savers to maintain its currency peg.

Relatedly, China's vast export earnings earn less than they ought to when they are invested in U.S. debt securities that offer modest yields, when investments in the Chinese economy can return 10 times as much (albeit on riskier terms). Seen from that view, the people of China, who earn on average just one-fortieth what Americans do, are indirectly subsidizing the insatiable shopping of Americans, who acquire ever more goods at the same time that Chinese consumers are hampered from buying goods from abroad.

The people of China are indirectly subsidizing the insatiable shopping of Americans.

The obverse of this peculiar relationship is that China lends America all the money it needs to spend itself silly. The cycle of codependency, which former U.S Treasury Secretary Lawrence Summers labels a "balance of financial terror," isn't sustainable. The U.S. cannot take on ever-bigger debt and amass huge trade deficits indefinitely. In the worst scenario, the U.S.'s willingness to fritter away its national wealth to finance private consumption and unproductive government spending would extract a permanent price on the economy, sending the U.S. in a downward spiral that would be hard to escape.

Thus do the routes to prosperity chosen by China and the U.S. put both countries at risk. Without the U.S. to buy Chinese goods, China cannot sustain its growth; without China to lend money to the U.S., Americans cannot spend. Without the twin engines of the U.S. and China stoking the fortunes of other nations, the rest of the world might also sputter.

How can the U.S., perhaps with its traditional allies, adjust to a competitive challenger that has strengths unlike any other that America has faced? Are the transfers of talent, technology, and capital part of an inevitable dynamic? Or does the U.S., or any other country, have the power to shape a future in which everyone prospers?

Americans looking for answers and action must also find a way to move America's leadership to see China's rise as every bit as worthy of national attention as the rumblings in more obvious political hot spots. While all eyes turn to the so-called clash of civilizations between Islam and the West, China will have the more profound impact on the world in the long run. And yet, despite occasional misgivings offered in factory towns and tariffs slapped on imports at the height of campaign season, American leaders tend to view China's rise as the fulfillment of a free marketer's dream, where global investors will shepherd the country into wealth, democracy, and peaceful interdependence with the rest of the free world.

It is a lovely theory, and it may ultimately be true. There is, however, no evidence upon which to base such a prediction. Which exactly of the world's large, highly nationalistic, dictatorial, Communist-capitalist countries offers a historical analogue? Answer: There is no such country.

This article was adapted from **TED C. FISHMAN'S** book, *CHINA, INC.*, published by Scribner, an imprint of Simon & Schuster.

Three Dimensional

The markets of Japan, Korea, and China are far from homogeneous.

MASAAKI KOTABE AND CRYSTAL JIANG

Asia is one of the world's most dynamic regions, and offers multiple opportunities for businesses and investors. In terms of its nominal gross domestic product (GDP) in 2005, Japan has the largest economy ($4.80 trillion), followed by China ($1.84 trillion) and Korea ($.72 trillion). China's real purchasing power exceeds $7 trillion, Japan's is estimated at $4 trillion, and Korea's is estimated at $1 trillion. These giants' combined purchasing power is comparable to the $12 trillion U.S. economy.

One of the challenges faced by American and other Western multinational companies is a tendency to lump together these markets and assume that Asian consumers have similar tastes and preferences, moderated by different income levels. This is not only a very shortsighted view, but also a risky assumption when entering these markets.

Asian countries have distinct cultural, social, and economic characteristics that affect consumer behavior, with consumers in Japan, Korea, and China differing in brand orientations, attitudes toward domestic and foreign products, quality and price perceptions, and technology feature preferences. A comparative analysis of consumer behaviors can help companies identify effective marketing strategies, and enable them to successfully tackle these Asian markets (see Table 1).

Brand Orientation

Japan. Of all the developed countries, this is the most brand-conscious and status-conscious. It is also intensely style-conscious: Consumers love high-end luxury goods (especially from France and Italy), purchasing items such as designer handbags, shoes, and jewelry. Since 2001, Hermes, Louis Vuitton (commonly referred to as LVMH), and Coach have opened glitzy flagship stores in Tokyo and enjoyed double-digit sales growth. And the country represents 20% of Gucci's worldwide revenue, 15% of LVMH's, and 12% of Chanel's. It seems that a slumping economy has not inhibited its consumers.

Eager to "know who they are," they prefer brands that contribute to their senses of identity and self-expression. These highly group-oriented consumers are apt to select prestigious

Executive Briefing

Globalizing markets might not mean that markets have become similar. Although multinational companies tend to believe that all Asian markets are the same, a comparative analysis proves that consumers in Japan, Korea, and China differ in their brand orientations, attitudes toward domestic and foreign products, quality and price perceptions, and product feature preferences. To ensure success, companies must set aside narrow and risky assumptions, and tailor country-specific strategies to target these consumers.

merchandise based on social class standards, and prefer products that enhance their status. Accordingly, they attach more importance to the reputation of the merchandise than to their personal social classes.

Noticeably, the country's consumer markets have expanded to China and Korea. In Shanghai or Seoul, you can see the influence of Japan's fashion trends and products. There's even a Chinese word for this phenomenon: ha-ri, which means the adoration of Japanese style.

Korea. Consumers have very sophisticated tastes, show immense passion for new experiences, and favor premium and expensive imported products. In 2004, the Korean Retail Index showed continuous growth of premium brands in certain product categories, such as whiskey, shampoo, and cosmetics. Consumers also demonstrate great interest in generational fads (expressions of their generations and cultures, not just of their economics or regions), thereby selecting products that follow their generations' judgments and preferences.

China. Roughly 10 million–13 million Chinese consumers prefer luxury goods. The majority of them are entrepreneurs or young professionals working for foreign multinational firms. Recent studies found that 24% of the population, mostly in their 20s and 30s, prefers new products and considers technology an important part of life. (Those in their 40s

Table 1 Market Characteristics of the Three Largest Asian Economies

	Japan	Korea	China
Population (2005)	127 million	48 million	1,306 million
Nominal GDP (2005)	$4.80 trillion	$ .72 trillion	$1.84 trillion
GDP purchasing power parity (2004)	$3.7 trillion	$ .92 trillion	$7.3 trillion
GDP per capita purchasing power parity (2004)	$29,400	$19,200	$5,600
GDP real growth rate of country (2004)	2.9%	4.6%	9.1%
Degree of luxury brand consciousness	Very strong	Strong	Varied
Preference for foreign products	Strong (particularly for European products)	Weak	Very strong
Price/quality perception	Extremely quality demanding	Polarization of consumption	Very price conscious
Importance of high-tech features on new products	Very high	Very high	Varied

Sources: Central Intelligence Agency, World Factbook, and Index Mundi

and 50s are price-conscious, brand loyal, and less sensitive to technology.) With higher education and purchasing power, this generation is brand- and status-conscious. It considers luxury goods to be personal achievements, bringing higher social status.

Purchasing behavior tends to vary regionally. Consumers in metropolitan areas follow fashions/trends/styles, prefer novelty items, and are aware of brand image and product quality. These consumers live on the eastern coast—in major cities such as Shanghai, Beijing, Shenzhen, and Dalian. There, luxury brands such as Armani, Prada, and LVMH are considered prominent logos for high-income clientele.

According to LVMH, this country is its fourth-largest market in terms of worldwide sales. It's no wonder that many high-end firms label these consumers "the new Japanese": a group of increasingly wealthy people hungry for brands and fanatical about spending.

Domestic vs. Foreign

Japan. Although consumers are extremely demanding and have different perceptions of products made in other countries, they are generally accepting of quality foreign products. However, Japan is mostly dominated by well-established companies

such as Canon, Sony, and Toyota. Many globally successful firms experience great difficulty gaining footholds.

In this market, Häagen-Dazs Japan Inc. succeeded the exit of competitor Ben & Jerry's, dominating the premium ice cream market with a 90% market share. It successfully delivered the message of a "lifestyle-enhancement product" with word-of-mouth advertising, garnering a flood of free publicity. The company flourished by promoting high quality with local appeal.

Korea. These consumers hold negative attitudes toward foreign businesses; the majority believes that these businesses transfer local wealth to other countries, and crowd out small establishments. Consumers are very proud, and demonstrate a complicated love-hate relationship with foreign brands.

Very few consumers understand or speak English, let alone the languages of their closest trading partners: Japan and China. Often, Korean campaigns require significant rebranding—use of localized brands—to influence local perceptions. According to an official at Carrefour (the world's second-largest retailer), the company has difficulty expanding its investments into other provinces because of excessive regulations, and hasn't done enough research to keep up with Korean consumers' needs.

Nevertheless, the country is increasingly comfortable with the presence of foreign companies in previously closed industries. (In fact, the society is much too uncritical and passive in the acceptance of foreign—especially American—products.) And consumers are far less brand-conscious than before, and will embrace new products from unknown companies.

China. Attitudes toward foreign products differ, depending on consumers' age groups. Companies can no longer view this country's youth through the lens of traditional cultural values; this generation considers international taste a key factor in making decisions. Conversely, the mature generation (55 years and older) expresses a definite preference for locally made products. In general, consumers believe imported products under foreign brand names are more dependable.

Many foreign companies (e.g., Nike, Nokia, Sony, McDonald's) have replaced unknown local brands. The country retains more than 300 licensed Starbucks outlets, and chairman Howard Schultz says of this market: "In addition to the 200 million middle-to-upper-class segments of the population that are typically customers for upscale brands, there is a growing affinity from the younger, affluent consumer for Western brands."

However, some foreign companies—with an increased focus on local appeal—have lost their prominent brands' images to domestic rivals, ultimately forfeiting their market share. After all, when this country's consumers are inspired by design and function, they prefer domestic brands because of their good value for the money.

Quality and Price

Japan. These consumers are the world's strictest when it comes to demand for product quality, and they clearly articulate their needs/desires about a product or packaging operation.

They view information other than price (e.g., brand, packaging, advertising) as important variables in assessing quality and making decisions. Compared with Chinese and Korean consumers, they have much higher expectations for products—and are willing to pay premium prices for them. In agricultural produce, for example, they are less tolerant of skin blemishes, small size, and uniformity.

Foreign companies that don't fully understand and meet consumers' needs/expectations struggle with their investments. Although Wal-Mart dwarfs the competition (with $285 billion in 2004 global sales) and owns 42% of all Japanese supermarket chains, it faces losses there. Its "everyday low prices" philosophy doesn't seem to attract Japanese consumers, because they often associate low price with low quality: yasu-karou, warukarou—cheap price, cheap product.

To cater to these consumers, manufacturers have adopted a total quality approach. To survive fierce local competition, Procter & Gamble sought the best available materials for product formulations and packaging. In the process, it learned some invaluable lessons on how to improve operations, and obtained new product ideas from consumers. (Interestingly, the company took this education on the Japanese way of interacting with consumers and applied it globally.) Today, the country serves as Procter & Gamble's major technical center in Asia, where it develops certain global technologies.

And McDonald's opened its first store in Tokyo's Ginza district, which is identified with luxury brand-name goods. It purchased expensive land—not justified by the limited profits of a hamburger establishment—to boost the quality image of its product. Today, McDonald's Japan has grown to become the country's largest fast-food chain.

In terms of cost, the younger generation prefers low-priced products—everything priced at 100 yen (similar to U.S. dollar stores). The "two extreme price markets" segmentation model explains how consumers value lower prices for their practical use while paying premium prices for self-satisfaction, social status, and the quality of products—especially those from Europe. As a result, anything that falls in the middle of the price range—such as the country's designer brands—generates petty profits.

Korea. Consumption has been sluggish since the Asian financial crisis of 1997–1999. However, the younger generation is at the forefront of a new and emerging pattern; it holds opposing expectations of/preferences for low-priced and high-priced goods. When purchasing high-tech or fashion-related items, these consumers prefer well-known brands, and tend to purchase expensive goods to attain psychological satisfaction. Yet they are willing to purchase unbranded goods with low prices, as long as the basic features are guaranteed. It has taken several decades for discount stores to surpass the retail market.

China. Most consumers are price sensitive, and try to safeguard part of their income for investment. In 2005, many global automakers readjusted their strategies in this country, based on demand predictions that most consumers would purchase cars priced less than $12,000. One popular Chinese automaker, Chery, priced its QQ model between $5,500 and $7,500; another aggressive domestic automaker, Xiali, priced its cars at similarly affordable prices.

Although this market is lucrative with growing demand, foreign brands (e.g., Honda, General Motors, Volkswagen Group) cannot compete with Chinese automakers' competitive prices. And when the younger generation worships Western and luxury brands—in eagerness to establish its social identity—it might prefer pirated versions to domestic ones, making anticounterfeiting control a major issue for companies.

Technology Features

Japan. Because of the country's harmonic convergence of the domestic market and the industrial sector, consumers have always preferred high-tech gadgets. According to an estimate by The World Bank Group, the country possesses 410,000 of the world's 720,000 working robots (which perform useful chores and provide companionship). Its electronics companies create gizmos by borrowing new concepts from the computer industry, such as personal video recorders, interactive pagers, and Internet radios.

Instead of looking for cost or value, consumers are willing to pay for better and cooler features and technological sophistication. Largely because of Japan's small living quarters, manufacturers have become experts at miniaturizing and creating multifunction devices. For instance, Sony's PlayStation Portable compacts the power of the original PlayStation into a palm-sized package. According to the company, it can deliver music and MPEG-4 video, can display photos, and even offers a Wi-Fi connection for wireless gaming and messaging. It's also no wonder that the country welcomed Baroke, the first company to successfully produce quality sparkling and still wine in a can.

Korea. The most wired country in the world is a leader in Internet usage and high-tech industries such as mobile phones, liquid crystal displays, and semiconductors. It also has widespread broadband, and high volumes of personal computer ownership. While mobile phone sales have cooled in Japan, these consumers continue to trade in phones for newer models about every six months.

Largely because of Japan's small living quarters, manufacturers have become experts at miniaturizing and creating multifunction devices.

According to a Samsung Research Institute survey, consumers prefer to express themselves without following social conventions. The Cyworld virtual community Web site, for instance, provides a subscriber with a private room, a circle of friends, and an endless range of "home" decoration possibilities and cool music. Ever-widening cyberspace reaches more than one-fourth of the population. The younger generation in particular enjoys virtual shopping malls and e-commerce.

China. It is imperative for companies to understand the major differences in consumer behavior between generations. Young Chinese consumers (typically affluent segments in the prosperous cities) are passionate about the latest developments. Recent studies found that 24% of the population—most with ages in the early 20s or 30s—prefer new products and consider technology an important part of life. Those in their 40s–50s, on the other hand, are price conscious, brand loyal, and less sensitive to technology.

Advice and Recommendations

Marketers need to tailor country-specific strategies to target consumers in Japan, Korea, and China. The existence of strategically equivalent segments (e.g., the younger generation, with its propensity to purchase high-quality, innovative, and foreign products) suggests a geocentric approach to global markets. These similarities allow for standardized strategies across national boundaries. By aggregating such segments, companies not only preserve consumer orientation, but also reduce the number of marketing mixes they have to offer—without losing market share, marketing, advertising, research and development, and production throughout Asia.

Moreover, because product design, function, and quality determine consumers' experiences, companies must simultaneously incorporate all areas—such as product development and marketing—to establish commanding positions in mature markets. Once they create positive images in these countries, success will be forthcoming.

Japan:
- This is the most profitable market for luxury goods companies. The key to success is promotion of high quality, local appeal, and a sense of extravagance.
- As one of the most volatile markets, it requires a steady flow of new stimuli with an improved rhythm of innovations. To survive, companies must continuously develop new products and establish prestigious brand value. If they can succeed there, then they can do so anywhere.
- Picky Japanese consumers clearly articulate their requirements about products or packaging operations. As a result, companies can use the country as their technical center—to gain firsthand experience in satisfying consumers in the region.
- These consumers are willing to pay for better and cooler features and technological sophistication. Companies can win their hearts by introducing gizmos.
- Because significant differences exist among generations, and those differences will translate into diverse consumer behaviors, segmentation marketing (identifying variations based on age, region, and gender) is best. Companies must be aware of these

differences, and understand what kinds of products/ services can meet the market segment's needs. For example: Coca-Cola has introduced more products here than anywhere else, including coffee and green tea beverages that appeal to Japanese tastes. As a result, its net operating revenue represents more than 60% of the total Asian segment (20% of its worldwide revenue).

Korea:
- A consumer-oriented approach is crucial for identifying tastes and blending in, rather than being viewed as foreign. Careful market, brand, and advertising testing is imperative.
- It can be difficult to enter this market alone; strategic alliances with domestic companies are a practical way to understand local preferences when introducing a global brand.
- If foreign companies make greater efforts to intensify their involvements with—and long-term commitments to—the country's economic development, then consumers' perceptions of an "invasion" will dissipate over time.
- Product design directly affects a company's competitiveness. This and brand power can overcome product quality, and even product functions. To present the best product design to its consumers, Samsung Electronics hired an influential British industrial designer. According to the company's Economic Research Institute, a good design "provides a good experience for consumers"; it looks different, feels good, is easy to use, and has an identity.

China:
- Foreign companies can no longer wait; the market for consumer goods is growing rapidly, stimulated by a strong economy.
- Its diversity and the vastness of its consumer base make it critical for companies to segment consumers based on demographic, geographic, and psychographic/ lifestyle variations.
- Because of the younger generation's brand orientation, promoting symbolic value is imperative for conspicuous and inconspicuous foreign products.
- Multinational companies can't assume that their first-mover advantages will be rewarded for brand recognition and established distribution channels.
- Cost-conscious consumers are quite unpredictable, so companies should avoid a too-high premium price strategy. Instead, they should research quantitatively acceptable price/value trade-offs by category.
- Because local brands are on the rise, foreign companies must work harder to localize research and development and the contents of their products. They must also better evaluate the market and the potential for long-term

growth. Without competitive pricing and world-class product design/quality, companies will have a tough time surviving.

Company executives must remember that not all countries are created equally. By understanding and learning to appreciate the differences and similarities between these three Asian purchasing giants, companies from other countries can immerse their organizations seamlessly.

MASAAKI KOTABE is the Washburn Chair of International Business and Marketing and director of research at the Institute of Global Management Studies at Temple University's Fox School of Business and Management in Philadelphia. He may be reached at mkotabe@ temple.edu. **CRYSTAL JIANG** is a PhD candidate in strategy and international business at the Fox School of Business and Management. She may be reached at crystalj@temple.edu. To join the discussion on this article, please visit www.marketingpower.com/marketingmanagementblog.

From *Marketing Management,* Vol. 15, no. 2, March/April 2006, pp. 39–43. Copyright © 2006 by American Marketing Association. Reprinted by permission.

Tech's Future

With affluent markets maturing, tech's next 1 billion customers will be Chinese, Indian, Brazilian, Thai . . . In reaching them, the industry will be deeply transformed

STEVE HAMM

In recent months, the Andhra Pradesh province in southern India has been the site of a rash of farmer suicides. Drought and low-quality seeds have left poor farmers with failed crops and no way to pay their debts. Many have swallowed lethal doses of pesticides as their only escape. Government officials estimate the toll since May at more than 60.

Against this bleak backdrop, a ray of hope: Neelamma, a 26-year-old woman, has found opportunity as a new type of entrepreneur. She's one of a dozen itinerant photographers who walk the streets of their farming communities carrying small backpacks stuffed with a digital camera, printer, and solar battery charger. As part of an experiment organized by Hewlett-Packard Co., Neelamma and the others are able to double their family incomes by charging the equivalent of 70¢ apiece for photos of newborns, weddings, and other proud moments of village life.

To make this happen, HP had to throw out its notions of how the tech business works. Anand Tawker, the company's director of emerging-market solutions in India, and his colleagues wrestled with fundamental questions: Does computing technology have a place in villages where electricity is fitful? Could it improve people's lives? How could villagers living in poverty pay for the latest digital wonders? And they came up with answers. In place of standard electricity, HP designers created the portable solar charger. Instead of selling the gear outright, HP rents the equipment to the photographers for $9 a month. "We asked people what they needed. One thing kept coming up: 'We want more money in our pockets,'" says Tawker. "So we do experiments. We launch and learn."

Why go to all that trouble? The answer is fast becoming obvious. During the first 50 years of the info-tech era, about 1 billion people have come to use computers, the vast majority of them in North America, Western Europe, and Japan. But those markets are maturing. Computer industry sales in the U.S. are expected to increase just 6% per year from now to 2008, according to market researcher IDC. To thrive, the industry must reach out to the next 1 billion customers. And many of those people will come not from the same old places but from far-flung frontiers like Shanghai, Cape Town, and Andhra Pradesh. "The robust growth opportunities are clearly shifting to the developing world," says Paul A. Laudicina, managing director at management consultant A.T. Kearney Inc.

Tech companies are scrambling to cash in on what they hope will be the next great growth wave. Led by China, India, Russia, and Brazil, emerging markets are expected to see tech sales surge 11% per year over the next half decade, to $230 billion, according to IDC. What makes these markets so appealing is not just the poor, but also the growing ranks of the middle-class consumers. Already, there are 60 million in China and 200 million in India, and their numbers are growing fast. These newly wealthy consumers are showing a taste for fashionable brands and for products every bit as capable as those available to Americans, Japanese, and Germans.

That tantalizing opportunity is drawing all of tech's big players. Microsoft is hawking software in Malaysia, Intel is pushing its chips in India, Cisco Systems is in Sri Lanka, and on and on. IBM says emerging markets are now a top priority. "We'll be even more aggressive," says IBM Chief Executive Samuel J. Palmisano. In Brazil, where IBM's revenues just zoomed past $1 billion, Big Blue plans on hiring 2,000 people and spending an additional $100 million on market development.

A Rival in Every Port

For tech's giants, this is the equivalent of America's basketball stars playing Argentina in the Olympics under international rules. The leaders are just as vulnerable to upset because they're facing companies that grew up in these markets and know them intimately. Just look to China, where homegrown Lenovo Group Ltd. has fought off Dell and other invaders to remain the top PC player. The Western powers may be accustomed to dominating in the developed world, but as the competition shifts to new terrain, their lock on the future is far from secure. They face stiff challenges from service companies in India, online gaming pioneers in Korea, security outfits in Eastern Europe, and network gearmakers in China. Even mighty Microsoft is vulnerable. Open-source software, with growing support in developing countries, could stunt its growth.

How the Tech Industry Is Changing

The rapid growth of sales in developing countries is having a profound impact on the tech industry. Companies must reimagine how they design products and do business.

Design

Products have to be simpler and more durable. TVS Electronics, an Indian printer maker, is producing devices for India's 1.2 million small shops. They're an all-in-one computer, cash register, and inventory-management system. They can be operated with icons, because many clerks are illiterate. And they tolerate dust and heat.

Innovation

Companies have to innovate for the peculiarities of emerging markets. Electricity often is unavailable or unreliable. That prompted Hewlett-Packard to design a small solar panel to charge digital printers for itinerant photographers in India. In South Africa, HP is working with a solar fabric that's cheaper and less fragile.

Pricing

There's pressure on prices, so some companies are using pay-as-you-go schemes. Poland needed to modernize its drivers' licensing system but couldn't afford it. So Hewlett-Packard agreed to install Poland's new computer system in exchange for a cut of the fees drivers pay each time they get a new license or renew an old one.

Business Development

The old strategies may not work anymore, so companies are trying new ones. IBM figures it can do well in China by supplying technology to local companies. Example: It developed a low-cost, $12 microprocessor and a simple network computer for China's Culturecom, which is selling computers and Net-access services in the country's rural backwaters.

Competition

Companies like Cisco, Dell, and Microsoft dominate in the developed world. But now a host of new challengers are using their low costs and intimate knowledge of local markets to give the giants trouble. Chinese networking upstart Huawei can charge 50% less for gear than Cisco, and is starting to make inroads worldwide.

The closest historical precedent for what's happening now is the PC revolution of the late 1970s and early 1980s. Before the PC, computers were the province of technical druids in giant corporations and government offices. Then with Apple Computer Inc.'s Macintosh and IBM's PC, the tech industry underwent a huge market-expanding shift. Computers began to show up on the desktops of everyone from schoolchildren to small-business owners. The result was seismic change. Microsoft, Intel, and Dell became the new champions, while dinosaurs like Digital Equipment lumbered off to the tar pits. Now, with rapid diffusion of technology into emerging economies, the industry is again reaching a gigantic new audience. And a new generation of companies will try to kick their elders in the teeth.

Expect a power shift from West to East. That's because the PC-centric era, dominated by U.S. companies, is fast giving way to the wireless age. The trend is most apparent in Asia, where cell phones with Net access are the computing gizmo of choice. While 30 million PCs are expected to be sold there this year, that pales in comparison to the 200 million cell phones capable of handling e-mail and Web surfing that researcher Yankee Group projects. That gives an advantage to Korea's Samsung Group and LG, which make cell phones as well as PCs. In the past four years they've come from nowhere to become the No. 3 and No. 6 mobile-phone makers in the world. "In the 20th century the torch came across the Atlantic from Europe to America. Now the torch is crossing the Pacific," says Geoffrey A. Moore, managing director at tech consultancy TCG Advisors LLC.

The challenges of succeeding in emerging markets are forcing the Western powers to come up with bold new strategies.

They're under pressure to innovate like crazy, pioneer new ways of doing business, and outmaneuver their feisty new competitors. "The pattern in the past was to sell the same stuff to the same kind of customers. But that won't work, and it has to change," says C.K. Prahalad, business professor at the University of Michigan Business School and author of *The Fortune at the Bottom of the Pyramid*, a book about commerce in the developing world. "What's required is a fundamental rethinking of how to design products and make money."

The result is an outpouring of innovation, from both the old guard and the up-and-comers, that could rival that of the PC era. The Indian photographer's setup is just the start. New innovations designed for the developing world range from the Simputer, a durable handheld being sold in India, to e-Town, a package of all of the products and services rural Chinese towns need to provide Net access for their residents. And who would have thought up a cell phone designed for the world's 1.4 billion Muslims? Nobody—until now. Tiny Dubai-based Ilkone Mobile Telecommunication has just started selling a phone that not only comes loaded with the Koran but also alerts people at prayer times and, with the help of a compass, points them toward Mecca.

BRAZIL
IBM's revenues here recently sailed past $1 billion. No wonder it has plans to hire 2,000 people and spend big bucks here.

Developing countries require new business strategies as well as new products. Most families in rural China or India can't afford a PC. In many instances, a handful of computers have to be shared by a whole village to be economically feasible. A new class of businesses—tech kiosk operators—is emerging to provide computing as a service. With cash often in short supply, pay-as-you-go programs are not only boosting cell-phone usage but are catching on with computers and Web access as well.

When these technologies cycle back into the mature markets, it could change everything from pricing to product design. To succeed in the developing world, devices and software have to be better in many ways: cheaper, easier to use, extra-durable, more compact—and still packed with powerful features. The resulting improvements will ultimately benefit everybody from New Delhi to New York. One possibility: HP is testing a solar fabric with itinerant photographers in South Africa that costs 80% less than the traditional solar panels that they use in India and won't crack. If this works out, people around the world could recharge their portable electronics by dropping them into carrying cases made of the material.

Creating Consumers

For tech's powerhouses, this shift to emerging markets cuts both ways. They have a chance to round up many new customers, but only if they're smarter than their new competitors. They'll have to invest substantial sums of money up front. Yet, for many products, prices will of necessity be very low. While the first billion customers produced an industry with more than $1 trillion in annual revenues, sales for the second billion won't be anything close to that. And ultimately, lower prices in the emerging markets will put pressure on prices everywhere. You could end up with an industry that, while it delivers a lot of value to a lot of people, it won't be able sustain the revenue growth rates or the profit margins of its glorious past.

On the brighter side, tech's spread into emerging markets could have a snowball effect on the world economy and the tech industry's fortunes. Investments in technology stoke national economies—boosting productivity, gross domestic product, and consumption of all sorts of products, including more technology. And as computer-factory workers in China and software programmers in India increase their incomes, they become consumers. A.T. Kearney figures that the number of people with the equivalent of $10,000 in annual income will double, to 2 billion, by 2015—and 900 million of those newcomers to the consumer class will be in emerging markets. "If you have a middle class that provides a sufficient market for consumer goods, you have the basis for rapid industrial expansion and jobs for poor people," says Sarbuland Khan, head of the information-technology task force at the U.N. "It becomes a virtuous cycle rather than a vicious cycle."

Strategic Rethinking

Cintia Arantes and Eduardo Severino de Santana are the embodiment of that hope. The Brazilians, both 22, grew up poor in Recife, on the country's northeastern coast. But both are climbing the social ladder thanks to a local program that trains disadvantaged Brazilian youths in computer skills. De Santana, who had been unemployed last year, quickly turned one computer course into a job helping to manage the tech facilities at a national law firm.

RUSSIA
The nation's large companies are beginning to see the point of investing in information technology.

Arantes' trajectory could take her even higher. Her laborer father doesn't have steady work, so she helps support the family of six by working nights at a phone company call center. Thanks to a tip from a teacher at a school where she was an administrative assistant, she started taking computer courses last year. Now she's an intern at a local software company in the mornings, takes courses in the afternoon, and hopes to enter a university computer engineering program next year. Her goal: to become a programmer. "I'll keep on battling until I get there," she vows. In the meantime, she's trying to save up the $700 or so it would cost to buy a PC.

In many cases, tech companies will only succeed in emerging markets if they're willing to ditch the strategies that made them successful in the developed world. Take Dell. In 2000 it introduced a consumer PC in China, called SmartPC, that was different from any it had sold before. It came preconfigured rather than built to order, and it was manufactured not by Dell but by Taiwanese companies. At less than $600, the SmartPC has helped Dell become the top foreign supplier in China. Its share of the PC market there rose from less than 1% in 1998 to 7.4% today.

Still, Dell is anything but the dominant force in China that it is in the U.S. A key reason is that Dell's practice of selling direct to customers, over the Net or the phone, doesn't work very well in the Middle Kingdom. Chinese typically want to lay their hands on computers before they buy them. That means the best way to reach them is via vast retailing operations—the strength of local players Lenovo and Founder Electronics, which both rank ahead of Dell with market shares of 25.7% and 11.3%, respectively, according to IDC. Dell set up kiosks to demonstrate its SmartPC and other products. But in August, the company withdrew from the consumer market in the face of competitors selling stripped-down PCs for as little as $362. "In the fastest-growing large market in the world, the local PC makers are winning," says Philippe de Marcillac, a senior vice-president at IDC.

Cultural Customization

There's no easy formula for selling in emerging markets. Some corporate or government customers in Russia and Brazil are as big as any in the U.S., and their needs are just as sophisticated. Russian Railways, with 1.2 million employees, spent $2 billion over the last three years building a modern data communications system. "We're very proud," says Anna Belova, deputy minister of the railway. "We have a huge scale of tasks, and we find creative solutions." Now other giant Russian enterprises see it as a role model and are boosting their tech purchases, too.

To target innovations that will resonate in these markets, companies are conducting in-depth studies of peoples' needs. Intel, for instance, has a team of 10 ethnographers traveling the world to find out how to redesign existing products or come up with new ones that fit different cultures or demographic groups. One of its ethnographers, Genevieve Bell, visited 100 homes in Asia over the past three years and noticed that many Chinese families were reluctant to buy PCs, even if they could afford them. Parents were concerned that their children would listen to pop music or surf the Web, distracting them from school work.

Intel turned that insight into a product. At its User-Centered Design Group in Hillsboro, Ore., industrial designers and other specialists created "personas" of typical Chinese families and pasted pictures that Bell had taken of Chinese households on their walls. They even built sample Chinese kitchens—the room where a computer is most often used. The result: Late this year, Intel expects a leading Chinese PC maker to start selling the China Home Learning PC. It comes with four education applications and a physical lock and key that allows parents to prevent their kids from goofing off when they should be studying.

Many products designed for consumers and small businesses in emerging markets will have to fit some demanding specifications: They need to be simple to use and capable of operating in harsh environments. A handful of products have already come out with these factors in mind—and many more are on the way. India's TVS Electronics Ltd., for instance, is selling a new kind of all-in-one business machine called Sprint designed especially for that country's 1.2 million small shopkeepers. It's part cash register and part computer, designed to tolerate heat, dust, and power outages. The cost: just $180 for the smallest of three models.

Pricing is often the make-or-break factor. In rural South Africa, where HP has set up a pilot program similar to the one in India for developing technologies for poor people, the average person makes less than $1 a day. Clearly, not too many can afford to buy their own personal computers. HP's solution? The 441 PC (as in four users for one computer). It's a machine set up in a school or library that connects to four keyboards and four screens, so multiple people can get on the Net or send e-mail at the same time.

Some of the best ideas for the developing world have the potential for catching on everywhere—including the U.S. It's already starting to happen. Kishore Kumar first developed a simple PC-based remote health-monitoring system for distant villages in his native India. Now his company, TeleVital Inc. of Milpitas, Calif., is marketing the technology in the States. The first U.S. customer, Battle Mountain General Hospital in Battle Mountain, Nev., couldn't afford patient-monitoring equipment—or people to operate it. Now it's hooking up with a hospital 100 miles away to track its patients. Says Battle Mountain administrator Peggy Lindsey: "We in rural America can really use equipment like this."

When tech companies modify their existing products for emerging markets, they can end up with improvements that have a broader impact. That's what happened at Nokia Corp. when it set out to reduce the costs of setting up and operating wireless telephone networks. One improvement, called Smart Radio technology, can cut in half the number of signal-transmission sites operators need. Wrap that and other new technologies together, and operators can build networks for up to 50% less than before. Nokia has been rolling out these innovations from Thailand to Peru. DTAC, the No. 2 Thai cellular operator, is installing the new gear around Bangkok. "If this works, we can use this concept to penetrate into much more remote areas up-country," says Sigve Brekke, the company's co-CEO.

Dell already has translated emerging-market innovations into successes in its traditional markets. After SmartPC took off in China, Dell in 2001 introduced a version for the U.S., for the first time going after bargain hunters. A year later, Dell absorbed the SmartPC into its mainstream consumer product line as sales took off. "We try to take some of the best ideas we have seen that are happening in local environments and make it a global product," says Dell Senior Vice-President William J. Amelio.

Dell, Nokia, and other Western giants need all of the innovations they can muster, especially as the field of competition shifts to emerging markets, and they're confronted by a stampede of aggressive challengers. Chinese communications-equipment maker Huawei is giving Westerners fits in its home market, where it has captured a 16% share in the crucial router business, second only to mighty Cisco, according to IDC. And thanks to prices up to 50% lower than rivals', Huawei is expanding everywhere from Russia to Brazil. It already ranks No. 2 worldwide in broadband networking gear, says market researcher RHK. "Huawei is being very aggressive," says Cicero Olivieri, director of engineering and planning for GVT, a large telecom company in Brazil.

Momentum Shift

The most serious challenge lies ahead. Huawei is pouring money into Internet Protocol version 6, or IPv6, the standard for the next-generation of the Internet that will have more security, speed, and capacity. China is planning to adopt IPv6 more rapidly than any other country in the world. And if Huawei's close ties to the Chinese government help it become the early leader in the technology, it could get the jump on rivals such as Cisco, Alcatel, and Lucent. "The Ciscos of the world will have to change their business models to compete—and try to out-innovate these small, nimble companies," says William Nuti, a former Cisco senior vice-president and now CEO of Symbol Technologies.

Throughout the developing world, new players are popping up like obstacles in a *Super Mario Brothers* game. Take the online game business itself. Upstart NCsoft has taken advantage of Korea's lead in broadband penetration to build the world's largest online game business, with more than 5 million monthly subscriptions. NCsoft CEO Kim Tack Jin is now expanding in Taiwan, China, Japan, and the U.S.—where 228,000 copies of its *City of Heroes* game were sold in the first three months after

Up-and-Comers

With the tech action in emerging markets, local players have a chance to become players on the world stage. Here are some bright prospects:

	Business	Global Expansion
NCSOFT	The world's No. 1 seller of online PC games, with more than 5 million monthly subscribers. The South Korean company is predicting revenue growth of 55% this year, to $221 million, and 70% growth outside its home market.	After taking off in Korea, NCsoft is expanding in Taiwan, China, Japan, and the U.S. China and Japan present the most growth opportunity. In the U.S., its *City of Heroes* was an instant hit when it launched in April.
I-FLEX SOLUTIONS	The Indian company, which offers banking software and services, claims the world's top software suite for managing consumer, corporate, Internet, and investment banking. In a slow-growth worldwide enterprise software industry, revenues grew 26% last quarter.	I-flex sells in 108 countries and just inked a $10 million deal with Banco Du Chile, the largest commercial bank in the country. Prospects are bright: i-flex's Internet-based systems and low-cost Indian programming give it a huge advantage.
TCL MOBILE	A subsidiary of electronics conglomerate TCL Corp., it's one of the top two Chinese handset makers, specializing in moderately priced phones. It recently formed a joint venture with Alcatel to expand into higher-end products.	It's starting to expand into developing markets in Asia, Africa, and the former Soviet Union. Though TCL faces tough competition, its solid position in the No. 1 cellular market gives it a decent chance at emerging as a strong global player.
KASPERSKY LABS	Anti-virus software. Founded by Eugene Kaspersky, one of the world's leading experts on computer security, the Russian company's products protect computers against viruses, hackers, and spam. Sales are forecast to grow 50% this year.	Kaspersky is expanding in Europe, the U.S., China, and Japan, targeting consumers and small businesses. With viruses rampant, Kaspersky is well placed to tap growing demand for security products by capitalizing on Russia's renowned programming skills.

its April release, according to market researcher NPD Group. The key to NCsoft's success: It has come up with a combo of fantasy and action gaming that's a hit with players.

Even mighty Microsoft is vulnerable to the competitive threats. Linux is emerging as a viable alternative to its Windows in developing markets and could cut into its market share. China, Japan, and Korea are collaborating on a version of the free open-source software package. A number of governments are considering policies that favor open-source software packages, and one, Israel, has already decided to stop using Microsoft's products. While that affects only tens of thousands of government workers, if other countries take the same path, millions of their employees could end up using open-source software, rather than Windows and Office.

Microsoft doesn't have an answer—at least not yet. In October the company, which declined to comment for this story, will begin to sell a cheaper Windows in Thailand, Indonesia, and Malaysia in an effort to beat back the open-source threat. But it so far refuses to follow suit in China—where it has had four general managers in six years. "Business as usual won't

work there. They have to find new ways to do things," warns Jack Gao, who ran Microsoft China from 1999 to 2003 and now heads up software maker Autodesk's China operations.

It may turn out that patience is the most important attribute for tech companies trying to get things going in emerging markets. IBM, after all, has been in Brazil for 87 years. Hewlett-Packard has spent three years establishing pilot programs in India and South Africa and, finally, they're starting to yield products and to improve the lives of the locals. Take Neelamma, the itinerant photographer. She has become a star in the two-room house with a dirt floor that she and her stonecutter husband, Krishnamurthy, share with his parents and brother. What are Neelamma's dreams? "I want to buy a television and a ceiling fan. And I want to build a small photo studio in my home," she says. One young woman's life and aspirations have been changed by the arrival of technology. Another 1 billion new consumers may not be too far behind.

—With Manjeet Kripalani, in Bombay; Bruce Einhorn, in Hong Kong and Andy Reinhardt in Paris, and bureau reports.

The Great Wal-Mart of China

For the world's biggest company, the key to growth lies in the world's biggest country.

Clay Chandler

"This way, ladies! Follow me!" It's two weeks before the opening of Wal-Mart's first supercenter in Chongqing, and Baker Jiang, Wal-Mart's manager for western China, has invited a delegation of women on a tour. A small army of red-shirted associates greets the ladies at the door with a rousing Wal-Mart cheer. Inside, Jiang whisks the group around shelves piled with toys, sporting goods, and household appliances, past the new film-processing machines, and down the escalator to the produce department, butcher shop, and bakery where, donning mask and hairnet, he beckons visitors to inspect for cleanliness. Wal-Mart, he says, "will never use tap water to make your bread." By tour's end, it is the women who are cheering. "This blouse is so cheap," says one. "Can I buy it now?" Another gives Jiang a coquettish nudge. "We've waited so many years for this. What took you so long?"

Wal-Mart doesn't get that kind of reception in many parts of the U.S. these days. In its home market the giant retailer is under siege, blamed for evils from squeezing suppliers and crushing the corner grocer to busting unions and driving down wages. But good luck convincing Chinese consumers that the arrival of a supercenter should be cause for public outcry. In Chongqing, a metropolis of 31 million where shopping options have long been limited to dank, state-run stores with surly clerks or open-air markets where the tomatoes may or may not be as fresh as the garbage, the locals say, "Bring it on!"

"So what if they take business from other shopkeepers?" says 51-year-old Sheng Xuehua. "They should, if they can do a better job." Out on the street, construction worker Li Daping agrees. "We can't wait for Wal-Mart to open. We're practically counting the days."

Opening day, when it arrives June 30, brings pandemonium. There's a giddy rush when doors swing wide at 7:30 A.M. Thousands of shoppers scamper from aisle to aisle, heaping carts with spinach, cooking oil, whatever they can grasp. A truckload of roasted ducks sells out in minutes. By 8 A.M. the queue for rotisserie chicken at 85 cents a bird is 50 people long. Shoppers snatch five-kilogram sacks of rice as fast as employees can unload them. At tanks near the entrance, housewives lunge at live grass fish as long as their arms. At 9:30, a cadre of local officials joins Wal-Mart's Asia CEO, Joe Hatfield, for a ceremony on the public square outside. There's a brass band, fire-breathing Sichuan opera dancers, and a traditional lion dance. Hatfield paints the eye of a lion's head to bring good luck. But the gesture seems superfluous: Inside, each of the store's 75 checkout lanes is backed up 15 customers deep. By closing time at 10 P.M., 120,000 customers have trooped through the doors. But there is little time to savor success. Wal-Mart opens its next supercenter in Shanghai in less than a month. In the world's most populous market, the world's biggest retailer is playing catch-up.

Wal-Mart plans to roll out 15 new stores in China this year, including its first supercenters in Beijing and Shanghai, and it has enticed analysts with talk of increasing floor space by as much as 50% a year. Company executives won't elaborate on expansion plans, but Hatfield, a chain-smoking 30-year Wal-Mart veteran who has run the China operation since 1995, says his orders from Bentonville, Ark., are clear. At last year's annual meeting, held in Shenzhen, members of Wal-Mart's board admonished him to "get a lot more aggressive."

And no wonder. Wal-Mart can't sustain the astronomical U.S. growth rates of the past decade forever. Sooner rather than later, the company will need help from overseas. But the Beast of Bentonville has yet to emerge as a dominant player in any of the foreign markets that account for about 20% of its global sales. In Germany it is still struggling to stanch losses at the two retailers it acquired in the 1990s. In Japan it has yet to articulate a clear strategy for its 38% stake in the troubled Seiyu chain. The company has had better luck in emerging economies, such as Mexico, where there are fewer entrenched incumbents. But executives have long viewed China, with its vast population and booming economy, as their best bet for long-term global growth. In an interview with FORTUNE last year, former Wal-Mart CEO David Glass proclaimed China "the one place in the world where you could replicate Wal-Mart's success in the U.S."

It was slow going at first. The company sent an advance team of executives to China in 1994 and, two years later, opened the first Wal-Mart supercenter in Shenzhen, the gritty boomtown across the border from Hong Kong. Before the first store opened, an alliance with a Thai supermarket chain collapsed, forcing Wal-Mart to surrender planned developments in Shanghai and Shenyang. Beijing checked Wal-Mart's expansion with regulations, limiting foreign retailers to a handful of large cities and obliging them to offer at least 35% of each store to local partners. The Sam's Club format, with its emphasis on membership fees and high-volume sales, left Chinese customers cold. By the end of last year, Wal-Mart could boast just 43 stores in China—a far cry from the 3,719 it operates in the U.S. The company doesn't disclose financial results for China. But China's chamber of commerce reported in its annual retail ranking that Wal-Mart grossed $916 million last year—less than 2% of the company's international sales, and a tiny sliver of its $288 billion total revenue.

Those numbers have nowhere to go but up. The demographics are dazzling: 100 cities with populations of more than a million; 150 million urban families with annual incomes of more than $10,000 within the next ten years; more than $6 trillion in total retail spending this year, and growing at a 15% annual clip. And unlike India, which forbids foreign direct investment in the retail sector, China is opening its doors to outside players. The crucial turning point came last December, when Beijing, in keeping with terms of its admission to the World Trade Organization, granted foreign retailers permission to invest independently in any city they choose.

But many hurdles remain. Hatfield says his biggest challenge is finding qualified managers. Each supercenter, which mixes produce and general merchandise, requires hiring and training 500 employees. Locating sites is just as tricky. In most Chinese cities, municipal governments control prime real estate, giving an edge to state-owned retailers. And then there's the competition. In America, Wal-Mart may be the 800-pound gorilla, but in China, it's still a chimp, jostling with Chinese conglomerates such as the state-run Shanghai Brilliance group, as well as with foreign rivals such as France's Carrefour. Wang Zongnan, president of Brilliance, China's largest retailer with 3,300 stores and sales of $8.1 billion, says he doesn't lose much sleep worrying about Wal-Mart. "Local retailers have the advantage in all large economies," he says. "I see no reason to doubt that will be the case in China too."

Wal-Mart no longer sells snake, but the fare is pretty exotic. *Spicy chicken feet* and stinky tofu are perennial favorites.

Wal-Mart hopes to prove that thinking wrong. By opening in Chongqing, on the upper reaches of the Yangtze River, it is establishing a beachhead for expansion well beyond China's densely populated eastern seaboard. And to get it right, Hatfield and his lieutenants pulled out all the stops, working with development partners from Shenzhen and Singapore to secure a prime location at Nine Dragon Plaza, a public square across from the municipal zoo.

The store is surrounded by residential developments and lies at the terminus of a new light-rail line. Store manager Sunny Han estimates that more than a million people live within a four-mile radius. But that same circle includes three stores operated by New Century, a retail group owned by the local government, as well as a lively street market and a gleaming new Carrefour as big as Wal-Mart. To lure customers, Wal-Mart will open an hour and a half earlier and close later, and it will deploy a fleet of free shuttle buses to ferry residents to the store.

At the open-air market on nearby Go Forward Street, peddlers hawking long beans and acorn squash were bracing for the worst a few weeks before the opening. "I'll definitely switch to Wal-Mart," said Liu Bijuan, a stocky housewife picking through baskets of eggplants and cucumbers. In a stall nearby, a butcher scratched himself lazily as flies swarmed over slabs of beef. But at the Carrefour up the road, it was a different story. The space is vast and well stocked. Shoppers thronged the food counter, and prices for many items were comparable to those in Wal-Mart stores.

Carrefour came to China a year after Wal-Mart but has expanded more rapidly. The French retailer's China CEO, Jean Luc Chereau, credits his success to the 12 years he spent building Carrefour's business in Taiwan. "It was in Taiwan that we discovered Chinese culture," he says. "By the time I moved to Shanghai in 1999, I was well prepared." But Carrefour has also demonstrated superior operating savvy and a greater tolerance for risk. By forging alliances with local governments, it circumvented many of Beijing's restrictions, fashioning a network of 60 hypermarkets in 25 cities, with sales last year of nearly $2 billion. This year China's largest foreign retailer vows to match Wal-Mart's China expansion store for store.

Still, it's early days, and Wal-Mart has deep pockets. More important, perhaps, is that Hatfield and his team have become adept at replicating Wal-Mart's corporate culture and figuring out what Chinese consumers want. Headquarters for Wal-Mart's retail operation—a dingy warren tucked behind the first supercenter in Shenzhen—reflect the company's reputation for pinching pennies. But Hatfield spends little time there. Most days you'll find him roaming Wal-Mart stores, scouting the competition, or foraging for products in urban street markets. "I'm a big believer in Sam's philosophy that when it comes to good ideas, you should steal shamelessly," he says. "You have to get out there and ask, 'What are our competitors doing that we're not?' You have to be hungry for new knowledge every day."

Hatfield's pursuit of local knowledge has produced surprising differences in the look and feel of Wal-Mart's stores in China. Chinese customers tend to do their shopping on foot, not by car. They have smaller apartments and smaller refrigerators, so they buy in smaller quantities and are accustomed to going to market every one or two days. So Wal-Mart supercenters in China devote lots of floor space to food. Perishable products get pride of place and come in a mind-boggling assortment of shapes, colors, and flavors. Except for the prices and the smiley faces, a U.S. customer venturing into the produce department at a Chinese Wal-Mart might think he had stumbled into a Whole Foods store in San Francisco.

"I'm a believer in Sam's philosophy that when it comes to good ideas, you should *steal shamelessly,"* Hatfield says.

Wal-Mart's managers have learned a lot about Chinese customers. One early discovery: They want to put their hands on the merchandise, shucking each corncob before putting it in their basket, or demanding that associates not only take a fitted sheet out of the plastic but demonstrate it on an actual bed. Chinese shoppers also have a thing for clamor. Often managers can goose sales simply by dispatching associates to restack an item noisily in the middle of the floor. And at the Chongqing opening, bottles of red wine moved briskly when bundled with free cans of Sprite. (In China they like their cabernet carbonated.)

The fare can get a lot more exotic than that. Since the SARS epidemic two years ago, Wal-Mart's China stores have stopped slaughtering poultry on the premises and no longer offer rabbits or snakes. But spicy chicken feet and stinky tofu are perennial favorites. In Chongqing, those who come too late to catch a grass fish can choose from a selection of lobsters, turtles, and live bullfrogs the size of soccer balls. At most supercenters, the bestselling items are prepared lunches served in Styrofoam containers: two meats, two vegetables, rice, and a cup of hot soup, freshly prepared onsite—all for less than $1. A typical supercenter sells more than 1,000 a day. Hatfield says the sight of truck and taxi drivers retching on the side of the road helped convince him that there was an opportunity for Wal-Mart to boost midday store traffic by luring customers from local street vendors.

Another innovation is what Wal-Mart calls "retail-tainment." Stores provide space for local school groups to perform, and they organize daily activities for the elderly. Residents are welcome to wander in and freeload on air conditioning. It's savvy marketing, of course. But it may have long-term benefit: If Wal-Mart can succeed in weaving itself into the fabric of urban communities, it may head off the image problems that have arisen in other markets.

Unlike the merchandise, Wal-Mart's management practices have required little tinkering for China. If anything, the red shirts, mass cheering, incessant pep rallies, and veneration of a deceased founder seem characteristics far better suited to the People's Republic than the American South. Two hours of buttonholing Chongqing associates as they left work failed to identify anyone who would confess to feeling oppressed. What's striking about all this regimentation, though, is that it's so focused on answering the wants of individuals. At times, Baker and Sunny, with their folksy PR tours and community-outreach projects, seem like old-time Boston ward heelers.

Another constant is the obsession with *tian tian ping jia*—everyday low prices. Hatfield, darting around a supercenter in Shenzhen, ticks off item after item: "Men's dress slacks? Eight bucks—and that's including alterations. Those dress shoes? $4.80. They were three times that two years ago." Wal-Mart lured customers to the Chongqing opening by advertising DVD players for $23.97 and in-line skates for $11.93. Often products are displayed with signs declaring the value of the discount wrested from suppliers by Wal-Mart buyers.

Although Wal-Mart's shelves bristle with U.S. consumer brands—from Crest toothpaste and Clairol shampoos to Oreos and Gatorade—almost everything is made in China. And, as in the U.S., suppliers have trouble sorting out whether Wal-Mart's embrace is a bear hug or a death grip. Consider Dong Yongjian, the 33-year-old proprietor of a spicy-chicken-feet factory an hour's drive from the Chongqing store. Wal-Mart buyers stumbled on Dong's product four years ago at a rival retailer in Shenzhen. They sent a team of auditors to inspect his factory and began stocking his chicken feet in stores. Dong's chicken-feet recipe—which he guards as zealously as Colonel Sanders did his "secret blend of 11 herbs and spices"—was an immediate hit. Wal-Mart has become Dong's top customer. But while sales are booming, profits aren't. "They want the lowest prices I can possibly give them," says Dong. "I see this is a long-run relationship, so I'm doing my best to hold down costs." At the headquarters of Yunan Red Wine, a salesman says that to win Wal-Mart's business his company had to knock prices down 15%, undermining its pricing power with other customers.

If the associates on the sales battlefront in Chongqing represent one face of Wal-Mart's operation in China, suppliers waiting in the reception area of Wal-Mart's global procurement headquarters in Shenzhen are another. The room, with a poster of Sam Walton on one wall and Wal-Mart's latest share price on another, is an exporters' purgatory. Supplicants take a number and wait for an audience with Wal-Mart buyers or quality inspectors. Those whose products are deemed worthy of Wal-Mart's U.S. customers can see sales rocket almost overnight. Many come bearing items of whimsy—dancing Christmas trees, Jar Jar Binks action figures, Nerf dart sets. But this is a tense place. On a recent afternoon, there was no mirth in the eyes of Li Xiaolong as he stepped into a tiny conference room, strapped on the target-shaped vest manufactured by his Dongguan employer, and waited for a Wal-Mart buyer to fire Nerf darts into his chest. Last year Wal-Mart spent $18 billion on merchandise from China-based suppliers, most of it toys, footwear, Christmas decorations, and sporting equipment, accounting for 3% of China's total exports. If Wal-Mart were a country, it would be China's sixth-largest export market.

Wal-Mart buys only about 10% of what it sells in U.S. stores from suppliers in China. But at a March meeting for investment analysts in Shenzhen, company executives spoke of raising China purchases significantly—to perhaps double the current amount—over the next five years. Critics say that pits American workers against Chinese, who earn $5 a day. Andrew Tsuei, head of Wal-Mart's overseas procurement office, offers no apologies. "My job is to find the best value for our customers while sourcing in an ethical way," he says. "China gives us competitive products and meets our quality and ethical standards. There's no reason for us not to buy here."

Wal-Mart executives say they hold suppliers to U.S. standards for business ethics as well as product quality, dispatching hundreds of auditors to monitor working conditions, compensation, and safety records—though Tsuei acknowledges that gauging compliance is a challenge. In China, as in the U.S., Wal-Mart has resisted calls for labor unions. Chinese associates, however, aren't up in arms. That's because Chinese unions are creatures of the state, run to collect dues for the party and keep tabs on workers, not represent them. In November, after months of public sniping by the government-controlled All China Trade Federation, Beijing and Bentonville reached a compromise. Wal-Mart pledged to accept a union should workers formally request one. Thus far they have not.

The red shirts and *mass cheering* seem better suited to the People's Republic than the American South.

Given the scope of Wal-Mart's ambitions in China and the enthusiasm of Chinese shoppers at recent store openings, Bentonville's stated expansion plan looks way too timid. Merrill Lynch analyst Daniel Barry calculates that even if Wal-Mart adds stores at a rate faster than this year's pace, its China retail network will include no more than 230 stores by 2009. That's fewer than the number of stores Wal-Mart will add in the U.S. this year.

Maybe Wal-Mart is just playing its China cards close to the vest. In the U.S., the company's pattern has always been to keep its head down and its mouth shut—until it has piled up all the chips. Wal-Mart International spokesman Elizabeth Keck says that, although Wal-Mart doesn't make projections more than a year out, "it is not correct to assume that we only plan to open 15 new stores a year in China." She also hints at the possibility of growth through acquisition. But her boss, Wal-Mart's International CEO, John Menzer, isn't tipping his hand. "We'll take one store at a time," he told reporters in Beijing this spring.

Back in Chongqing, Joe Hatfield has few doubts about the company's success. Walking into the store after the opening ceremony, he is almost run over by a couple wheeling two large shopping carts piled high with sacks of rice. Does it worry him that on opening day customers have loaded up so heavily they won't need to return to the store for months? "Nah," he laughs, waving to the pair. "Those two'll be back tomorrow. They gotta buy vegetables."

Reporter associates Susan M. Kaufman; Joan Levinstein and Wang Ting

Selling to the Poor

Searching for new customers eager to buy your products? Forget Tokyo's schoolgirls and Milan's fashionistas. Instead, try the world's 4 billion poor people, the largest untapped consumer market on Earth. To reach them, CEOs must shed old concepts of marketing, distribution, and research. Getting it right can both generate big profits and help end economic isolation throughout the developing world.

ALLEN L. HAMMOND AND C.K. PRAHALAD

When the Indian industrial and technology conglomerate ITC started building a network of Internet-connected computers called "e-Choupals" in farming villages in India's rural state of Madhya Pradesh in 2001, soy farmers were suddenly able to check fair market prices for their crops. Some farmers began tracking soy futures on the Chicago Board of Trade, and soon most of them were bypassing local auction markets and selling their crops directly to ITC for about $6 more per ton than they previously received. The same ITC network enables farmers to buy seeds, fertilizers, and other materials directly, at considerable savings, as well as to purchase formerly unavailable soil-testing services. Today, the growing e-Choupal network reaches 1.8 million farmers, and ITC is receiving demands from rural farmers for new products and services—the beginnings of consumer market power at the poorest level of Indian society.

The ITC network is one example of how access to information can increase productivity and raise incomes. It also reveals what happens when large businesses stop regarding the world's 4 billion poor people as victims and start eyeing them as consumers. For decades, corporate executives at the world's largest companies—and their counterparts running wealthy governments—have thought of poor people as powerless and desperately in need of handouts. But turning the poor into customers and consumers is a far more effective way of reducing poverty.

Why hasn't the business world caught on? The explanations are well known: Infrastructure in the developing world is often poor or nonexistent, creating the need for substantial upfront investment. Illiteracy tends to be high, requiring nontraditional marketing approaches. Tribal, racial, and religious tensions, as well as rampant crime, complicate hiring and business operations. Governments—especially local and provincial authorities—often do not function effectively or transparently. Corruption is widespread.

Yet many multinational companies already overcome such problems to serve middle-class customers in developing countries. The fundamental barriers to serving poor customers in low-income nations exist within companies and governments in rich nations, where leaders have uncritically accepted the myth that the poor have no money. In reality, low-income households collectively possess most of the buying power in many developing countries, including such emerging economies as China and India. If businesses ignore the bottom of the economic pyramid, they miss most of the market. Another myth is that the poor resist new products and services, when in truth poor consumers are rarely offered products designed for their lifestyles and circumstances, leaving them unable to interact with the global economy. Perhaps the greatest misperception of all is that selling to the poor is not profitable or, worse yet, exploitative. Selling to the world's poorest people can be very lucrative and a key source of growth for global companies, even while this interaction benefits and empowers poor consumers.

The market for goods and services among the world's poor—families with an annual household income of less than $6,000—is enormous. The 18 largest emerging and transition countries include 680 million such households, with a total annual income of $1.7 trillion—roughly equal to Germany's annual gross domestic product. Brazil's poorest citizens comprise nearly 25 million households with a total annual income of $73 billion. India has 171 million poor households with a combined $378 billion in income. China's poor residents account for 286 million households with a combined annual income of $691 billion. Surveys show that poor households spend most of their income on housing, food, healthcare, education, finance charges, communications, and consumer goods. Multinational corporations have largely failed to tap this market, even though the rewards for doing so could be substantial.

Fortune Sellers

Developing nations offer multinational corporations a vast, untapped market. But consumers, even poor ones, often associate particular brands with unsavory business practices. Increasingly, corporations seek moral and ethical legitimacy—and try to avoid charges of exploitation—when marketing their goods and services to the poor. "Customers are searching for organizations that they can trust," explains Raoul Pinnell, vice president of global brands and communications at Shell International.

Multilateral initiatives aimed at improving corporate behavior and boosting consumer acceptance, such as the United Nations Global Compact or the Caux Round Table's Principles for Business, have met with mixed results. Alternatively, some corporations that work in poor markets are undertaking innovative and transparent self-regulation projects, sometimes with assistance from governments in the developing world. In 1993, when Avon sent an army of direct-selling cosmetics merchants paddling up Amazon tributaries to sell perfumes and makeup to miners and prostitutes, Avon ladies answered only to themselves. Today, direct sellers arriving to "Avon-gelize" remote Indian villages are subject to sanctioning by an Indian judge—effectively a corporate ombudsman—if they break a code of ethics formulated by the Indian Direct Selling Association. (The code aims to weed out "fraudulent elements" among direct sellers and prevent pyramid schemes.) "It's protection for the company, the consumer, and the sales force," says David Gosling, Avon India's managing director.

Similarly, the Switzerland-based Nestlé Group, a longtime target of human rights advocates for their marketing of baby formula over mother's milk in poor countries, appointed an ombudsman in 2002 to expose any unethical promotional activities. Coca-Cola India is attempting to, in their words, regain public trust and credibility after allegations of pesticide contamination incited angry consumers in Bombay to smash thousands of Coke bottles in 2003. The company recently formed an advisory board—led by former Indian Cabinet Secretary Naresh Chandra—that will oversee Coca-Cola's practices in India. The company also appointed former chief justice of the Indian Supreme Court B.N. Kirpal to lead an advisory body called the India Environment Council, which will guide Coca-Cola India's social-responsibility practices.

In poor countries, the distribution of households by income level is heavily skewed toward the bottom rungs of the economy. With the bulk of the population—and buying power—residing in the low-income segments of poor nations, smart companies need to start concentrating their efforts there, where demand is high and competition is sparse. Governments, too, should take note. Poor people are asking why they should not share the benefits of globalization, and there is growing awareness that traditional development solutions have not worked. The private sector can and must do better.

Business School Basics

Markets in the developing world can nurture global business through their sheer size, rate of growth, and consumer demands. Consider three examples: cell phones, table salt, and cosmetics.

Cellular technology was originally developed as a luxury for the rich, but today poor countries drive the explosion in wireless communications. Sub-Saharan Africa is now a leading region in percentage growth of cell phone usage, expanding 37 percent during 2003. India boasts 22 million cellular customers and is adding around 1.5 million new customers every month. By 2005, China, India, and Brazil will have a combined 500 million cell phone users, compared to 150 million in the United States. The sheer size of these markets will necessarily change the dynamics of the business—shifting to the poor the power to determine both the preferred features of cell phones and their technological makeup. The pacesetting customers will no longer be found in Tokyo and Rome, but rather in Xian and Bangalore.

The cellular industry proves that if companies wish to engage poorer markets, they must shed traditional business models developed with wealthy consumers in mind. Prepaid phone cards are now the dominant business model for the cell phone market worldwide. Such cards crush the perception that business with the poor is risky; prepaid cards eliminate phone companies' collection costs and debt, and firms are paid before they connect a call. Yet even with prepaid cards, some companies initially misjudged the nature and depth of the market. In Venezuela in 1995, for example, U.S.-based BellSouth International started selling $10 and $20 phone cards, largely aimed at the middle class. Today the company sells enormously popular $4 phone cards at more than 30,000 retail outlets, reaching even Venezuela's poorest citizens and, because of the lower unit price, reaching a far larger market. By forcing corporations to rethink costs, business models, and industry standards, poor consumers are initiating a revolution in cellular communications.

Selling to poor consumers also requires innovative research and development. In rural India, for example, only four out of 10 households use iodized table salt, even though iodized salt provides a critical and convenient nutritional supplement. Due to India's environmental conditions, much of the iodine in salt is lost during transport and storage. The remainder often disappears in the Indian cooking process. To overcome this problem, Hindustan Lever Ltd., a subsidiary of Europe's Unilever Corp., has developed a way to encapsulate iodine, protecting it from transportation, storage, and cooking, and releasing the iodine only when salted food is ingested. The new salt required Hindustan Lever to invest in two years of advanced research and development, but if its salt sells successfully, the company could sharply reduce iodine deficiency disorder, a disease that affects more than 70 million people in India and is the country's leading cause of mental retardation. The lesson: Successful product development requires a deep understanding of local circumstances, so that critical features and functionality—salt with protected iodine—can be incorporated into the product's design.

Modernizing distribution channels is also crucial for companies hoping to reach low-income markets in the developing world. "Person-to-person" cosmetic giants Amway Corp. and Avon Products, Inc. use direct-distribution strategies in India

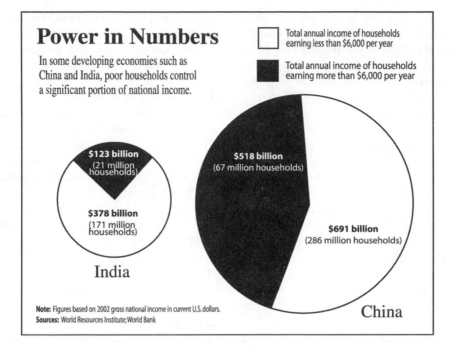

Power in Numbers

In some developing economies such as China and India, poor households control a significant portion of national income.

☐ Total annual income of households earning less than $6,000 per year

■ Total annual income of households earning more than $6,000 per year

$123 billion (21 million households)

$378 billion (171 million households)

India

$518 billion (67 million households)

$691 billion (286 million households)

China

Note: Figures based on 2002 gross national income in current U.S. dollars.
Sources: World Resources Institute; World Bank

and Brazil, respectively, to sell beauty products among a wider circle of customers—increasing the corporations' reach and employing poor people as entrepreneurs. Amway, for example, has enlisted around 600,000 self-employed individual distributors in India. Hindustan Lever is mimicking the approach with a direct-distribution system for personal-care products. The company expects to sign on more than 500,000 self-employed Indian distributors within five years.

Similar transformations in business models, research and development, and product distribution are underway or imminent in healthcare, education, finance, agriculture, building materials, and other goods and services. But these changes will only lead to a true business revolution if corporate perceptions regarding the world's poor shift dramatically. Managers in multinational corporations are conditioned to think mainly of rich consumers. They are prisoners of their own logic. Poor consumers challenge virtually every preconception parroted by business schools and marketing seminars. Yet, thanks in part to role models such as Brazilian entrepreneur Samuel Klein, the number of firms doing well by doing good is growing. Klein started Casas Bahia, a successful retail chain, when he fled Europe's Holocaust and started selling inexpensive linens and blankets to poor Brazilians. Klein learned quickly that the poor are willing to pay but they are often unable to afford lump sums for purchases. Allowing customers to pay in installments was the obvious solution. What started as a one-man blanket operation has grown into a business with more than $2 billion in sales last year. Casas Bahia employs more than 22,000 people, operates over 350 stores with 10 million customers, and the company's credit system has one of the lowest default rates in Brazil.

Power to the Poor

When multinational corporations attempt to penetrate new markets in the developing world, critics sometimes condemn them for preaching the gospel of consumer culture to the poor, for exploiting the poor as cheap labor, and for extracting and despoiling natural resources without fairly compensating locals. In truth, some multinationals have been guilty on all these counts. But the private sector may do more harm by ignoring poor consumers than by engaging them. After all, if the poor can't participate in global markets, they can't benefit from them either.

Poor families benefit in several ways when large companies target them as consumers. Access to new products, expanded choices, and increased purchasing power improves one's quality of life. New services and information that improve efficiency help increase productivity and raise incomes among poor citizens. Processes that are fair to the consumer and treat poor customers with respect—as when ITC uses electronic scales that give accurate weights for grain and offers a farmer a chair to sit in while the sale is completed—builds loyalty and trust in the company and in the global economic system. And the exercising of collective consumer market power forces attention to the needs of poor people.

When a retail chain in Mexico started selling chicken parts instead of whole chickens in its outlets a few years ago, sales quadrupled. Smaller unit packages—enough for a single, immediate use—enable poor consumers to buy a product that they otherwise could not afford, thus unlocking their purchasing power. The same principle applies to personal-care products. In India, Hindustan Lever, Procter & Gamble, and most of their competitors make "single-serving" versions of their products, from detergents to shampoo. More than 60 percent of the value of the shampoo market and 95 percent of all shampoo units sold in India are now single-serve. Many are designed explicitly for the poor and do not even require hot water. Because of these efforts, nearly all Indians now enjoy access to shampoo. Companies selling small unit sizes at affordable prices make money, expand markets, and generate broader access to goods and services that improve people's quality of life.

Nowhere are the benefits of access to new services more evident than in banking and the Internet. Prodem FFP, a Bolivian financial organization that targets low-income customers, installs automatic teller machines that recognize fingerprints, communicate via text-to-speech technology in three local dialects, and display a color-coded touch screen that illiterate customers can use. Prodem has expanded its market, and now more Bolivians have access to professional, secure banking services. On the other side of the world, in India, the wireless Internet service company n-Logue found that its customers in rural villages were slow to appreciate e-mail (many villagers do not normally communicate in writing) but quick to accept e-mail photos and video conferencing. N-Logue's customers found value in sharing a photo of a new baby with distant relatives or sending a photo of a sick cow to a government agricultural agent for quick advice. Even in traditional business sectors such as construction materials, Mexico's Cemex is expanding its market by combining a "pay as you go" system with delivery of materials and instructions as needed, enabling the poor to build better quality housing.

Beyond such benefits as higher standards of living and greater purchasing power, poor consumers find real value in dignity and choice. In part, lack of choice is what being poor is all about. In India, a young woman working as a sweeper outdoors in the hot sun recently expressed pride in being able to use a fashion product—Fair and Lovely cream, which is part sunscreen, part moisturizer, and part skin-lightener—because, she says, her hard labor will take less of a toll on her skin than it did on her parents'. She has a choice and feels empowered because of an affordable consumer product formulated for her needs. Likewise, Amul, a large Indian dairy cooperative, found an instant market in 2001 when it introduced ice cream, a luxury in tropical India, at affordable prices (2 cents per serving). Poor people want to buy their children ice cream every bit as much as middle-class families, but before Amul targeted the poor as consumers, they lacked that option.

Globalization's New Frontier

In 2003, Thailand's Information and Communications Technology Minister Surapong Suebwonglee was looking for ways to extend the benefits of technology to the masses. So he challenged Thailand's computer industry to come up with a $260 personal computer and a $450 laptop. In return, Suebwonglee guaranteed a market of at least 500,000 machines. The Thai computer indus-

try met that price. But to do so, it had to omit Microsoft's widely used (and costly) Windows and Office operating software and offer the open-source Linux operating system instead. Not wanting to be left out, Microsoft cut the price for its software to a total of $38 in Thailand, dramatically below normal retail prices. The "people's PCs" are now selling briskly (most with Linux, some with Windows) throughout Thailand. Nearly 300,000 computers were sold through early fall of 2003, with projected first-year sales of 1 million machines. In March 2004, Microsoft announced plans for a "tailored and limited" Thai-language version of its Windows XP Home software at reduced prices.

The Thai example shows that the global economy is open to both innovation and consumer market power originating in poor countries. Consumers in developing nations are increasingly willing to exercise that power, not least of all by rejecting trade or investment deals they see as unfair. Just last year in Bolivia, for example, popular discontent with the terms of foreign investment in a new pipeline to carry natural gas to global markets, including the United States, triggered protests and unrest that ultimately brought down the government of President Gonzalo Sánchez de Lozada. The president's successor, Carlos Mesa, quickly canceled the deal.

The message for the private sector is clear: Ignore poor consumers at your peril. Blocs of poor consumers increasingly have the power to reject what a multinational corporation wants to buy or sell; via their governments, they can also empower a nontraditional competitor. It may not be wise for corporations to wait for governments to smooth the path of globalization, or to depend solely on formal trade talks to make developing markets safe for their products. Businesses must learn to serve poor markets by overcoming those markets' unique constraints as well as their own antiquated business models and misconceptions about the developing world.

Ending the economic isolation of poor populations and bringing them within the formal global economy will ensure that they also have the opportunity to benefit from globalization. That is the world's new entrepreneurial frontier.

ALLEN L. HAMMOND is vice president for innovation and director of the digital dividends project at the World Resources Institute. **C.K. PRAHALAD** is Harvey C. Fruehauf professor of business administraion at the University of Michigan Business School and author of *The Fortune at the Bottom of the Pyramid: Eradicating Poverty Through Profit* (Philadelphia: Wharton School Publishing, 2004). He is a member of the board of directors of Hindustan Lever Ltd.

Glossary

This glossary of marketing terms is included to provide you with a convenient and ready reference as you encounter general terms in your study of marketing that are unfamiliar or require a review. It is not intended to be comprehensive, but taken together with the many definitions included in the articles themselves, it should prove to be quite useful.

A

acceptable price range The range of prices that buyers are willing to pay for a product; prices that are above the range may be judged unfair, while prices below the range may generate concerns about quality.

adaptive selling A salesperson's adjustment of his or her behavior between and during sales calls, to respond appropriately to issues that are important to the customer.

advertising Marketing communication elements designed to stimulate sales through the use of mass media displays, direct individual appeals, public displays, give-aways, and the like.

advertorial A special advertising section in magazines that includes some editorial (nonadvertising) content.

Americans with Disabilities Act (ADA) Passed in 1990, this U.S. law prohibits discrimination against consumers with disabilities.

automatic number identification A telephone system that identifies incoming phone numbers at the beginning of the call, without the caller's knowledge.

B

bait and switch Advertising a product at an attractively low price to get customers into the store, but making the product unavailable so that the customers must trade up to a more expensive version.

bar coding A computer-coded bar pattern that identifies a product. *See also* universal product code.

barter The practice of exchanging goods and services without the use of money.

benefit segmentation Organizing the market according to the attributes or benefits consumers need or desire, such as quality, service, or unique features.

brand A name, term, sign, design, symbol, or combination used to differentiate the products of one company from those of its competition.

brand image The quality and reliability of a product as perceived by consumers on the basis of its brand reputation or familiarity.

brand name The element of a brand that can be vocalized.

break-even analysis The calculation of the number of units that must be sold at a certain price to cover costs (break even); revenues earned past the break-even point contribute to profits.

bundling Marketing two or more products in a single package at one price.

business analysis The stage of new product development where initial marketing plans are prepared (including tentative marketing strategy and estimates of sales, costs, and profitability).

business strategic plan A plan for how each business unit in a corporation intends to compete in the marketplace, based upon the vision, objectives, and growth strategies of the corporate strategic plan.

C

capital products Expensive items that are used in business operations but do not become part of any finished product (such as office buildings, copy machines).

cash-and-carry wholesaler A limited-function wholesaler that does not extend credit for or deliver the products it sells.

caveat emptor A Latin term that means "let the buyer beware." A principle of law meaning that the purchase of a product is at the buyer's risk with regard to its quality, usefulness, and the like. The laws do, however, provide certain minimum protection against fraud and other schemes.

channel of distribution *See* marketing channel.

Child Protection Act U.S. law passed in 1990 to regulate advertising on children's TV programs.

Child Safety Act Passed in 1966, this U.S. law prohibits the marketing of dangerous products to children.

Clayton Act Anticompetitive activities are prohibited by this 1914 U.S. law.

co-branding When two brand names appear on the same product (such as a credit card with a school's name).

comparative advertising Advertising that compares one brand against a competitive brand on at least one product attribute.

competitive pricing strategies Pricing strategies that are based on a organization's position in relation to its competition.

consignment An arrangement in which a seller of goods does not take title to the goods until they are sold. The seller thus has the option of returning them to the supplier or principal if unable to execute the sale.

consolidated metropolitan statistical area (CMSA) Based on census data, the largest designation of geographic areas. *See also* primary metropolitan statistical area.

consumer behavior The way in which buyers, individually or collectively, react to marketplace stimuli.

Consumer Credit Protection Act A 1968 U.S. law that requires full disclosure of the financial charges of loans.

consumer decision process This four-step process includes recognizing a need or problem, searching for information, evaluating alternative products or brands, and purchasing a product.

Consumer Product Safety Commission (CPSC) A U.S. government agency that protects consumers from unsafe products.

consumerism A social movement in which consumers demand better information about the service, prices, dependability, and quality of the products they buy.

convenience products Consumer goods that are purchased at frequent intervals with little regard for price. Such goods are relatively standard in nature and consumers tend to select the most convenient source when shopping for them.

cooperative advertising Advertising of a product by a retailer, dealer, distributor, or the like, with part of the advertising cost paid by the product's manufacturer.

corporate strategic plan A plan that addresses what a company is and wants to become, and then guides strategic planning at all organizational levels.

Glossary

countersegmentation A concept that combines market segments to appeal to a broad range of consumers, assuming that there will be an increasing consumer willingness to accept fewer product and service choices for lower prices.

customer loyalty concept To focus beyond customer satisfaction toward customer retention as a way to generate sales and profit growth.

D

demand curve A relationship that shows how many units a market will purchase at a given price in a given period of time.

demographic environment The study of human population densities, distributions, and movements that relate to buying behavior.

derived demand The demand for business-to-business products that is dependent upon a demand for other products in the market.

differentiated strategy Using innovation and points of difference in product offerings, advanced technology, superior service, or higher quality in wide areas of market segments.

direct mail promotion Marketing goods to consumers by mailing unsolicited promotional material to them.

direct marketing The sale of products to carefully targeted consumers who interact with various advertising media without salesperson contact.

discount A reduction from list price that is given to a buyer as a reward for a favorable activity to the seller.

discretionary income The money that remains after taxes and necessities have been paid for.

disposable income That portion of income that remains after payment of taxes to use for food, clothing, and shelter.

dual distribution The selling of products to two or more competing distribution networks, or the selling of two brands of nearly identical products through competing distribution networks.

dumping The act of selling a product in a foreign country at a price lower than its domestic price.

durable goods Products that continue in service for an appreciable length of time.

E

economy The income, expenditures, and resources that affect business and household costs.

electronic data interchange (EDI) A computerized system that links two different firms to allow transmittal of documents; a quick-response inventory control system.

entry strategy An approach used to begin marketing products internationally.

environmental scanning Obtaining information on relevant factors and trends outside a company and interpreting their potential impact on the company's markets and marketing activities.

European Union (EU) The world's largest consumer market, consisting of 16 European nations: Austria, Belgium, Britain, Denmark, Finland, France, Germany, Greece, Italy, Ireland, Luxembourg, the Netherlands, Norway, Portugal, Spain, and Sweden.

exclusive distribution Marketing a product or service in only one retail outlet in a specific geographic marketplace.

exporting Selling goods to international markets.

F

Fair Packaging and Labeling Act of 1966 This law requires manufacturers to state ingredients, volume, and manufacturer's name on a package.

family life cycle The progress of a family through a number of distinct phases, each of which is associated with identifiable purchasing behaviors.

Federal Trade Commission (FTC) The U.S. government agency that regulates business practices; established in 1914.

five C's of pricing Five influences on pricing decisions: customers, costs, channels of distribution, competition, and compatibility.

FOB (free on board) The point at which the seller stops paying transportation costs.

four I's of service Four elements to services: intangibility, inconsistency, inseparability, and inventory.

four P's *See* marketing mix.

franchise The right to distribute a company's products or render services under its name, and to retain the resulting profit in exchange for a fee or percentage of sales.

freight absorption Payment of transportation costs by the manufacturer or seller, often resulting in a uniform pricing structure.

functional groupings Groupings in an organization in which a unit is subdivided according to different business activities, such as manufacturing, finance, and marketing.

G

General Agreement on Tariffs and Trade (GATT) An international agreement that is intended to limit trade barriers and to promote world trade through reduced tariffs; represents over 80 percent of global trade.

geodemographics A combination of geographic data and demographic characteristics; used to segment and target specific markets.

green marketing The implementation of an ecological perspective in marketing; the promotion of a product as environmentally safe.

gross domestic product (GDP) The total monetary value of all goods and services produced within a country during one year.

growth stage The second stage of a product life cycle that is characterized by a rapid increase in sales and profits.

H

hierarchy of effects The stages a prospective buyer goes through when purchasing a product, including awareness, interest, evaluation, trial, and adoption.

I

idea generation An initial stage of the new product development process; requires creativity and innovation to generate ideas for potential new products.

implied warranties Warranties that assign responsibility for a product's deficiencies to a manufacturer, even though the product was sold by a retailer.

imports Purchased goods or services that are manufactured or produced in some other country.

integrated marketing communications A strategic integration of marketing communications programs that coordinate all promotional activities—advertising, personal selling, sales promotion, and public relations.

internal reference prices The comparison price standards that consumers remember and use to judge the fairness of prices.

introduction stage The first product life cycle stage; when a new product is launched into the marketplace.

ISO 9000 International Standards Organization's standards for registration and certification of manufacturer's quality management and quality assurance systems.

J

joint venture An arrangement in which two or more organizations market products internationally.

just-in-time (JIT) inventory control system An inventory supply system that operates with very low inventories and fast, on-time delivery.

L

Lanham Trademark Act A 1946 U.S. law that was passed to protect trademarks and brand names.

late majority The fourth group to adopt a new product; representing about 34 percent of a market.

lifestyle research Research on a person's pattern of living, as displayed in activities, interests, and opinions.

limit pricing This competitive pricing strategy involves setting prices low to discourage new competition.

limited-coverage warranty The manufacturer's statement regarding the limits of coverage and noncoverage for any product deficiencies.

logistics management The planning, implementing, and moving of raw materials and products from the point of origin to the point of consumption.

loss-leader pricing The pricing of a product below its customary price in order to attract attention to it.

M

Magnuson-Moss Act Passed in 1975, this U.S. law regulates warranties.

management by exception Used by a marketing manager to identify results that deviate from plans, diagnose their cause, make appropriate new plans, and implement new actions.

manufacturers' agent A merchant wholesaler that sells related but noncompeting product lines for a number of manufacturers; also called manufacturers' representatives.

market The potential buyers for a company's product or service; or to sell a product or service to actual buyers. The place where goods and services are exchanged.

market penetration strategy The goal of achieving corporate growth objectives with existing products within existing markets by persuading current customers to purchase more of the product or by capturing new customers.

marketing channel Organizations and people that are involved in the process of making a product or service available for use by consumers or industrial users.

marketing communications planning A seven-step process that includes marketing plan review; situation analysis; communications process analysis; budget development; program development integration and implementation of a plan; and monitoring, evaluating, and controlling the marketing communications program.

marketing concept The idea that a company should seek to satisfy the needs of consumers while also trying to achieve the organization's goals.

marketing mix The elements of marketing: product, brand, package, price, channels of distribution, advertising and promotion, personal selling, and the like.

marketing research The process of identifying a marketing problem and opportunity, collecting and analyzing information systematically, and recommending actions to improve an organization's marketing activities.

marketing research process A six-step sequence that includes problem definition, determination of research design, determination

of data collection methods, development of data collection forms, sample design, and analysis and interpretation.

mission statement A part of the strategic planning process that expresses the company's basic values and specifies the operation boundaries within marketing, business units, and other areas.

motivation research A group of techniques developed by behavioral scientists that are used by marketing researchers to discover factors influencing marketing behavior.

N

nonprice competition Competition between brands based on factors other than price, such as quality, service, or product features.

nondurable goods Products that do not last or continue in service for any appreciable length of time.

North American Free Trade Agreement (NAFTA) A trade agreement among the United States, Canada, and Mexico that essentially removes the vast majority of trade barriers between the countries.

North American Industry Classification System (NAICS) A system used to classify organizations on the basis of major activity or the major good or service provided by the three NAFTA countries— Canada, Mexico, and the United States; replaced the Standard Industrial Classification (SIC) system in 1997.

O

observational data Market research data obtained by watching, either mechanically or in person, how people actually behave.

odd-even pricing Setting prices at just below an even number, such as $1.99 instead of $2.

opinion leaders Individuals who influence consumer behavior based on their interest in or expertise with particular products.

organizational goals The specific objectives used by a business or nonprofit unit to achieve and measure its performance.

outbound telemarketing Using the telephone rather than personal visits to contact customers.

outsourcing A company's decision to purchase products and services from other firms rather than using in-house employees.

P

parallel development In new product development, an approach that involves the development of the product and production process simultaneously.

penetration pricing Pricing a product low to discourage competition.

personal selling process The six stages of sales activities that occur before and after the sale itself: prospecting, preapproach, approach, presentation, close, and follow-up.

point-of-purchase display A sales promotion display located in high-traffic areas in retail stores.

posttesting Tests that are conducted to determine if an advertisement has accomplished its intended purpose.

predatory pricing The practice of selling products at low prices to drive competition from the market and then raising prices once a monopoly has been established.

prestige pricing Maintaining high prices to create an image of product quality and appeal to buyers who associate premium prices with high quality.

pretesting Evaluating consumer reactions to proposed advertisements through the use of focus groups and direct questions.

Glossary

price elasticity of demand An economic concept that attempts to measure the sensitivity of demand for any product to changes in its price.

price fixing The illegal attempt by one or several companies to maintain the prices of their products above those that would result from open competition.

price promotion mix The basic product price plus additional components such as sales prices, temporary discounts, coupons, favorable payment and credit terms.

price skimming Setting prices high initially to appeal to consumers who are not price-sensitive and then lowering prices to appeal to the next market segments.

primary metropolitan statistical area (PMSA) Major urban area, often located within a CMSA, that has at least one million inhabitants.

PRIZM A potential rating index by ZIP code markets that divides every U.S. neighborhood into one of 40 distinct cluster types that reveal consumer data.

product An idea, good, service, or any combination that is an element of exchange to satisfy a consumer.

product differentiation The ability or tendency of manufacturers, marketers, or consumers to distinguish between seemingly similar products.

product expansion strategy A plan to market new products to the same customer base.

product life cycle (PLC) A product's advancement through the introduction, growth, maturity, and decline stages.

product line pricing Setting the prices for all product line items.

product marketing plans Business units' plans to focus on specific target markets and marketing mixes for each product, which include both strategic and execution decisions.

product mix The composite of products offered for sale by a firm or a business unit.

promotional mix Combining one or more of the promotional elements that a firm uses to communicate with consumers.

proprietary secondary data The data that is provided by commercial marketing research firms to other firms.

psychographic research Measurable characteristics of given market segments in respect to lifestyles, interests, opinions, needs, values, attitudes, personality traits, and the like.

publicity Nonpersonal presentation of a product, service, or business unit.

pull strategy A marketing strategy whose main thrust is to strongly influence the final consumer, so that the demand for a product "pulls" it through the various channels of distribution.

push strategy A marketing strategy whose main thrust is to provide sufficient economic incentives to members of the channels of distribution, so as to "push" the product through to the consumer.

Q

qualitative data The responses obtained from in-depth interviews, focus groups, and observation studies.

quality function deployment (QFD) The data collected from structured response formats that can be easily analyzed and projected to larger populations.

quotas In international marketing, they are restrictions placed on the amount of a product that is allowed to leave or enter a country; the total outcomes used to assess sales representatives' performance and effectiveness.

R

regional marketing A form of geographical division that develops marketing plans that reflect differences in taste preferences, perceived needs, or interests in other areas.

relationship marketing The development, maintenance, and enhancement of long-term, profitable customer relationships.

repositioning The development of new marketing programs that will shift consumer beliefs and opinions about an existing brand.

resale price maintenance Control by a supplier of the selling prices of his branded goods at subsequent stages of distribution, by means of contractual agreement under fair trade laws or other devices.

reservation price The highest price a consumer will pay for a product; a form of internal reference price.

restraint of trade In general, activities that interfere with competitive marketing. Restraint of trade usually refers to illegal activities.

retail strategy mix Controllable variables that include location, products and services, pricing, and marketing communications.

return on investment (ROI) A ratio of income before taxes to total operating assets associated with a product, such as inventory, plant, and equipment.

S

sales effectiveness evaluations A test of advertising efficiency to determine if it resulted in increased sales.

sales forecast An estimate of sales under controllable and uncontrollable conditions.

sales management The planning, direction, and control of the personal selling activities of a business unit.

sales promotion An element of the marketing communications mix that provides incentives or extra value to stimulate product interest.

samples A small size of a product given to prospective purchasers to demonstrate a product's value or use and to encourage future purchase; some elements that are taken from the population or universe.

scanner data Proprietary data that is derived from UPC bar codes.

scrambled merchandising Offering several unrelated product lines within a single retail store.

selected controlled markets Sites where market tests for a new product are conducted by an outside agency and retailers are paid to display that product; also referred to as forced distribution markets.

selective distribution This involves selling a product in only some of the available outlets; commonly used when after-the-sale service is necessary, such as in the case of home appliances.

seller's market A condition within any market in which the demand for an item is greater than its supply.

selling philosophy An emphasis on an organization's selling function to the exclusion of other marketing activities.

selling strategy A salesperson's overall plan of action, which is developed at three levels: sales territory, customer, and individual sales calls.

services Nonphysical products that a company provides to consumers in exchange for money or something else of value.

share points Percentage points of market share; often used as the common comparison basis to allocate marketing resources effectively.

Sherman Anti-Trust Act Passed in 1890, this U.S. law prohibits contracts, combinations, or conspiracies in restraint of trade and actual monopolies or attempts to monopolize any part of trade or commerce.

shopping products Consumer goods that are purchased only after comparisons are made concerning price, quality, style, suitability, and the like.

single-channel strategy Marketing strategy using only one means to reach customers; providing one sales source for a product.

single-zone pricing A pricing policy in which all buyers pay the same delivered product price, regardless of location; also known as uniform delivered pricing or postage stamp pricing.

slotting fees High fees manufacturers pay to place a new product on a retailer's or wholesaler's shelf.

social responsibility Reducing social costs, such as environmental damage, and increasing the positive impact of a marketing decision on society.

societal marketing concept The use of marketing strategies to increase the acceptability of an idea (smoking causes cancer); cause (environmental protection); or practice (birth control) within a target market.

specialty products Consumer goods, usually appealing only to a limited market, for which consumers will make a special purchasing effort. Such items include, for example, stereo components, fancy foods, and prestige brand clothes.

Standard Industrial Classification (SIC) system Replaced by NAICS, this federal government numerical scheme categorized businesses.

standardized marketing Enforcing similar product, price, distribution, and communications programs in all international markets.

stimulus-response presentation A selling format that assumes that a customer will buy if given the appropriate stimulus by a salesperson.

strategic business unit (SBU) A decentralized profit center of a company that operates as a separate, independent business.

strategic marketing process Marketing activities in which a firm allocates its marketing mix resources to reach a target market.

strategy mix A way for retailers to differentiate themselves from others through location, product, services, pricing, and marketing mixes.

subliminal perception When a person hears or sees messages without being aware of them.

SWOT analysis An acronym that describes a firm's appraisal of its internal strengths and weaknesses and its external opportunities and threats.

synergy An increased customer value that is achieved through more efficient organizational function performances.

systems-designer strategy A selling strategy that allows knowledgeable sales reps to determine solutions to a customer's problems or to anticipate opportunities to enhance a customer's business through new or modified business systems.

T

target market A defined group of consumers or organizations toward which a firm directs its marketing program.

team selling A sales strategy that assigns accounts to specialized sales teams according to a customers' purchase-information needs.

telemarketing An interactive direct marketing approach that uses the telephone to develop relationships with customers.

test marketing The process of testing a prototype of a new product to gain consumer reaction and to examine its commercial viability and marketing strategy.

TIGER (Topologically Integrated Geographic Encoding and Reference) A minutely detailed U.S. Census Bureau computerized map of the U.S. that can be combined with a company's own database to analyze customer sales.

total quality management (TQM) Programs that emphasize long-term relationships with selected suppliers instead of short-term transactions with many suppliers.

total revenue The total of sales, or unit price, multiplied by the quantity of the product sold.

trade allowance An amount a manufacturer contributes to a local dealer's or retailer's advertising expenses.

trade (functional) discounts Price reductions that are granted to wholesalers or retailers that are based on future marketing functions that they will perform for a manufacturer.

trademark The legal identification of a company's exclusive rights to use a brand name or trade name.

truck jobber A small merchant wholesaler who delivers limited assortments of fast-moving or perishable items within a small geographic area.

two-way stretch strategy Adding products at both the low and high end of a product line.

U

undifferentiated strategy Using a single promotional mix to market a single product for the entire market; frequently used early in the life of a product.

uniform delivered price The same average freight amount that is charged to all customers, no matter where they are located.

universal product code (UPC) An assigned number to identify a product, which is represented by a series of bars of varying widths for optical scanning.

usage rate The quantity consumed or patronage during a specific period, which can vary significantly among different customer groups.

utilitarian influence To comply with the expectations of others to achieve rewards or avoid punishments.

V

value added In retail strategy decisions, a dimension of the retail positioning matrix that refers to the service level and method of operation of the retailer.

vertical marketing systems Centrally coordinated and professionally managed marketing channels that are designed to achieve channel economies and maximum marketing impact.

vertical price fixing Requiring that sellers not sell products below a minimum retail price; sometimes called resale price maintenance.

W

weighted-point system The method of establishing screening criteria, assigning them weights, and using them to evaluate new product lines.

wholesaler One who makes quantity purchases from manufacturers (or other wholesalers) and sells in smaller quantities to retailers (or other wholesalers).

Z

zone pricing A form of geographical pricing whereby a seller divides its market into broad geographic zones and then sets a uniform delivered price for each zone.

Test Your Knowledge Form

We encourage you to photocopy and use this page as a tool to assess how the articles in *Annual Editions* expand on the information in your textbook. By reflecting on the articles you will gain enhanced text information. You can also access this useful form on a product's book support Web site at *http://www.mhcls.com/online/*.

NAME: DATE:

_____

TITLE AND NUMBER OF ARTICLE:

_____

BRIEFLY STATE THE MAIN IDEA OF THIS ARTICLE:

_____

LIST THREE IMPORTANT FACTS THAT THE AUTHOR USES TO SUPPORT THE MAIN IDEA:

_____

WHAT INFORMATION OR IDEAS DISCUSSED IN THIS ARTICLE ARE ALSO DISCUSSED IN YOUR TEXTBOOK OR OTHER READINGS THAT YOU HAVE DONE? LIST THE TEXTBOOK CHAPTERS AND PAGE NUMBERS:

_____

LIST ANY EXAMPLES OF BIAS OR FAULTY REASONING THAT YOU FOUND IN THE ARTICLE:

_____

LIST ANY NEW TERMS/CONCEPTS THAT WERE DISCUSSED IN THE ARTICLE, AND WRITE A SHORT DEFINITION:

We Want Your Advice

ANNUAL EDITIONS revisions depend on two major opinion sources: one is our Advisory Board, listed in the front of this volume, which works with us in scanning the thousands of articles published in the public press each year; the other is you—the person actually using the book. Please help us and the users of the next edition by completing the prepaid article rating form on this page and returning it to us. Thank you for your help!

ANNUAL EDITIONS: Marketing 08/09

ARTICLE RATING FORM

Here is an opportunity for you to have direct input into the next revision of this volume.
We would like you to rate each of the articles listed below, using the following scale:

1. **Excellent: should definitely be retained**
2. **Above average: should probably be retained**
3. **Below average: should probably be deleted**
4. **Poor: should definitely be deleted**

Your ratings will play a vital part in the next revision.
Please mail this prepaid form to us as soon as possible.
Thanks for your help!

RATING	ARTICLE	RATING	ARTICLE
	1. Hot Stuff		24. He Came. He Sawed. He Took on the Whole Power-Tool Industry
	2. The World's Most Innovative Companies		25. In Praise of the Purple Cow
	3. The Next 25 Years		26. Starbucks' 'Venti' Problem
	4. Customers at Work		27. Making Cents of Pricing
	5. Marketing Myopia		28. Customer-Centric Pricing: The Surprising Secret for Profitability
	6. Customer Connection		29. Boost Your Bottom Line by Taking the Guesswork Out of Pricing
	7. The Big Opportunity		30. Pricing Gets Creative
	8. Listening to Starbucks		31. The Old Pillars of New Retailing
	9. Surviving in the Age of Rage		32. Why Costco Is So Damn Addictive
	10. Nonprofits Can Take Cues from Biz World		33. A Sales Channel They Can't Resist
	11. Fidelity Factor		34. Direct Mail Still Has Its Place
	12. Trust in the Marketplace		35. The Online Ad Surge
	13. 6 Strategies Marketers Use to Get Kids to Want Stuff *Bad*		36. Behind the Magic
	14. Wrestling With Ethics		37. Got Advertising That Works?
	15. The Science of Desire		38. Managing Differences
	16. Team Spirit		39. Segmenting Global Markets: Look Before You Leap
	17. Eight Tips Offer Best Practices for Online MR		40. How China Will Change Your Business
	18. A New Age for the Ad Biz		41. Three Dimensional
	19. The Halo Effect		42. Tech's Future
	20. Gen Y Sits on Top of Consumer Food Chain		43. The Great Wal-Mart of China
	21. You Choose, You Lose		44. Selling to the Poor
	22. Marketing: Consumers in the Mist		
	23. The Very Model of a Modern Marketing Plan		

‖‖‖

BUSINESS REPLY MAIL
FIRST CLASS MAIL PERMIT NO. 551 DUBUQUE IA

POSTAGE WILL BE PAID BY ADDRESSEE

McGraw-Hill Contemporary Learning Series
2460 KERPER BLVD
DUBUQUE, IA 52001-9902

ABOUT YOU

Name _____ Date _____

Are you a teacher? ❏ A student? ❏
Your school's name _____

Department _____

Address _____ City _____ State _____ Zip _____

School telephone # _____

YOUR COMMENTS ARE IMPORTANT TO US!

Please fill in the following information:
For which course did you use this book?

_____

Did you use a text with this ANNUAL EDITION? ❏ yes ❏ no
What was the title of the text?

_____

What are your general reactions to the Annual Editions concept?

_____

Have you read any pertinent articles recently that you think should be included in the next edition? Explain.

_____

Are there any articles that you feel should be replaced in the next edition? Why?

_____

Are there any World Wide Web sites that you feel should be included in the next edition? Please annotate.

_____

May we contact you for editorial input? ❏ yes ❏ no
May we quote your comments? ❏ yes ❏ no